INJUSTICE

GODS AMONG US: YEAR THREE

VOLUME 1

INJU
GODS AMO

Tom Taylor
Writer

Bruno Redondo Mike S. Miller
Xermanico Juan Albarran Vicente Cifuentes
Artists

J. Nanjan (NS Studios) Rex Lokus
Colorists

Wes Abbott
Letterer

Neil Googe and Rex Lokus

STICE

US: YEAR THREE
VOLUME 1

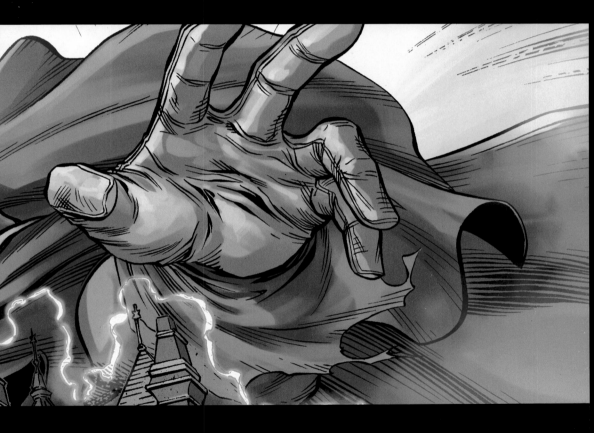

SUPERMAN Created by JERRY SIEGEL and JOE SHUSTER.
By Special Arrangement with the Jerry Siegel Family.

BASED ON THE VIDEOGAME INJUSTICE: GODS AMONG US

Jim Chadwick Editor – Original Series
Aniz Ansari Assistant Editor – Original Series
Jeb Woodard Group Editor – Collected Editions
Paul Santos Editor – Collected Edition
Louis Prandi Publication Design

Bob Harras Senior VP – Editor-in-Chief, DC Comics

Diane Nelson President
Dan DiDio and Jim Lee Co-Publishers
Geoff Johns Chief Creative Officer
Amit Desai Senior VP – Marketing & Global Franchise Management
Nairi Gardiner Senior VP – Finance
Sam Ades VP – Digital Marketing
Bobbie Chase VP – Talent Development
Mark Chiarello Senior VP – Art, Design & Collected Editions
John Cunningham VP – Content Strategy
Anne DePies VP – Strategy Planning & Reporting
Don Falletti VP – Manufacturing Operations
Lawrence Ganem VP – Editorial Administration & Talent Relations
Alison Gill Senior VP – Manufacturing & Operations
Hank Kanalz enior VP – Editorial Strategy & Administration
Jay Kogan VP – Legal Affairs
Derek Maddalena Senior VP – Sales & Business Development
Jack Mahan VP – Business Affairs
Dan Miron VP – Sales Planning & Trade Development
Nick Napolitano VP – Manufacturing Administration
Carol Roeder VP – Marketing
Eddie Scannell VP – Mass Account & Digital Sales
Courtney Simmons Senior VP – Publicity & Communications
Jim (Ski) Sokolowski VP – Comic Book Specialty & Newsstand Sales
Sandy Yi Senior VP – Global Franchise Management

INJUSTICE: GODS AMONG US YEAR THREE VOLUME 1

Published by DC Comics. Cover and compilation Copyright © 2015 DC
Comics. All Rights Reserved.

Originally published in single magazine form in INJUSTICE: GODS
AMONG US YEAR THREE 1-7. Copyright © 2014 DC Comics. All Rights
Reserved. All characters, their distinctive likenesses and related
elements featured in this publication are trademarks of DC Comics.
The stories, characters and incidents featured in this publication are
entirely fictional. DC Comics does not read or accept unsolicited ideas,
stories or artwork.

DC Comics, 4000 Warner Blvd. | Burbank, CA 91522
A Warner Bros. Entertainment Company.
Printed by RR Donnelley, Salem, VA, USA. 9/25/15. First Printing.
ISBN: 978-1-4012-5851-1

Library of Congress Cataloging-in-Publication Data is Available.

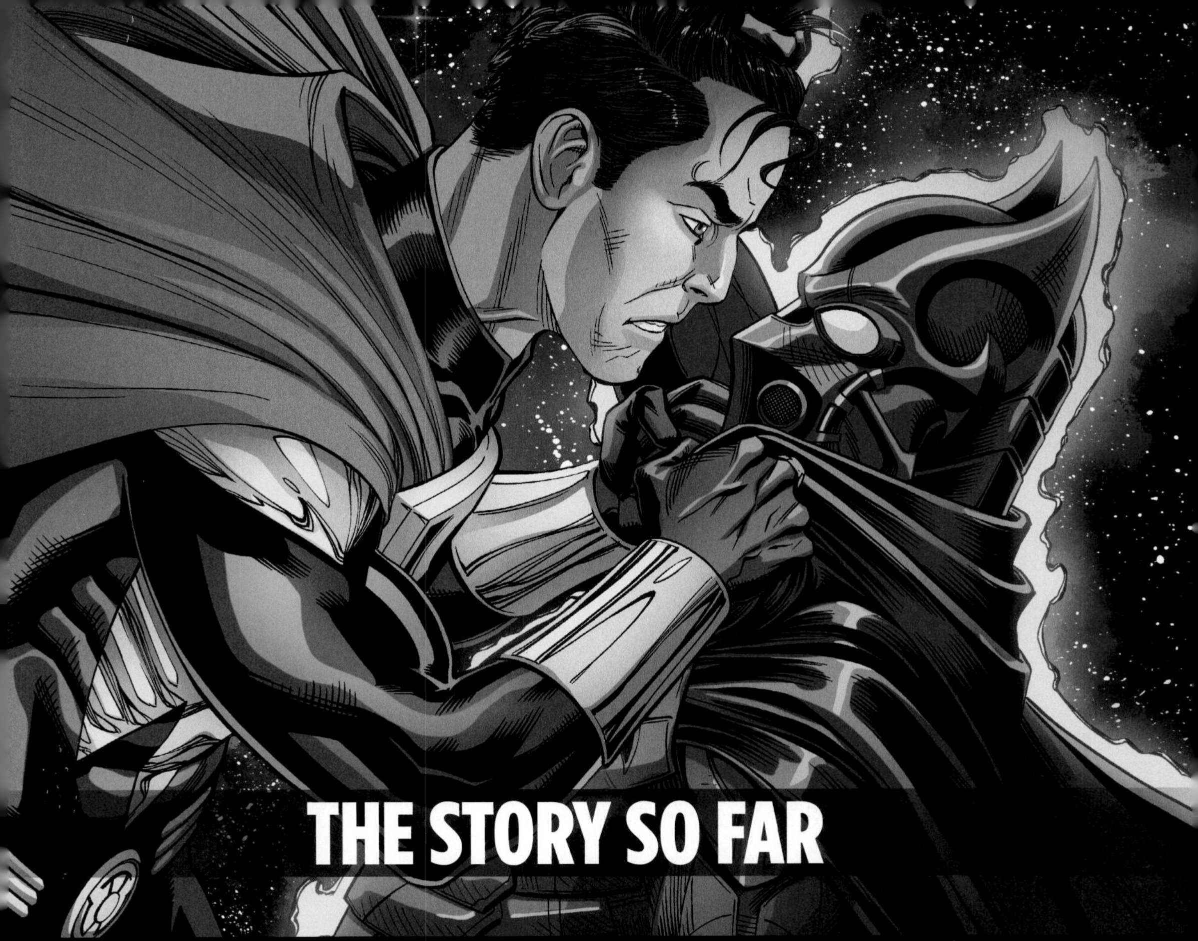

THE STORY SO FAR

When the Joker ditches Gotham and heads for Metropolis, Superman and Lois Lane are the victims of his most sinister plot to date. The aftermath unleashes an atomic explosion that destroys the City of Tomorrow, and with it, Lois Lane and their unborn child. Mad with grief, the Man of Steel does the unthinkable and murders the Joker in cold blood as Batman looks on in horror.

Superman begins a campaign to end violence the world over, involving himself in civil wars and international conflict, but Batman becomes concerned that this level of intervention is a slippery slope towards a police state. The Justice League becomes divided between those who believe in Superman's vision and those who share Batman's concerns, with Superman's team eventually coming under fire from the United States government.

As casualties begin to arise from the conflict, the schism between the two former friends grows even deeper. Batman and his resistance team manage to get their hands on a Kryptonite-powered pill that grants them superpowers, but at the cost of the lives of their teammates Green Arrow and Captain Atom...and of Batman's back being broken.

Faced with a growing resistance, Superman soon finds himself with an unexpected new ally: Sinestro, the former rogue Green Lantern who formed his own fear-powered Sinestro Corps. Sinestro recognizes his own history in Superman's struggle to save his planet from itself, and warns Superman that the Guardians of the Universe will soon send the Green Lantern Corps to intervene, even though Hal Jordan sides with Superman.

As the war between Green Lanterns and Superman's Justice League takes to the skies over Earth, a different war is being waged on the streets, where Superman's super-powered troops have turned Gotham into a totalitarian nightmare. Under the guidance of Jim Gordon, Batman's allies and the remnants of the Gotham City Police Department use the Kryptonite pills to empower themselves to fight back against the troops. But the pills accelerate Gordon's cancer, and he dies on the Watchtower, protecting his daughter Barbara from being traced by Cyborg.

Having earned Superman's trust, Sinestro manipulates Superman and his allies, resulting in the deaths of Earth's other Green Lanterns and in both Superman and Hal Jordan joining the Sinestro Corps. Although Batman's team is able to capture several of Superman's Justice League allies, they suffer a major loss of their own. When Black Canary confronts Superman over the death of her husband Green Arrow, Superman murders her in cold blood...an act broadcast around the world thanks to hidden cameras in her contacts.

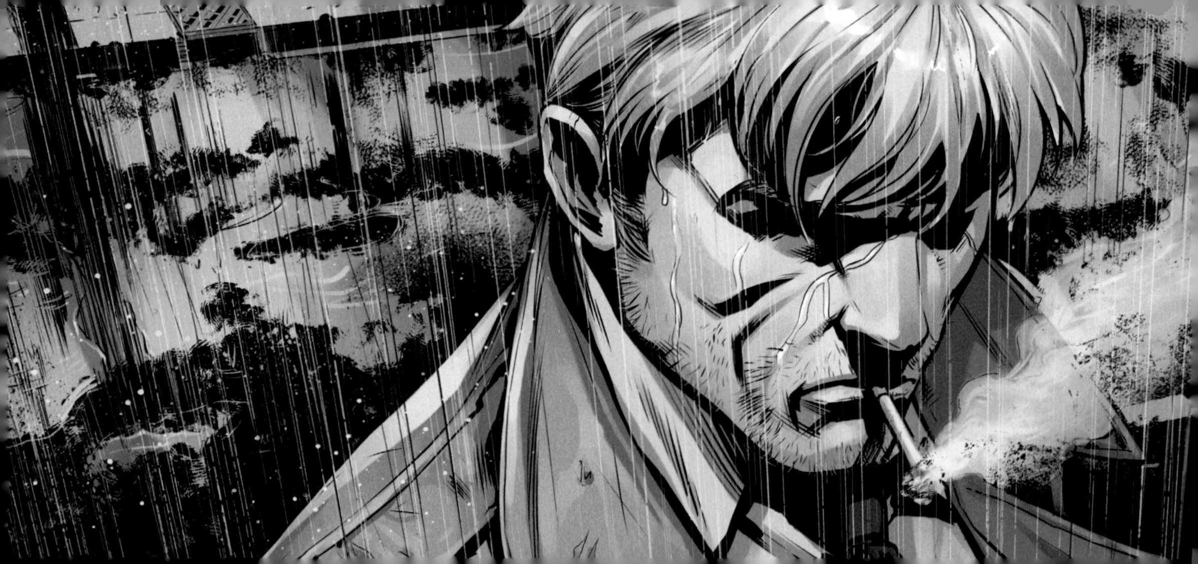

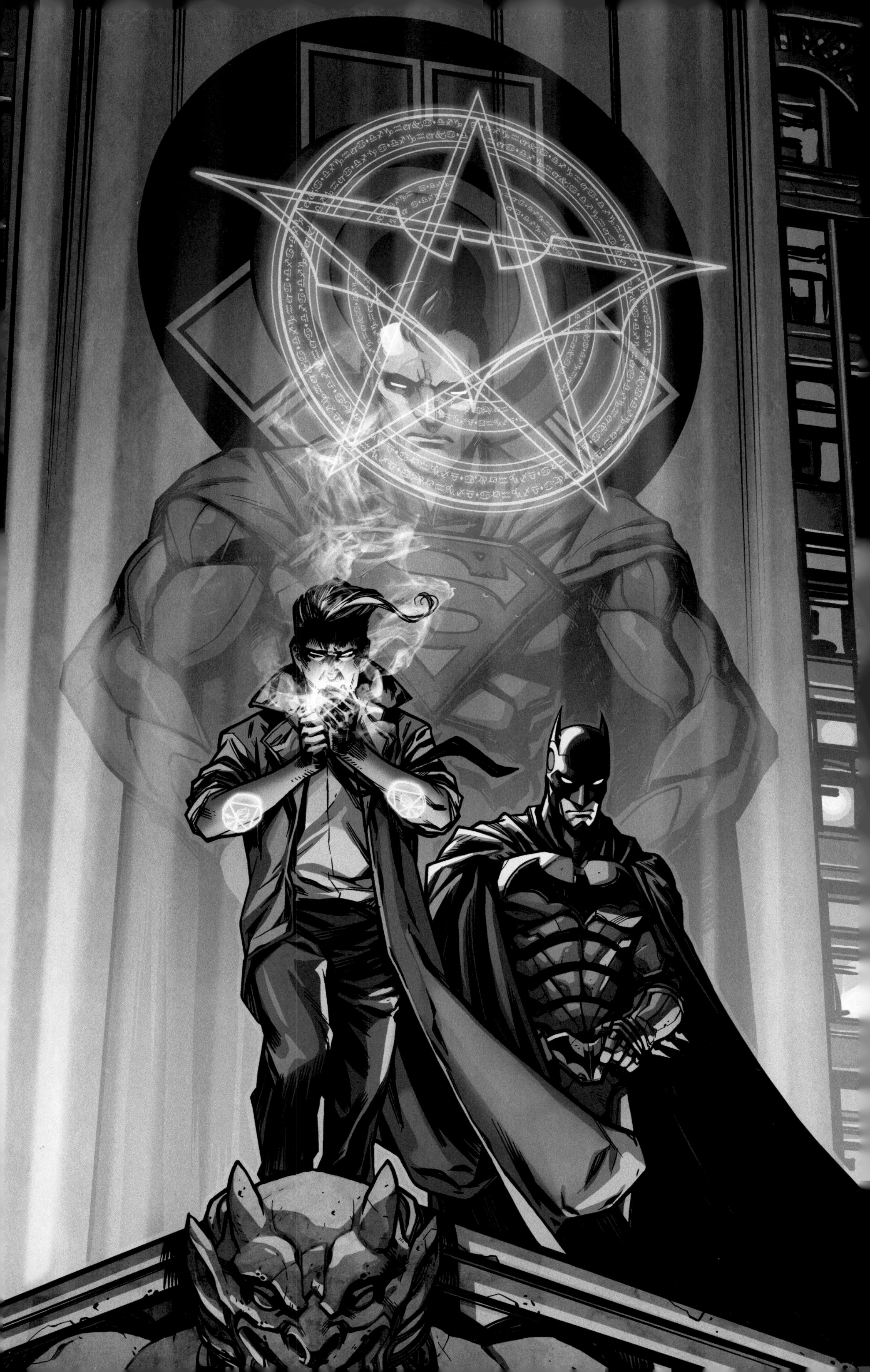

"Rose" **Bruno Redondo & Xermanico** Artists **J. Nanjan** Colorist
"Magic" **Bruno Redondo & Vicente Cifuentes** Artists **Rex Lokus** Colorist
Cover Art by **Neil Googe & Rex Lokus**

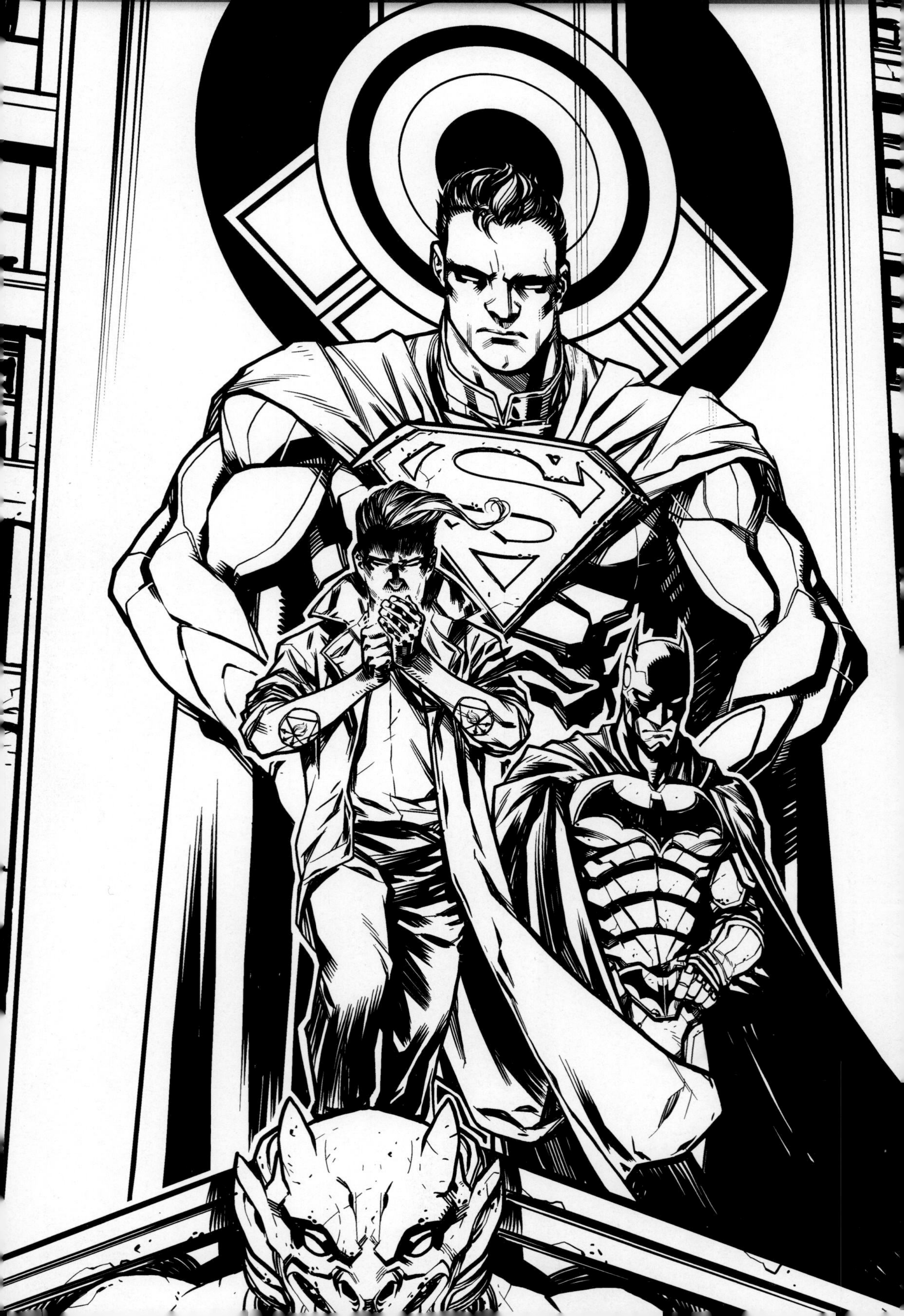

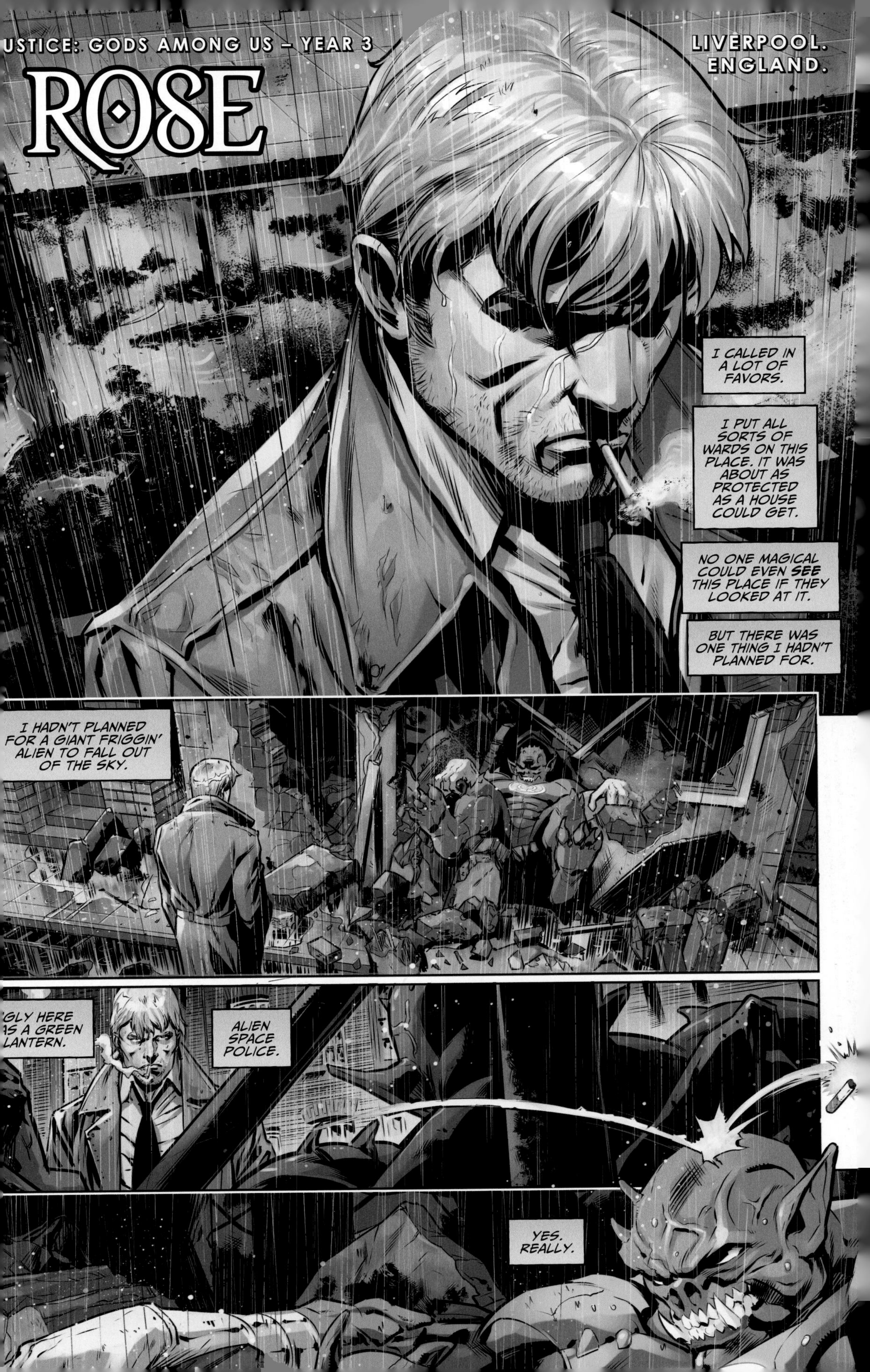
USTICE: GODS AMONG US – YEAR 3
ROSE
LIVERPOOL. ENGLAND.
I CALLED IN A LOT OF FAVORS.
I PUT ALL SORTS OF WARDS ON THIS PLACE. IT WAS ABOUT AS PROTECTED AS A HOUSE COULD GET.
NO ONE MAGICAL COULD EVEN SEE THIS PLACE IF THEY LOOKED AT IT.
BUT THERE WAS ONE THING I HADN'T PLANNED FOR.
I HADN'T PLANNED FOR A GIANT FRIGGIN' ALIEN TO FALL OUT OF THE SKY.
GLY HERE AS A GREEN LANTERN.
ALIEN SPACE POLICE.
YES. REALLY.

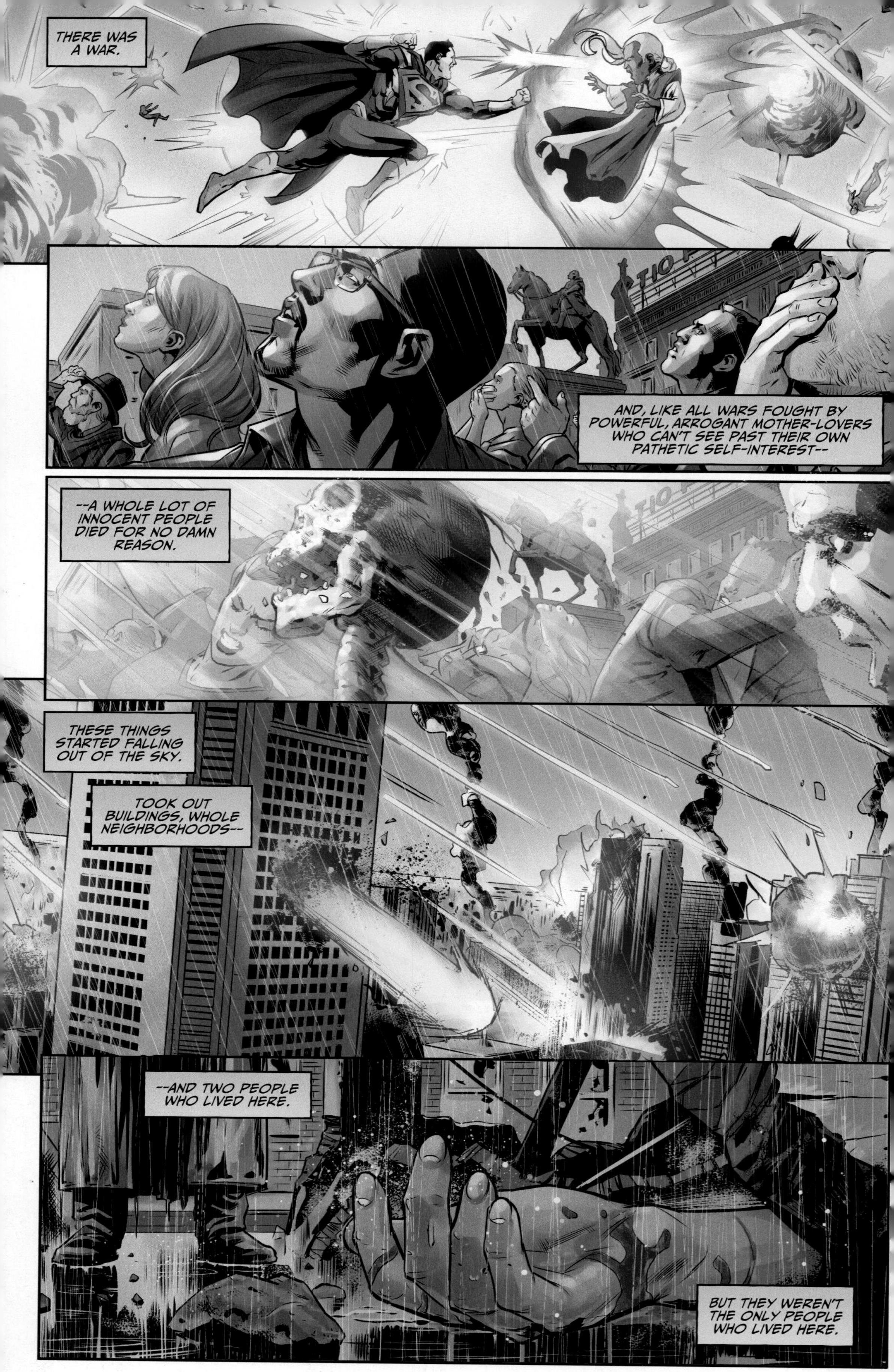
THERE WAS A WAR.
AND, LIKE ALL WARS FOUGHT BY POWERFUL, ARROGANT MOTHER-LOVERS WHO CAN'T SEE PAST THEIR OWN PATHETIC SELF-INTEREST--
--A WHOLE LOT OF INNOCENT PEOPLE DIED FOR NO DAMN REASON.
THESE THINGS STARTED FALLING OUT OF THE SKY.
TOOK OUT BUILDINGS, WHOLE NEIGHBORHOODS--
--AND TWO PEOPLE WHO LIVED HERE.
BUT THEY WEREN'T THE ONLY PEOPLE WHO LIVED HERE.

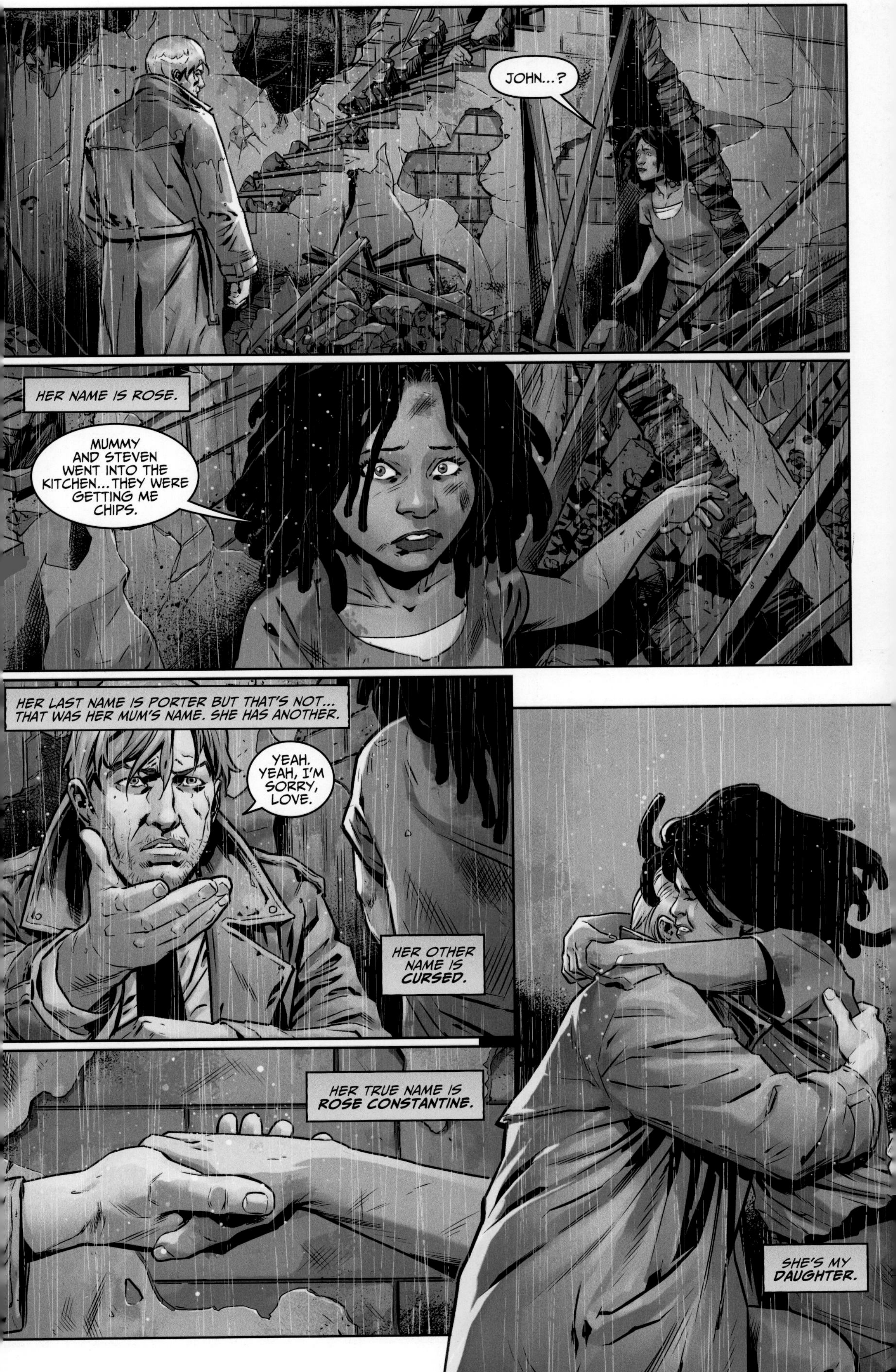
JOHN...?
HER NAME IS ROSE.
MUMMY AND STEVEN WENT INTO THE KITCHEN... THEY WERE GETTING ME CHIPS.
HER LAST NAME IS PORTER BUT THAT'S NOT... THAT WAS HER MUM'S NAME. SHE HAS ANOTHER.
YEAH. YEAH, I'M SORRY, LOVE.
HER OTHER NAME IS CURSED.
HER TRUE NAME IS ROSE CONSTANTINE.
SHE'S MY DAUGHTER.

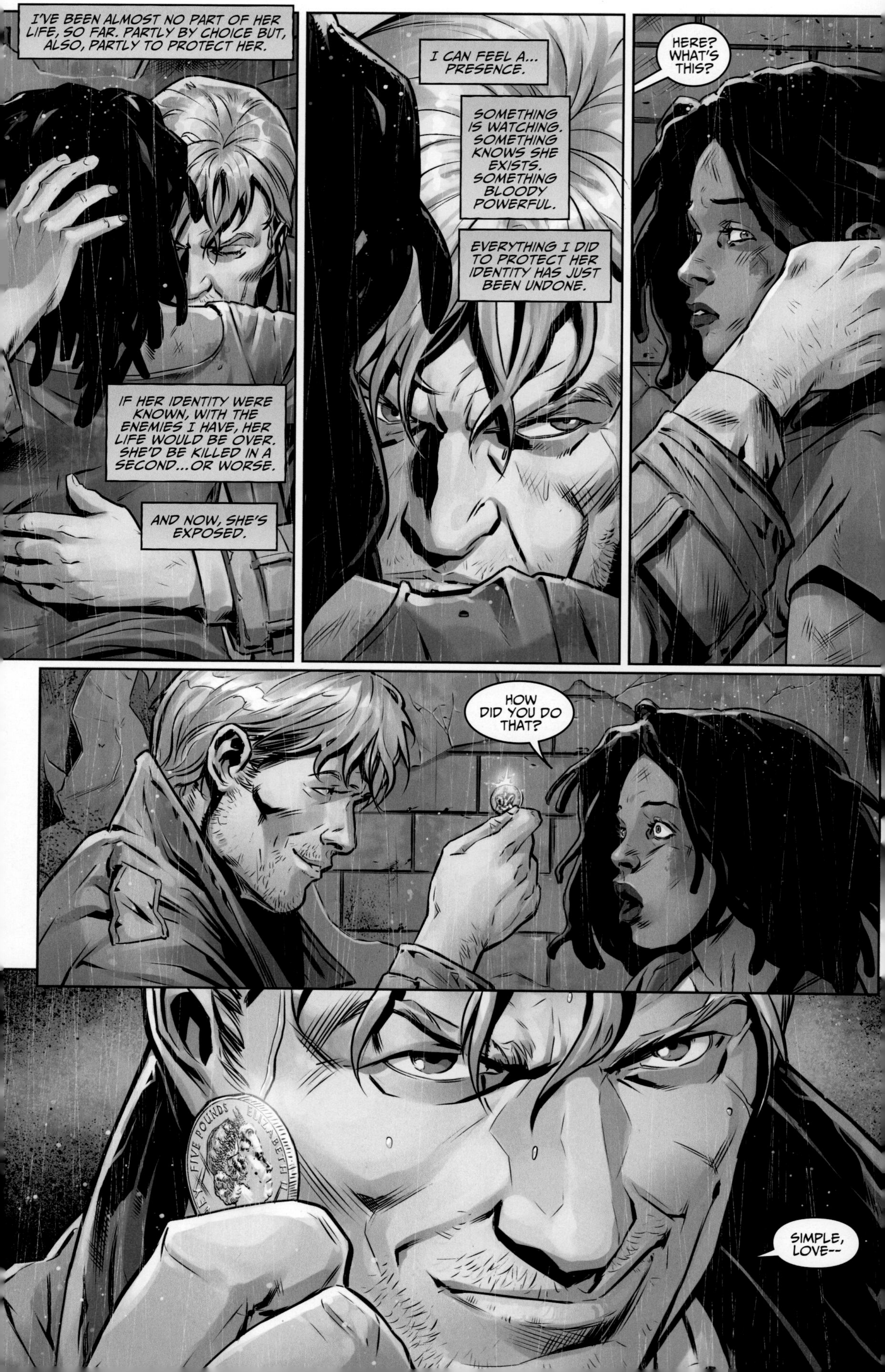
I'VE BEEN ALMOST NO PART OF HER LIFE, SO FAR. PARTLY BY CHOICE BUT, ALSO, PARTLY TO PROTECT HER.
IF HER IDENTITY WERE KNOWN, WITH THE ENEMIES I HAVE, HER LIFE WOULD BE OVER. SHE'D BE KILLED IN A SECOND...OR WORSE.
AND NOW, SHE'S EXPOSED.
I CAN FEEL A... PRESENCE.
SOMETHING IS WATCHING. SOMETHING KNOWS SHE EXISTS. SOMETHING BLOODY POWERFUL.
EVERYTHING I DID TO PROTECT HER IDENTITY HAS JUST BEEN UNDONE.
HERE? WHAT'S THIS?
HOW DID YOU DO THAT?
FIVE POUNDS ELIZABETH II
SIMPLE, LOVE--

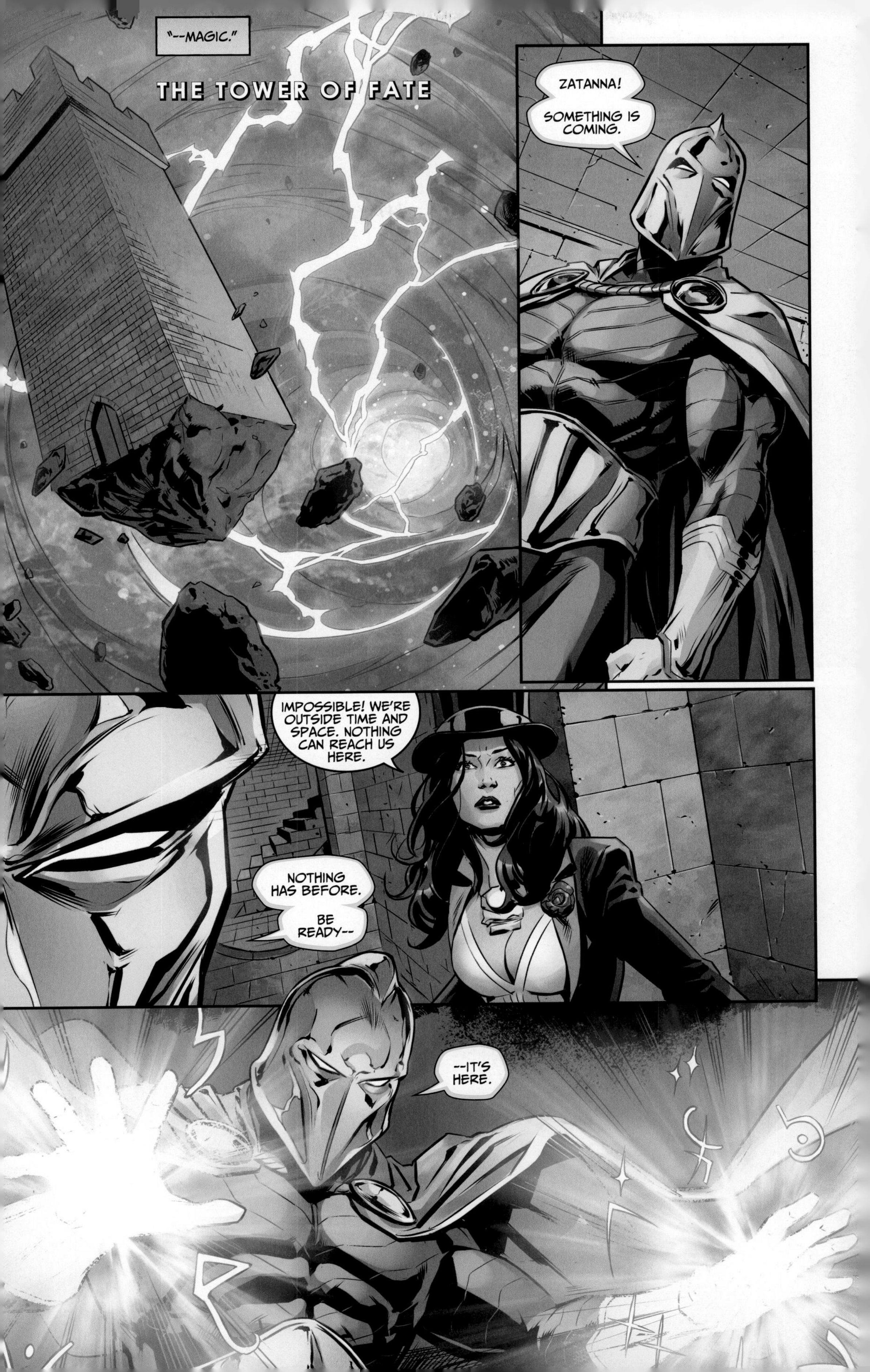
"--MAGIC."
THE TOWER OF FATE
ZATANNA!
SOMETHING IS COMING.
IMPOSSIBLE! WE'RE OUTSIDE TIME AND SPACE. NOTHING CAN REACH US HERE.
NOTHING HAS BEFORE.
BE READY--
--IT'S HERE.

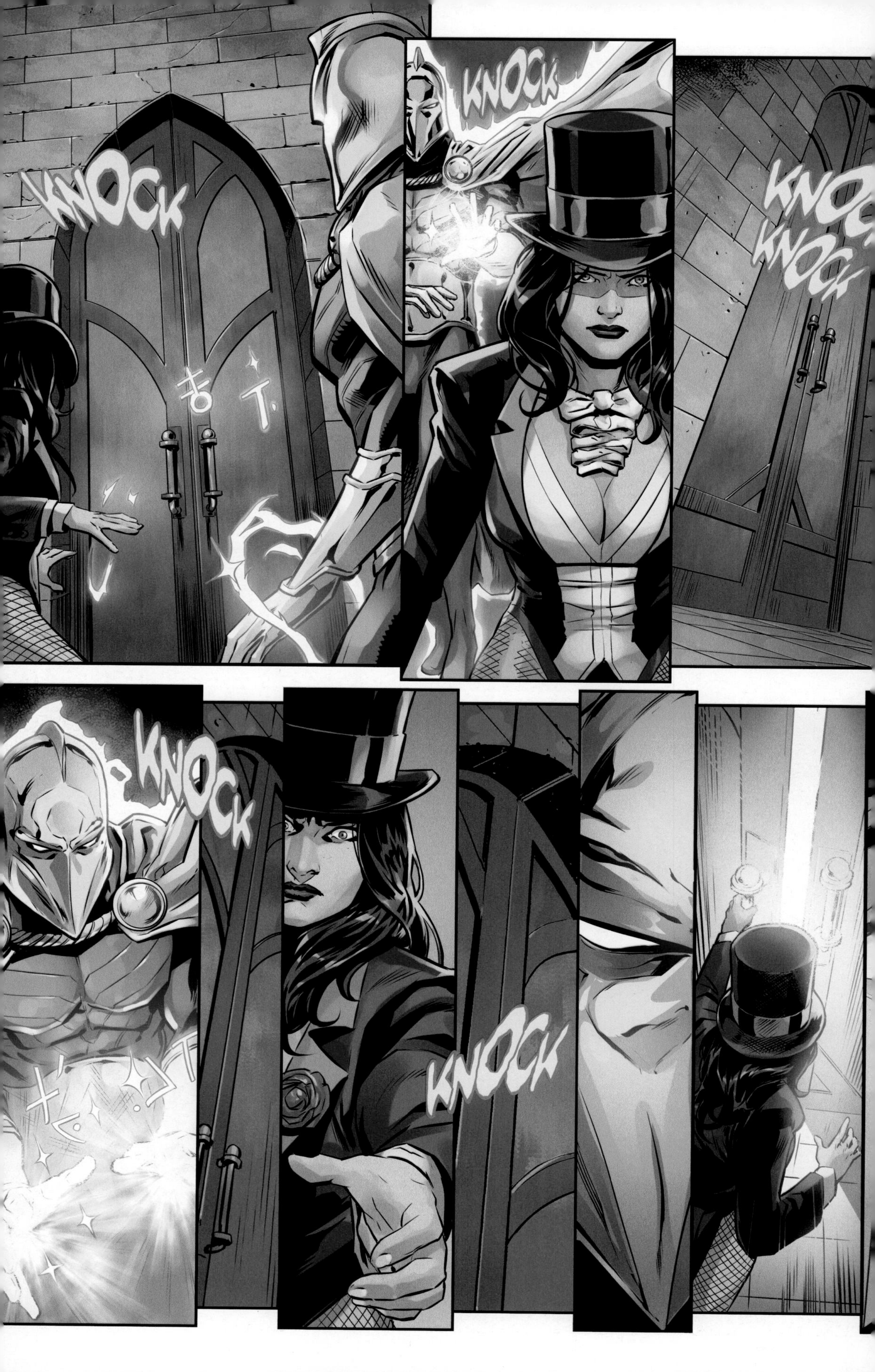
KNOCK
KNOCK
KNOCK
KNOCK
KNOCK
KNOCK

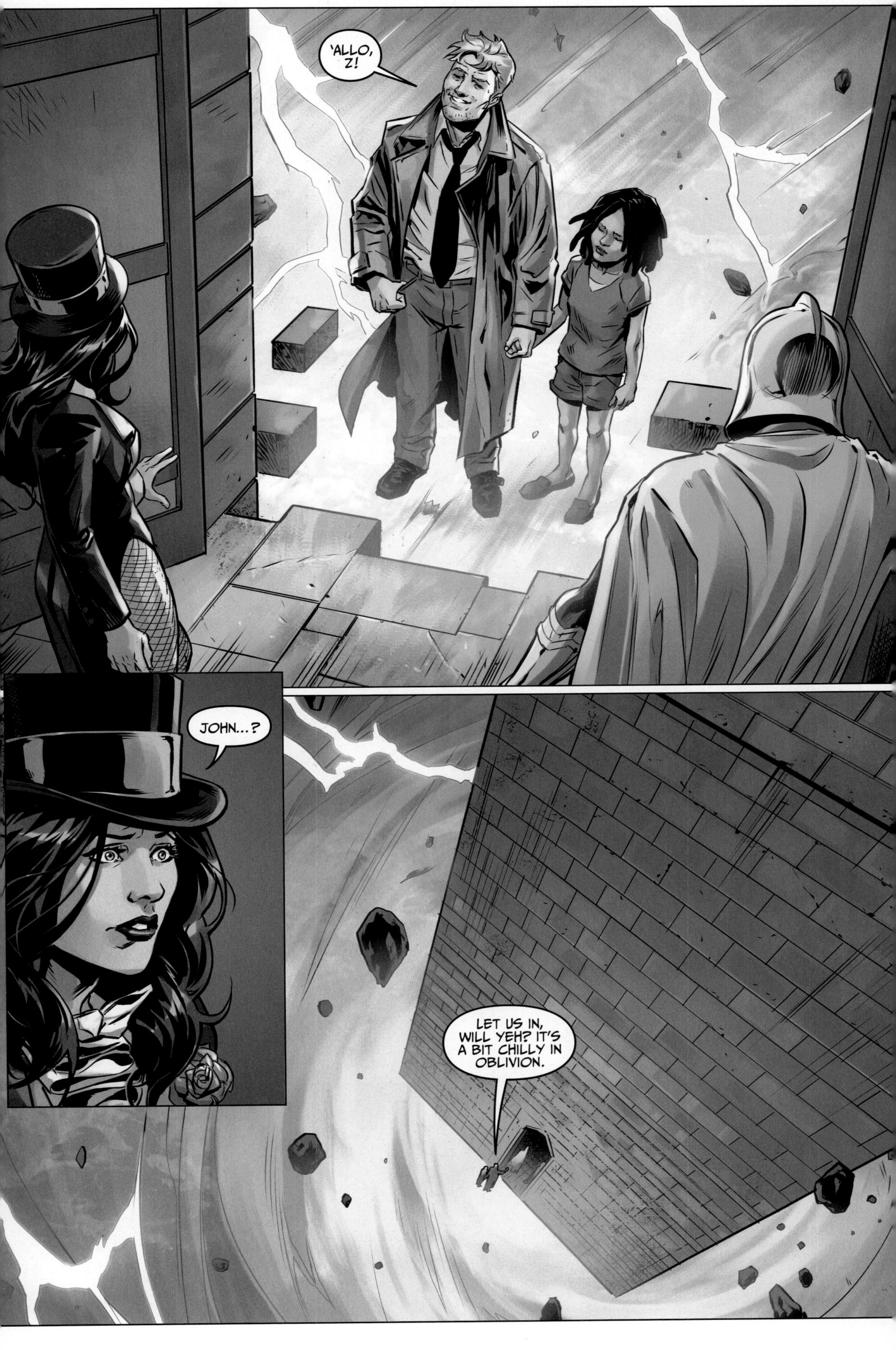
'ALLO, Z!
JOHN...?
LET US IN, WILL YEH? IT'S A BIT CHILLY IN OBLIVION.

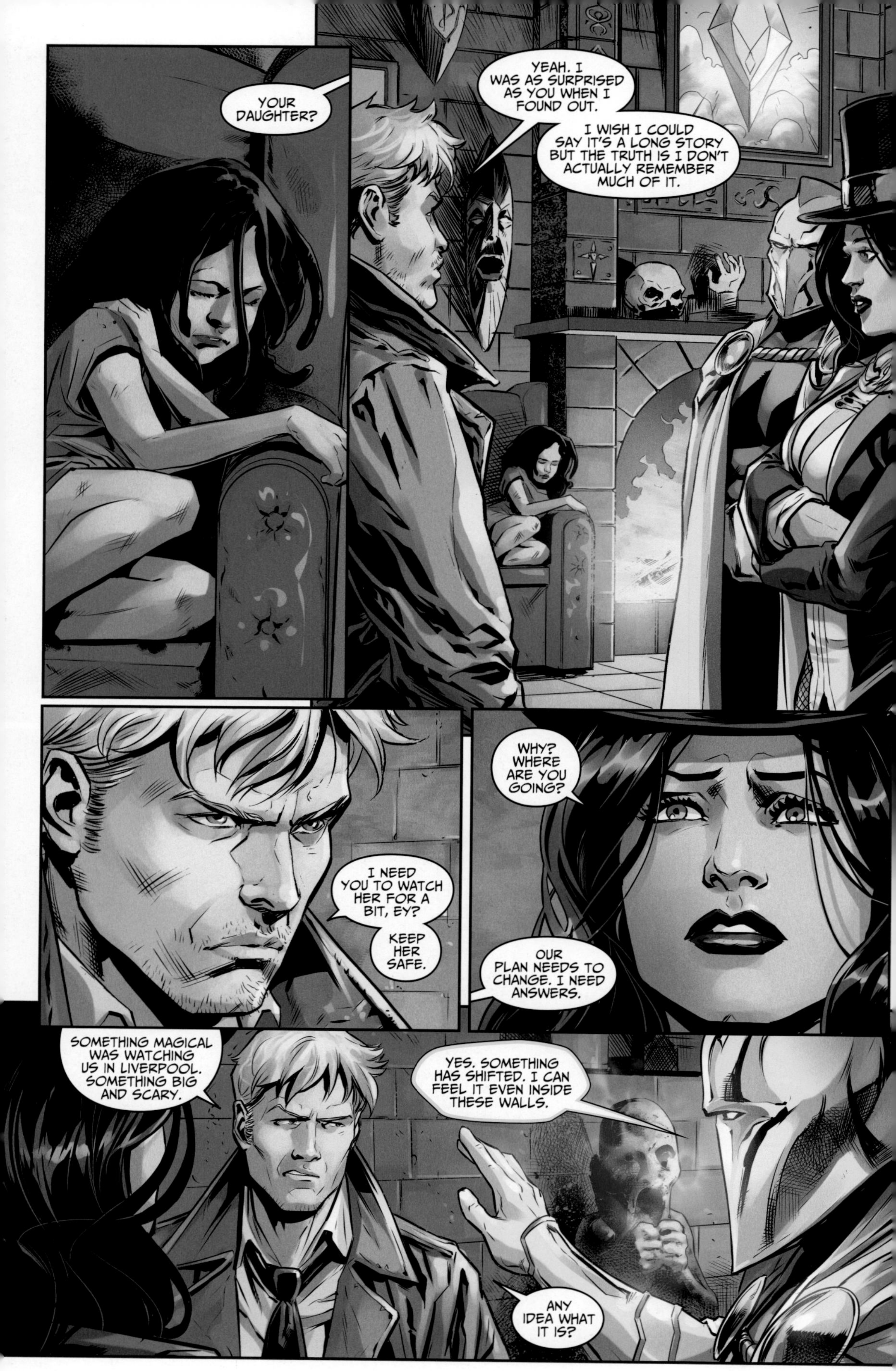
YOUR DAUGHTER?
YEAH. I WAS AS SURPRISED AS YOU WHEN I FOUND OUT.
I WISH I COULD SAY IT'S A LONG STORY BUT THE TRUTH IS I DON'T ACTUALLY REMEMBER MUCH OF IT.
I NEED YOU TO WATCH HER FOR A BIT, EY?
KEEP HER SAFE.
WHY? WHERE ARE YOU GOING?
OUR PLAN NEEDS TO CHANGE. I NEED ANSWERS.
SOMETHING MAGICAL WAS WATCHING US IN LIVERPOOL. SOMETHING BIG AND SCARY.
YES. SOMETHING HAS SHIFTED. I CAN FEEL IT EVEN INSIDE THESE WALLS.
ANY IDEA WHAT IT IS?

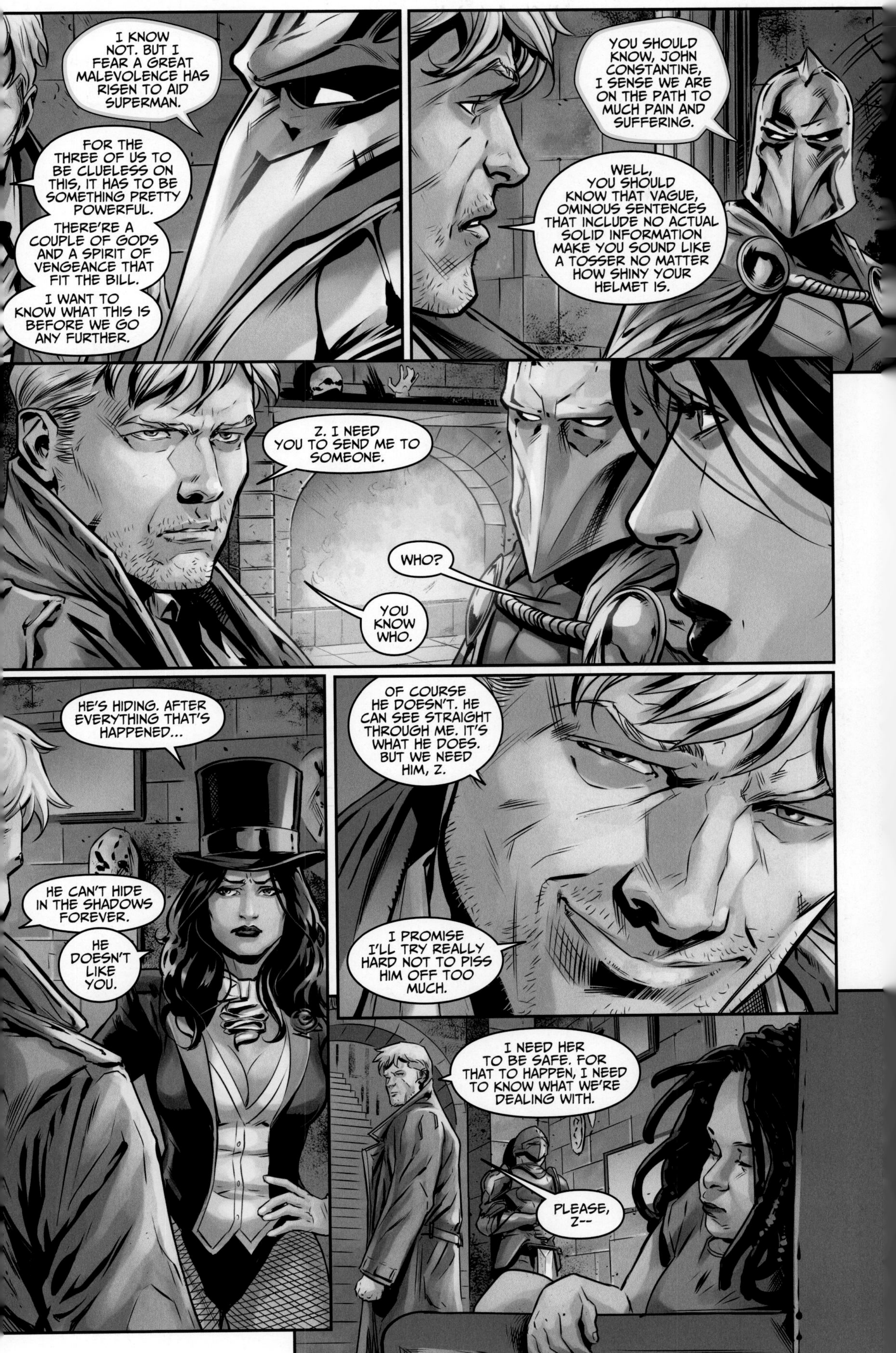
I KNOW NOT. BUT I FEAR A GREAT MALEVOLENCE HAS RISEN TO AID SUPERMAN.
FOR THE THREE OF US TO BE CLUELESS ON THIS, IT HAS TO BE SOMETHING PRETTY POWERFUL.
THERE'RE A COUPLE OF GODS AND A SPIRIT OF VENGEANCE THAT FIT THE BILL.
I WANT TO KNOW WHAT THIS IS BEFORE WE GO ANY FURTHER.
YOU SHOULD KNOW, JOHN CONSTANTINE, I SENSE WE ARE ON THE PATH TO MUCH PAIN AND SUFFERING.
WELL, YOU SHOULD KNOW THAT VAGUE, OMINOUS SENTENCES THAT INCLUDE NO ACTUAL SOLID INFORMATION MAKE YOU SOUND LIKE A TOSSER NO MATTER HOW SHINY YOUR HELMET IS.
Z. I NEED YOU TO SEND ME TO SOMEONE.
WHO?
YOU KNOW WHO.
HE'S HIDING. AFTER EVERYTHING THAT'S HAPPENED...
HE CAN'T HIDE IN THE SHADOWS FOREVER.
HE DOESN'T LIKE YOU.
OF COURSE HE DOESN'T. HE CAN SEE STRAIGHT THROUGH ME. IT'S WHAT HE DOES. BUT WE NEED HIM, Z.
I PROMISE I'LL TRY REALLY HARD NOT TO PISS HIM OFF TOO MUCH.
I NEED HER TO BE SAFE. FOR THAT TO HAPPEN, I NEED TO KNOW WHAT WE'RE DEALING WITH.
PLEASE, Z--

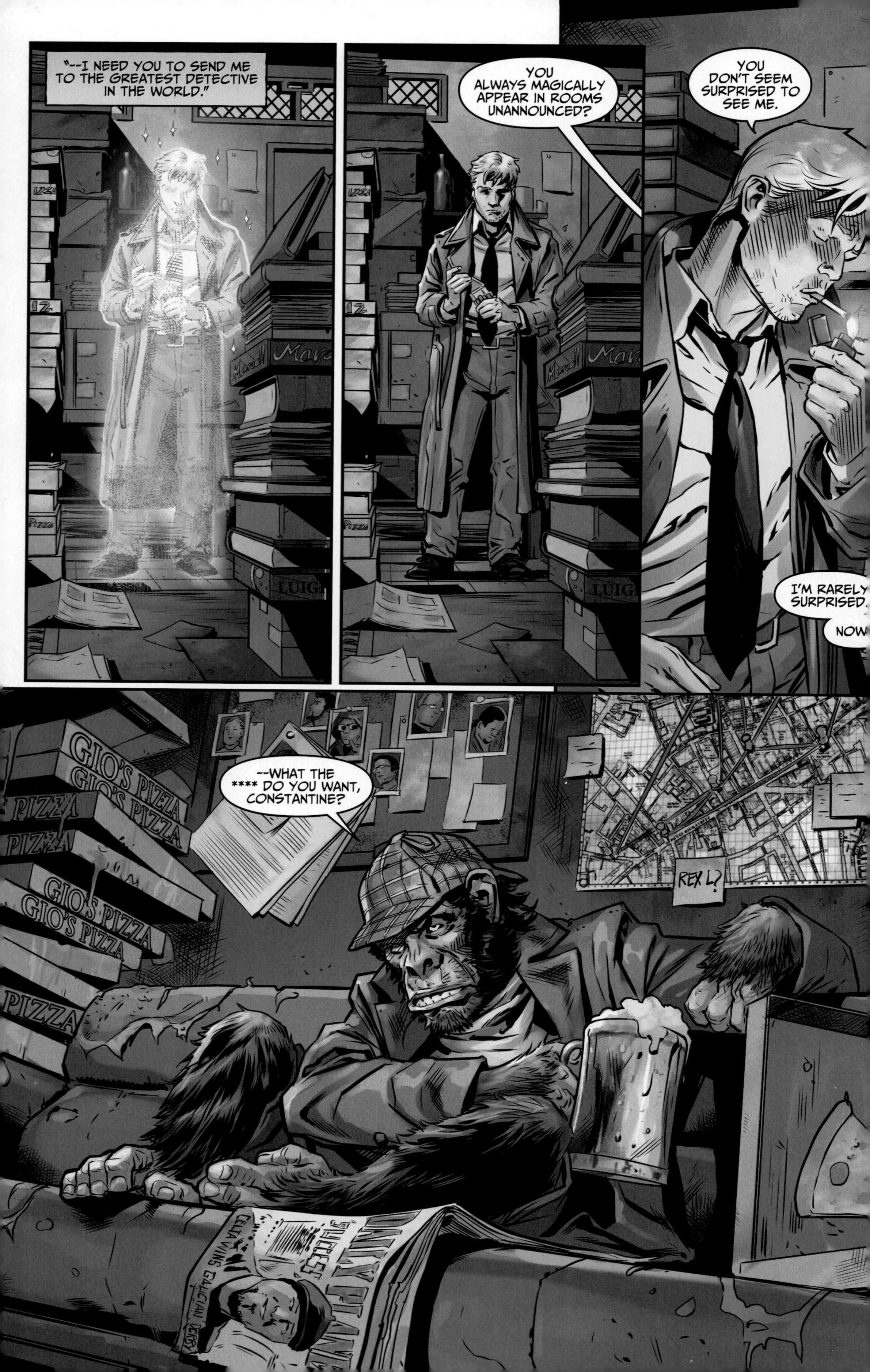
"--I NEED YOU TO SEND ME TO THE GREATEST DETECTIVE IN THE WORLD."
YOU ALWAYS MAGICALLY APPEAR IN ROOMS UNANNOUNCED?
YOU DON'T SEEM SURPRISED TO SEE ME.
I'M RARELY SURPRISED.
NOW
--WHAT THE **** DO YOU WANT, CONSTANTINE?
GIO'S PIZZA
GIO'S PIZZA
PIZZA
REX L?

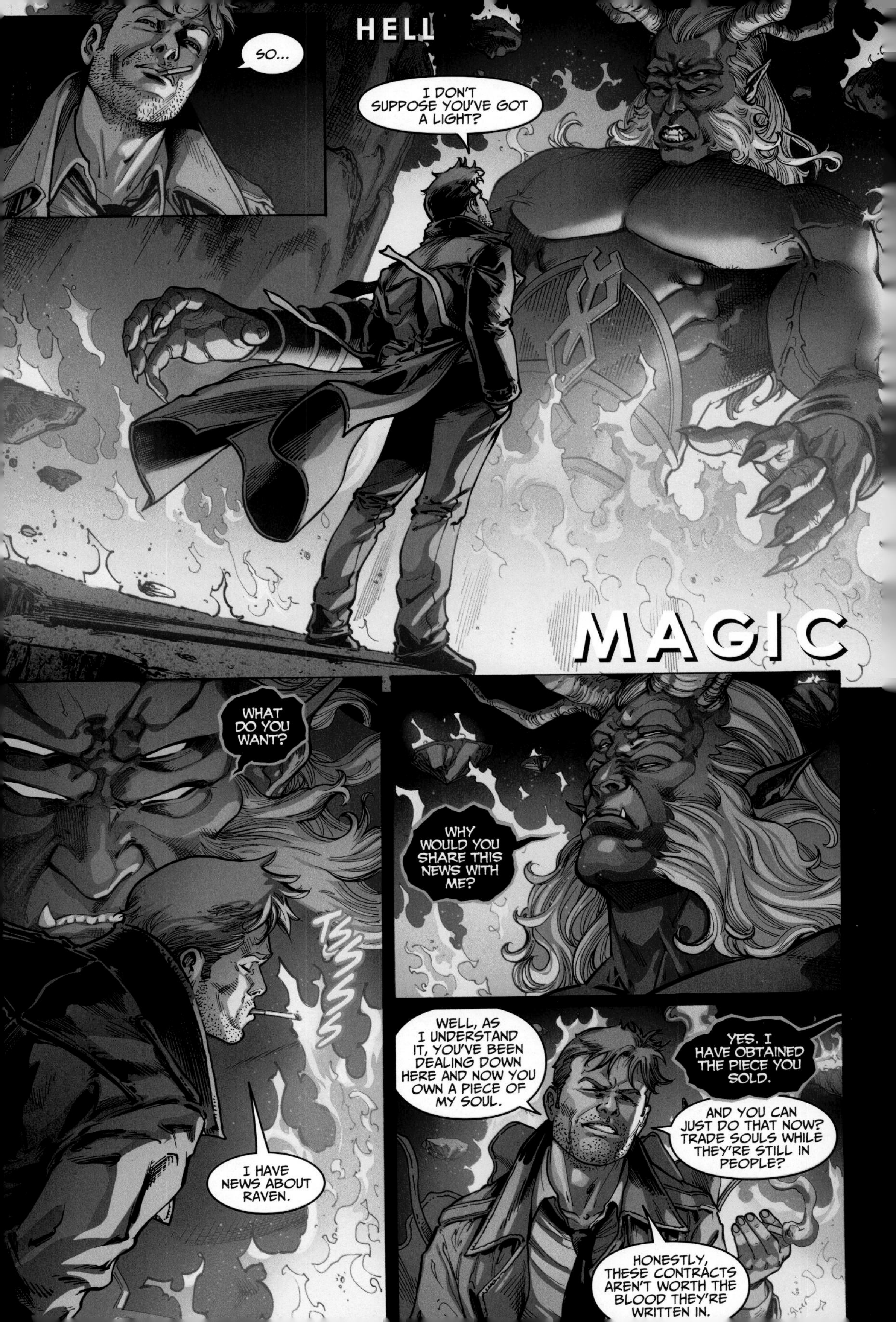
HELL
SO...
I DON'T SUPPOSE YOU'VE GOT A LIGHT?
MAGIC
WHAT DO YOU WANT?
TSSSSSS
I HAVE NEWS ABOUT RAVEN.
WHY WOULD YOU SHARE THIS NEWS WITH ME?
WELL, AS I UNDERSTAND IT, YOU'VE BEEN DEALING DOWN HERE AND NOW YOU OWN A PIECE OF MY SOUL.
YES. I HAVE OBTAINED THE PIECE YOU SOLD.
AND YOU CAN JUST DO THAT NOW? TRADE SOULS WHILE THEY'RE STILL IN PEOPLE?
HONESTLY, THESE CONTRACTS AREN'T WORTH THE BLOOD THEY'RE WRITTEN IN.

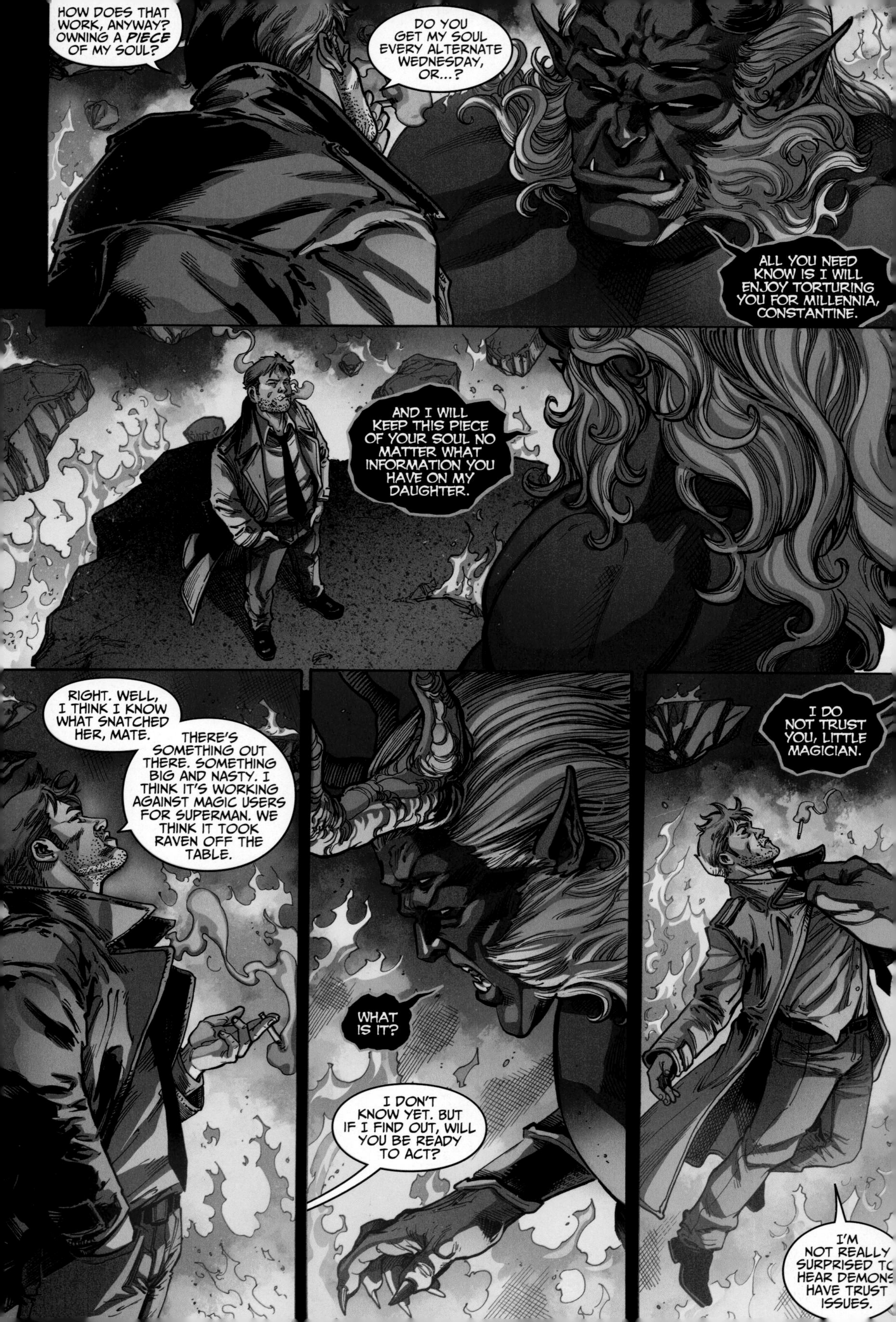

HOW DOES THAT WORK, ANYWAY? OWNING A *PIECE* OF MY SOUL?
DO YOU GET MY SOUL EVERY ALTERNATE WEDNESDAY, OR...?
ALL YOU NEED KNOW IS I WILL ENJOY TORTURING YOU FOR MILLENNIA, CONSTANTINE.
AND I WILL KEEP THIS PIECE OF YOUR SOUL NO MATTER WHAT INFORMATION YOU HAVE ON MY DAUGHTER.
RIGHT. WELL, I THINK I KNOW WHAT SNATCHED HER, MATE.
THERE'S SOMETHING OUT THERE. SOMETHING BIG AND NASTY. I THINK IT'S WORKING AGAINST MAGIC USERS FOR SUPERMAN. WE THINK IT TOOK RAVEN OFF THE TABLE.
WHAT IS IT?
I DON'T KNOW YET. BUT IF I FIND OUT, WILL YOU BE READY TO ACT?
I DO NOT TRUST YOU, LITTLE MAGICIAN.
I'M NOT REALLY SURPRISED TO HEAR DEMONS HAVE TRUST ISSUES.

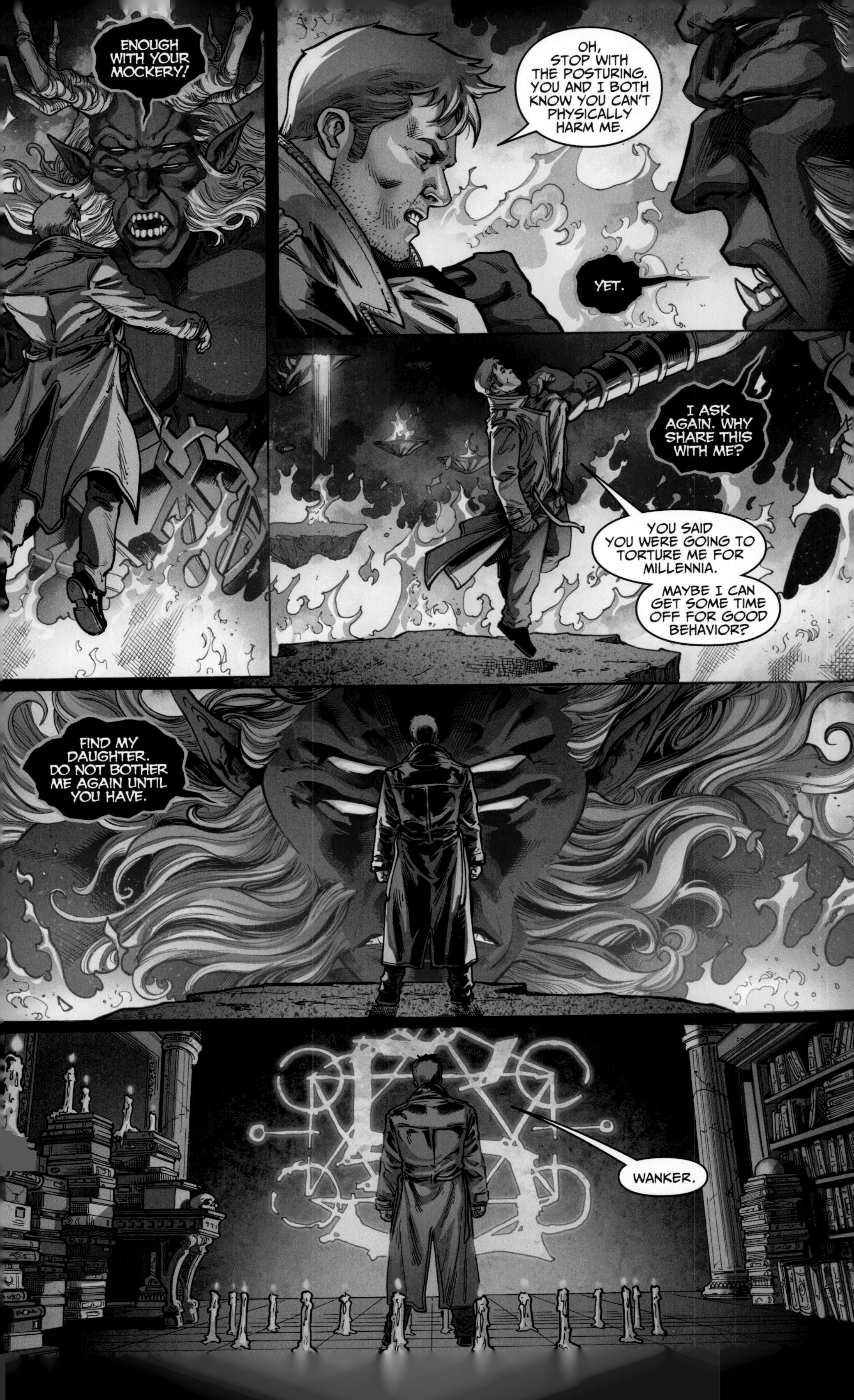
ENOUGH WITH YOUR MOCKERY!
OH, STOP WITH THE POSTURING. YOU AND I BOTH KNOW YOU CAN'T PHYSICALLY HARM ME.
YET.
I ASK AGAIN. WHY SHARE THIS WITH ME?
YOU SAID YOU WERE GOING TO TORTURE ME FOR MILLENNIA.
MAYBE I CAN GET SOME TIME OFF FOR GOOD BEHAVIOR?
FIND MY DAUGHTER. DO NOT BOTHER ME AGAIN UNTIL YOU HAVE.
WANKER.

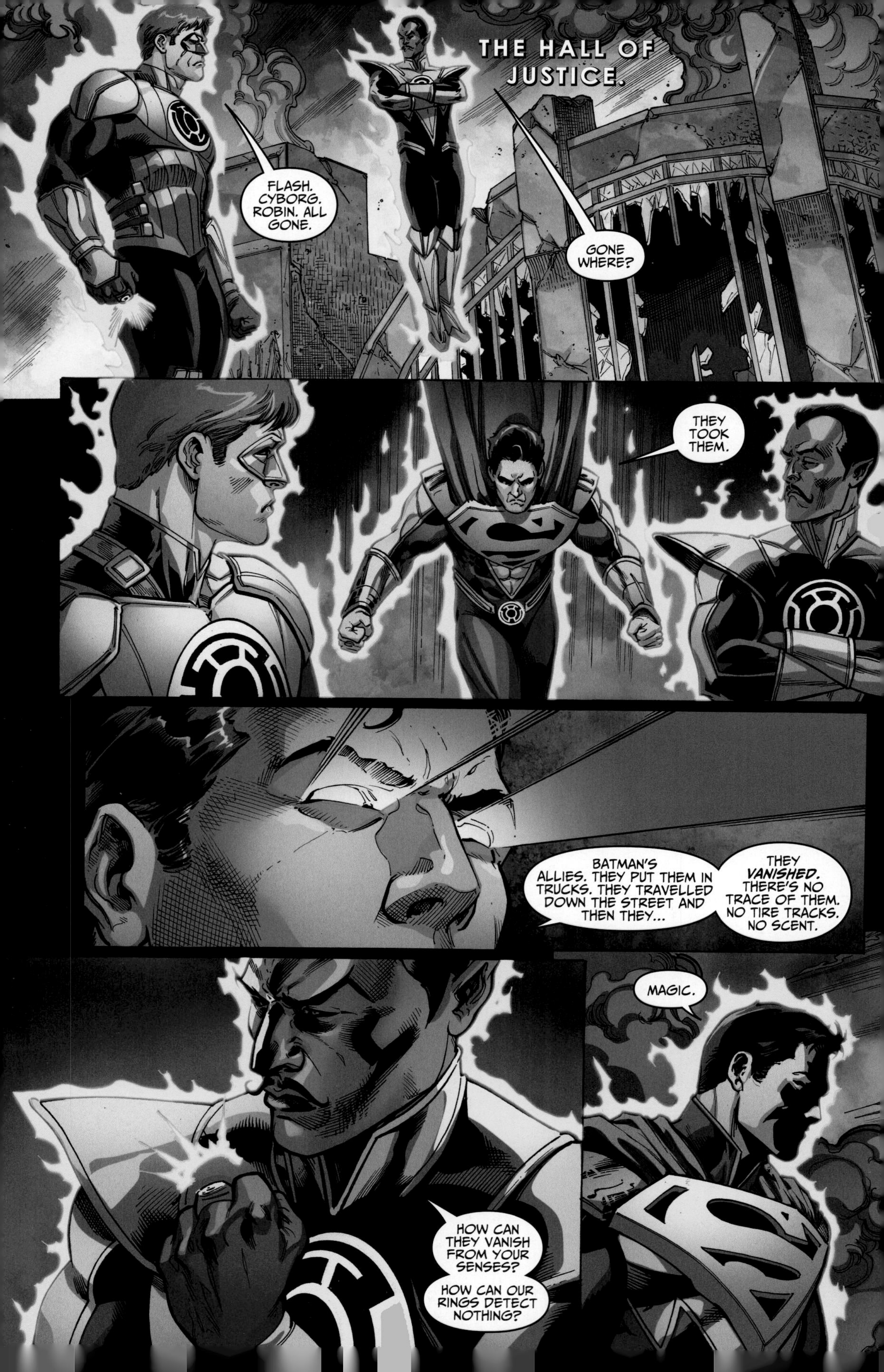
THE HALL OF JUSTICE.
FLASH. CYBORG. ROBIN. ALL GONE.
GONE WHERE?
THEY TOOK THEM.
BATMAN'S ALLIES. THEY PUT THEM IN TRUCKS. THEY TRAVELLED DOWN THE STREET AND THEN THEY...
THEY *VANISHED.* THERE'S NO TRACE OF THEM. NO TIRE TRACKS. NO SCENT.
MAGIC.
HOW CAN THEY VANISH FROM YOUR SENSES?
HOW CAN OUR RINGS DETECT NOTHING?

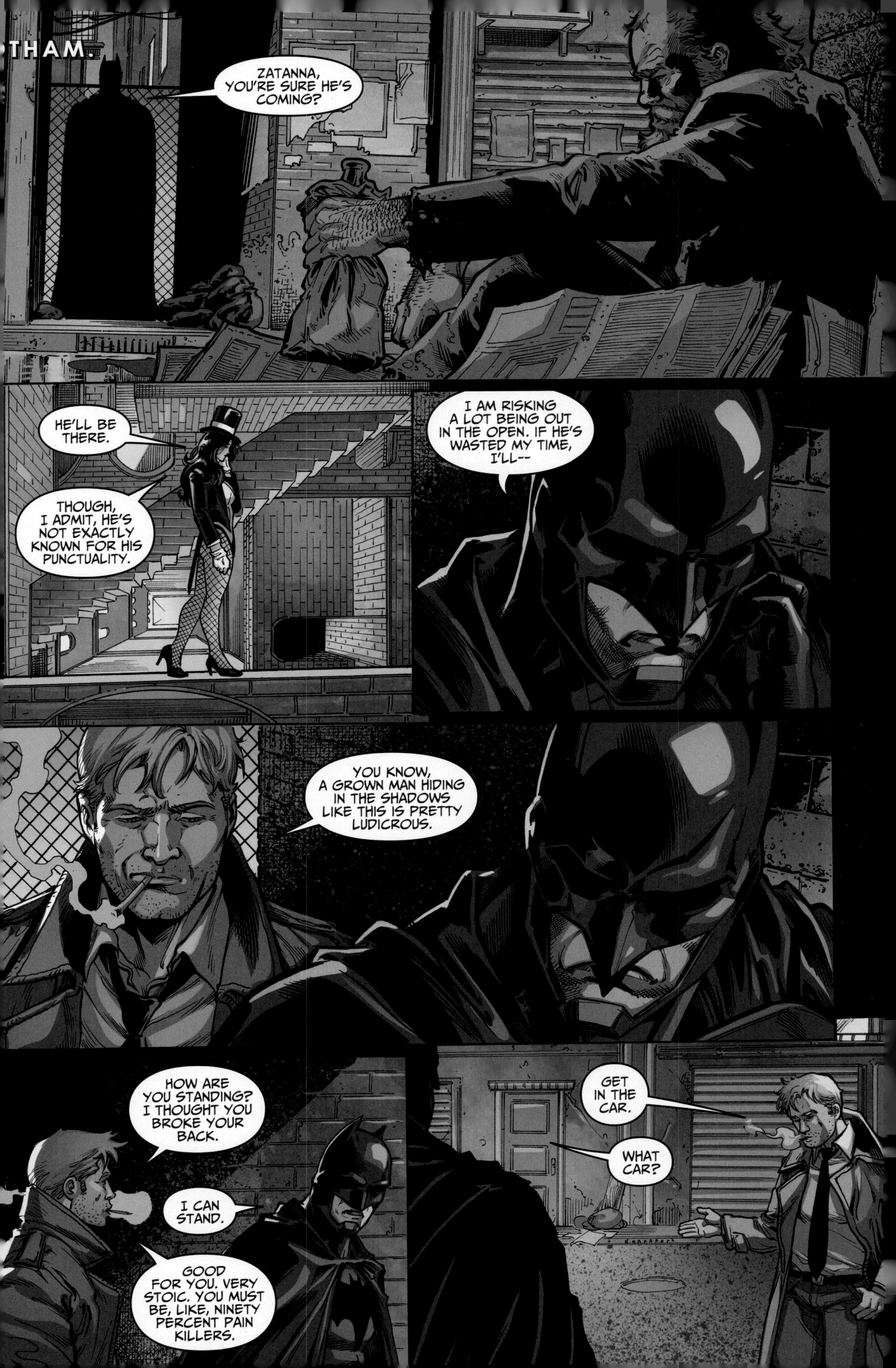
THAM.
ZATANNA, YOU'RE SURE HE'S COMING?
HE'LL BE THERE.
THOUGH, I ADMIT, HE'S NOT EXACTLY KNOWN FOR HIS PUNCTUALITY.
I AM RISKING A LOT BEING OUT IN THE OPEN. IF HE'S WASTED MY TIME, I'LL--
YOU KNOW, A GROWN MAN HIDING IN THE SHADOWS LIKE THIS IS PRETTY LUDICROUS.
HOW ARE YOU STANDING? I THOUGHT YOU BROKE YOUR BACK.
I CAN STAND.
GOOD FOR YOU. VERY STOIC. YOU MUST BE, LIKE, NINETY PERCENT PAIN KILLERS.
GET IN THE CAR.
WHAT CAR?

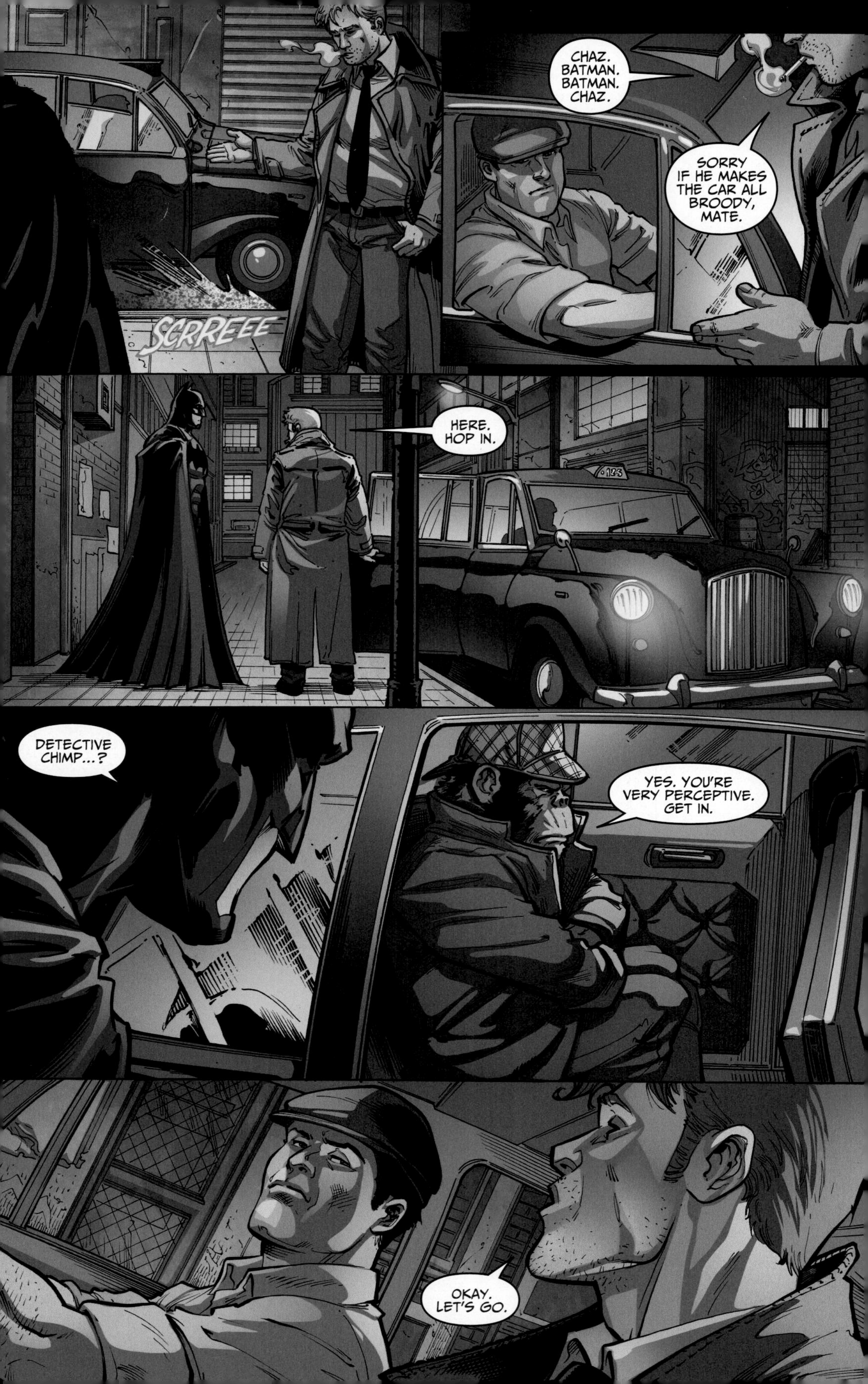
SCRREEE
CHAZ. BATMAN. BATMAN. CHAZ.
SORRY IF HE MAKES THE CAR ALL BROODY, MATE.
HERE. HOP IN.
DETECTIVE CHIMP...?
YES. YOU'RE VERY PERCEPTIVE. GET IN.
OKAY. LET'S GO.

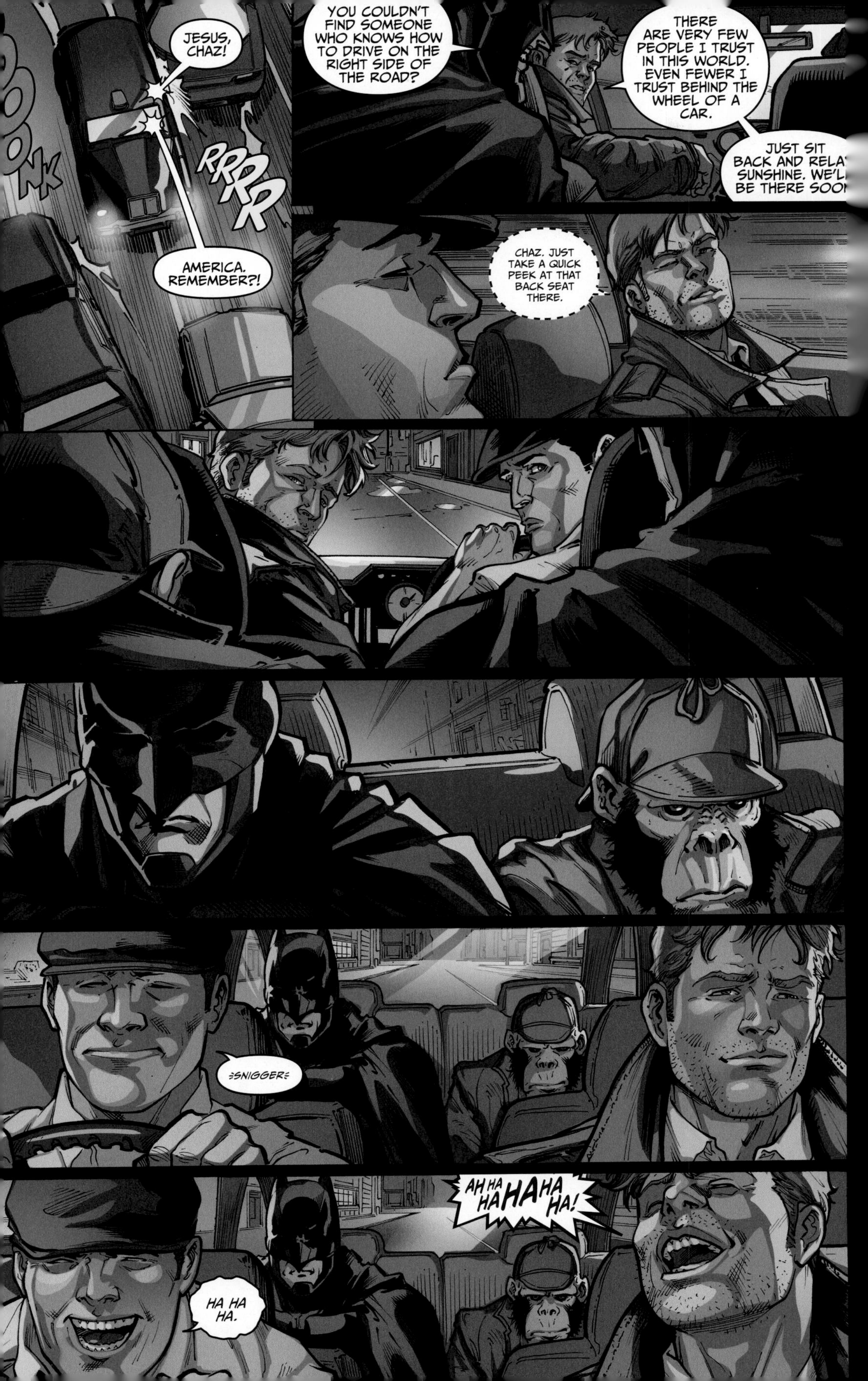
BOOONK
JESUS, CHAZ!
RRRR
AMERICA. REMEMBER?!
YOU COULDN'T FIND SOMEONE WHO KNOWS HOW TO DRIVE ON THE RIGHT SIDE OF THE ROAD?
THERE ARE VERY FEW PEOPLE I TRUST IN THIS WORLD. EVEN FEWER I TRUST BEHIND THE WHEEL OF A CAR.
JUST SIT BACK AND RELA SUNSHINE. WE'L BE THERE SOON
CHAZ. JUST TAKE A QUICK PEEK AT THAT BACK SEAT THERE.
SNIGGER
AH HA HA HA HA HA!
HA HA HA.

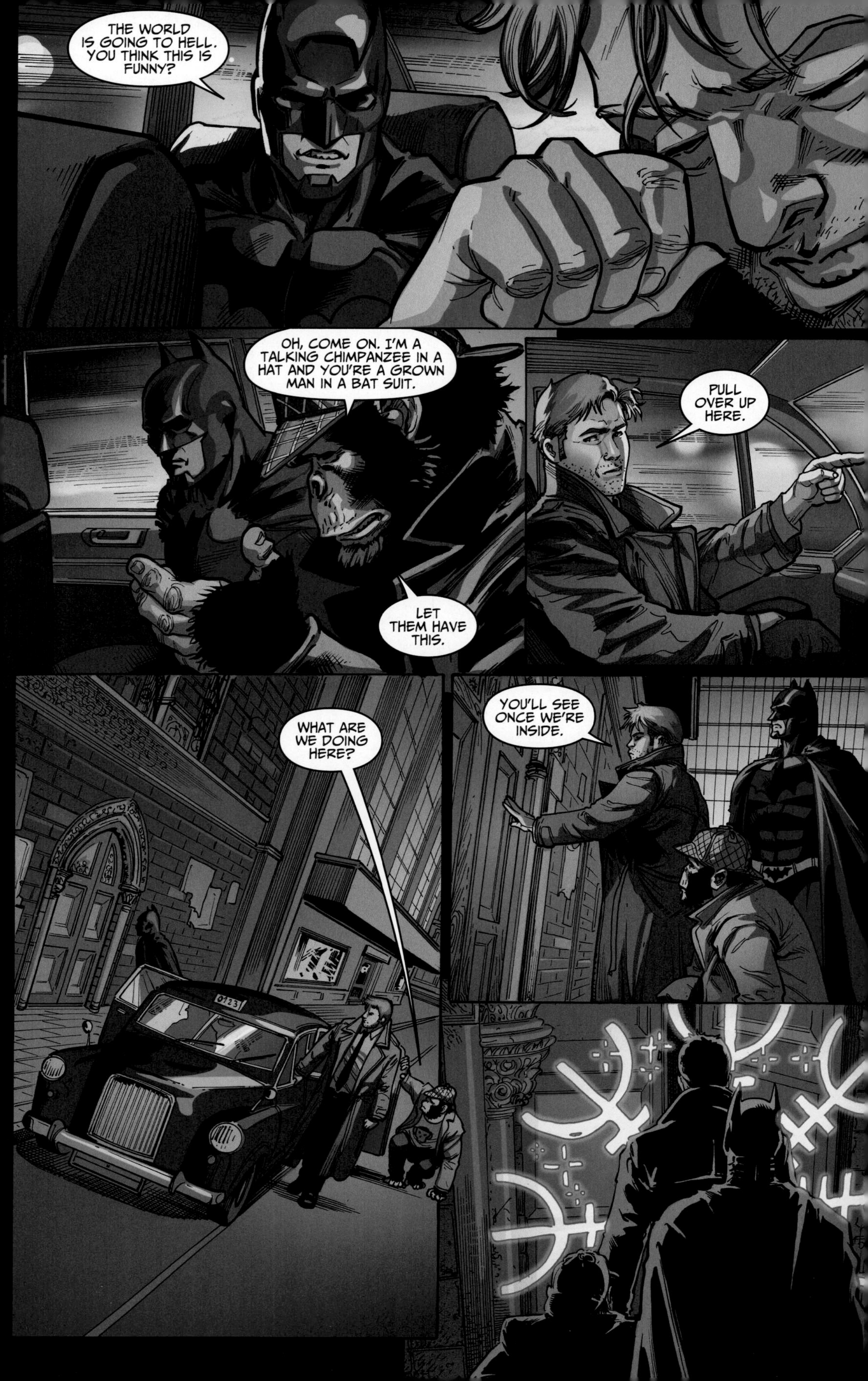
THE WORLD IS GOING TO HELL. YOU THINK THIS IS FUNNY?
OH, COME ON. I'M A TALKING CHIMPANZEE IN A HAT AND YOU'RE A GROWN MAN IN A BAT SUIT.
LET THEM HAVE THIS.
PULL OVER UP HERE.
WHAT ARE WE DOING HERE?
0123
YOU'LL SEE ONCE WE'RE INSIDE.

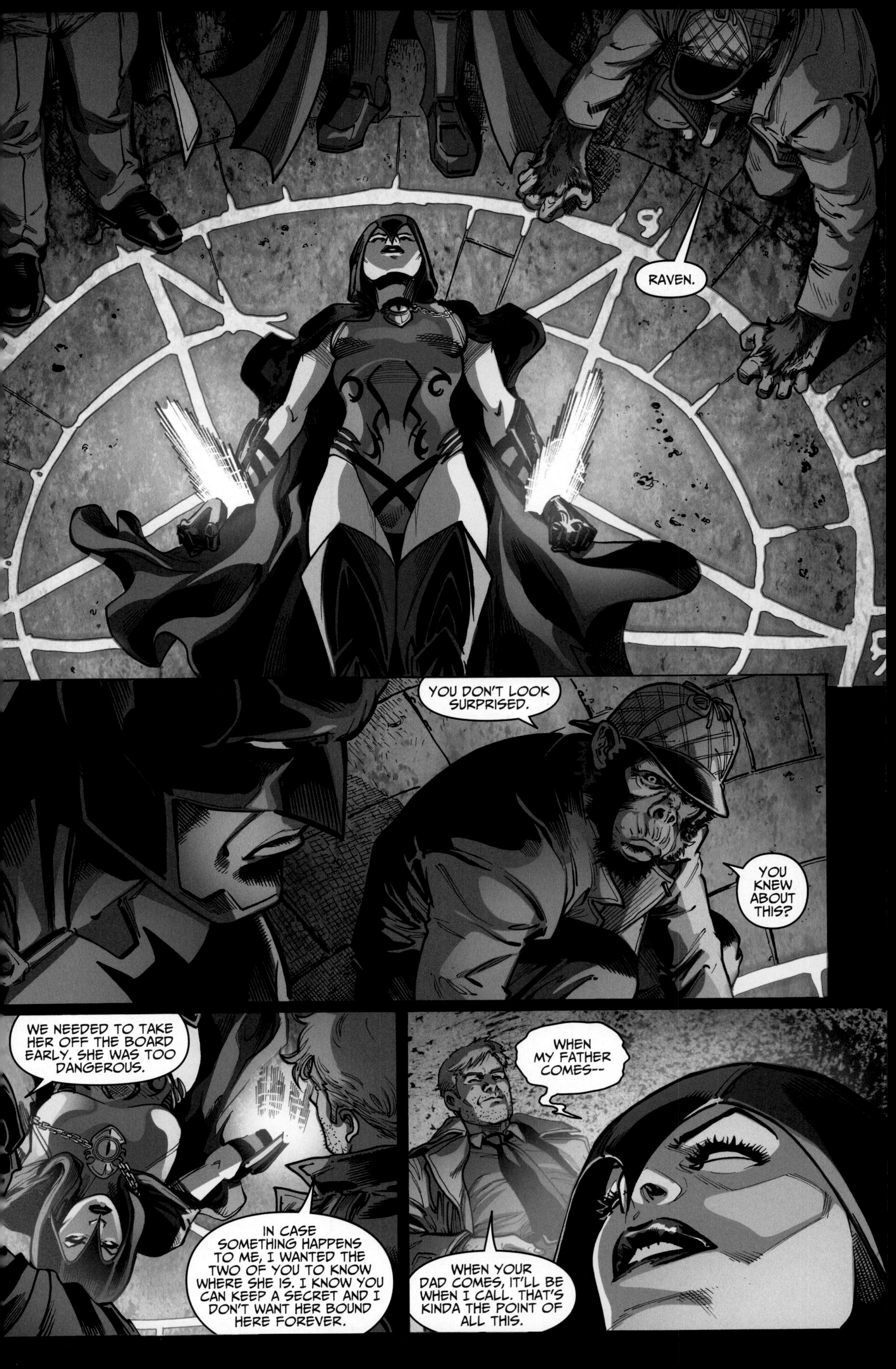
RAVEN.
YOU DON'T LOOK SURPRISED.
YOU KNEW ABOUT THIS?
WE NEEDED TO TAKE HER OFF THE BOARD EARLY. SHE WAS TOO DANGEROUS.
IN CASE SOMETHING HAPPENS TO ME, I WANTED THE TWO OF YOU TO KNOW WHERE SHE IS. I KNOW YOU CAN KEEP A SECRET AND I DON'T WANT HER BOUND HERE FOREVER.
WHEN MY FATHER COMES--
WHEN YOUR DAD COMES, IT'LL BE WHEN I CALL. THAT'S KINDA THE POINT OF ALL THIS.

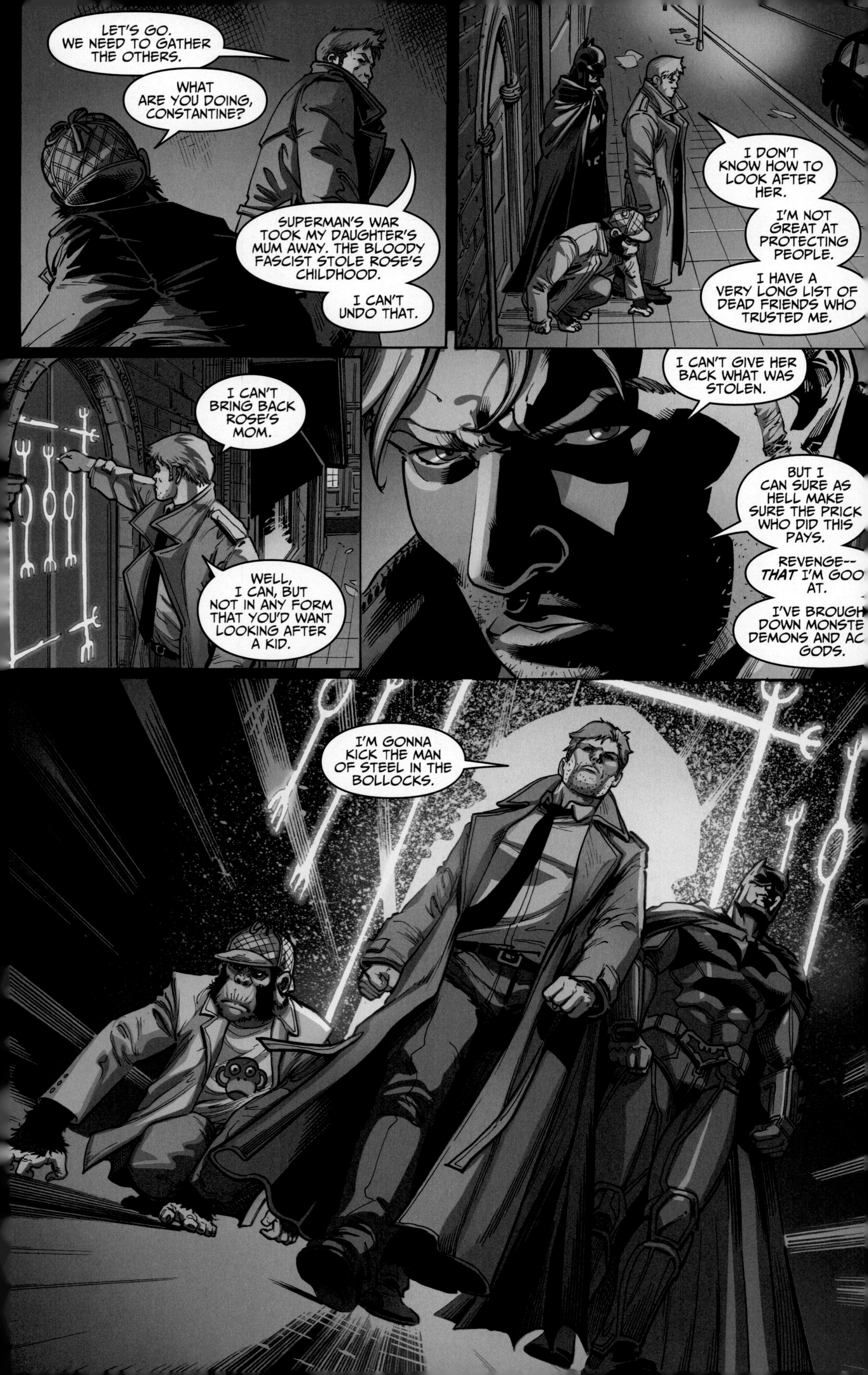
LET'S GO. WE NEED TO GATHER THE OTHERS.
WHAT ARE YOU DOING, CONSTANTINE?
SUPERMAN'S WAR TOOK MY DAUGHTER'S MUM AWAY. THE BLOODY FASCIST STOLE ROSE'S CHILDHOOD.
I CAN'T UNDO THAT.
I DON'T KNOW HOW TO LOOK AFTER HER.
I'M NOT GREAT AT PROTECTING PEOPLE.
I HAVE A VERY LONG LIST OF DEAD FRIENDS WHO TRUSTED ME.
I CAN'T BRING BACK ROSE'S MOM.
WELL, I CAN, BUT NOT IN ANY FORM THAT YOU'D WANT LOOKING AFTER A KID.
I CAN'T GIVE HER BACK WHAT WAS STOLEN.
BUT I CAN SURE AS HELL MAKE SURE THE PRICK WHO DID THIS PAYS.
REVENGE-- *THAT* I'M GOO AT.
I'VE BROUGH DOWN MONSTE DEMONS AND AC GODS.
I'M GONNA KICK THE MAN OF STEEL IN THE BOLLOCKS.

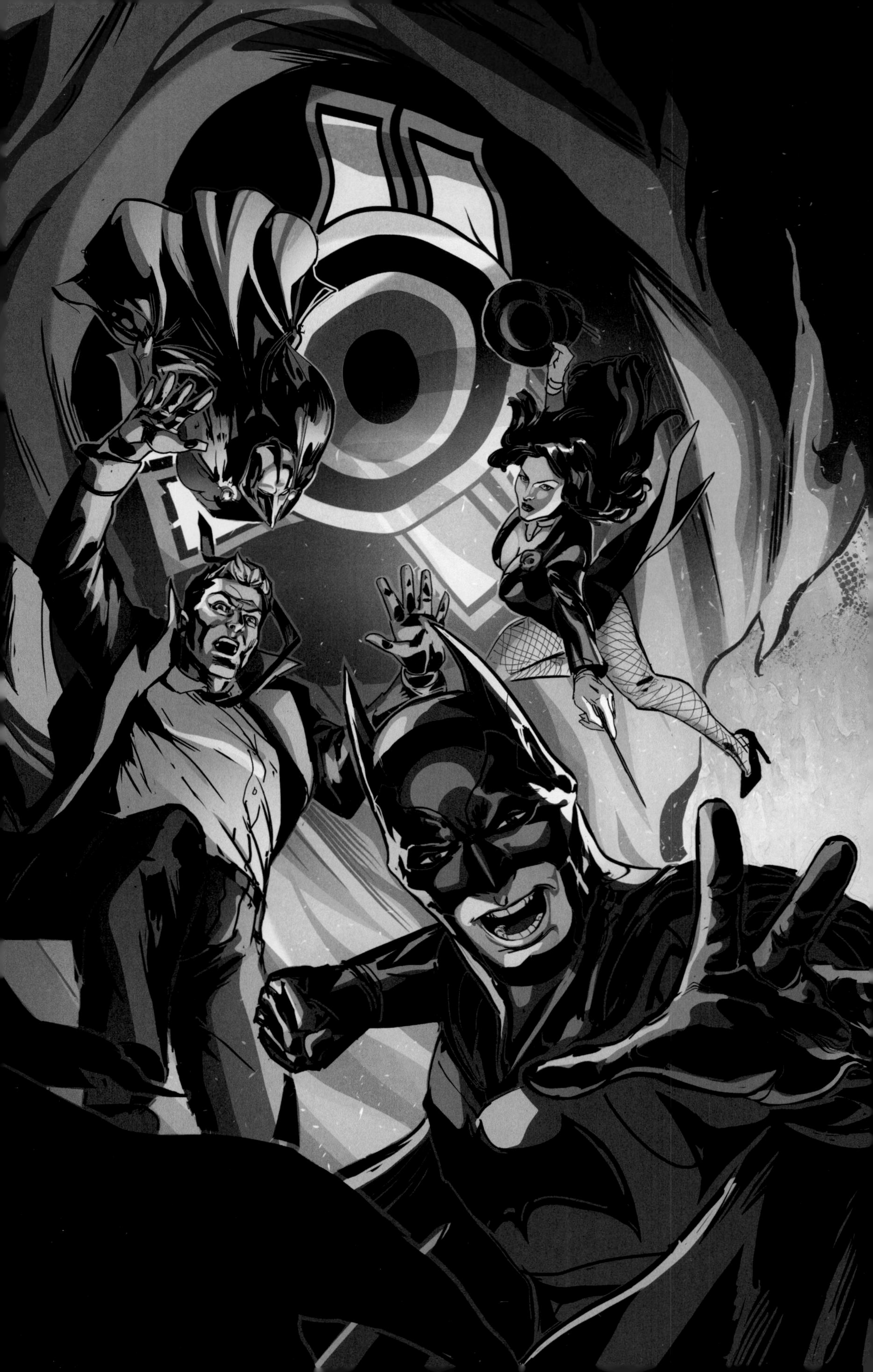

"Gathering Forces" **Mike S. Miller** Artist **J. Nanjan** Colorist
"Spirit of Vengeance" **Bruno Redondo & Xermanico** Artists **Rex Lokus** Colorist
Cover Art by **Trevor McCarthy & Rex Lokus**

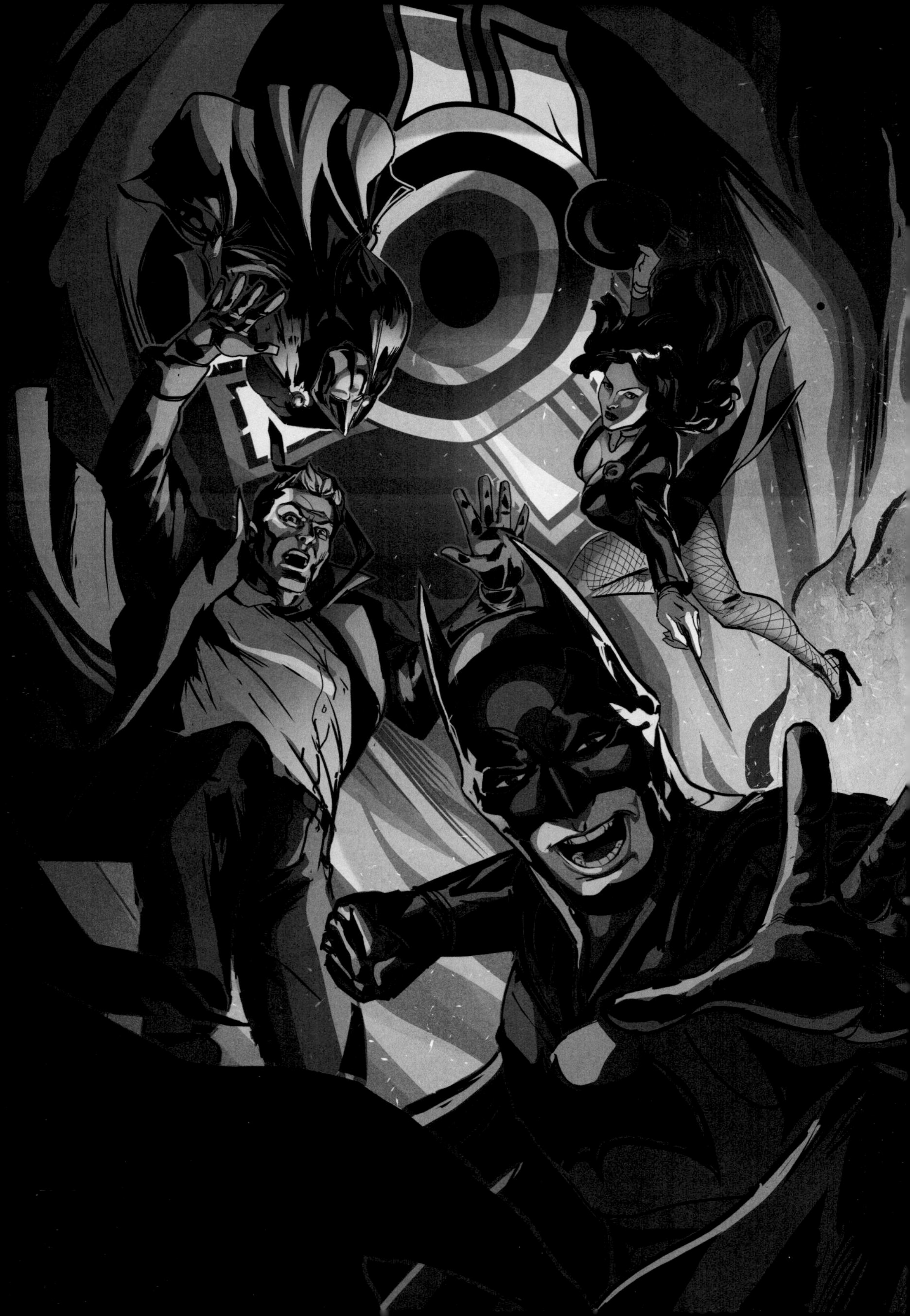

GATHERING FORCES

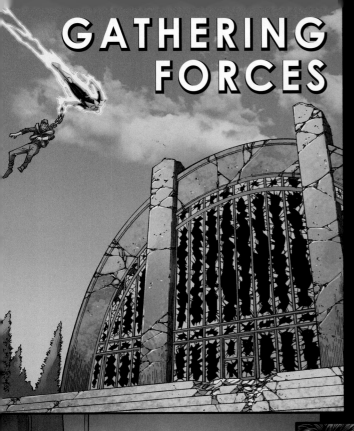

UNF!

OFFICER SPRAGUE. YOU WERE PART OF THE ATTACK ON THIS HALL AND ON ITS HEROES.

ANSWER HIM!

HNNG!

IT'S OKAY, SINESTRO.

LET HIM GO.

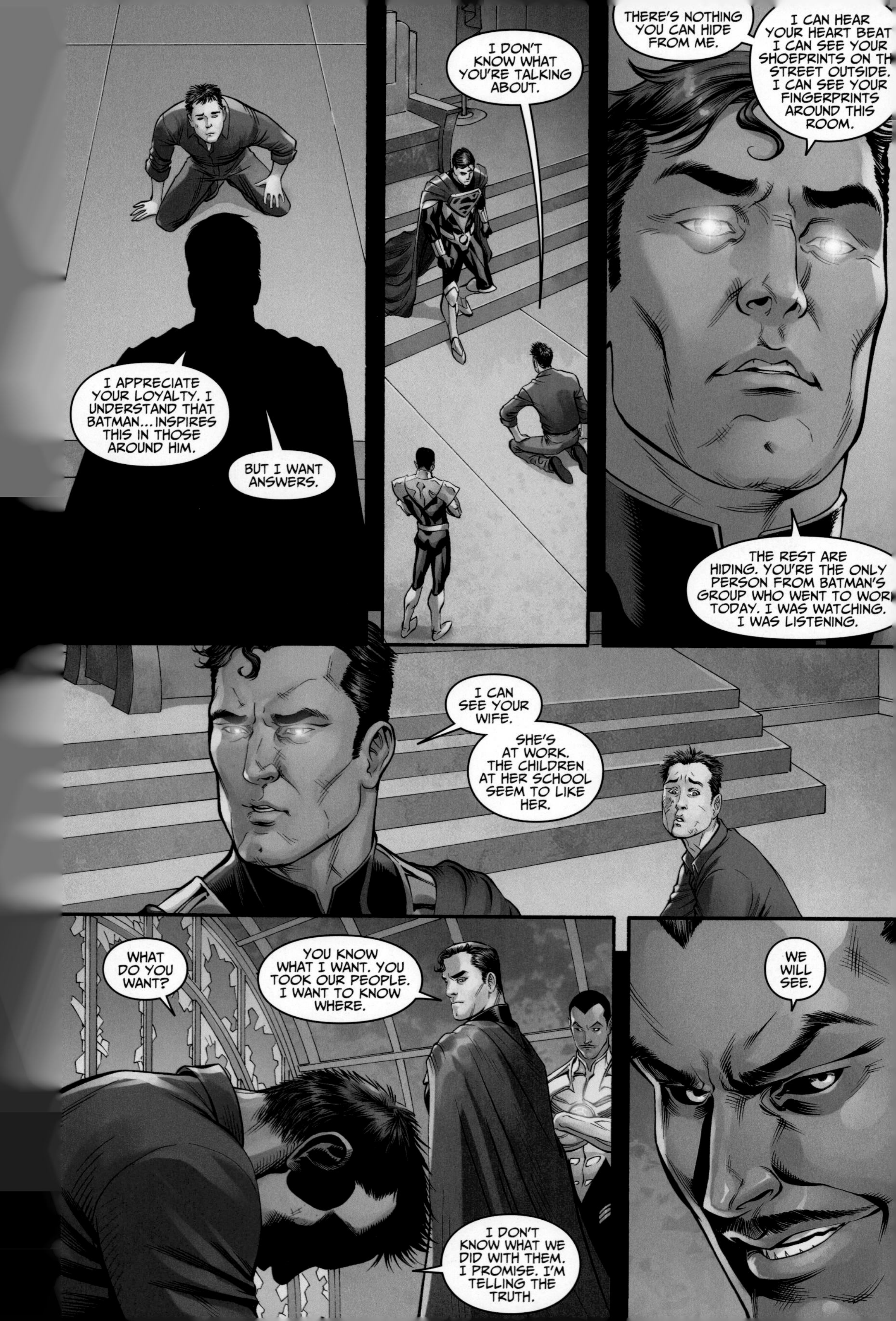
I APPRECIATE YOUR LOYALTY. I UNDERSTAND THAT BATMAN...INSPIRES THIS IN THOSE AROUND HIM.
BUT I WANT ANSWERS.
I DON'T KNOW WHAT YOU'RE TALKING ABOUT.
THERE'S NOTHING YOU CAN HIDE FROM ME.
I CAN HEAR YOUR HEART BEAT. I CAN SEE YOUR SHOEPRINTS ON TH STREET OUTSIDE. I CAN SEE YOUR FINGERPRINTS AROUND THIS ROOM.
THE REST ARE HIDING. YOU'RE THE ONLY PERSON FROM BATMAN'S GROUP WHO WENT TO WOR TODAY. I WAS WATCHING. I WAS LISTENING.
I CAN SEE YOUR WIFE.
SHE'S AT WORK. THE CHILDREN AT HER SCHOOL SEEM TO LIKE HER.
WHAT DO YOU WANT?
YOU KNOW WHAT I WANT. YOU TOOK OUR PEOPLE. I WANT TO KNOW WHERE.
I DON'T KNOW WHAT WE DID WITH THEM. I PROMISE. I'M TELLING THE TRUTH.
WE WILL SEE.

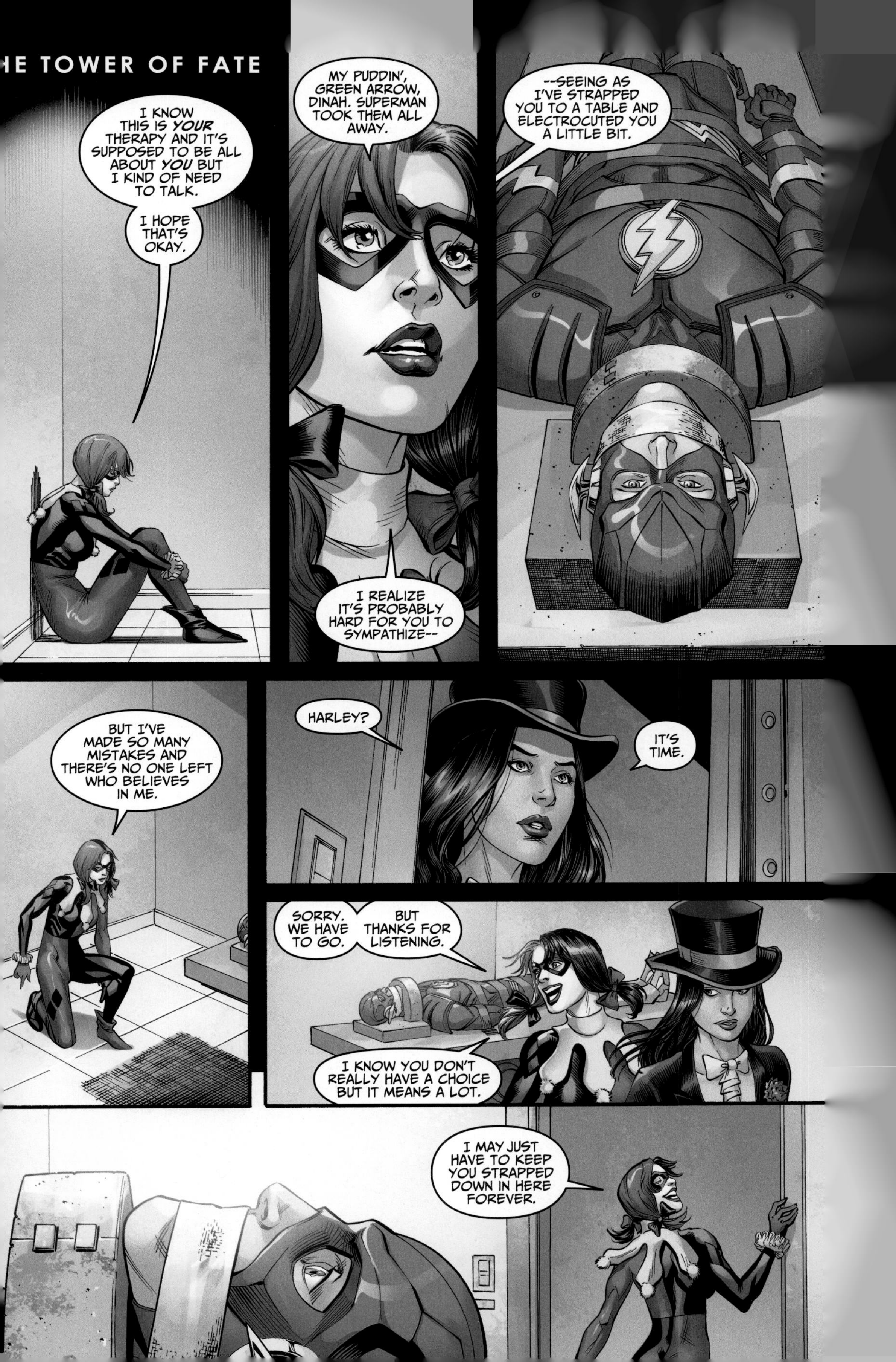
THE TOWER OF FATE
I KNOW THIS IS YOUR THERAPY AND IT'S SUPPOSED TO BE ALL ABOUT YOU BUT I KIND OF NEED TO TALK.
I HOPE THAT'S OKAY.
MY PUDDIN', GREEN ARROW, DINAH. SUPERMAN TOOK THEM ALL AWAY.
I REALIZE IT'S PROBABLY HARD FOR YOU TO SYMPATHIZE--
--SEEING AS I'VE STRAPPED YOU TO A TABLE AND ELECTROCUTED YOU A LITTLE BIT.
BUT I'VE MADE SO MANY MISTAKES AND THERE'S NO ONE LEFT WHO BELIEVES IN ME.
HARLEY?
IT'S TIME.
SORRY. WE HAVE TO GO.
BUT THANKS FOR LISTENING.
I KNOW YOU DON'T REALLY HAVE A CHOICE BUT IT MEANS A LOT.
I MAY JUST HAVE TO KEEP YOU STRAPPED DOWN IN HERE FOREVER.

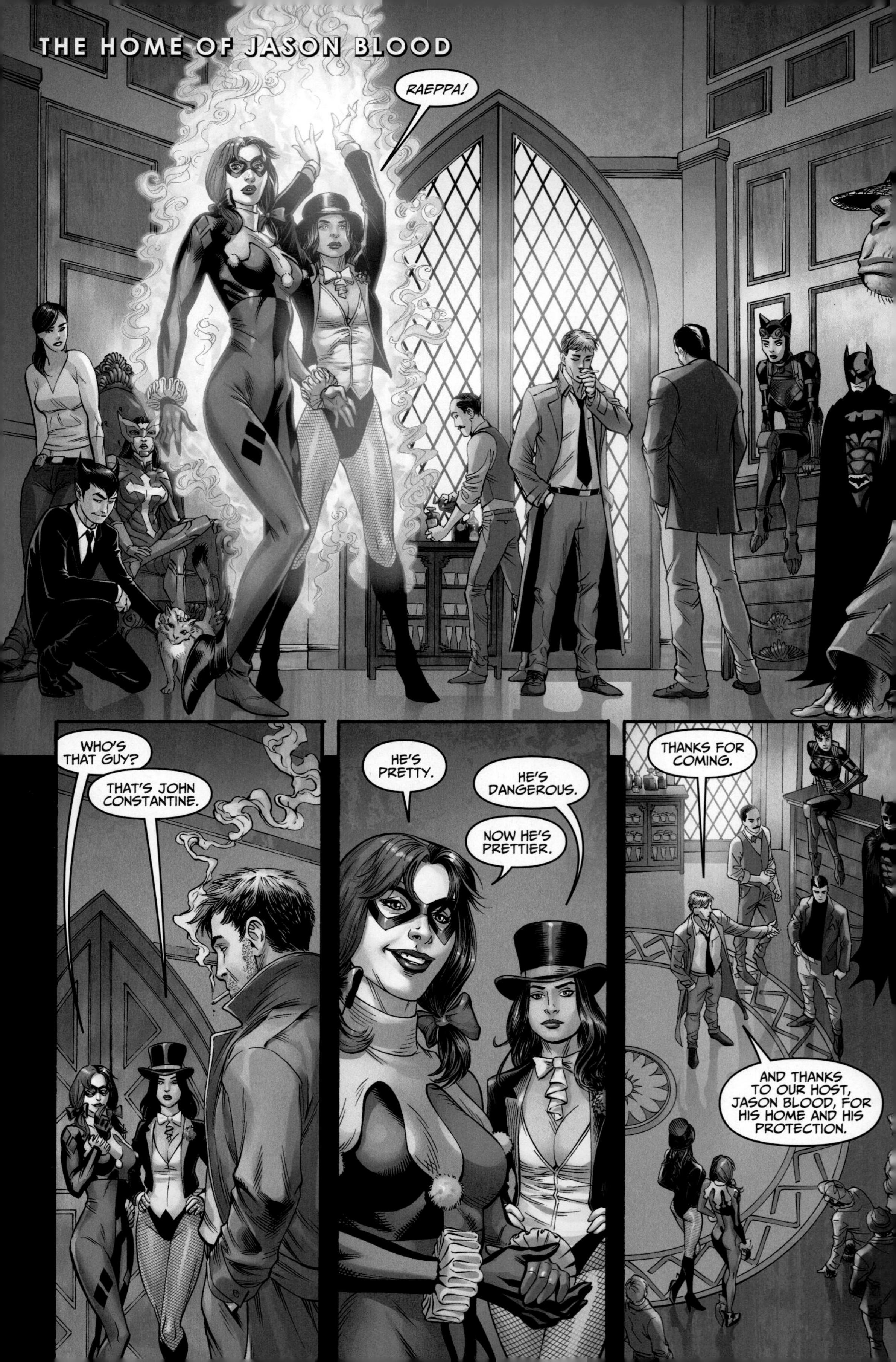
THE HOME OF JASON BLOOD
RAEPPA!
WHO'S THAT GUY?
THAT'S JOHN CONSTANTINE.
HE'S PRETTY.
HE'S DANGEROUS.
NOW HE'S PRETTIER.
THANKS FOR COMING.
AND THANKS TO OUR HOST, JASON BLOOD, FOR HIS HOME AND HIS PROTECTION.

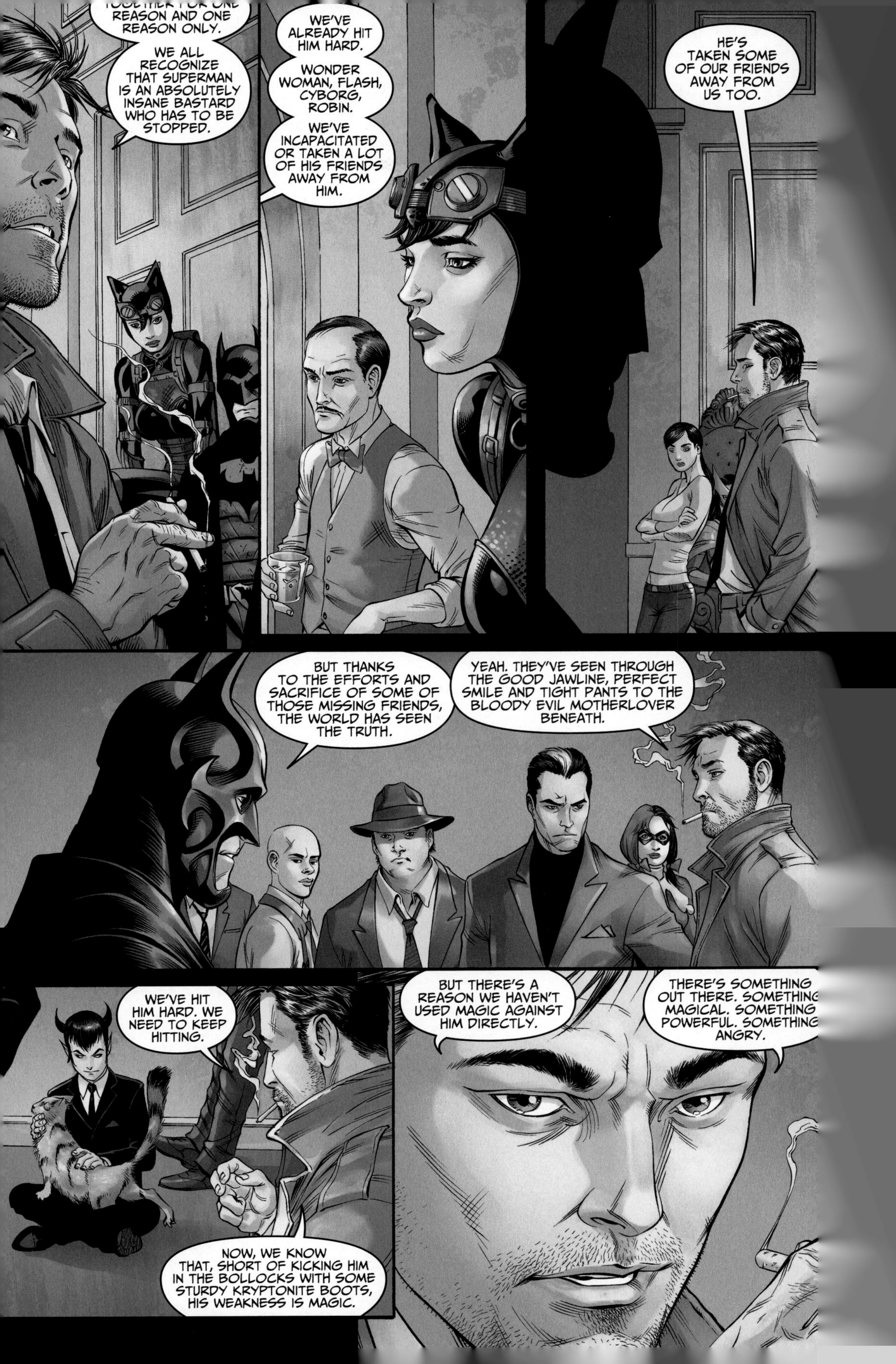
REASON AND ONE REASON ONLY.
WE ALL RECOGNIZE THAT SUPERMAN IS AN ABSOLUTELY INSANE BASTARD WHO HAS TO BE STOPPED.
WE'VE ALREADY HIT HIM HARD.
WONDER WOMAN, FLASH, CYBORG, ROBIN.
WE'VE INCAPACITATED OR TAKEN A LOT OF HIS FRIENDS AWAY FROM HIM.
HE'S TAKEN SOME OF OUR FRIENDS AWAY FROM US TOO.
BUT THANKS TO THE EFFORTS AND SACRIFICE OF SOME OF THOSE MISSING FRIENDS, THE WORLD HAS SEEN THE TRUTH.
YEAH. THEY'VE SEEN THROUGH THE GOOD JAWLINE, PERFECT SMILE AND TIGHT PANTS TO THE BLOODY EVIL MOTHERLOVER BENEATH.
WE'VE HIT HIM HARD. WE NEED TO KEEP HITTING.
NOW, WE KNOW THAT, SHORT OF KICKING HIM IN THE BOLLOCKS WITH SOME STURDY KRYPTONITE BOOTS, HIS WEAKNESS IS MAGIC.
BUT THERE'S A REASON WE HAVEN'T USED MAGIC AGAINST HIM DIRECTLY.
THERE'S SOMETHING OUT THERE. SOMETHING MAGICAL. SOMETHING POWERFUL. SOMETHING ANGRY.

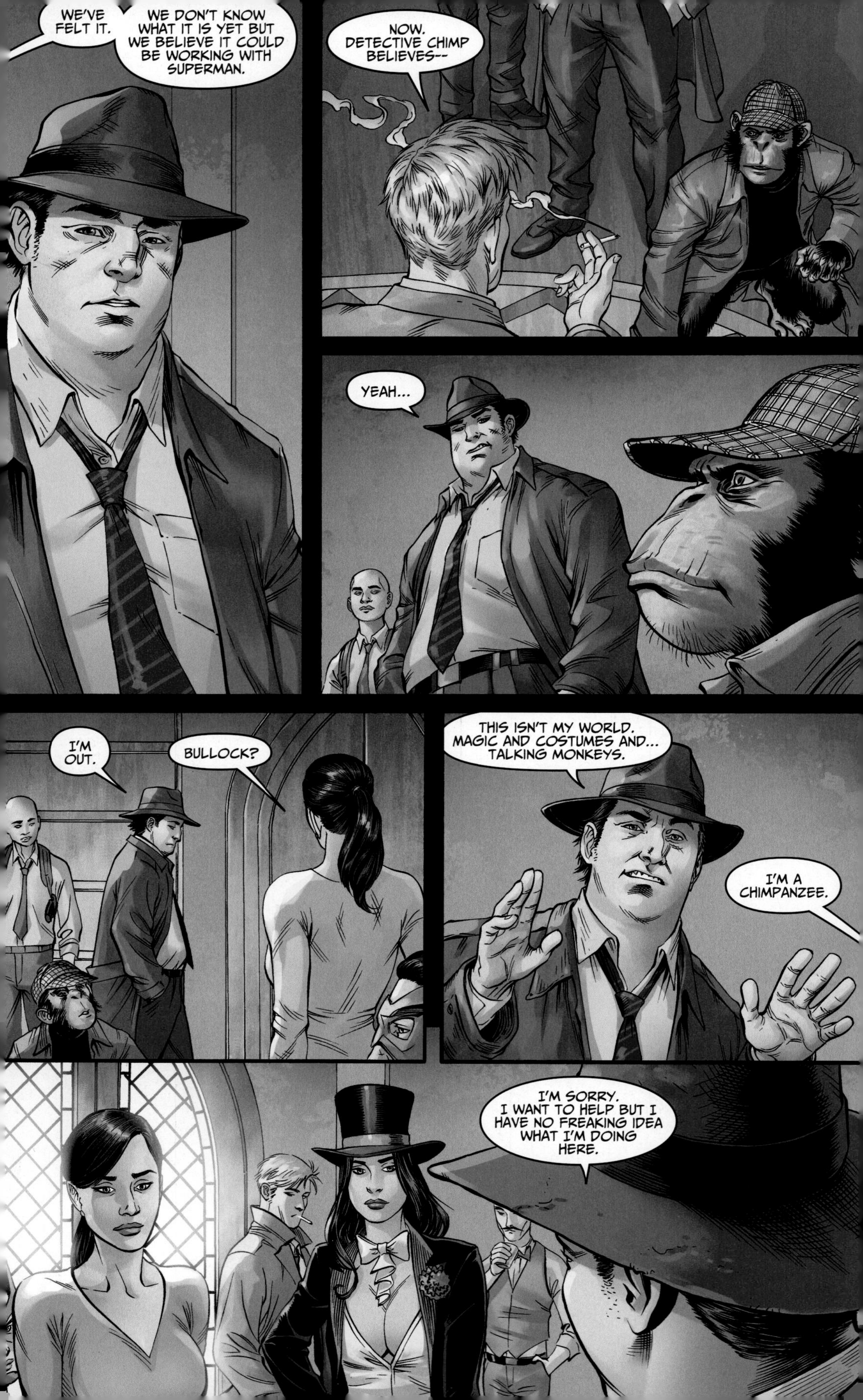
WE'VE FELT IT.
WE DON'T KNOW WHAT IT IS YET BUT WE BELIEVE IT COULD BE WORKING WITH SUPERMAN.
NOW. DETECTIVE CHIMP BELIEVES--
YEAH...
I'M OUT.
BULLOCK?
THIS ISN'T MY WORLD. MAGIC AND COSTUMES AND... TALKING MONKEYS.
I'M A CHIMPANZEE.
I'M SORRY. I WANT TO HELP BUT I HAVE NO FREAKING IDEA WHAT I'M DOING HERE.

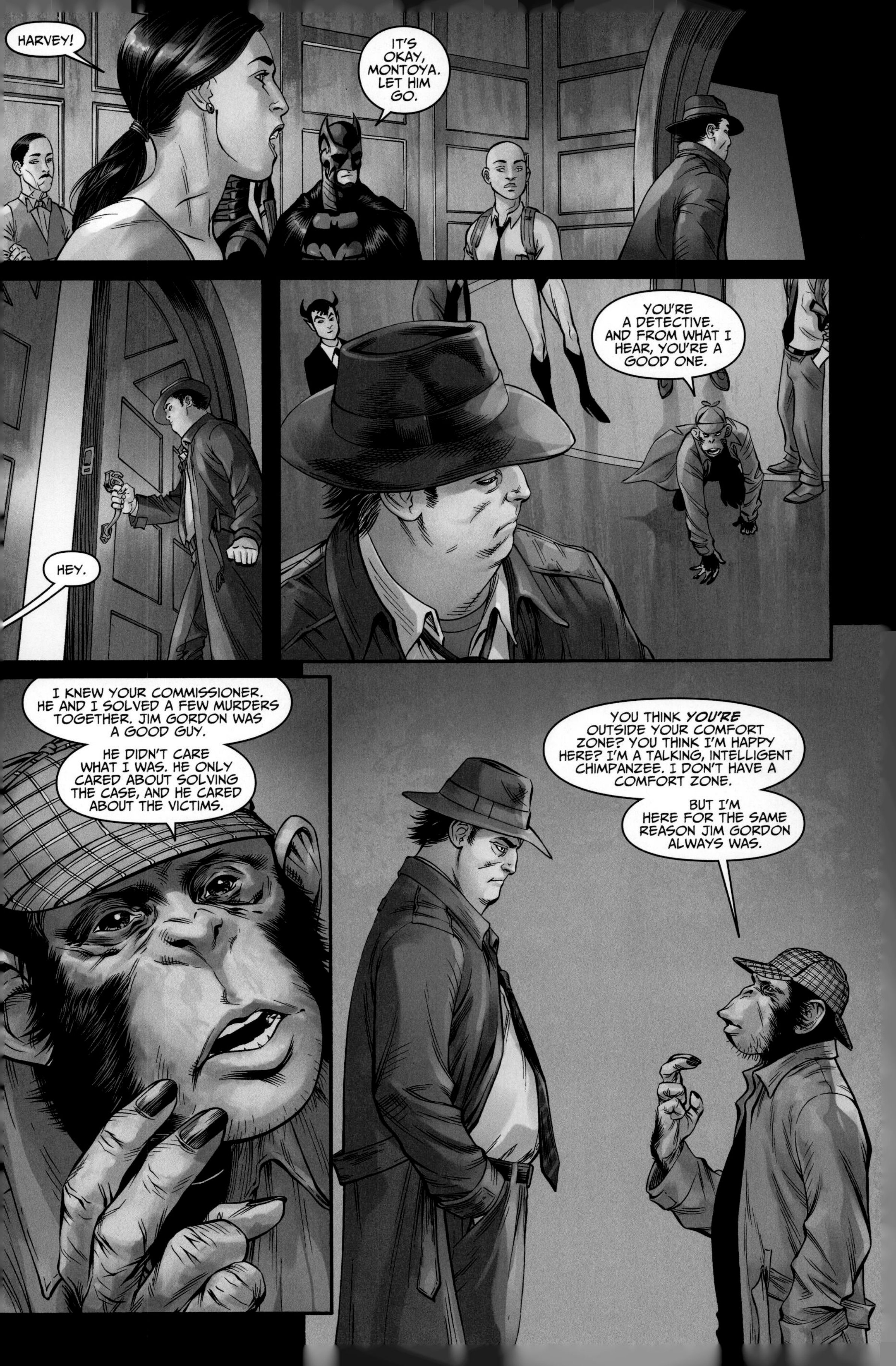
HARVEY!
IT'S OKAY, MONTOYA. LET HIM GO.
HEY.
YOU'RE A DETECTIVE. AND FROM WHAT I HEAR, YOU'RE A GOOD ONE.
I KNEW YOUR COMMISSIONER. HE AND I SOLVED A FEW MURDERS TOGETHER. JIM GORDON WAS A GOOD GUY.
HE DIDN'T CARE WHAT I WAS. HE ONLY CARED ABOUT SOLVING THE CASE, AND HE CARED ABOUT THE VICTIMS.
YOU THINK YOU'RE OUTSIDE YOUR COMFORT ZONE? YOU THINK I'M HAPPY HERE? I'M A TALKING, INTELLIGENT CHIMPANZEE. I DON'T HAVE A COMFORT ZONE.
BUT I'M HERE FOR THE SAME REASON JIM GORDON ALWAYS WAS.

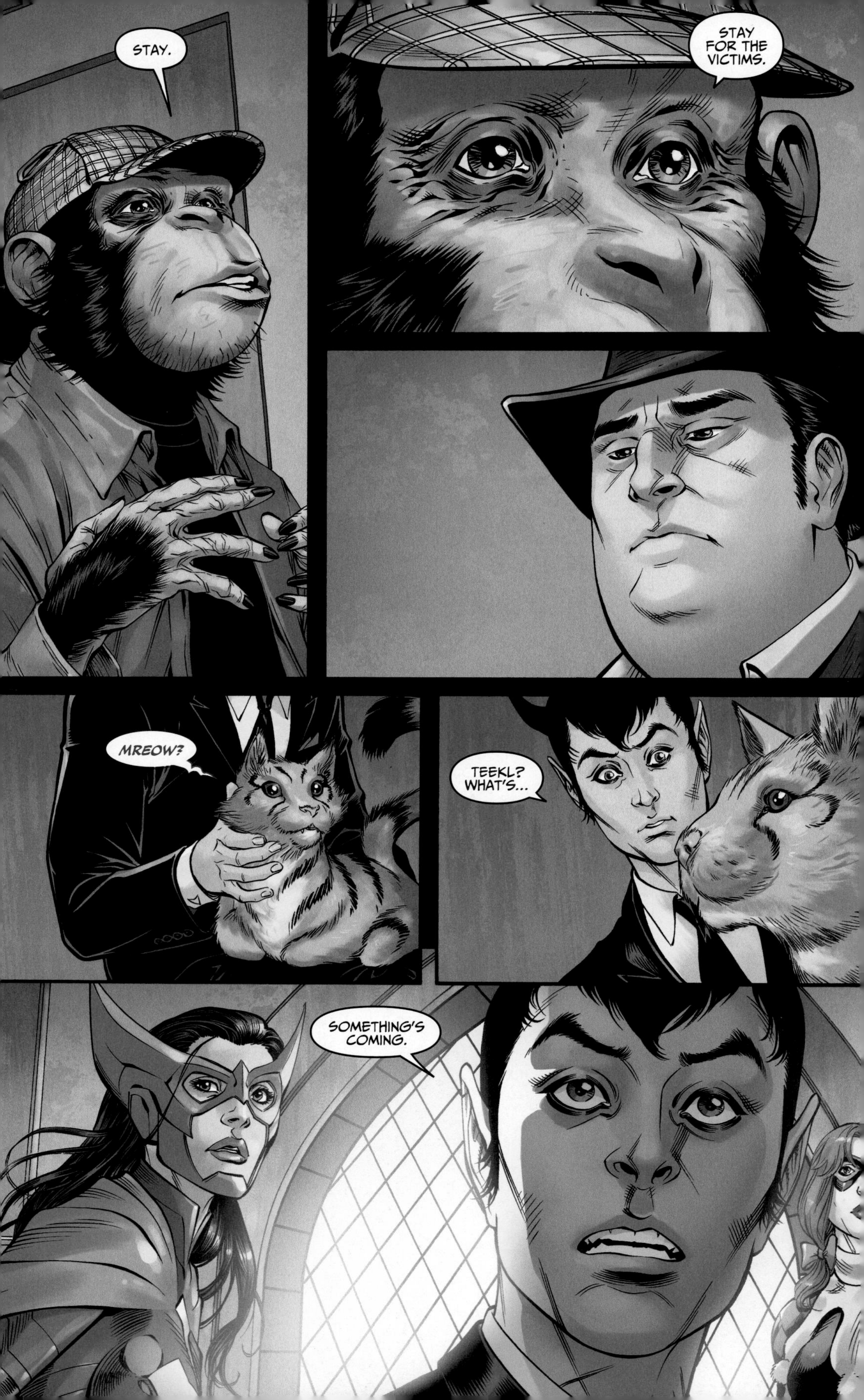
STAY.
STAY FOR THE VICTIMS.
MREOW?
TEEKL? WHAT'S...
SOMETHING'S COMING.

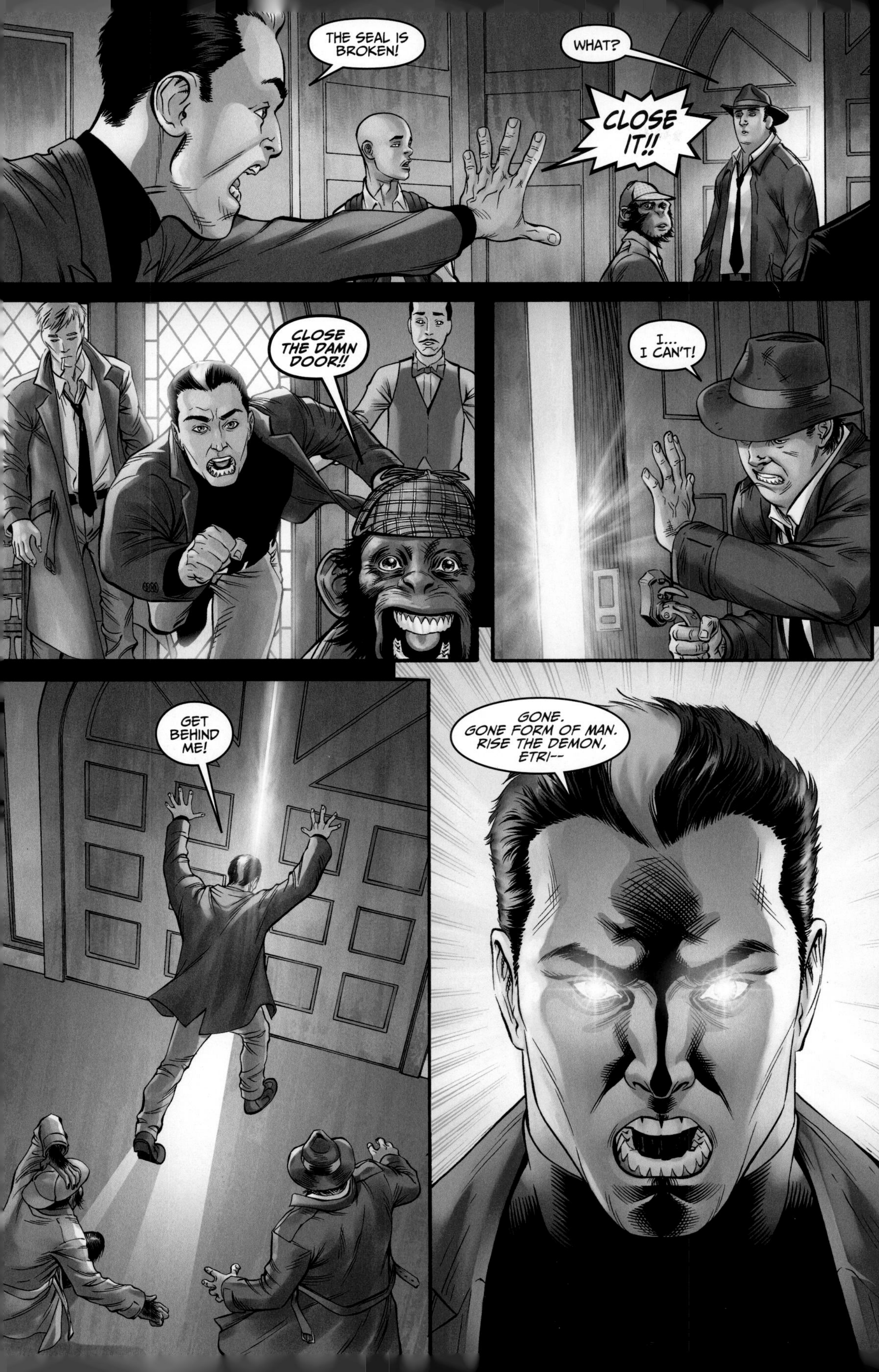
THE SEAL IS BROKEN!
WHAT?
CLOSE IT!!
CLOSE THE DAMN DOOR!!
I... I CAN'T!
GET BEHIND ME!
GONE. GONE FORM OF MAN. RISE THE DEMON, ETRI--

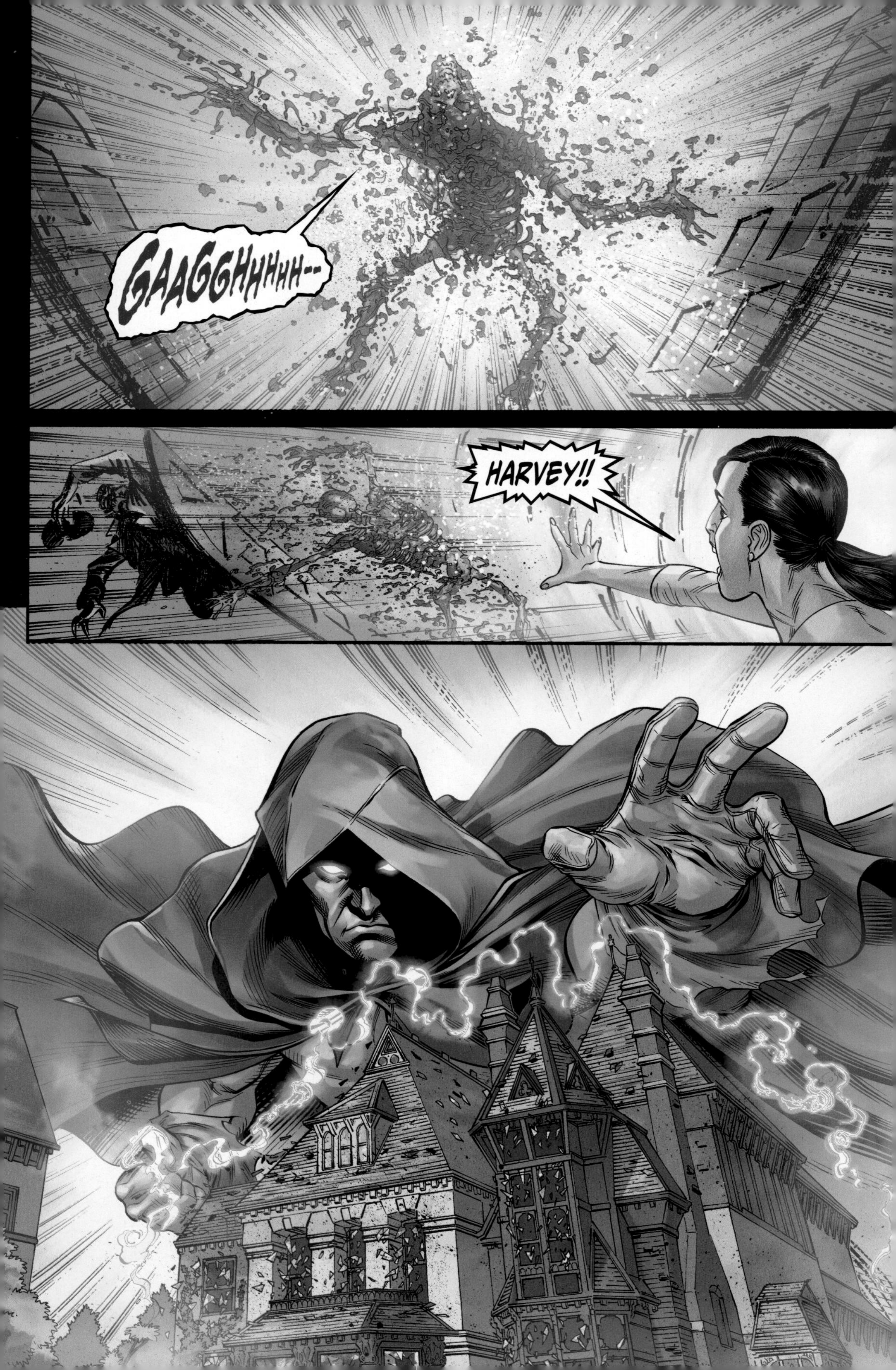
GAAGGHHHHH--
HARVEY!!

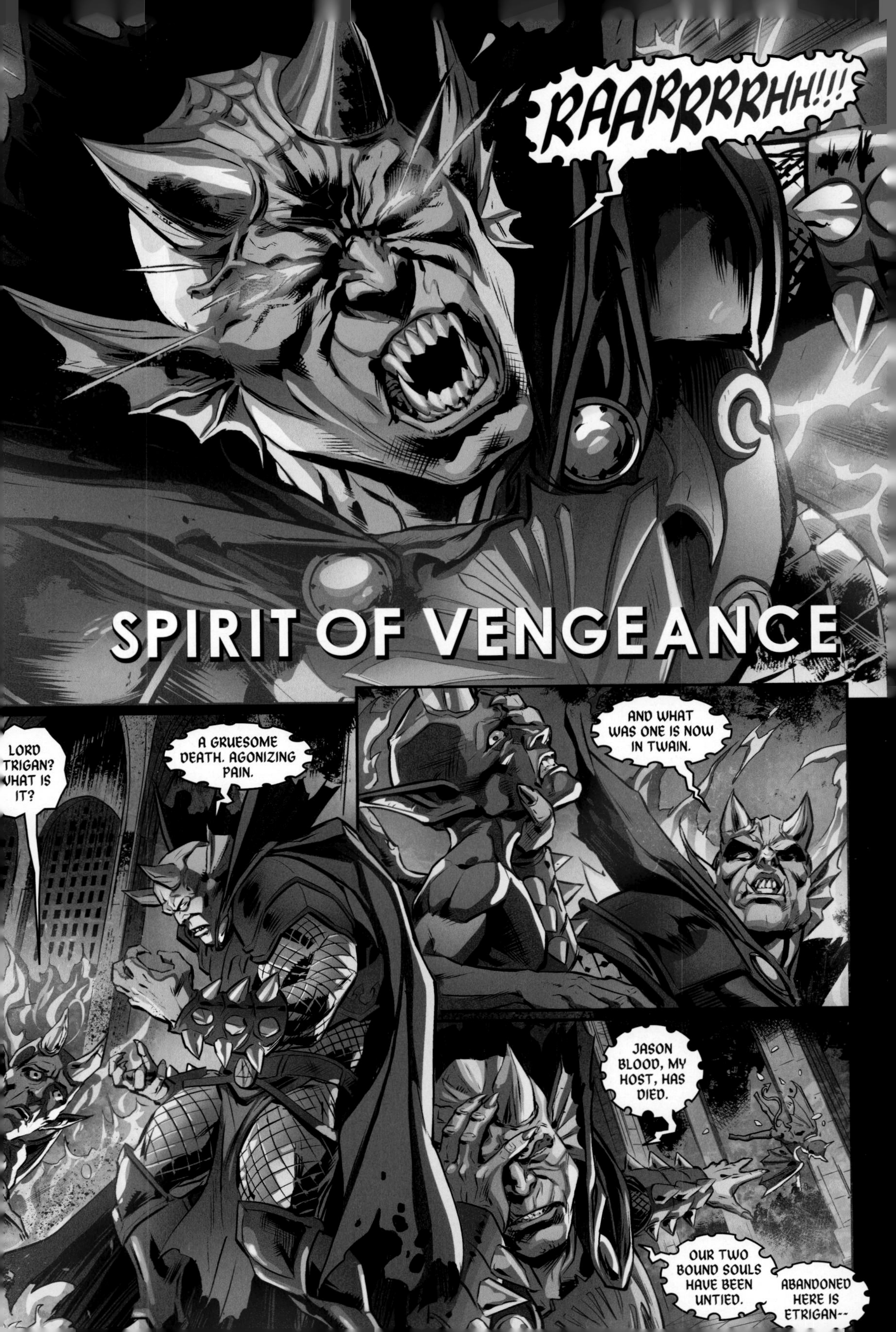
RAARRRRHH!!!
SPIRIT OF VENGEANCE
LORD TRIGAN? WHAT IS IT?
A GRUESOME DEATH. AGONIZING PAIN.
AND WHAT WAS ONE IS NOW IN TWAIN.
JASON BLOOD, MY HOST, HAS DIED.
OUR TWO BOUND SOULS HAVE BEEN UNTIED.
ABANDONED HERE IS ETRIGAN--

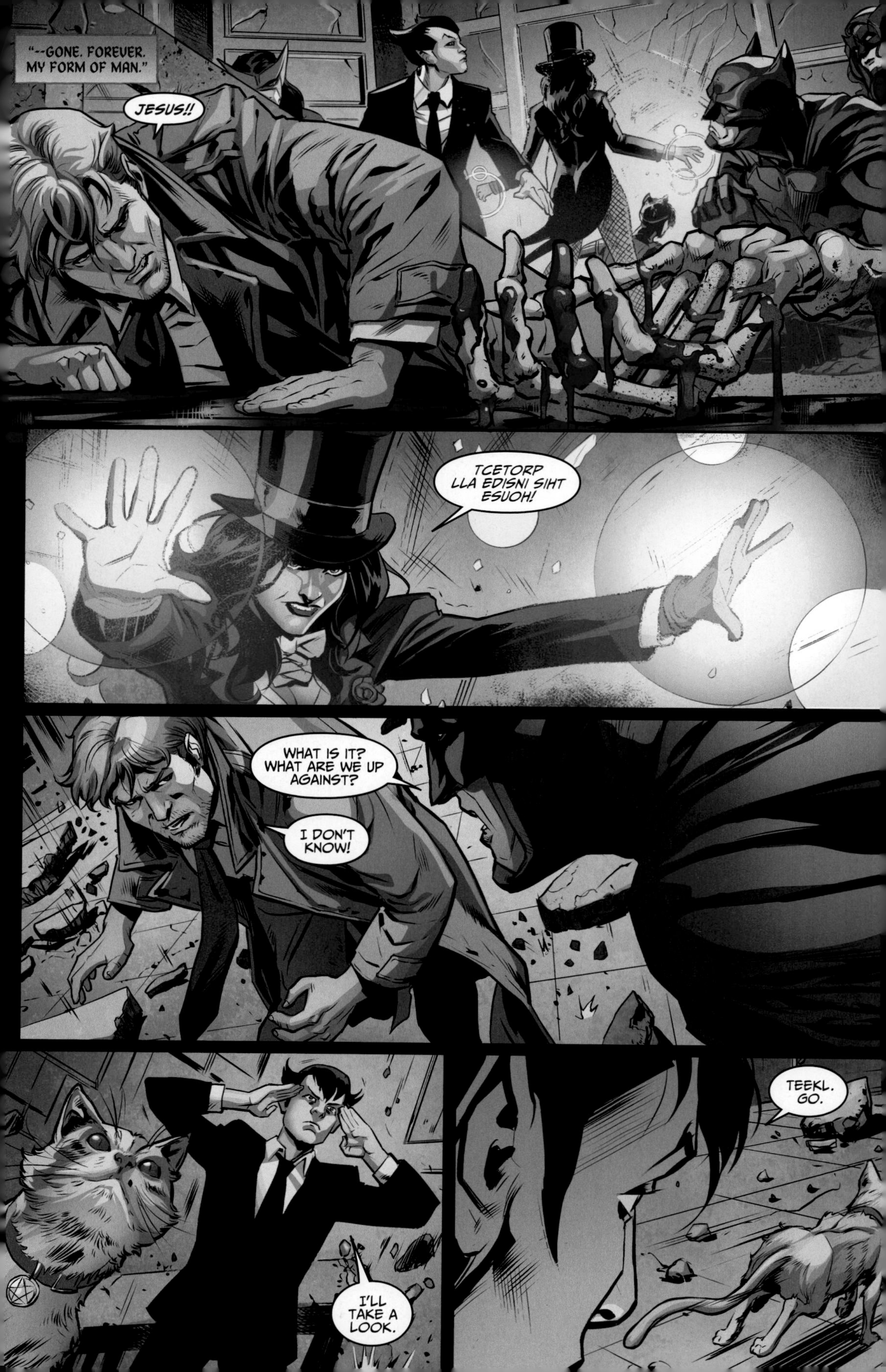
"--GONE. FOREVER. MY FORM OF MAN."
JESUS!!
TCETORP LLA EDISNI SIHT ESUOH!
WHAT IS IT? WHAT ARE WE UP AGAINST?
I DON'T KNOW!
I'LL TAKE A LOOK.
TEEKL. GO.

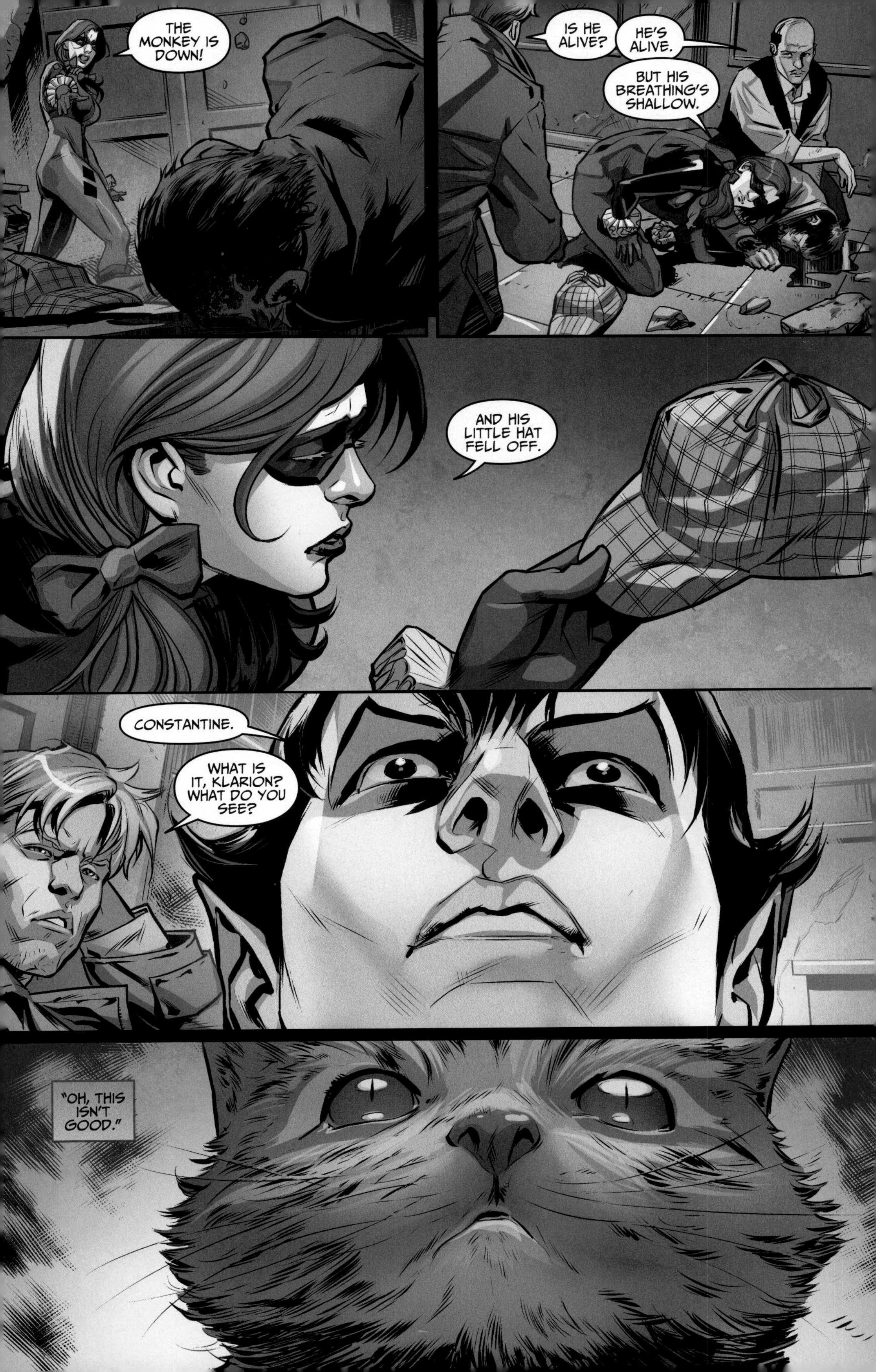
THE MONKEY IS DOWN!
IS HE ALIVE?
HE'S ALIVE.
BUT HIS BREATHING'S SHALLOW.
AND HIS LITTLE HAT FELL OFF.
CONSTANTINE.
WHAT IS IT, KLARION? WHAT DO YOU SEE?
"OH, THIS ISN'T GOOD."

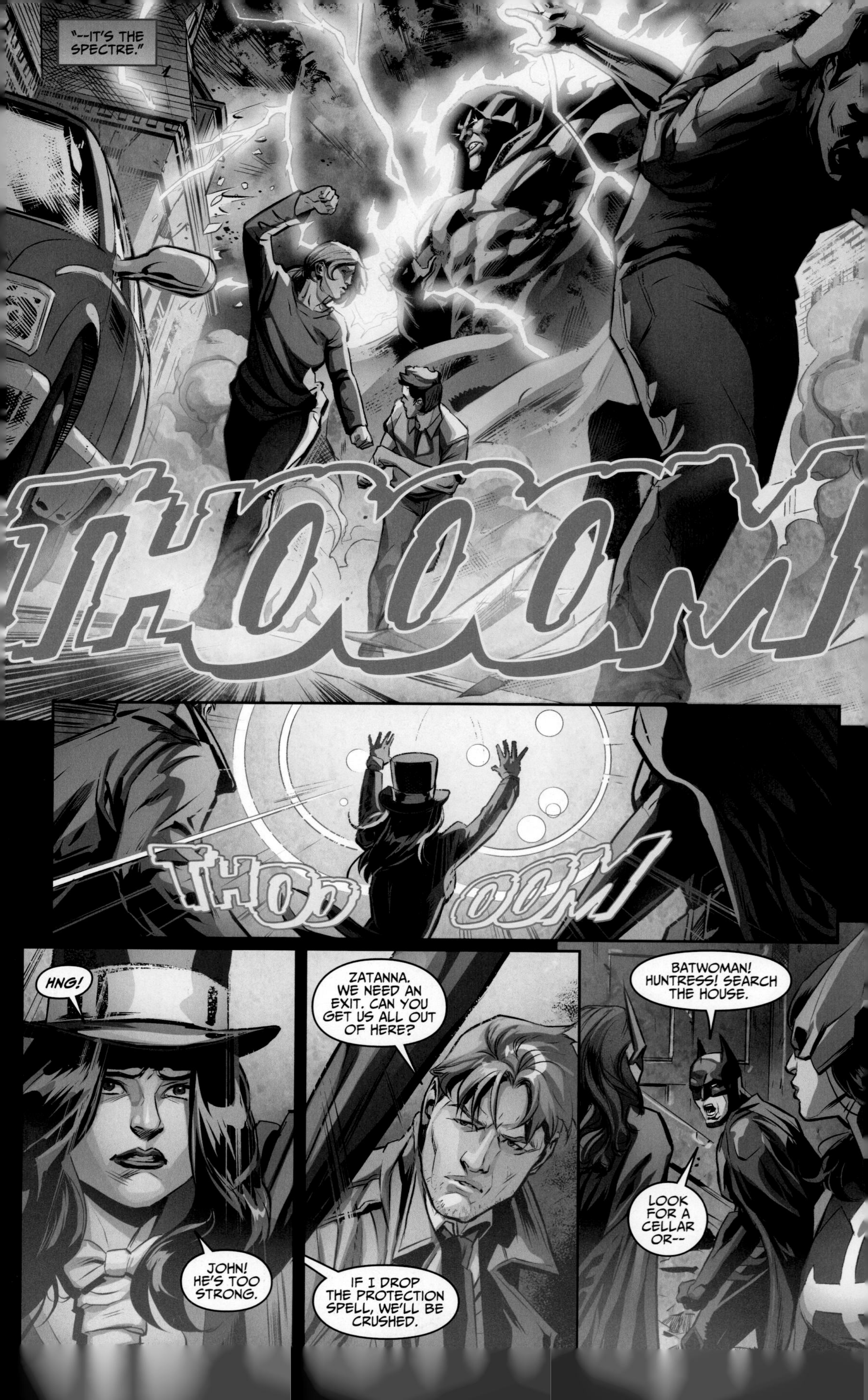
"--IT'S THE SPECTRE."
THOOOM
THOOOOM
HNG!
JOHN! HE'S TOO STRONG.
ZATANNA. WE NEED AN EXIT. CAN YOU GET US ALL OUT OF HERE?
IF I DROP THE PROTECTION SPELL, WE'LL BE CRUSHED.
BATWOMAN! HUNTRESS! SEARCH THE HOUSE.
LOOK FOR A CELLAR OR--

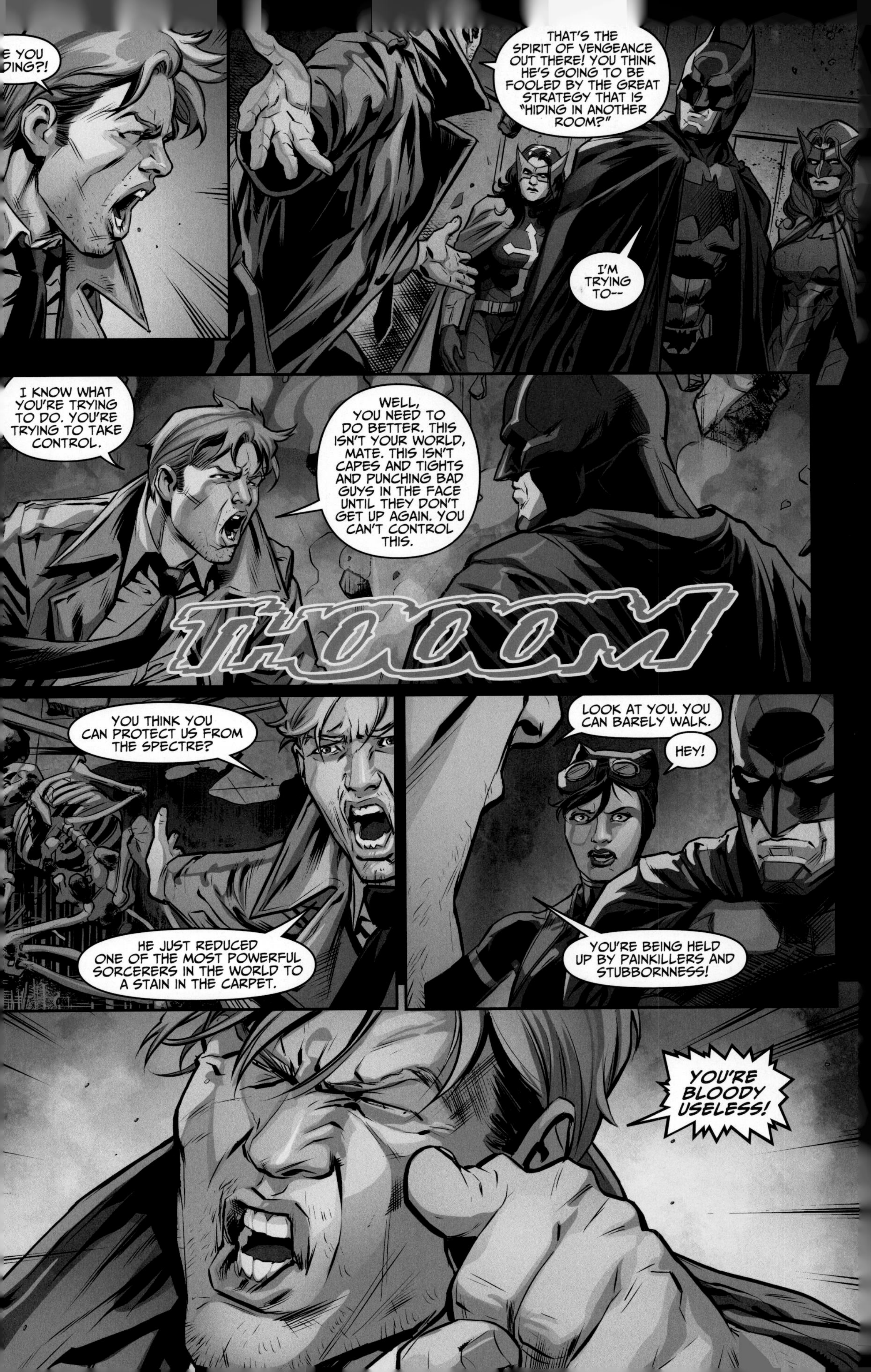
E YOU
DING?!
THAT'S THE SPIRIT OF VENGEANCE OUT THERE! YOU THINK HE'S GOING TO BE FOOLED BY THE GREAT STRATEGY THAT IS "HIDING IN ANOTHER ROOM?"
I'M TRYING TO--
I KNOW WHAT YOU'RE TRYING TO DO. YOU'RE TRYING TO TAKE CONTROL.
WELL, YOU NEED TO DO BETTER. THIS ISN'T YOUR WORLD, MATE. THIS ISN'T CAPES AND TIGHTS AND PUNCHING BAD GUYS IN THE FACE UNTIL THEY DON'T GET UP AGAIN. YOU CAN'T CONTROL THIS.
THOOOM
YOU THINK YOU CAN PROTECT US FROM THE SPECTRE?
HE JUST REDUCED ONE OF THE MOST POWERFUL SORCERERS IN THE WORLD TO A STAIN IN THE CARPET.
LOOK AT YOU. YOU CAN BARELY WALK.
HEY!
YOU'RE BEING HELD UP BY PAINKILLERS AND STUBBORNNESS!
YOU'RE BLOODY USELESS!

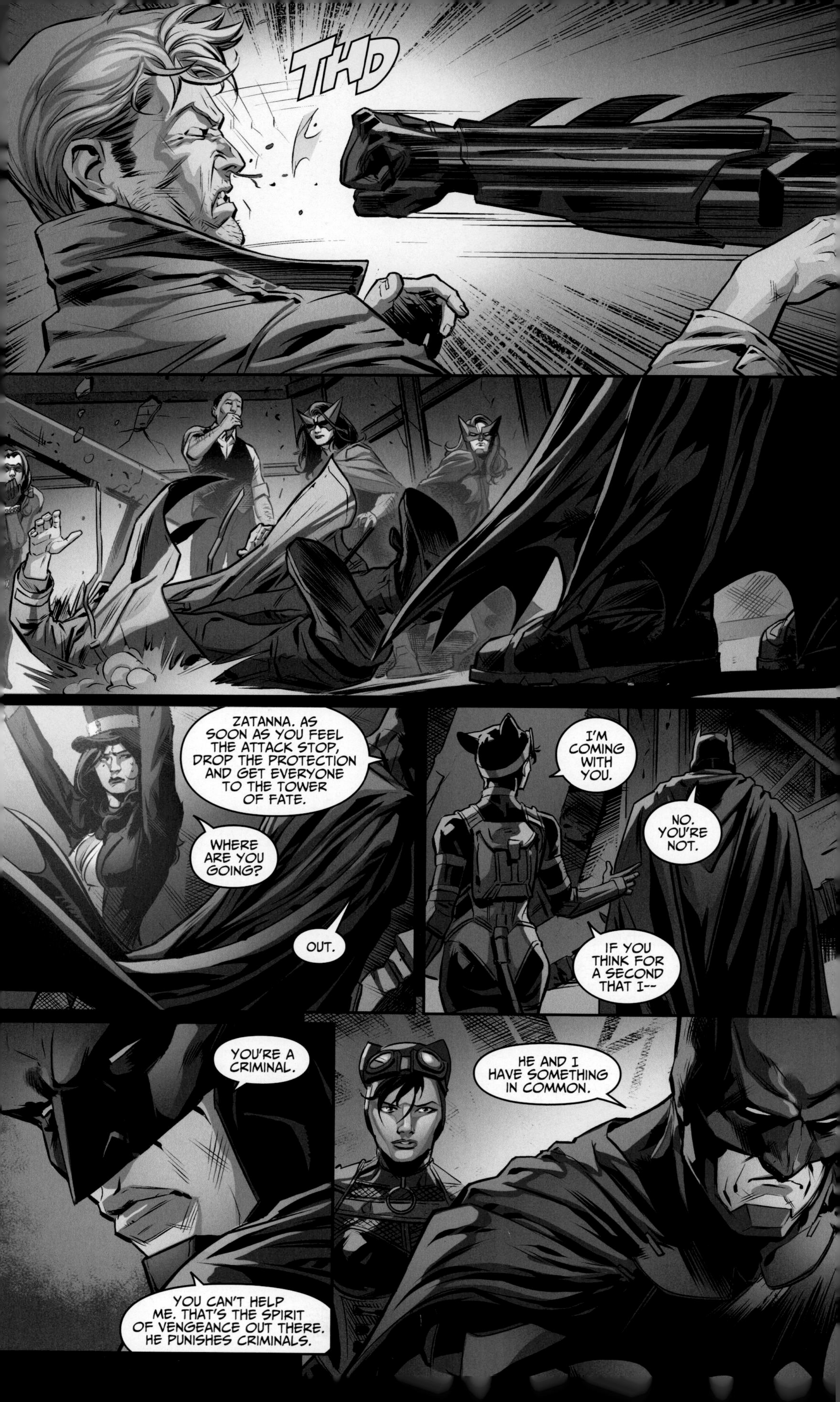
THD
ZATANNA. AS SOON AS YOU FEEL THE ATTACK STOP, DROP THE PROTECTION AND GET EVERYONE TO THE TOWER OF FATE.
WHERE ARE YOU GOING?
OUT.
I'M COMING WITH YOU.
NO. YOU'RE NOT.
IF YOU THINK FOR A SECOND THAT I--
YOU'RE A CRIMINAL.
HE AND I HAVE SOMETHING IN COMMON.
YOU CAN'T HELP ME. THAT'S THE SPIRIT OF VENGEANCE OUT THERE. HE PUNISHES CRIMINALS.

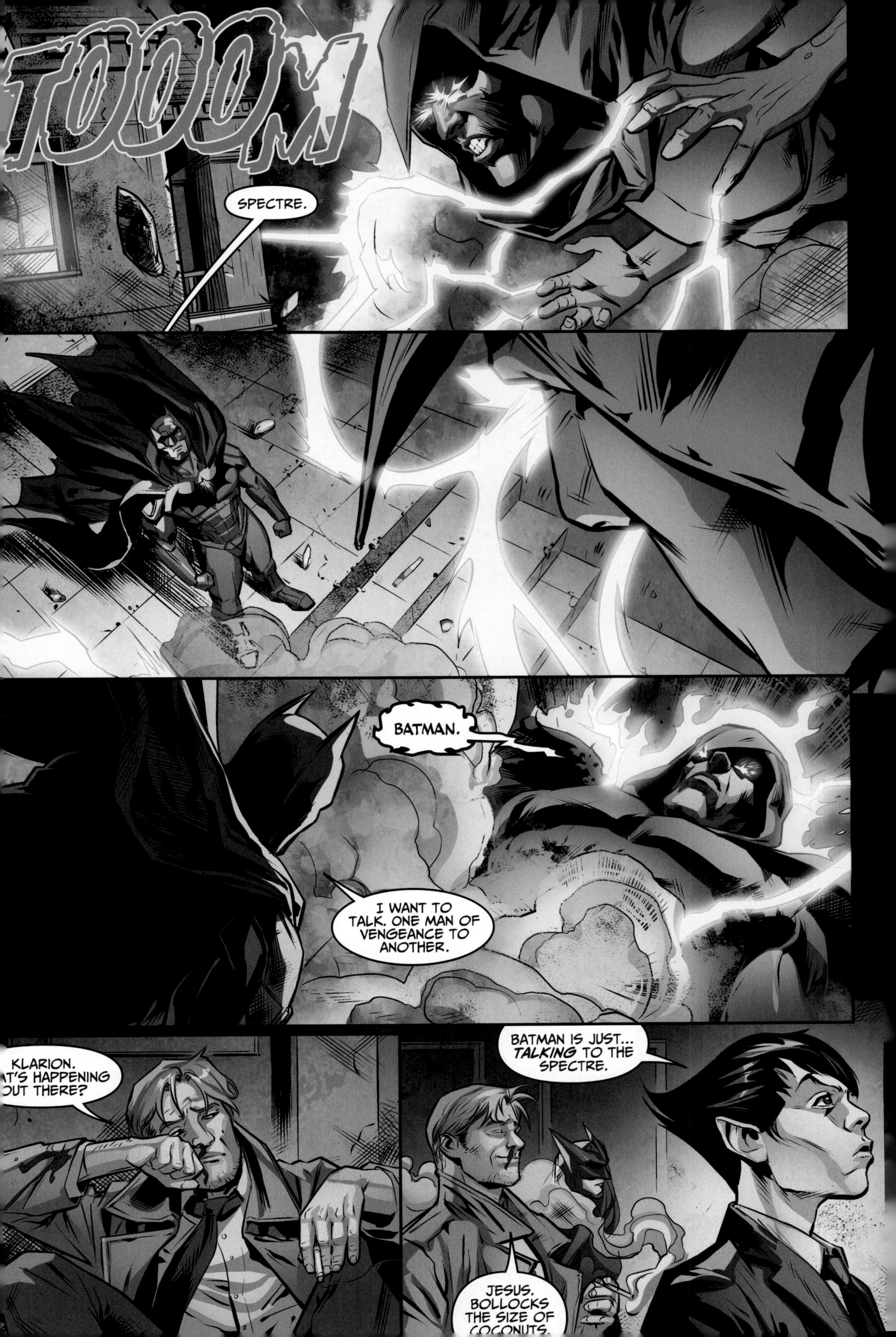
TOOOOM
SPECTRE.
BATMAN.
I WANT TO TALK. ONE MAN OF VENGEANCE TO ANOTHER.
KLARION. AT'S HAPPENING OUT THERE?
BATMAN IS JUST... *TALKING* TO THE SPECTRE.
JESUS. BOLLOCKS THE SIZE OF COCONUTS.

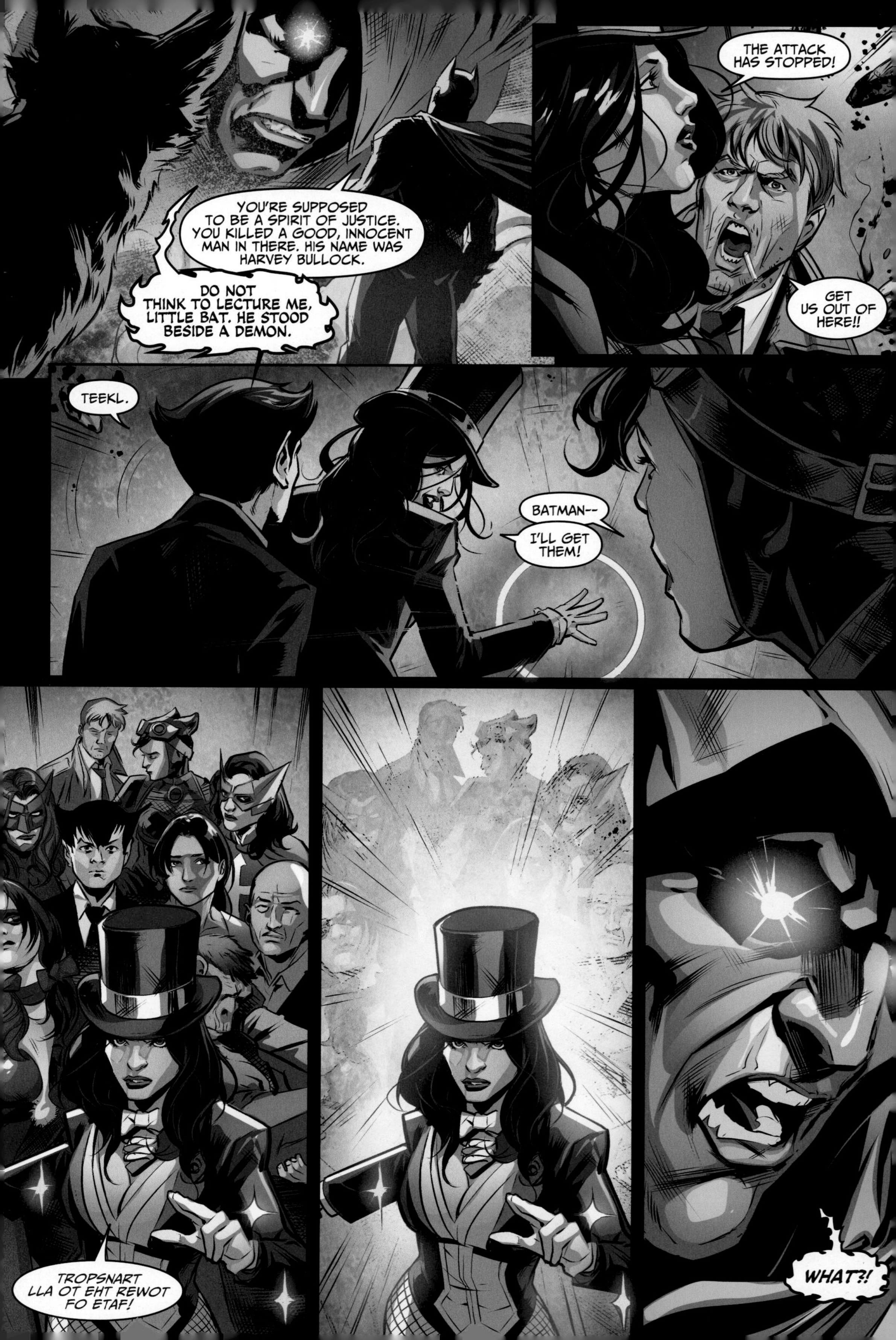
YOU'RE SUPPOSED TO BE A SPIRIT OF JUSTICE. YOU KILLED A GOOD, INNOCENT MAN IN THERE. HIS NAME WAS HARVEY BULLOCK.
DO NOT THINK TO LECTURE ME, LITTLE BAT. HE STOOD BESIDE A DEMON.
THE ATTACK HAS STOPPED!
GET US OUT OF HERE!!
TEEKL.
BATMAN--
I'LL GET THEM!
TROPSNART LLA OT EHT REWOT FO ETAF!
WHAT?!

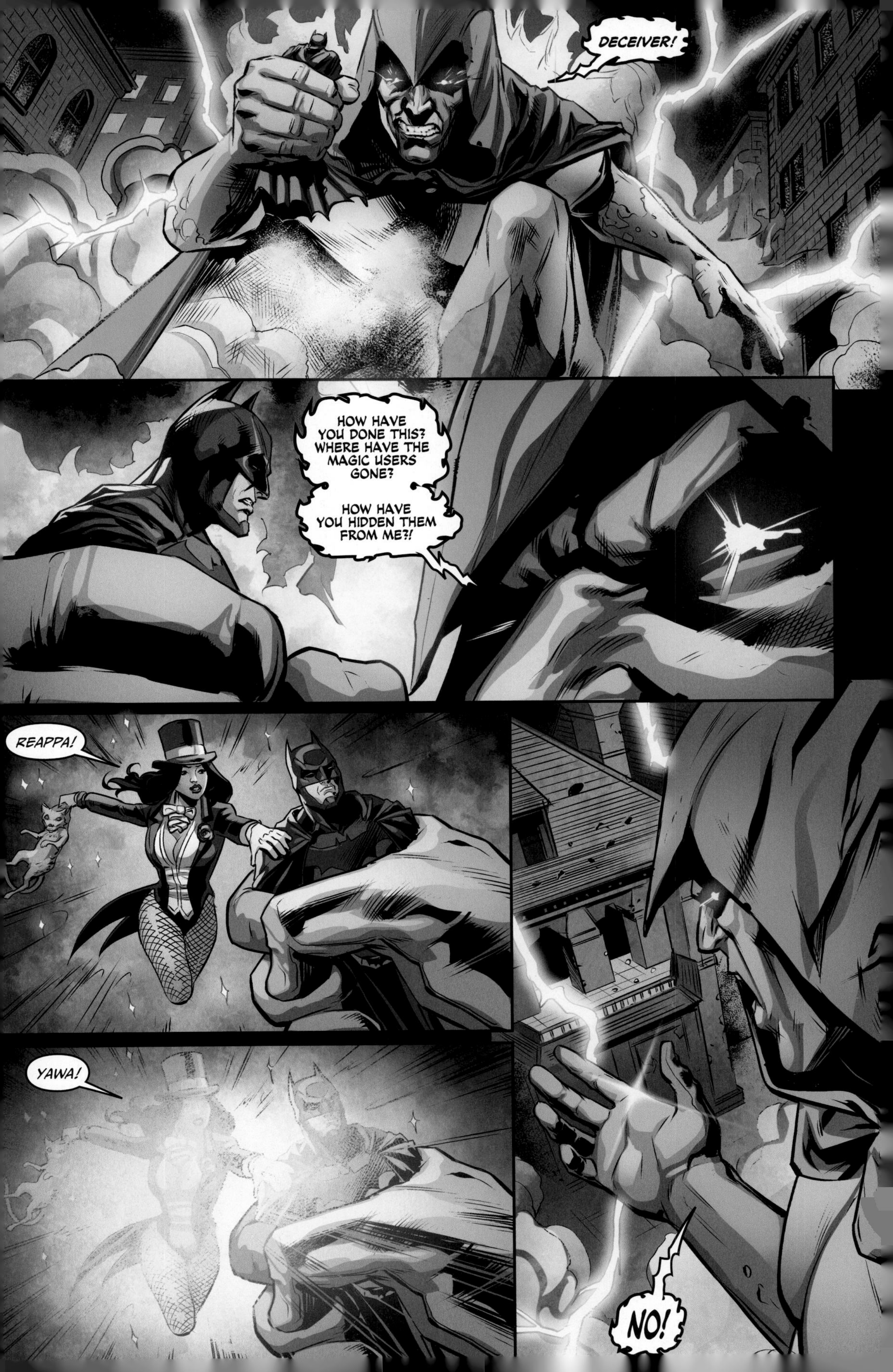
DECEIVER!
HOW HAVE YOU DONE THIS? WHERE HAVE THE MAGIC USERS GONE?
HOW HAVE YOU HIDDEN THEM FROM ME?!
REAPPA!
YAWA!
NO!

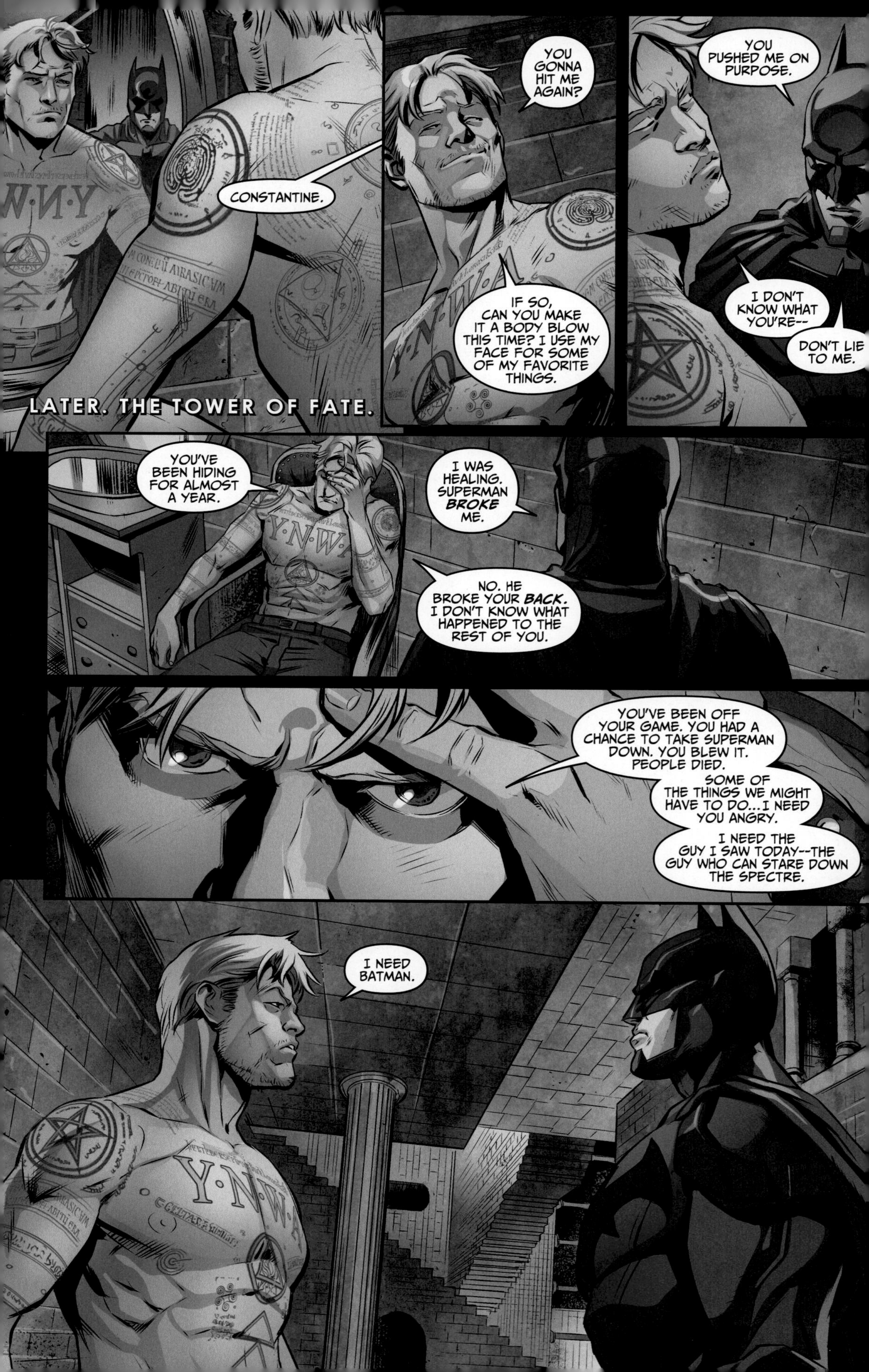
CONSTANTINE.
YOU GONNA HIT ME AGAIN?
IF SO, CAN YOU MAKE IT A BODY BLOW THIS TIME? I USE MY FACE FOR SOME OF MY FAVORITE THINGS.
YOU PUSHED ME ON PURPOSE.
I DON'T KNOW WHAT YOU'RE--
DON'T LIE TO ME.
LATER. THE TOWER OF FATE.
YOU'VE BEEN HIDING FOR ALMOST A YEAR.
I WAS HEALING. SUPERMAN BROKE ME.
NO. HE BROKE YOUR BACK. I DON'T KNOW WHAT HAPPENED TO THE REST OF YOU.
YOU'VE BEEN OFF YOUR GAME. YOU HAD A CHANCE TO TAKE SUPERMAN DOWN. YOU BLEW IT. PEOPLE DIED.
SOME OF THE THINGS WE MIGHT HAVE TO DO...I NEED YOU ANGRY.
I NEED THE GUY I SAW TODAY--THE GUY WHO CAN STARE DOWN THE SPECTRE.
I NEED BATMAN.

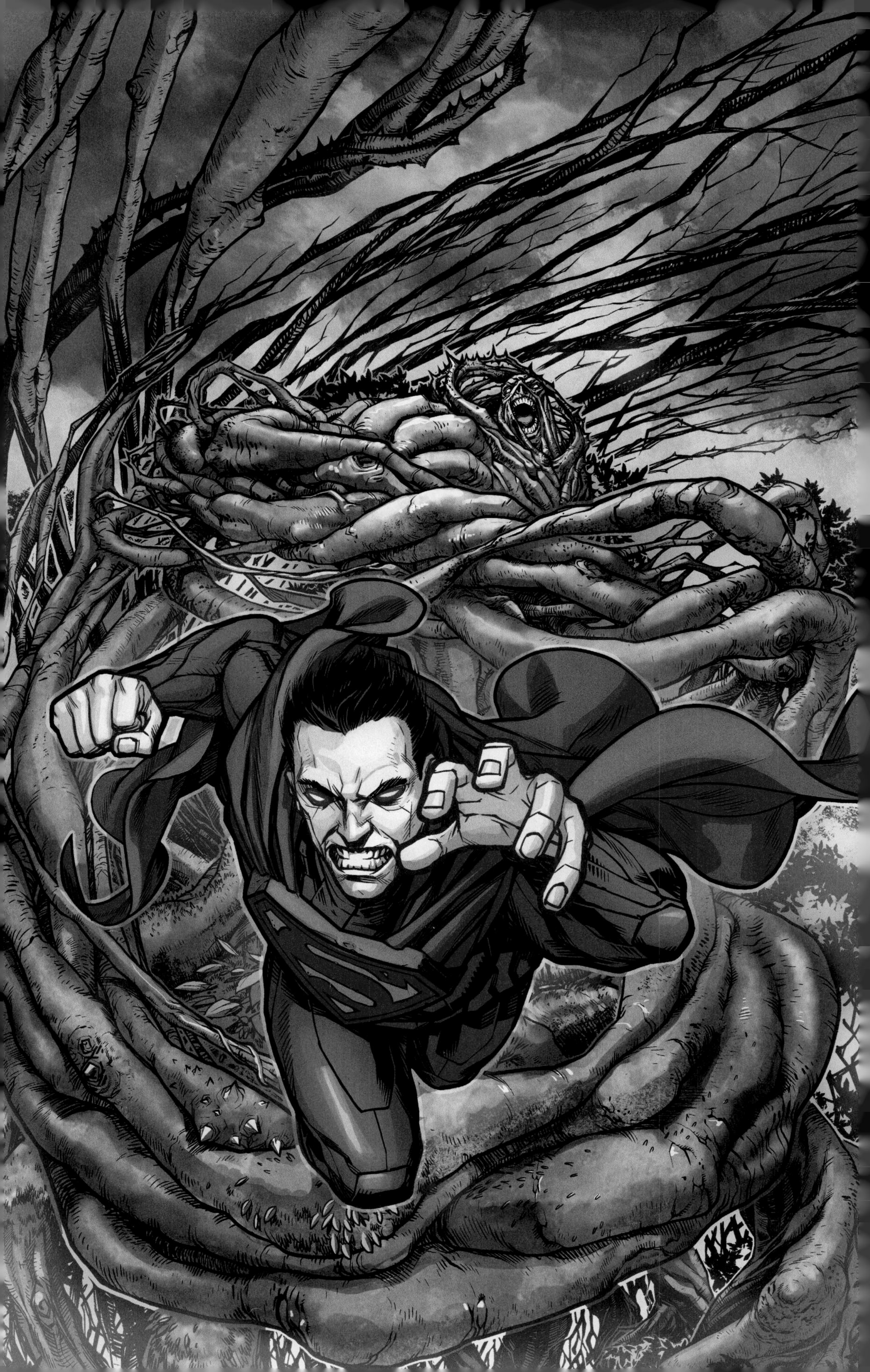

"The Coin" **Mike S. Miller** Artist **J. Nanjan** Colorist
"Xanadu" **Bruno Redondo, Xermanico, & Juan Albarran** Artists **Rex Lokus** Colorist
Cover Art by **Neil Googe & Rex Lokus**

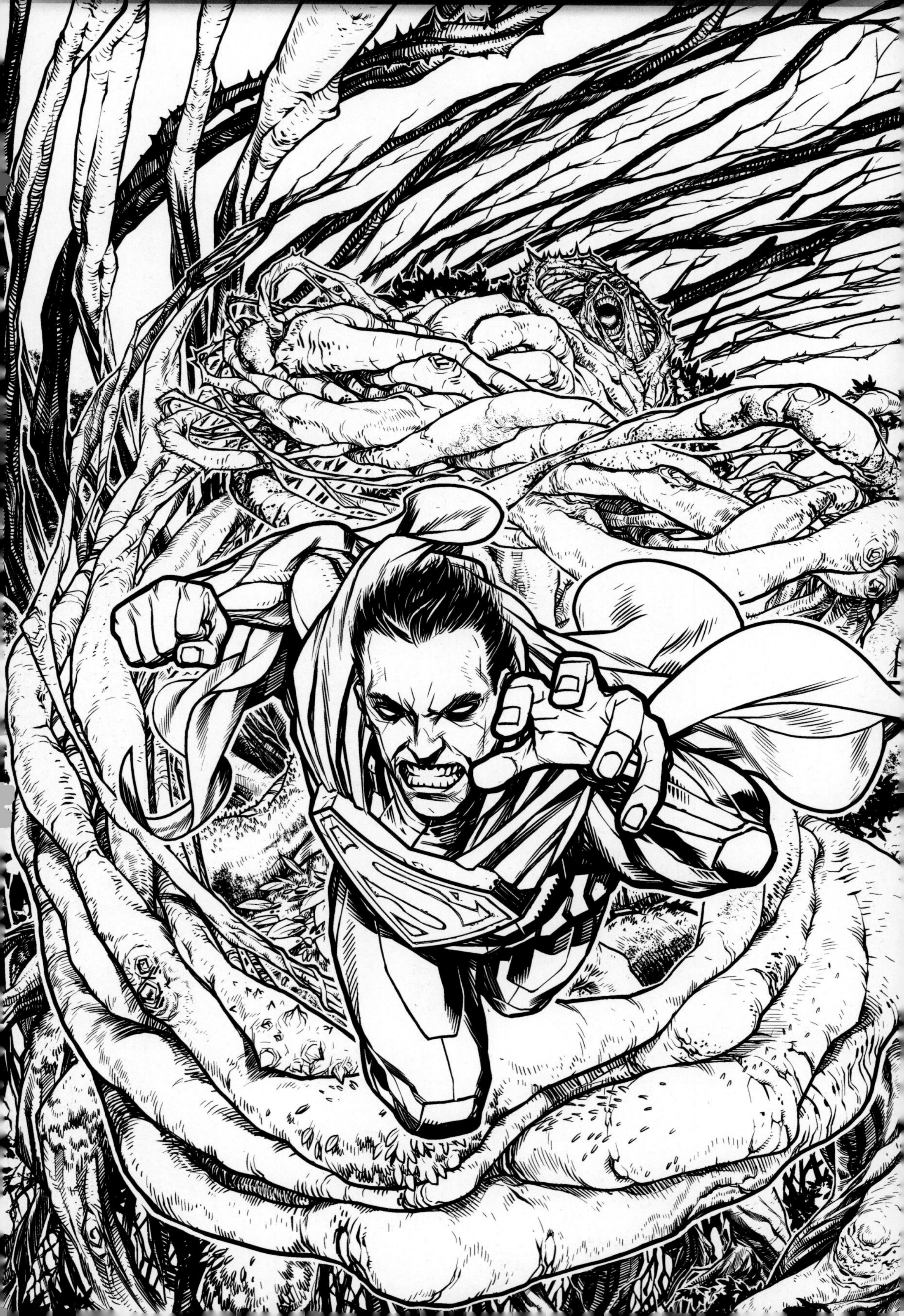

THE COIN

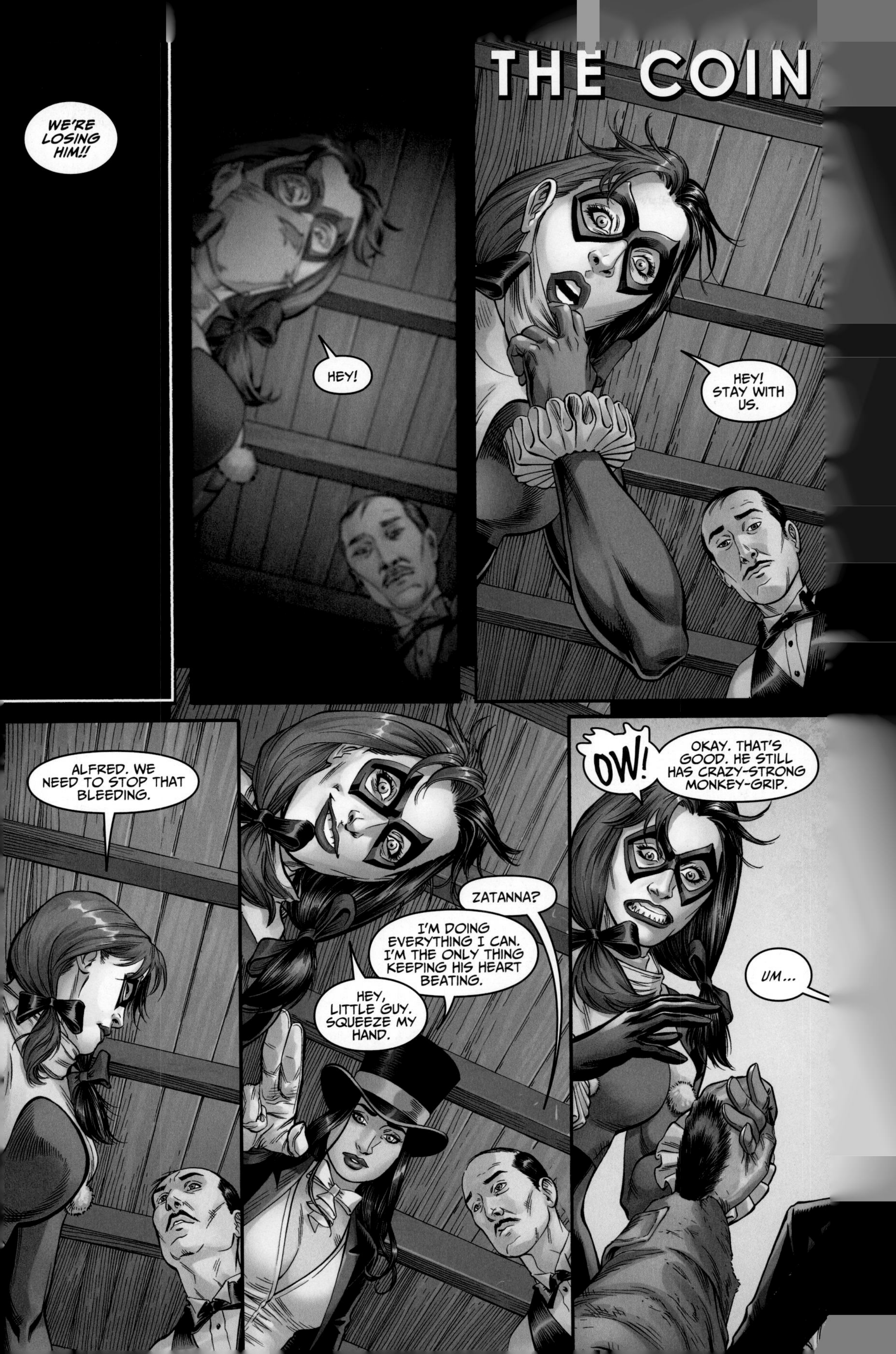
WE'RE LOSING HIM!!
HEY!
HEY! STAY WITH US.
ALFRED. WE NEED TO STOP THAT BLEEDING.
ZATANNA?
I'M DOING EVERYTHING I CAN. I'M THE ONLY THING KEEPING HIS HEART BEATING.
HEY, LITTLE GUY. SQUEEZE MY HAND.
OW!
OKAY. THAT'S GOOD. HE STILL HAS CRAZY-STRONG MONKEY-GRIP.
UM...

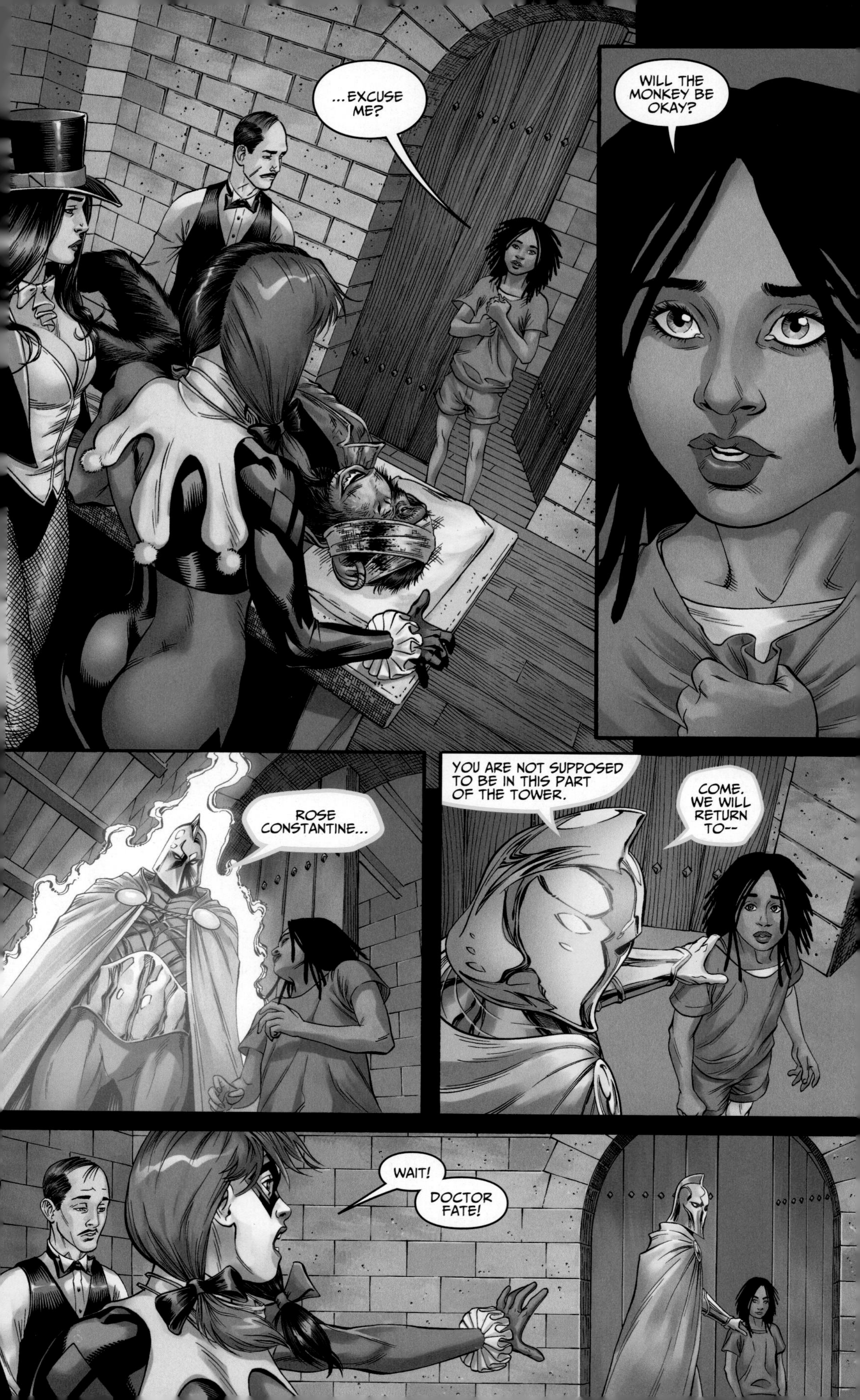

...EXCUSE ME?
WILL THE MONKEY BE OKAY?
ROSE CONSTANTINE...
YOU ARE NOT SUPPOSED TO BE IN THIS PART OF THE TOWER.
COME. WE WILL RETURN TO--
WAIT!
DOCTOR FATE!

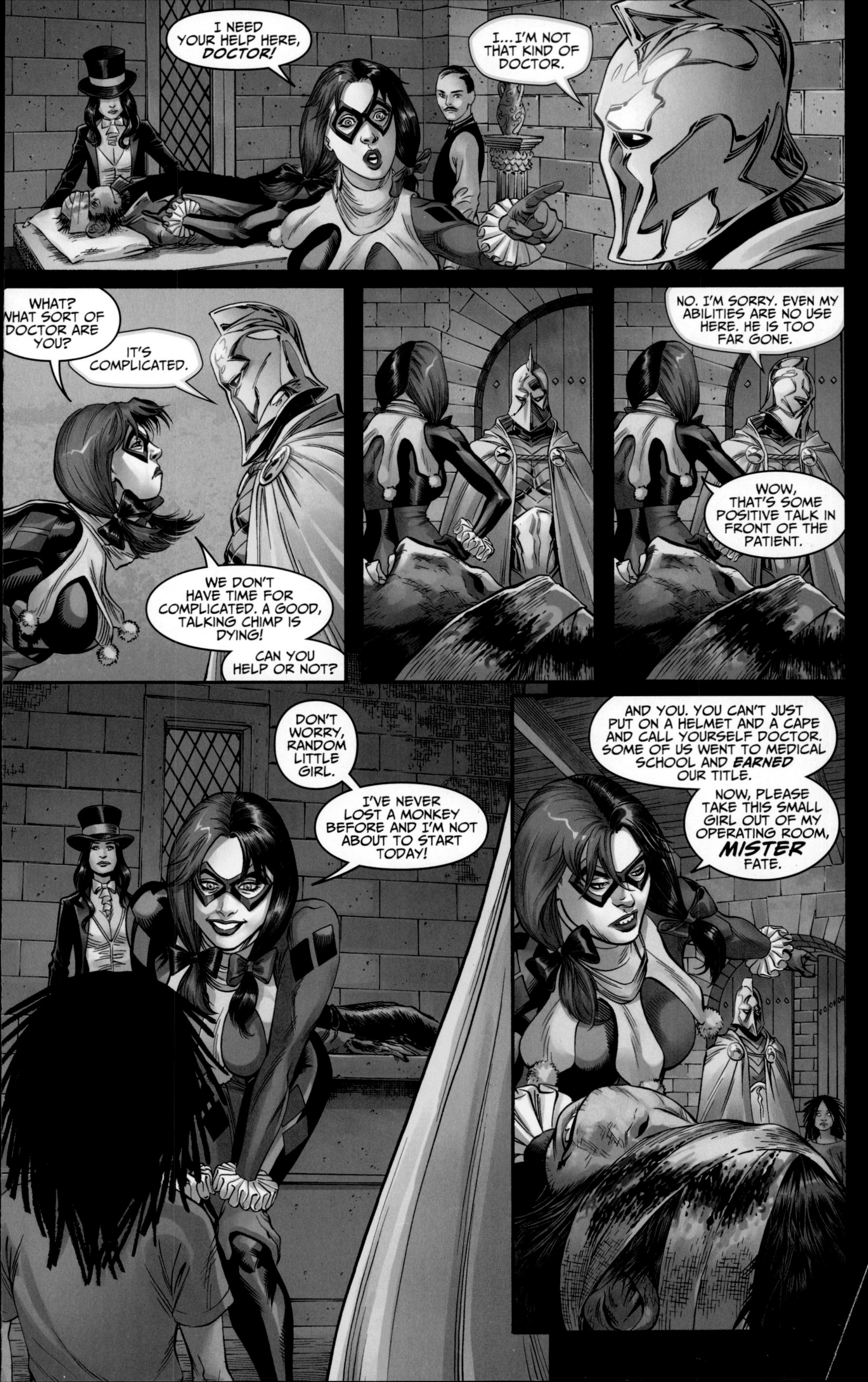

I NEED YOUR HELP HERE, DOCTOR!
I...I'M NOT THAT KIND OF DOCTOR.
WHAT? WHAT SORT OF DOCTOR ARE YOU?
IT'S COMPLICATED.
WE DON'T HAVE TIME FOR COMPLICATED. A GOOD, TALKING CHIMP IS DYING!
CAN YOU HELP OR NOT?
NO. I'M SORRY. EVEN MY ABILITIES ARE NO USE HERE. HE IS TOO FAR GONE.
WOW, THAT'S SOME POSITIVE TALK IN FRONT OF THE PATIENT.
DON'T WORRY, RANDOM LITTLE GIRL.
I'VE NEVER LOST A MONKEY BEFORE AND I'M NOT ABOUT TO START TODAY!
AND YOU. YOU CAN'T JUST PUT ON A HELMET AND A CAPE AND CALL YOURSELF DOCTOR. SOME OF US WENT TO MEDICAL SCHOOL AND EARNED OUR TITLE.
NOW, PLEASE TAKE THIS SMALL GIRL OUT OF MY OPERATING ROOM, MISTER FATE.

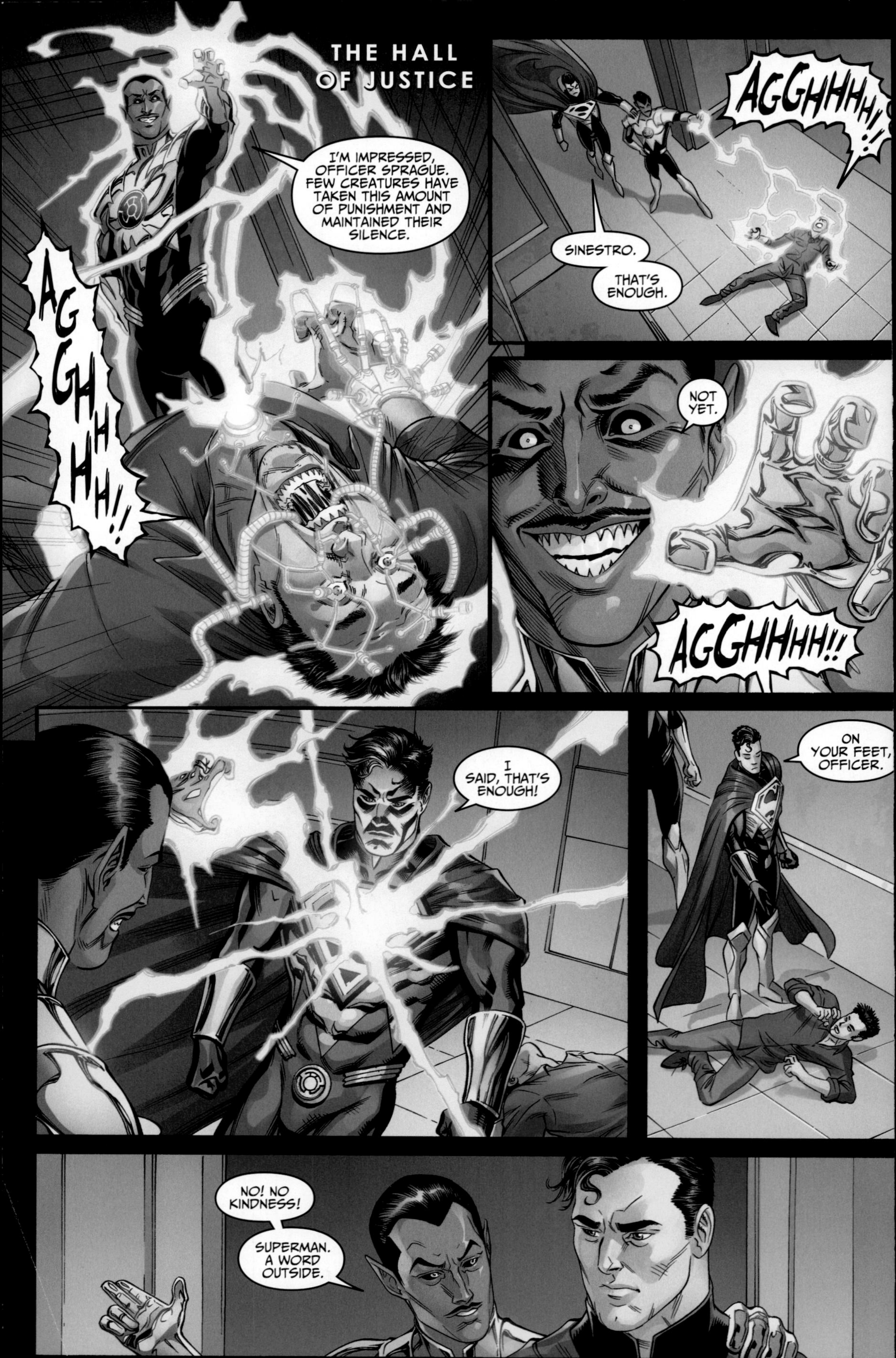
THE HALL OF JUSTICE
I'M IMPRESSED, OFFICER SPRAGUE. FEW CREATURES HAVE TAKEN THIS AMOUNT OF PUNISHMENT AND MAINTAINED THEIR SILENCE.
AGGHHHHH!!
AGGHHHH!!
SINESTRO.
THAT'S ENOUGH.
NOT YET.
AGGHHHH!!
I SAID, THAT'S ENOUGH!
ON YOUR FEET, OFFICER.
NO! NO KINDNESS!
SUPERMAN. A WORD OUTSIDE.

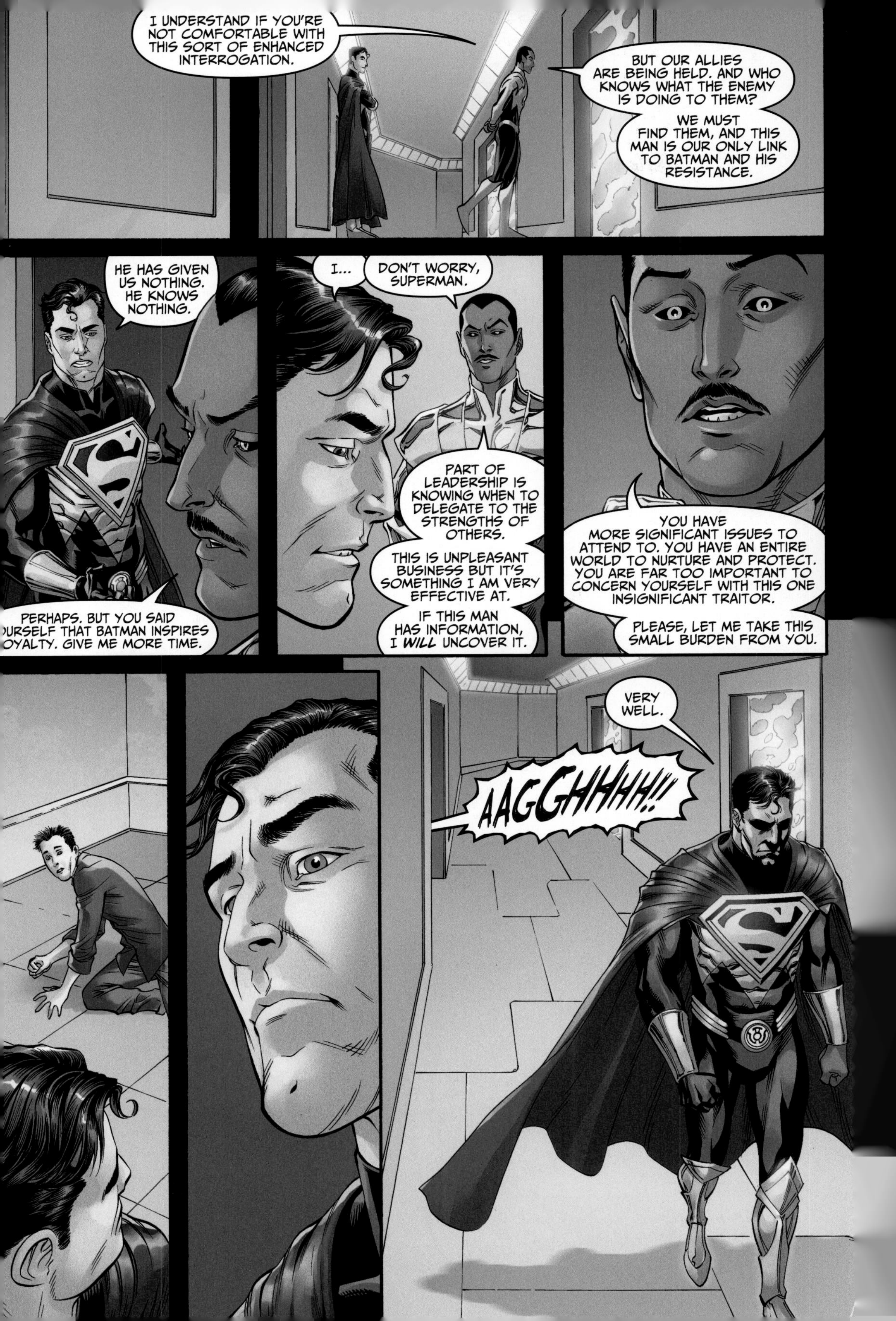

I UNDERSTAND IF YOU'RE NOT COMFORTABLE WITH THIS SORT OF ENHANCED INTERROGATION.
BUT OUR ALLIES ARE BEING HELD. AND WHO KNOWS WHAT THE ENEMY IS DOING TO THEM?
WE MUST FIND THEM, AND THIS MAN IS OUR ONLY LINK TO BATMAN AND HIS RESISTANCE.
HE HAS GIVEN US NOTHING. HE KNOWS NOTHING.
PERHAPS. BUT YOU SAID OURSELF THAT BATMAN INSPIRES OYALTY. GIVE ME MORE TIME.
I...
DON'T WORRY, SUPERMAN.
PART OF LEADERSHIP IS KNOWING WHEN TO DELEGATE TO THE STRENGTHS OF OTHERS.
THIS IS UNPLEASANT BUSINESS BUT IT'S SOMETHING I AM VERY EFFECTIVE AT.
IF THIS MAN HAS INFORMATION, I *WILL* UNCOVER IT.
YOU HAVE MORE SIGNIFICANT ISSUES TO ATTEND TO. YOU HAVE AN ENTIRE WORLD TO NURTURE AND PROTECT. YOU ARE FAR TOO IMPORTANT TO CONCERN YOURSELF WITH THIS ONE INSIGNIFICANT TRAITOR.
PLEASE, LET ME TAKE THIS SMALL BURDEN FROM YOU.
VERY WELL.
AAGGHHHH!!

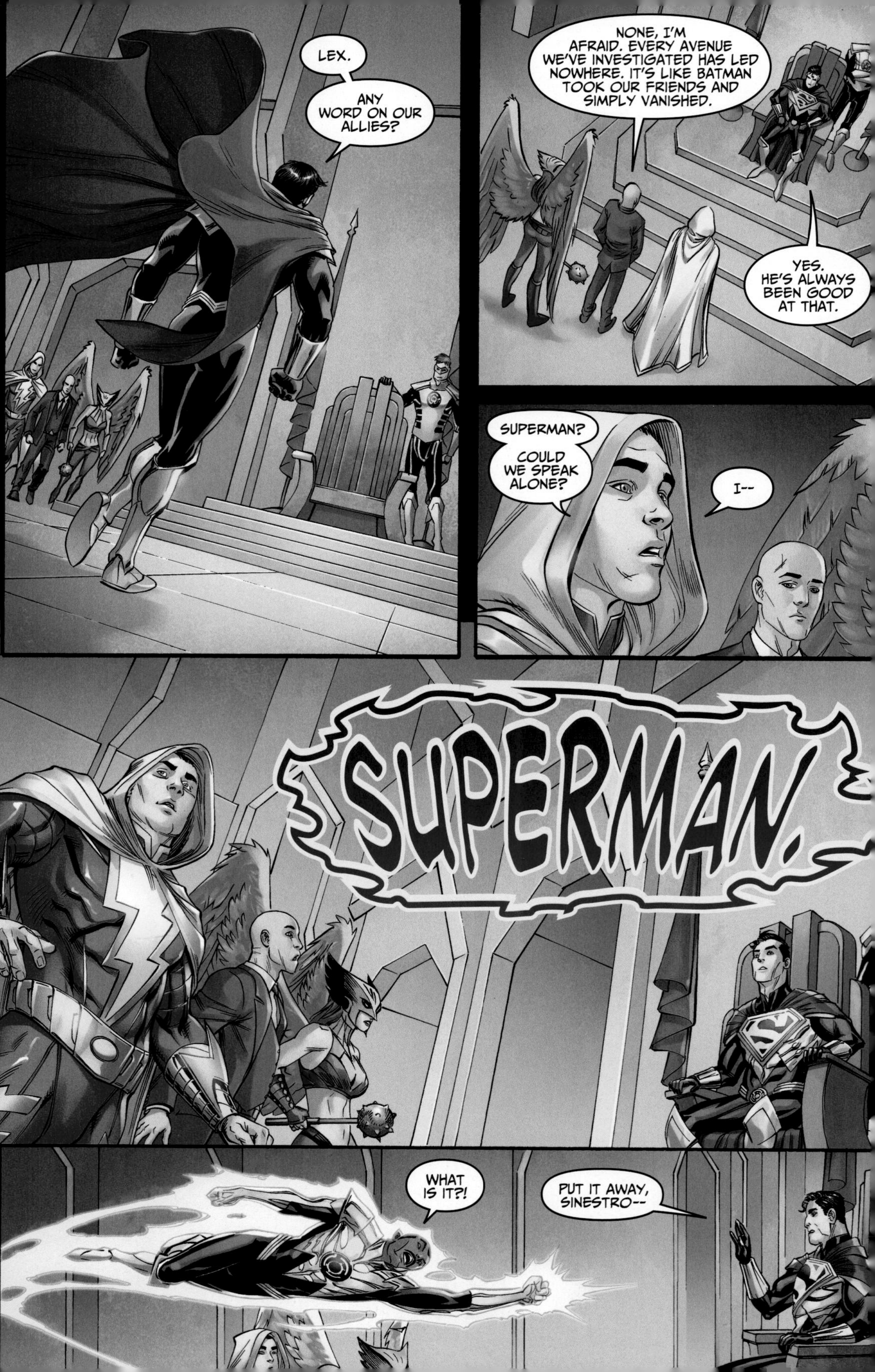
LEX.
ANY WORD ON OUR ALLIES?
NONE, I'M AFRAID. EVERY AVENUE WE'VE INVESTIGATED HAS LED NOWHERE. IT'S LIKE BATMAN TOOK OUR FRIENDS AND SIMPLY VANISHED.
YES. HE'S ALWAYS BEEN GOOD AT THAT.
SUPERMAN?
COULD WE SPEAK ALONE?
I--
SUPERMAN.
WHAT IS IT?!
PUT IT AWAY, SINESTRO--

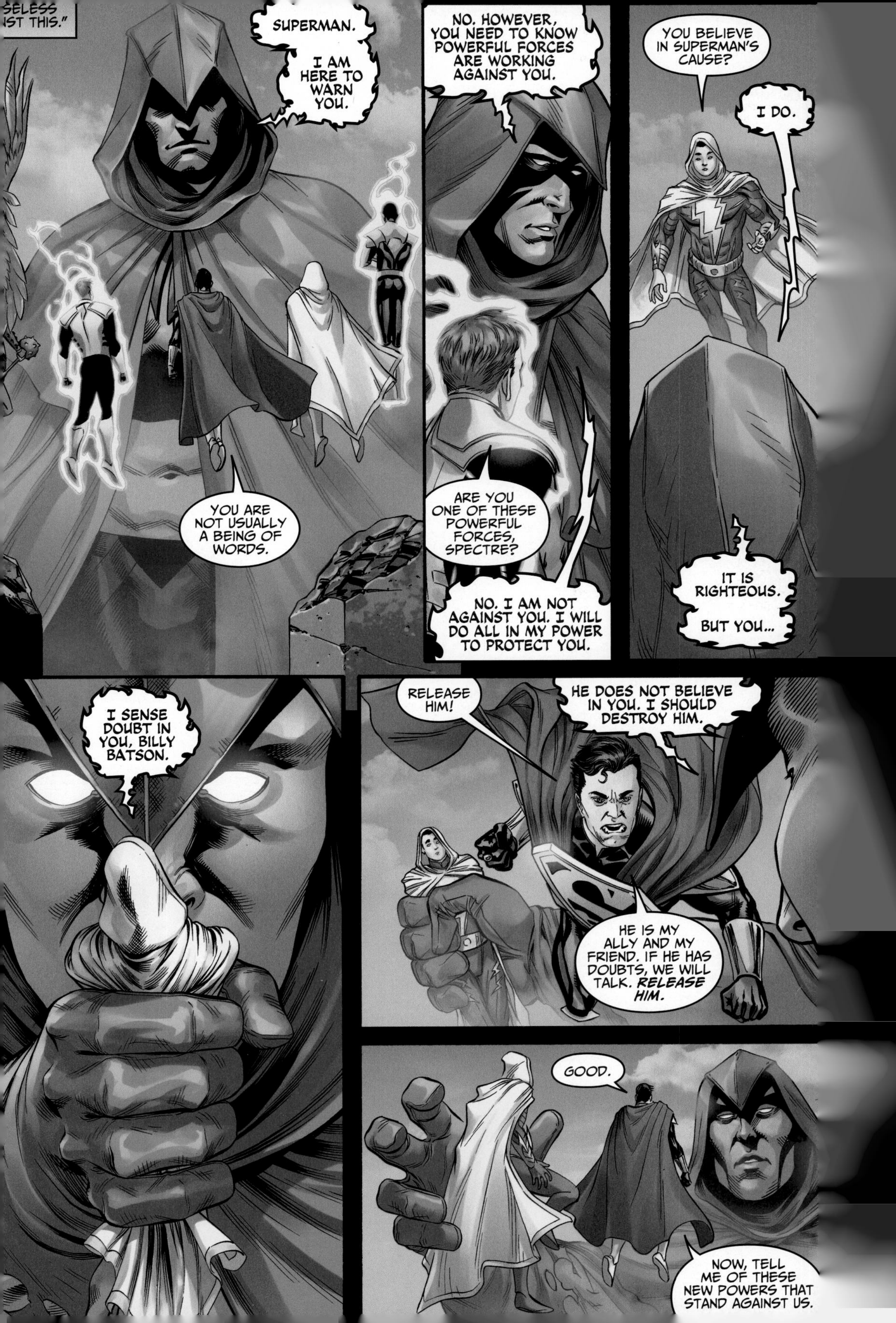
SELESS
IST THIS."
SUPERMAN. I AM HERE TO WARN YOU.
YOU ARE NOT USUALLY A BEING OF WORDS.
NO. HOWEVER, YOU NEED TO KNOW POWERFUL FORCES ARE WORKING AGAINST YOU.
ARE YOU ONE OF THESE POWERFUL FORCES, SPECTRE?
NO. I AM NOT AGAINST YOU. I WILL DO ALL IN MY POWER TO PROTECT YOU.
YOU BELIEVE IN SUPERMAN'S CAUSE?
I DO.
IT IS RIGHTEOUS. BUT YOU...
I SENSE DOUBT IN YOU, BILLY BATSON.
RELEASE HIM!
HE DOES NOT BELIEVE IN YOU. I SHOULD DESTROY HIM.
HE IS MY ALLY AND MY FRIEND. IF HE HAS DOUBTS, WE WILL TALK. *RELEASE HIM.*
GOOD.
NOW, TELL ME OF THESE NEW POWERS THAT STAND AGAINST US.

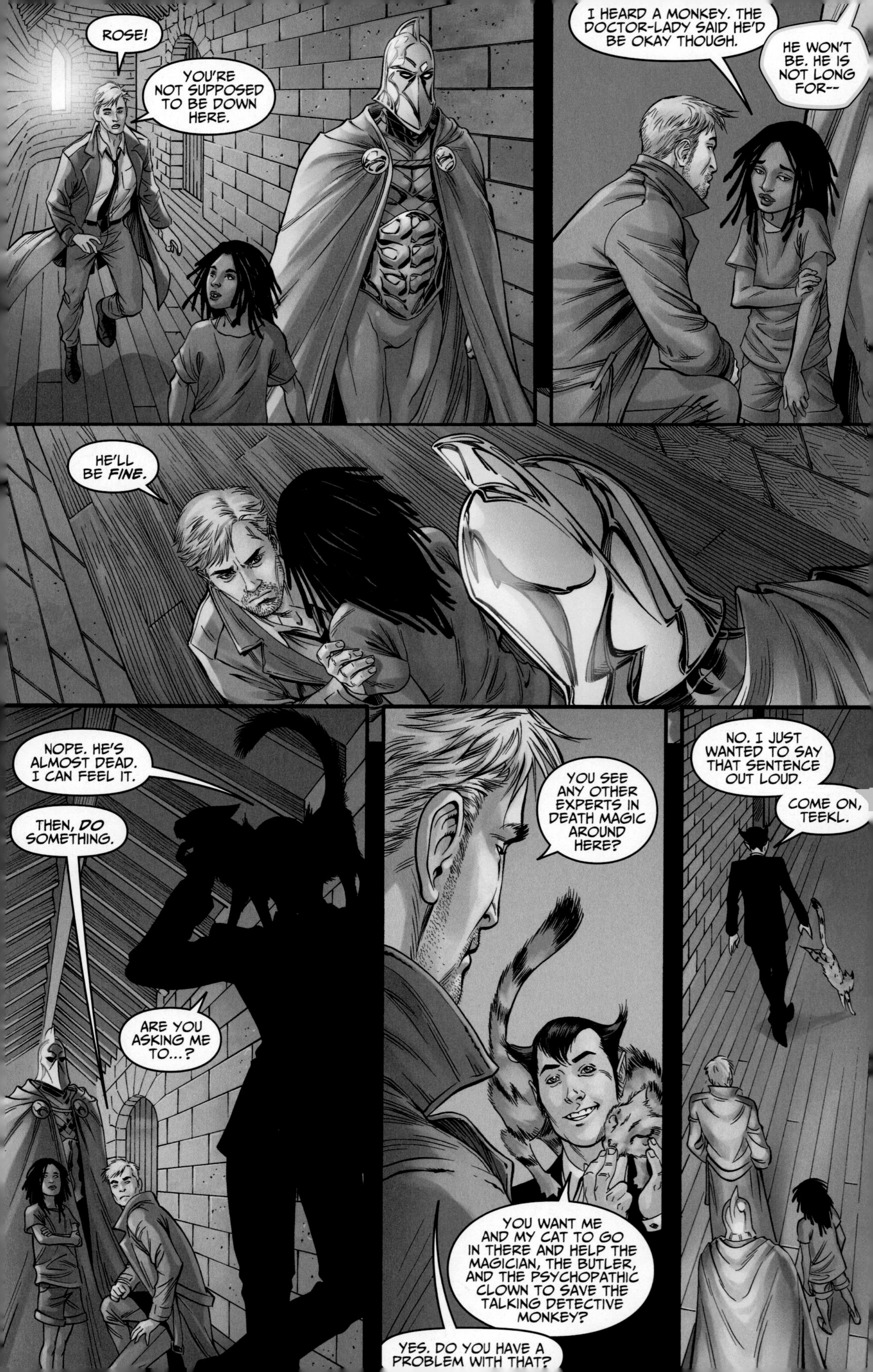

ROSE!
YOU'RE NOT SUPPOSED TO BE DOWN HERE.
I HEARD A MONKEY. THE DOCTOR-LADY SAID HE'D BE OKAY THOUGH.
HE WON'T BE. HE IS NOT LONG FOR--
HE'LL BE *FINE*.
NOPE. HE'S ALMOST DEAD. I CAN FEEL IT.
THEN, *DO* SOMETHING.
ARE YOU ASKING ME TO...?
YOU SEE ANY OTHER EXPERTS IN DEATH MAGIC AROUND HERE?
YOU WANT ME AND MY CAT TO GO IN THERE AND HELP THE MAGICIAN, THE BUTLER, AND THE PSYCHOPATHIC CLOWN TO SAVE THE TALKING DETECTIVE MONKEY?
YES. DO YOU HAVE A PROBLEM WITH THAT?
NO. I JUST WANTED TO SAY THAT SENTENCE OUT LOUD.
COME ON, TEEKL.

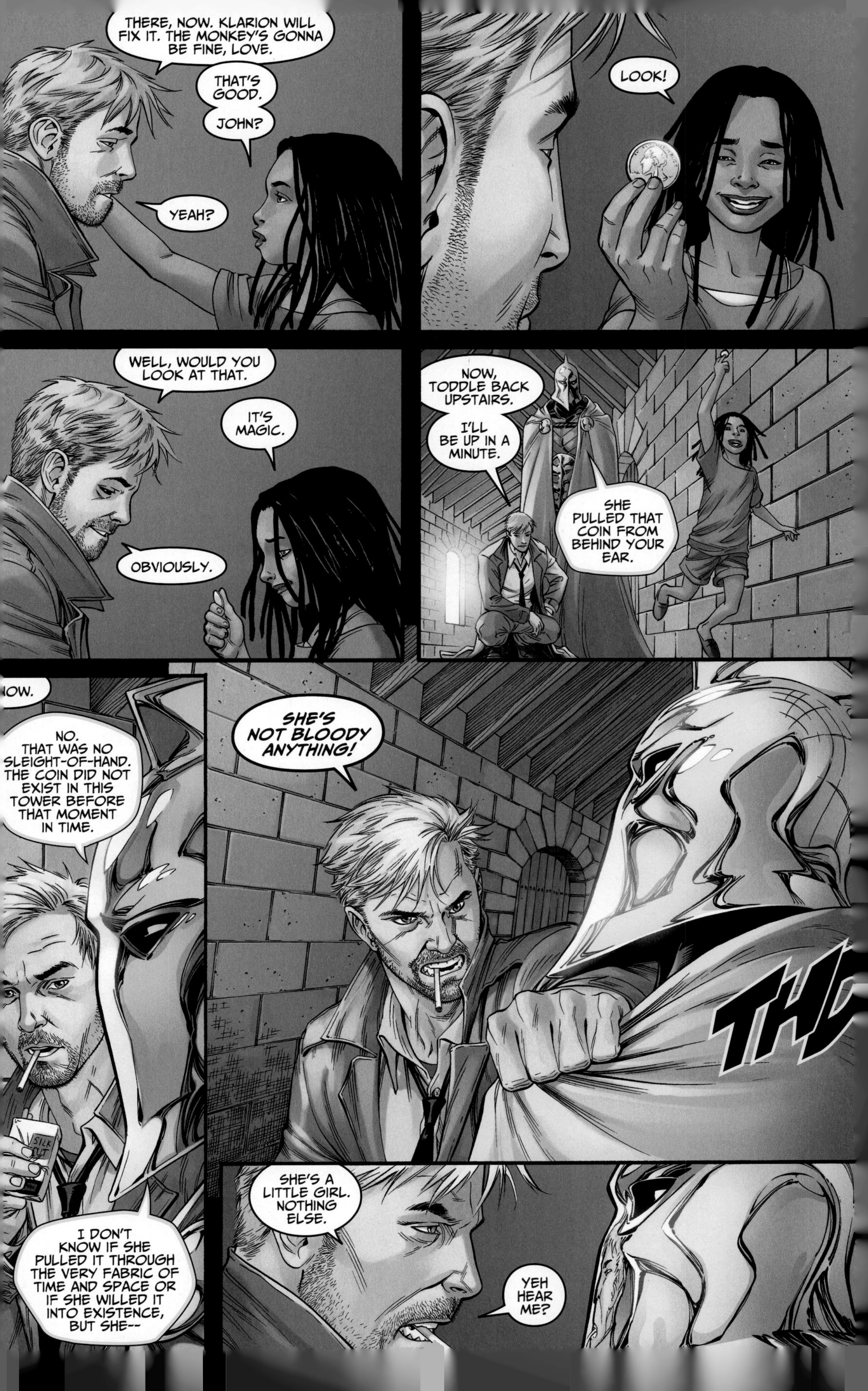
THERE, NOW. KLARION WILL FIX IT. THE MONKEY'S GONNA BE FINE, LOVE.
THAT'S GOOD.
JOHN?
YEAH?
LOOK!
WELL, WOULD YOU LOOK AT THAT.
IT'S MAGIC.
OBVIOUSLY.
NOW, TODDLE BACK UPSTAIRS.
I'LL BE UP IN A MINUTE.
SHE PULLED THAT COIN FROM BEHIND YOUR EAR.
NOW.
NO. THAT WAS NO SLEIGHT-OF-HAND. THE COIN DID NOT EXIST IN THIS TOWER BEFORE THAT MOMENT IN TIME.
I DON'T KNOW IF SHE PULLED IT THROUGH THE VERY FABRIC OF TIME AND SPACE OR IF SHE WILLED IT INTO EXISTENCE, BUT SHE--
SHE'S NOT BLOODY ANYTHING!
THD
SHE'S A LITTLE GIRL. NOTHING ELSE.
YEH HEAR ME?

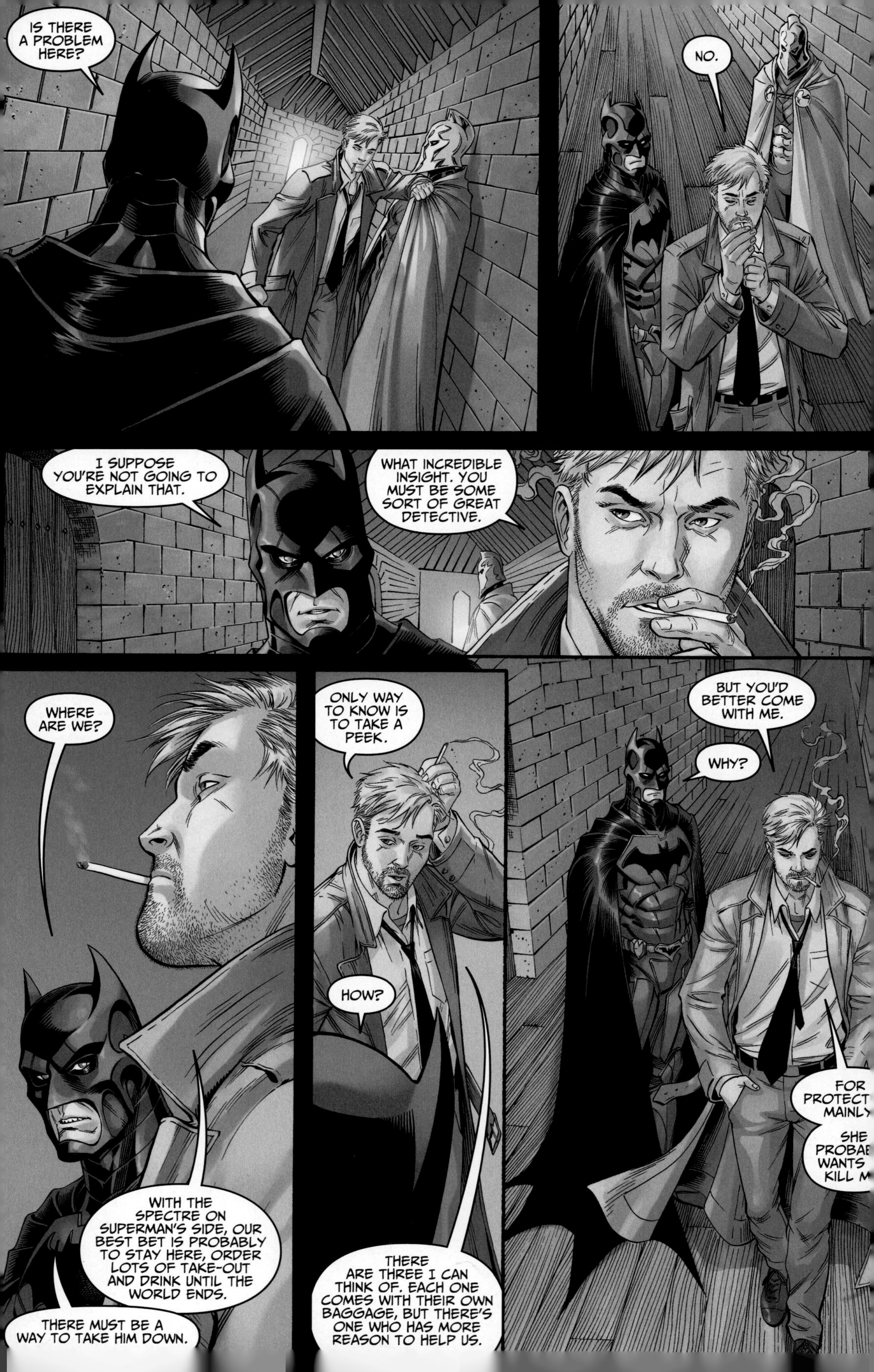
IS THERE A PROBLEM HERE?
NO.
I SUPPOSE YOU'RE NOT GOING TO EXPLAIN THAT.
WHAT INCREDIBLE INSIGHT. YOU MUST BE SOME SORT OF GREAT DETECTIVE.
WHERE ARE WE?
WITH THE SPECTRE ON SUPERMAN'S SIDE, OUR BEST BET IS PROBABLY TO STAY HERE, ORDER LOTS OF TAKE-OUT AND DRINK UNTIL THE WORLD ENDS.
THERE MUST BE A WAY TO TAKE HIM DOWN.
ONLY WAY TO KNOW IS TO TAKE A PEEK.
HOW?
THERE ARE THREE I CAN THINK OF. EACH ONE COMES WITH THEIR OWN BAGGAGE, BUT THERE'S ONE WHO HAS MORE REASON TO HELP US.
BUT YOU'D BETTER COME WITH ME.
WHY?

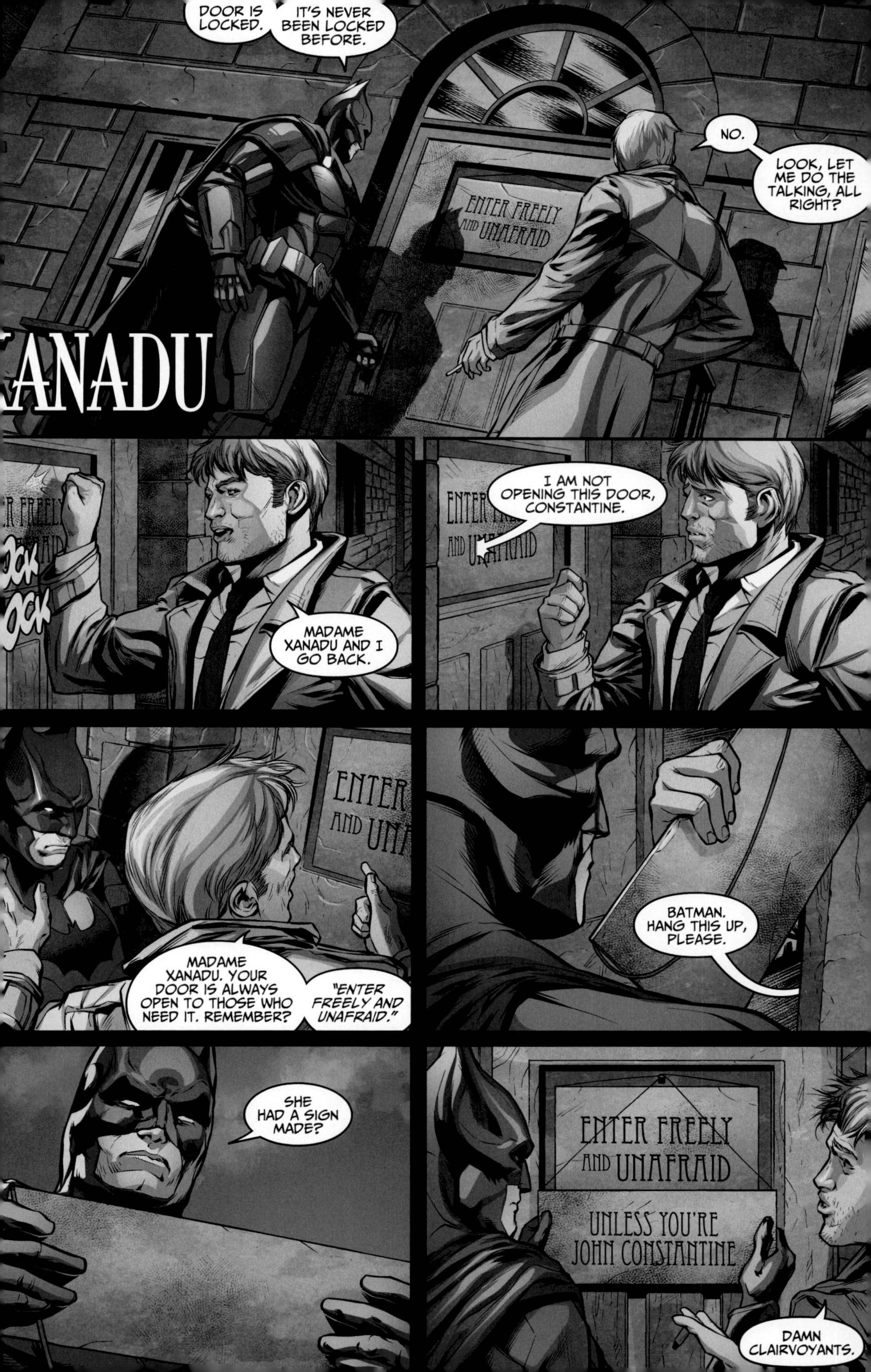
DOOR IS LOCKED.
IT'S NEVER BEEN LOCKED BEFORE.
NO.
LOOK, LET ME DO THE TALKING, ALL RIGHT?
ENTER FREELY AND UNAFRAID
XANADU
MADAME XANADU AND I GO BACK.
I AM NOT OPENING THIS DOOR, CONSTANTINE.
MADAME XANADU. YOUR DOOR IS ALWAYS OPEN TO THOSE WHO NEED IT. REMEMBER?
"ENTER FREELY AND UNAFRAID."
BATMAN. HANG THIS UP, PLEASE.
SHE HAD A SIGN MADE?
ENTER FREELY AND UNAFRAID
UNLESS YOU'RE JOHN CONSTANTINE
DAMN CLAIRVOYANTS.

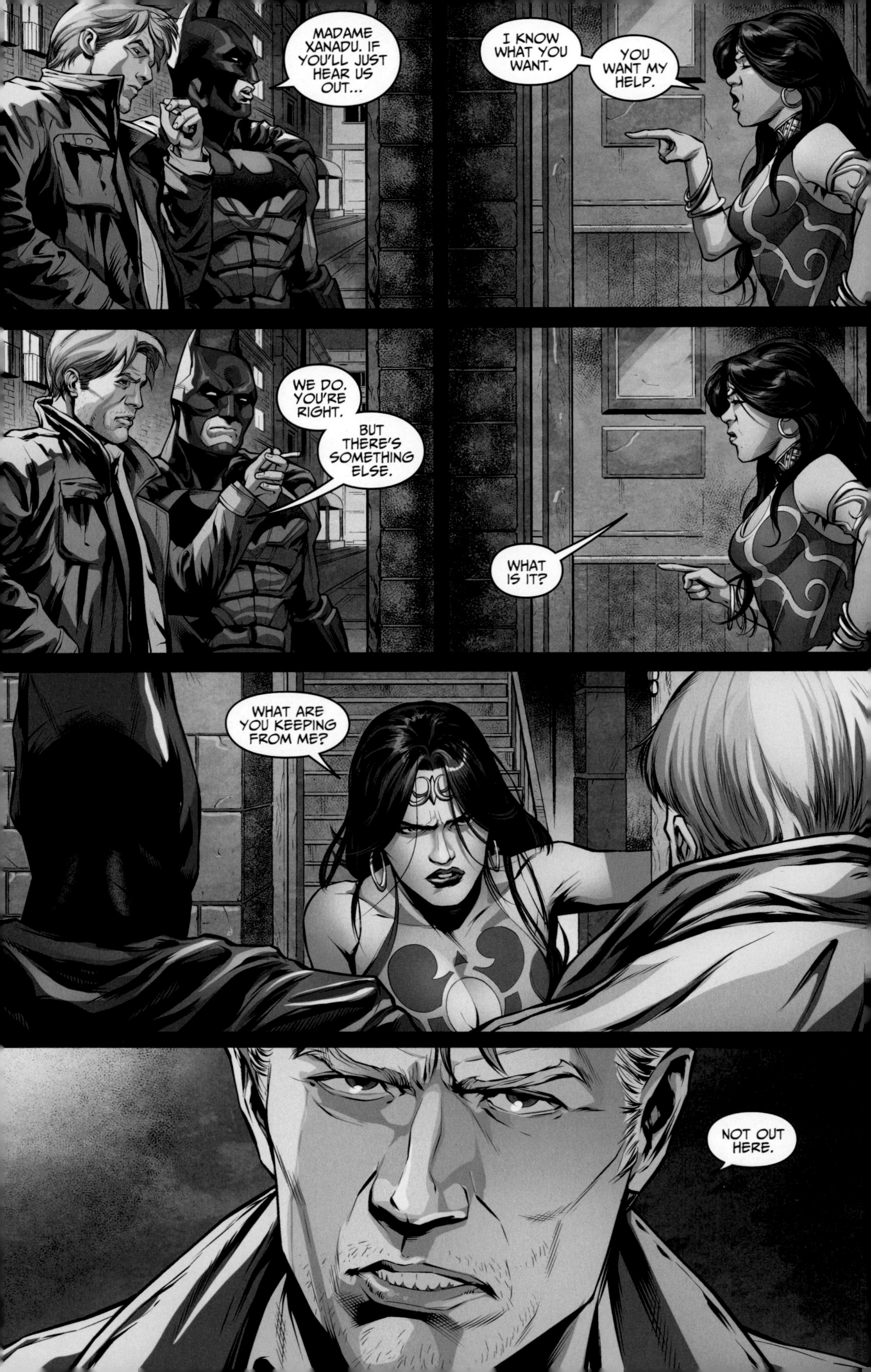
MADAME XANADU. IF YOU'LL JUST HEAR US OUT...
I KNOW WHAT YOU WANT.
YOU WANT MY HELP.
WE DO. YOU'RE RIGHT.
BUT THERE'S SOMETHING ELSE.
WHAT IS IT?
WHAT ARE YOU KEEPING FROM ME?
NOT OUT HERE.

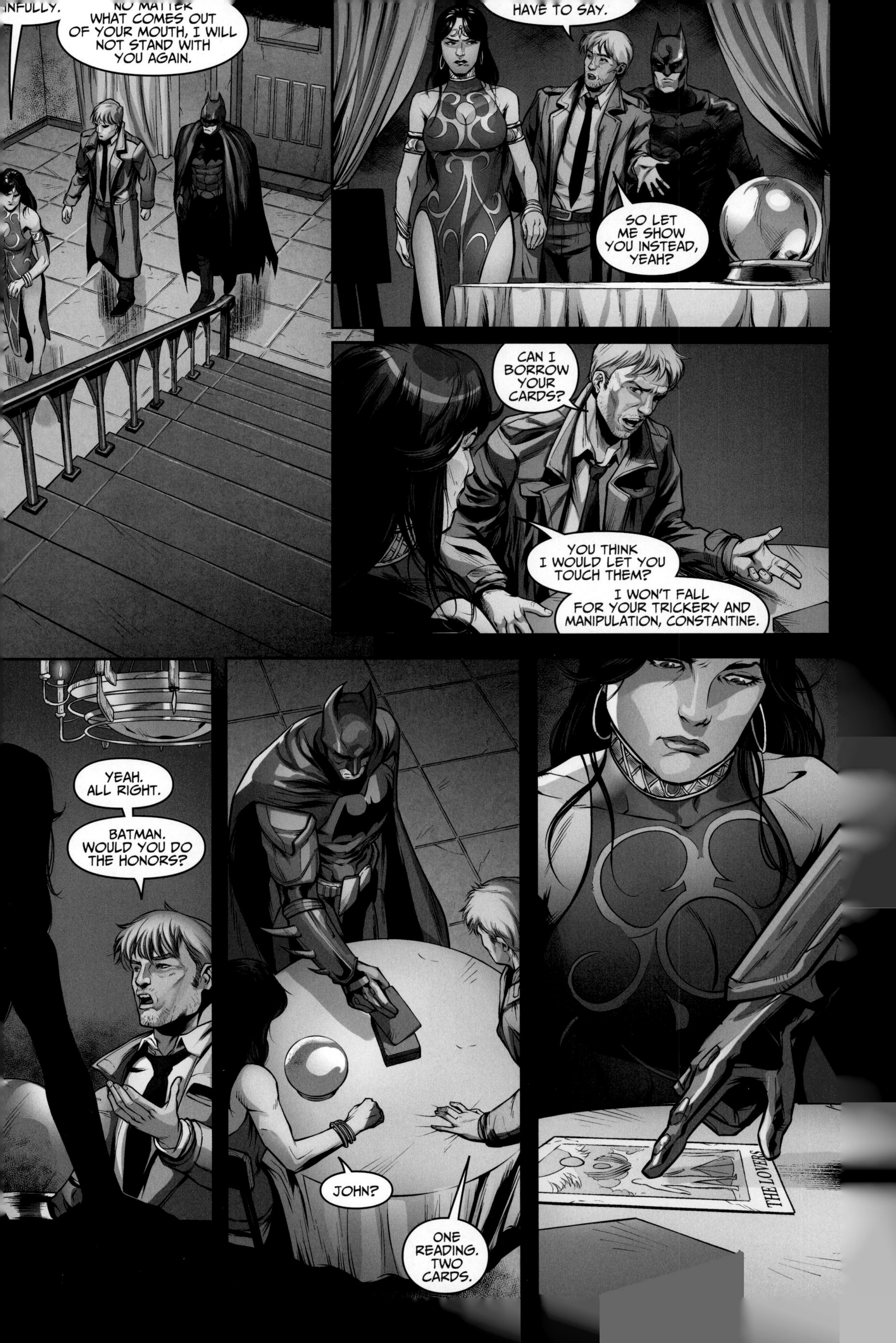

INFULLY.
NO MATTER WHAT COMES OUT OF YOUR MOUTH, I WILL NOT STAND WITH YOU AGAIN.
HAVE TO SAY.
SO LET ME SHOW YOU INSTEAD, YEAH?
CAN I BORROW YOUR CARDS?
YOU THINK I WOULD LET YOU TOUCH THEM?
I WON'T FALL FOR YOUR TRICKERY AND MANIPULATION, CONSTANTINE.
YEAH. ALL RIGHT.
BATMAN. WOULD YOU DO THE HONORS?
JOHN?
ONE READING. TWO CARDS.
THE LOVERS

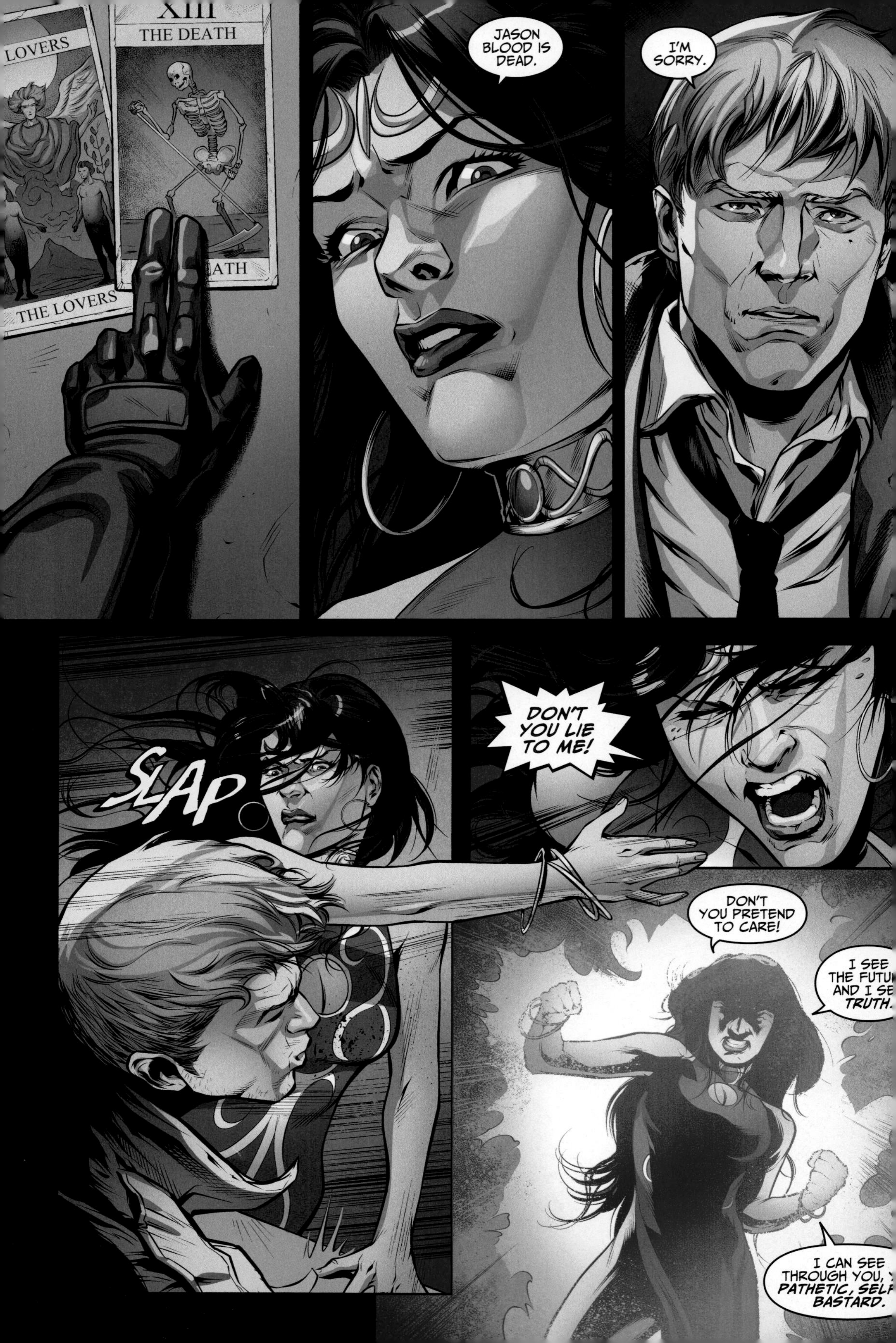

LOVERS
XIII
THE DEATH
THE LOVERS
EATH
JASON BLOOD IS DEAD.
I'M SORRY.
SLAP
DON'T YOU LIE TO ME!
DON'T YOU PRETEND TO CARE!
I SEE THE FUTU AND I SE TRUTH.
I CAN SEE THROUGH YOU, PATHETIC, SEL BASTARD.

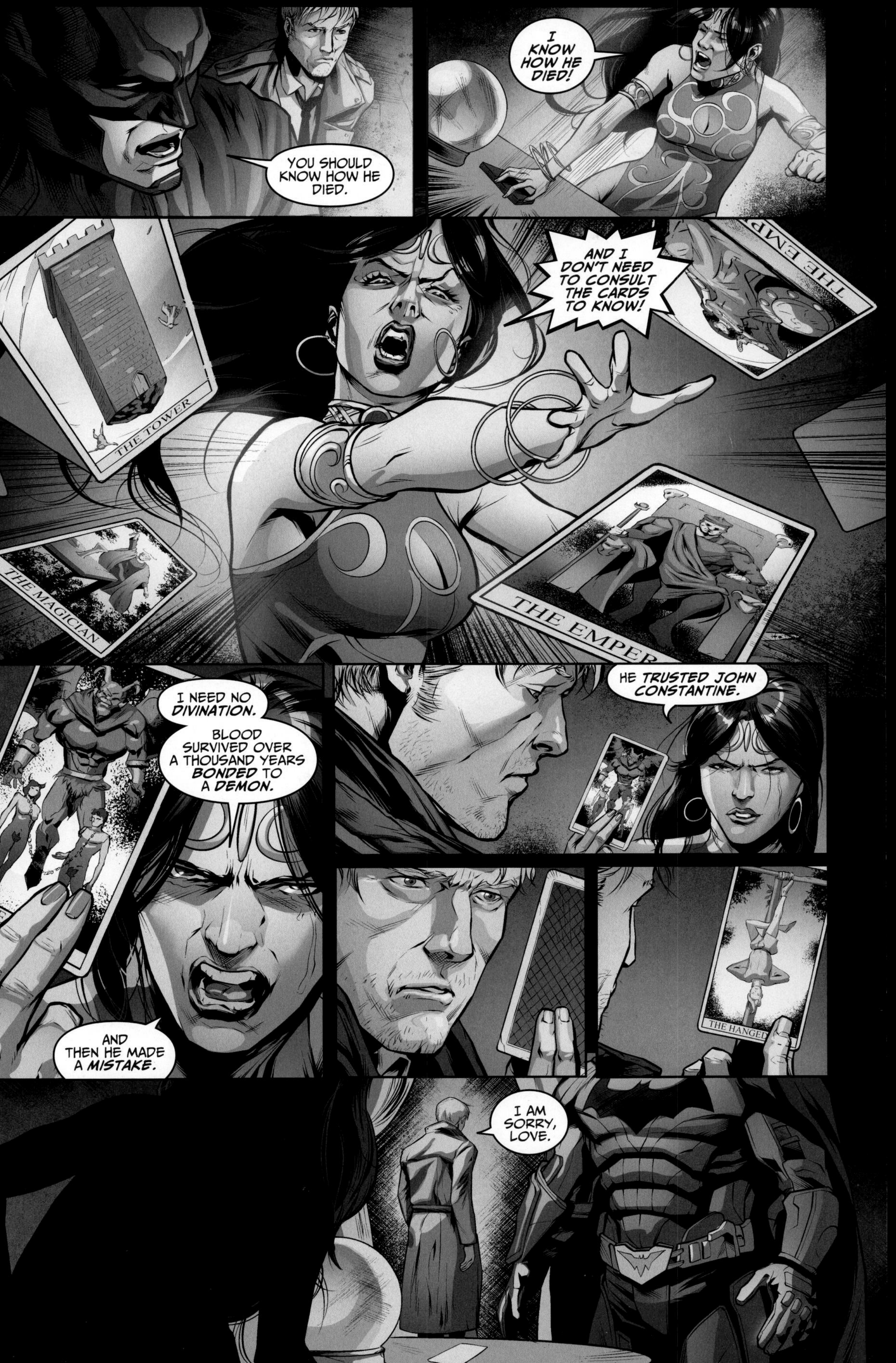
YOU SHOULD KNOW HOW HE DIED.
I KNOW HOW HE DIED!
AND I DON'T NEED TO CONSULT THE CARDS TO KNOW!
THE TOWER
THE MAGICIAN
THE EMPER
I NEED NO DIVINATION.
BLOOD SURVIVED OVER A THOUSAND YEARS BONDED TO A DEMON.
AND THEN HE MADE A MISTAKE.
HE TRUSTED JOHN CONSTANTINE.
THE HANGED
I AM SORRY, LOVE.

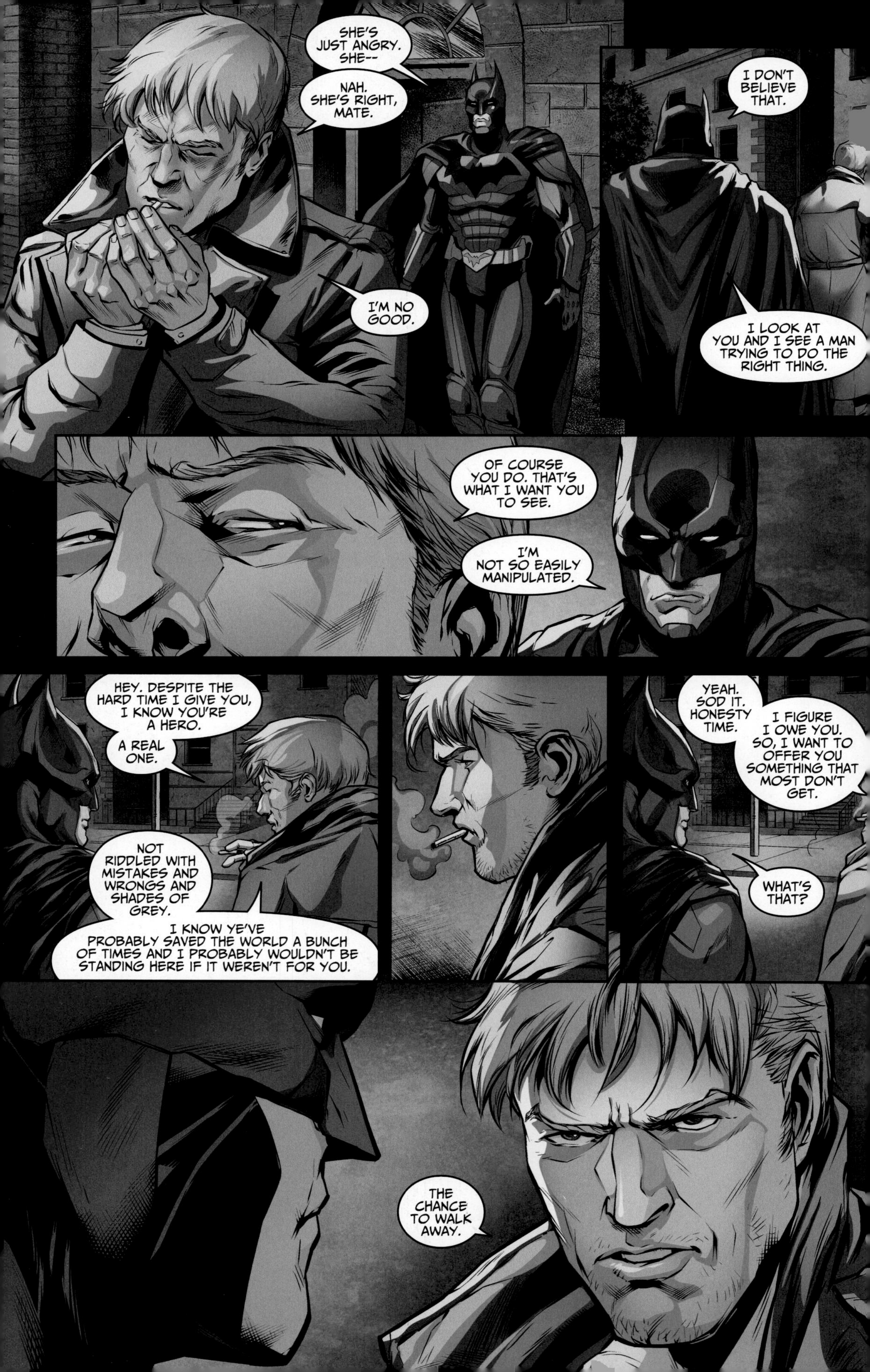
SHE'S JUST ANGRY. SHE--
NAH. SHE'S RIGHT, MATE.
I'M NO GOOD.
I DON'T BELIEVE THAT.
I LOOK AT YOU AND I SEE A MAN TRYING TO DO THE RIGHT THING.
OF COURSE YOU DO. THAT'S WHAT I WANT YOU TO SEE.
I'M NOT SO EASILY MANIPULATED.
HEY. DESPITE THE HARD TIME I GIVE YOU, I KNOW YOU'RE A HERO.
A REAL ONE.
NOT RIDDLED WITH MISTAKES AND WRONGS AND SHADES OF GREY.
I KNOW YE'VE PROBABLY SAVED THE WORLD A BUNCH OF TIMES AND I PROBABLY WOULDN'T BE STANDING HERE IF IT WEREN'T FOR YOU.
YEAH. SOD IT. HONESTY TIME.
I FIGURE I OWE YOU. SO, I WANT TO OFFER YOU SOMETHING THAT MOST DON'T GET.
WHAT'S THAT?
THE CHANCE TO WALK AWAY.

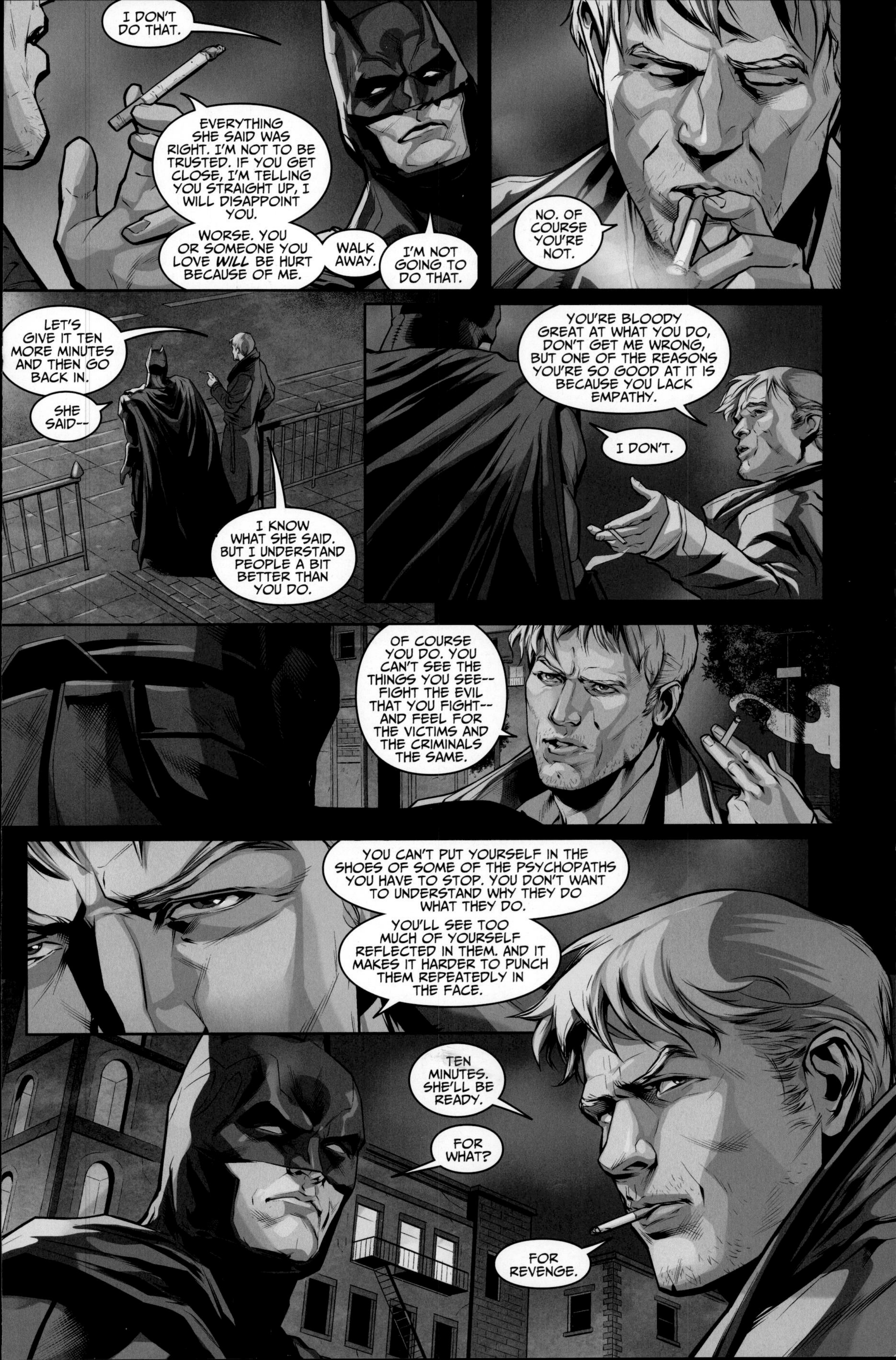

I DON'T DO THAT.
EVERYTHING SHE SAID WAS RIGHT. I'M NOT TO BE TRUSTED. IF YOU GET CLOSE, I'M TELLING YOU STRAIGHT UP, I WILL DISAPPOINT YOU.
WORSE. YOU OR SOMEONE YOU LOVE *WILL* BE HURT BECAUSE OF ME.
WALK AWAY.
I'M NOT GOING TO DO THAT.
NO. OF COURSE YOU'RE NOT.
LET'S GIVE IT TEN MORE MINUTES AND THEN GO BACK IN.
SHE SAID--
I KNOW WHAT SHE SAID. BUT I UNDERSTAND PEOPLE A BIT BETTER THAN YOU DO.
YOU'RE BLOODY GREAT AT WHAT YOU DO, DON'T GET ME WRONG, BUT ONE OF THE REASONS YOU'RE SO GOOD AT IT IS BECAUSE YOU LACK EMPATHY.
I DON'T.
OF COURSE YOU DO. YOU CAN'T SEE THE THINGS YOU SEE--FIGHT THE EVIL THAT YOU FIGHT--AND FEEL FOR THE VICTIMS AND THE CRIMINALS THE SAME.
YOU CAN'T PUT YOURSELF IN THE SHOES OF SOME OF THE PSYCHOPATHS YOU HAVE TO STOP. YOU DON'T WANT TO UNDERSTAND WHY THEY DO WHAT THEY DO.
YOU'LL SEE TOO MUCH OF YOURSELF REFLECTED IN THEM. AND IT MAKES IT HARDER TO PUNCH THEM REPEATEDLY IN THE FACE.
TEN MINUTES. SHE'LL BE READY.
FOR WHAT?
FOR REVENGE.

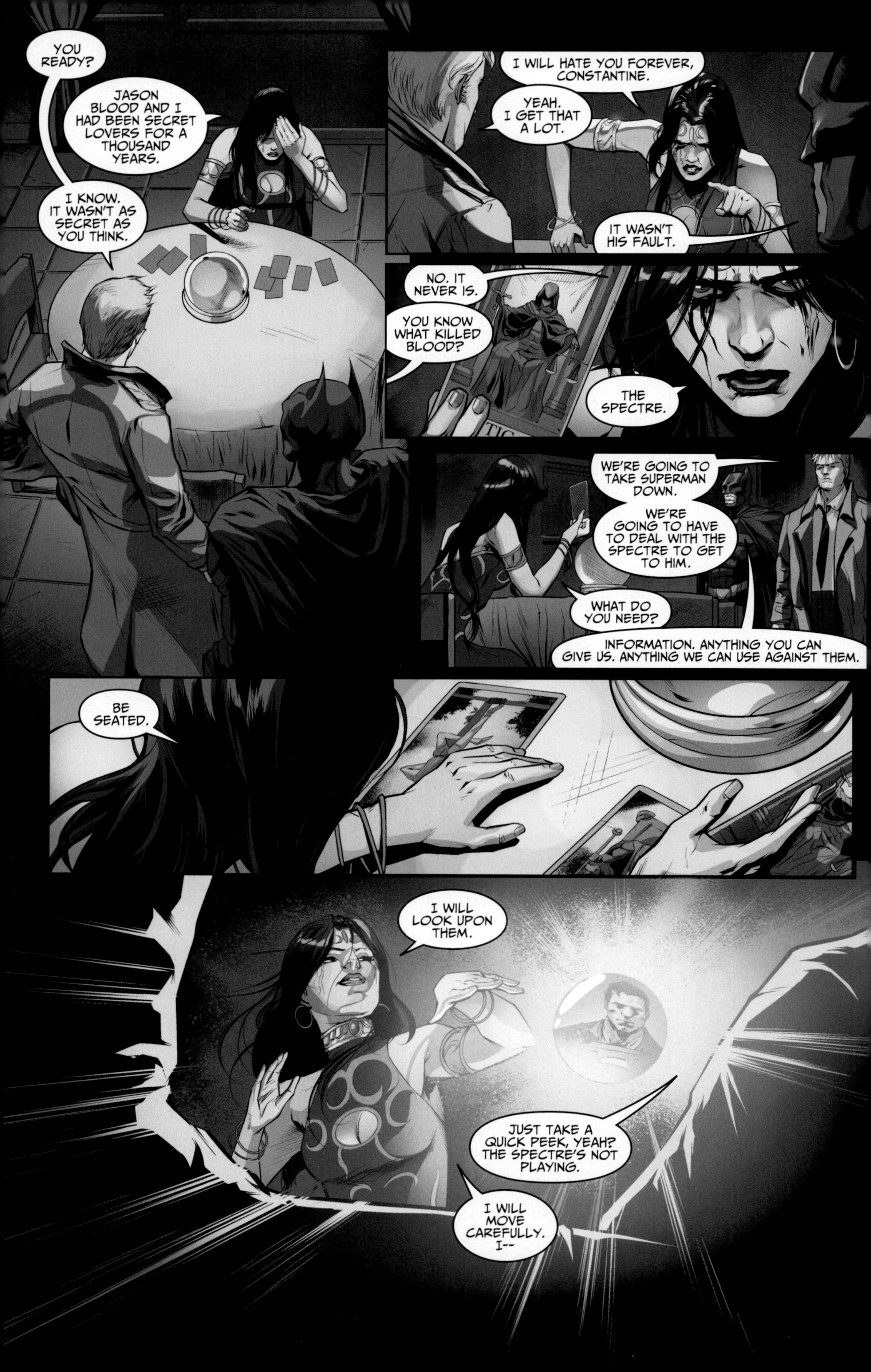
YOU READY?
JASON BLOOD AND I HAD BEEN SECRET LOVERS FOR A THOUSAND YEARS.
I KNOW. IT WASN'T AS SECRET AS YOU THINK.
I WILL HATE YOU FOREVER, CONSTANTINE.
YEAH. I GET THAT A LOT.
IT WASN'T HIS FAULT.
NO. IT NEVER IS.
YOU KNOW WHAT KILLED BLOOD?
THE SPECTRE.
WE'RE GOING TO TAKE SUPERMAN DOWN.
WE'RE GOING TO HAVE TO DEAL WITH THE SPECTRE TO GET TO HIM.
WHAT DO YOU NEED?
INFORMATION. ANYTHING YOU CAN GIVE US. ANYTHING WE CAN USE AGAINST THEM.
BE SEATED.
I WILL LOOK UPON THEM.
JUST TAKE A QUICK PEEK, YEAH? THE SPECTRE'S NOT PLAYING.
I WILL MOVE CAREFULLY. I--

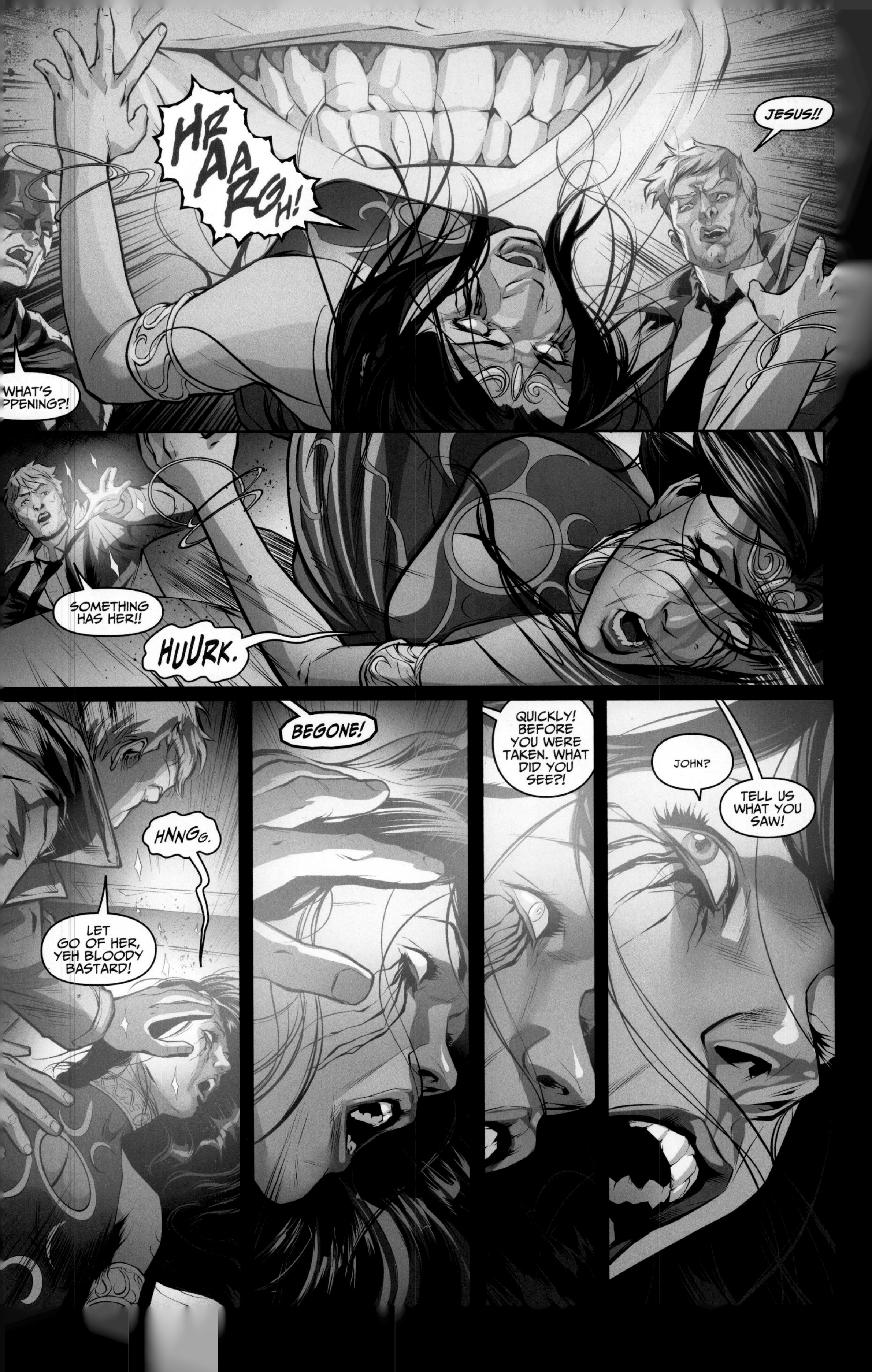
HRAARGH!
JESUS!!
WHAT'S
PPENING?!
SOMETHING HAS HER!!
HUURK.
HNNGG.
LET GO OF HER, YEH BLOODY BASTARD!
BEGONE!
QUICKLY! BEFORE YOU WERE TAKEN. WHAT DID YOU SEE?!
JOHN?
TELL US WHAT YOU SAW!

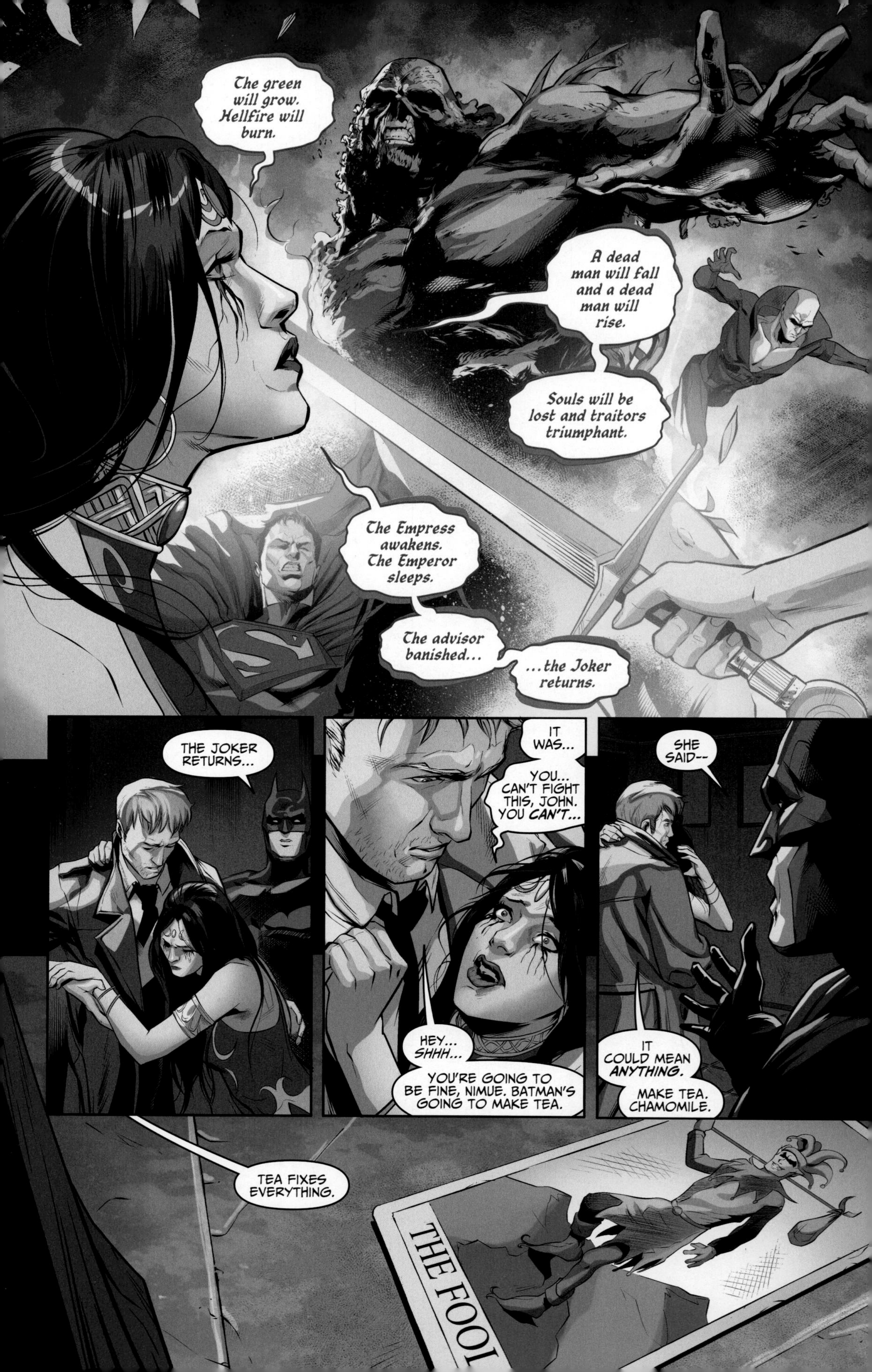
The green will grow. Hellfire will burn.
A dead man will fall and a dead man will rise.
Souls will be lost and traitors triumphant.
The Empress awakens. The Emperor sleeps.
The advisor banished...
...the Joker returns.
THE JOKER RETURNS...
IT WAS...
YOU... CAN'T FIGHT THIS, JOHN. YOU CAN'T...
HEY... SHHH...
YOU'RE GOING TO BE FINE, NIMUE. BATMAN'S GOING TO MAKE TEA.
SHE SAID--
IT COULD MEAN ANYTHING.
MAKE TEA. CHAMOMILE.
TEA FIXES EVERYTHING.
THE FOOL

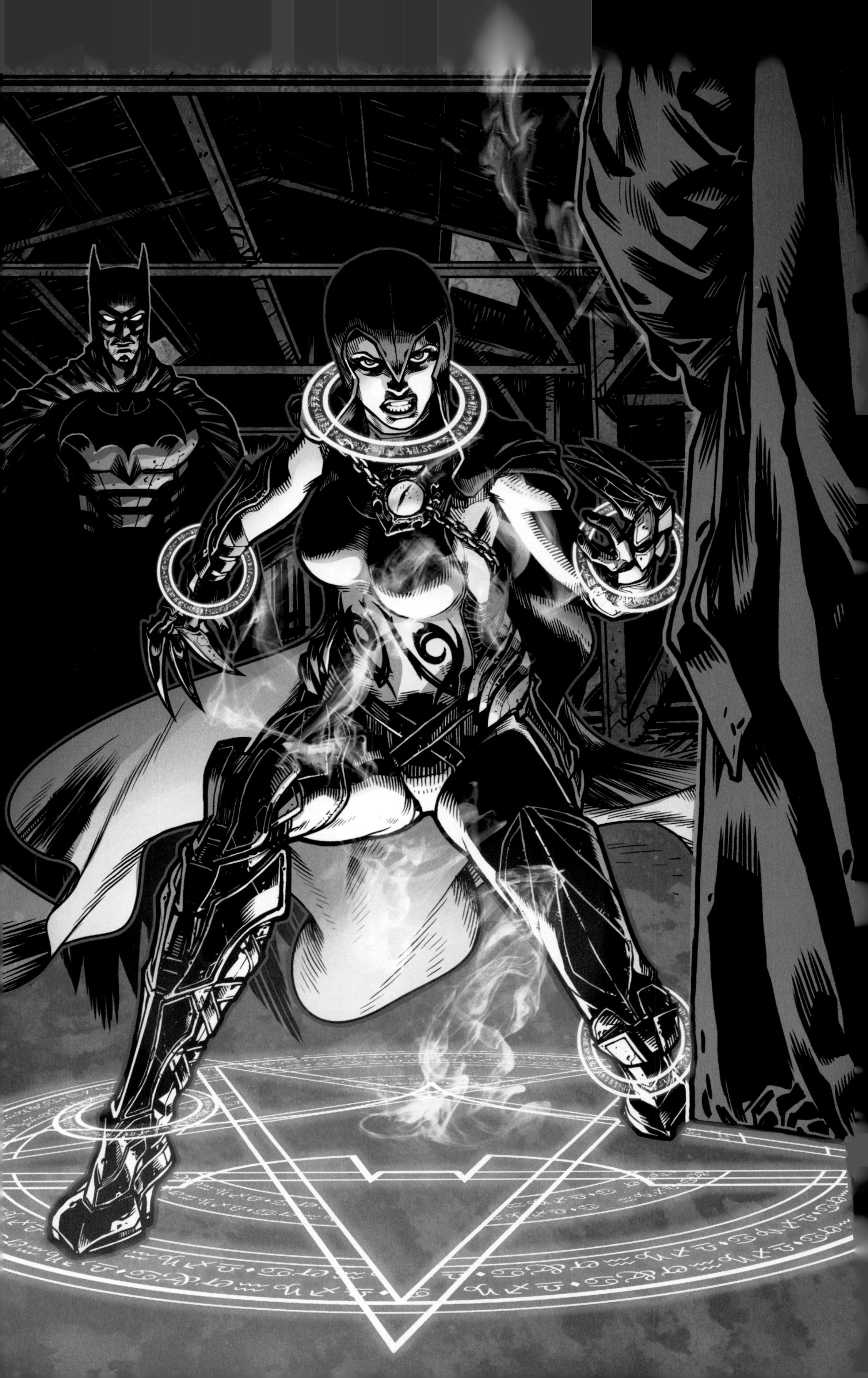

"Raven's Rescue" **Bruno Redondo & Xermanico** Artists **Rex Lokus** Colorist
"Ragman's Souls" **Mike S. Miller** Artist **J. Nanjan** Colorist
Cover Art by **Neil Googe & Rex Lokus**

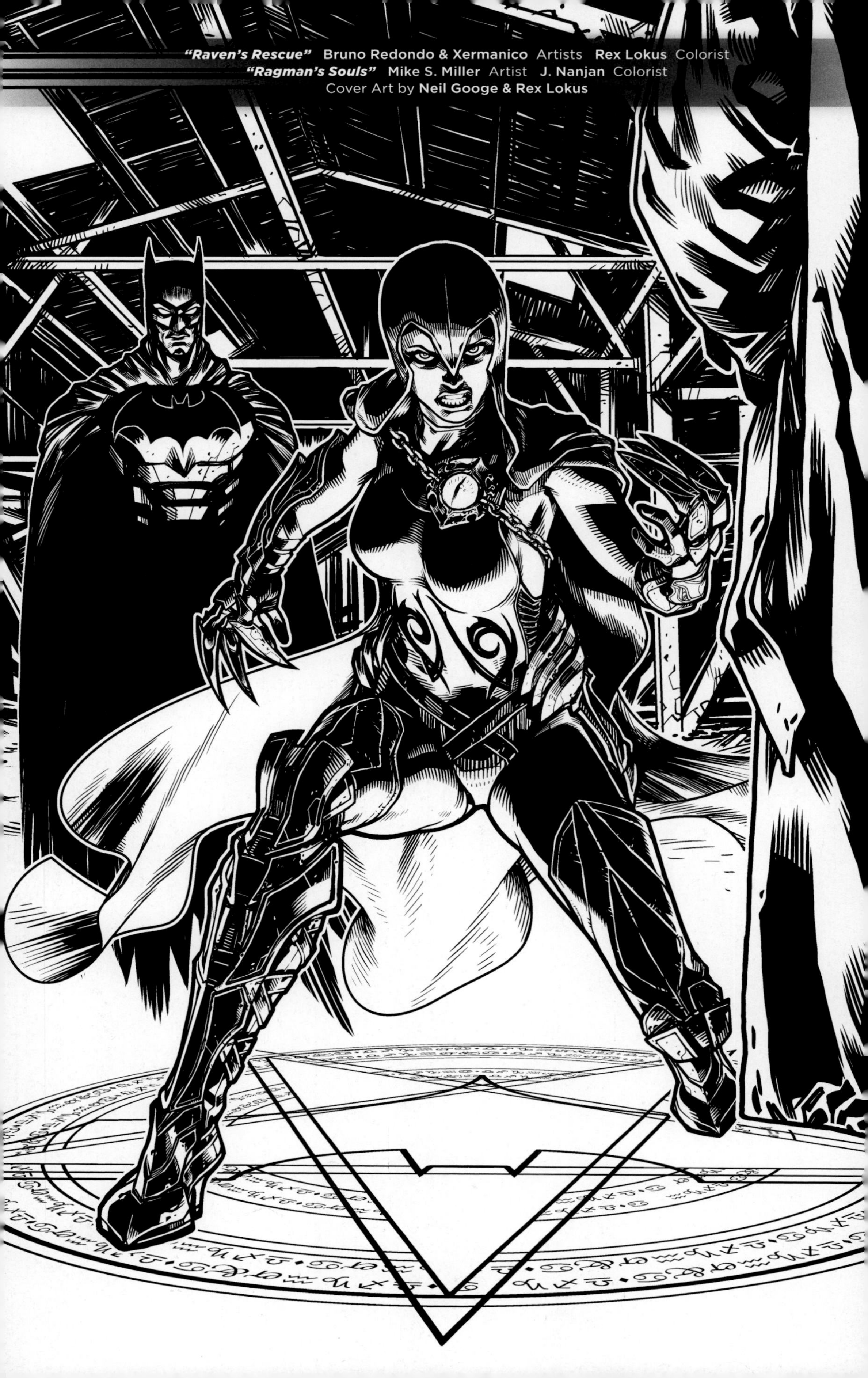

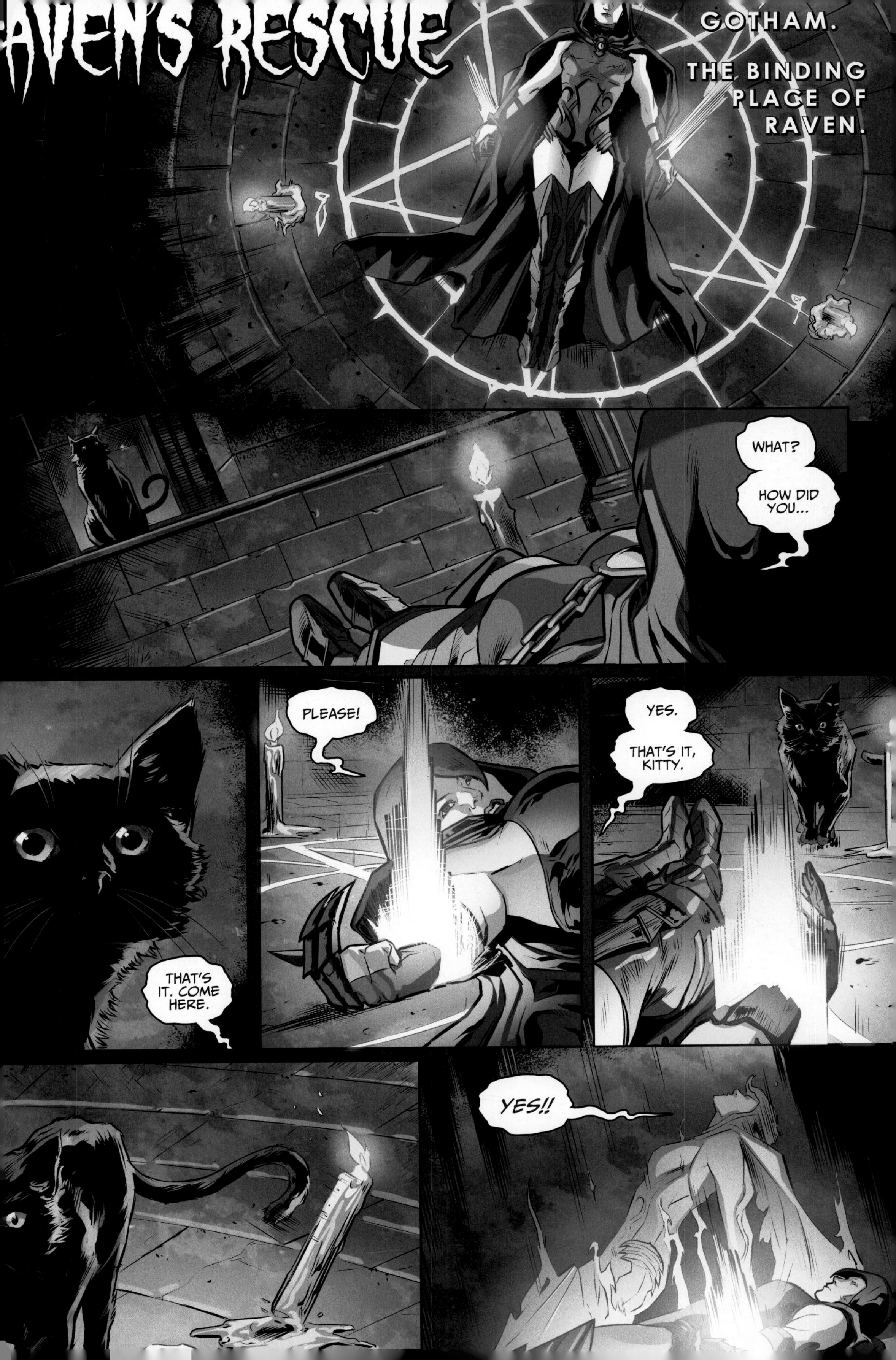
AVEN'S RESCUE
GOTHAM.
THE BINDING PLACE OF RAVEN.
WHAT?
HOW DID YOU...
THAT'S IT. COME HERE.
PLEASE!
YES.
THAT'S IT, KITTY.
YES!!

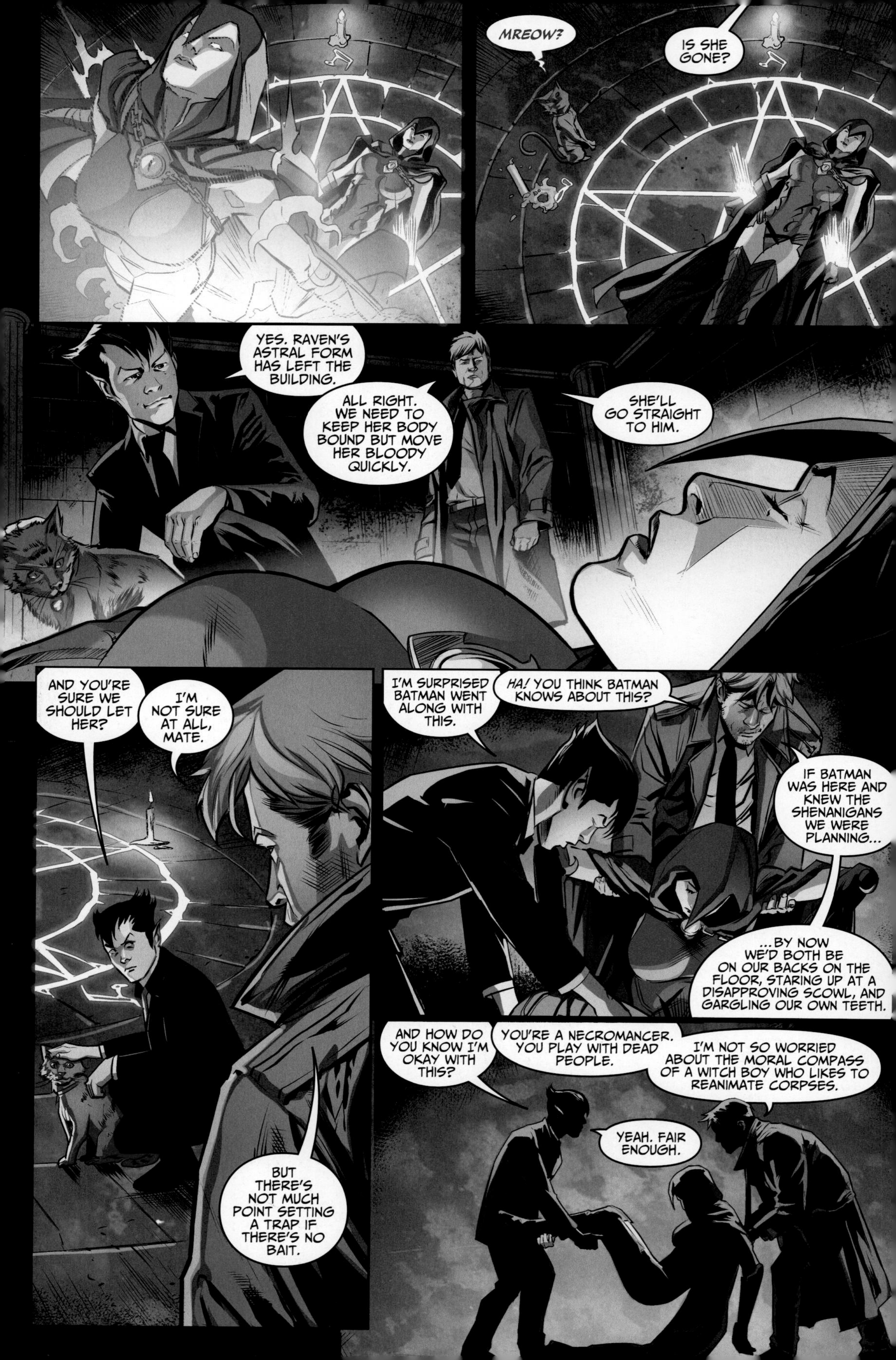
MREOW?
IS SHE GONE?
YES. RAVEN'S ASTRAL FORM HAS LEFT THE BUILDING.
ALL RIGHT. WE NEED TO KEEP HER BODY BOUND BUT MOVE HER BLOODY QUICKLY.
SHE'LL GO STRAIGHT TO HIM.
AND YOU'RE SURE WE SHOULD LET HER?
I'M NOT SURE AT ALL, MATE.
BUT THERE'S NOT MUCH POINT SETTING A TRAP IF THERE'S NO BAIT.
I'M SURPRISED BATMAN WENT ALONG WITH THIS.
HA! YOU THINK BATMAN KNOWS ABOUT THIS?
IF BATMAN WAS HERE AND KNEW THE SHENANIGANS WE WERE PLANNING...
...BY NOW WE'D BOTH BE ON OUR BACKS ON THE FLOOR, STARING UP AT A DISAPPROVING SCOWL, AND GARGLING OUR OWN TEETH.
AND HOW DO YOU KNOW I'M OKAY WITH THIS?
YOU'RE A NECROMANCER. YOU PLAY WITH DEAD PEOPLE.
I'M NOT SO WORRIED ABOUT THE MORAL COMPASS OF A WITCH BOY WHO LIKES TO REANIMATE CORPSES.
YEAH. FAIR ENOUGH.

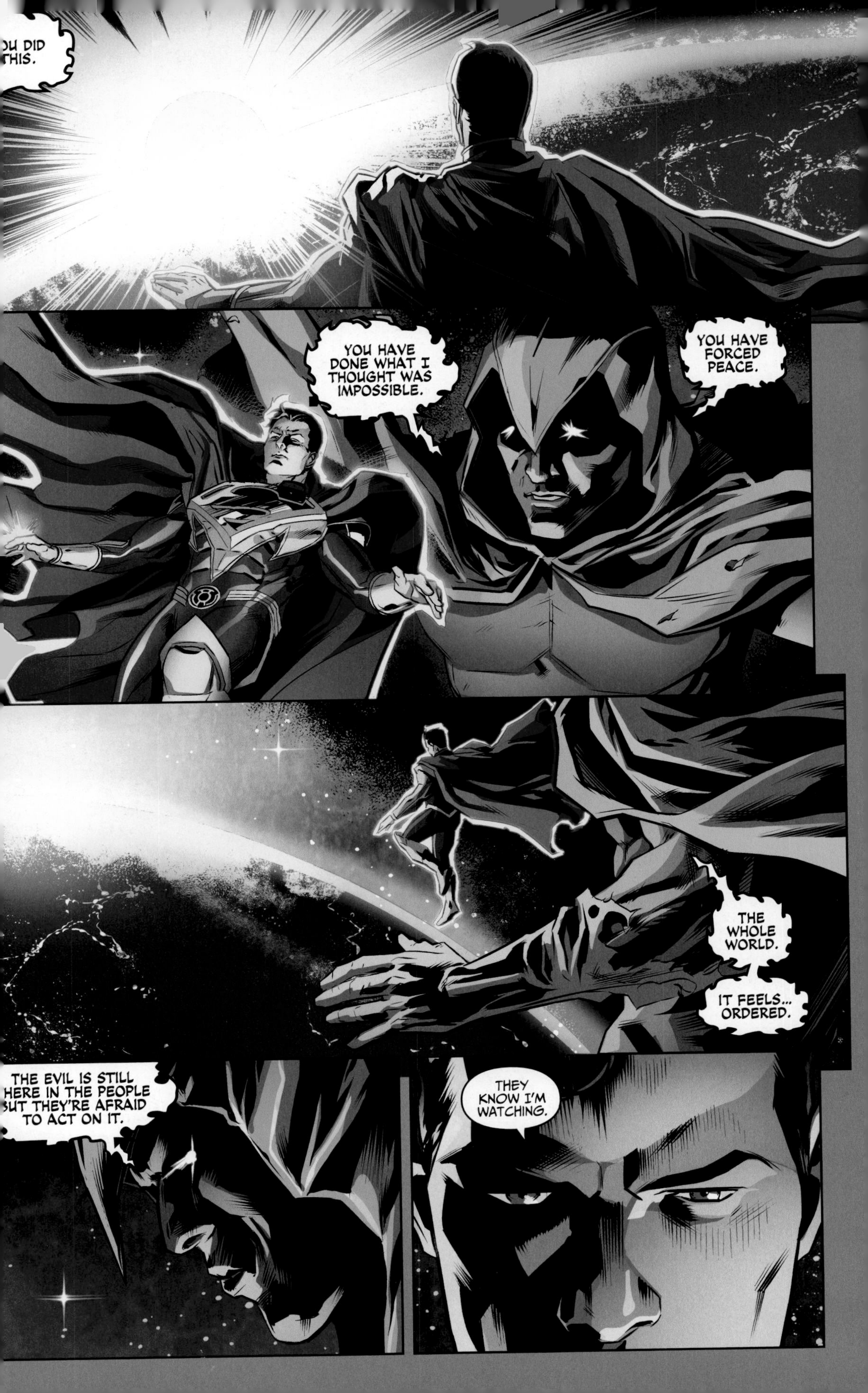

OU DID THIS.
YOU HAVE DONE WHAT I THOUGHT WAS IMPOSSIBLE.
YOU HAVE FORCED PEACE.
THE WHOLE WORLD.
IT FEELS... ORDERED.
THE EVIL IS STILL HERE IN THE PEOPLE BUT THEY'RE AFRAID TO ACT ON IT.
THEY KNOW I'M WATCHING.

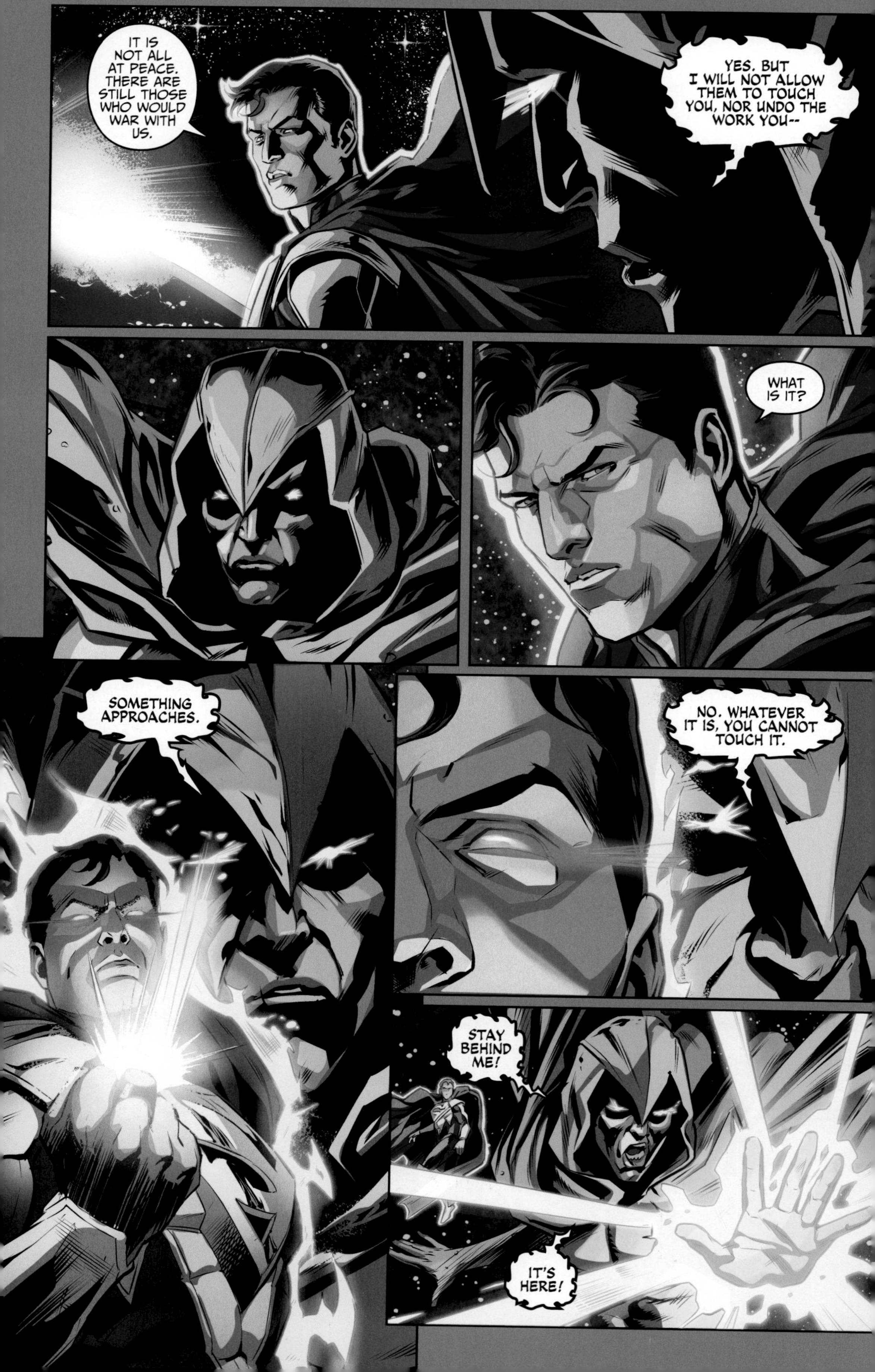
IT IS NOT ALL AT PEACE. THERE ARE STILL THOSE WHO WOULD WAR WITH US.
YES. BUT I WILL NOT ALLOW THEM TO TOUCH YOU, NOR UNDO THE WORK YOU--
WHAT IS IT?
SOMETHING APPROACHES.
NO. WHATEVER IT IS, YOU CANNOT TOUCH IT.
STAY BEHIND ME!
IT'S HERE!

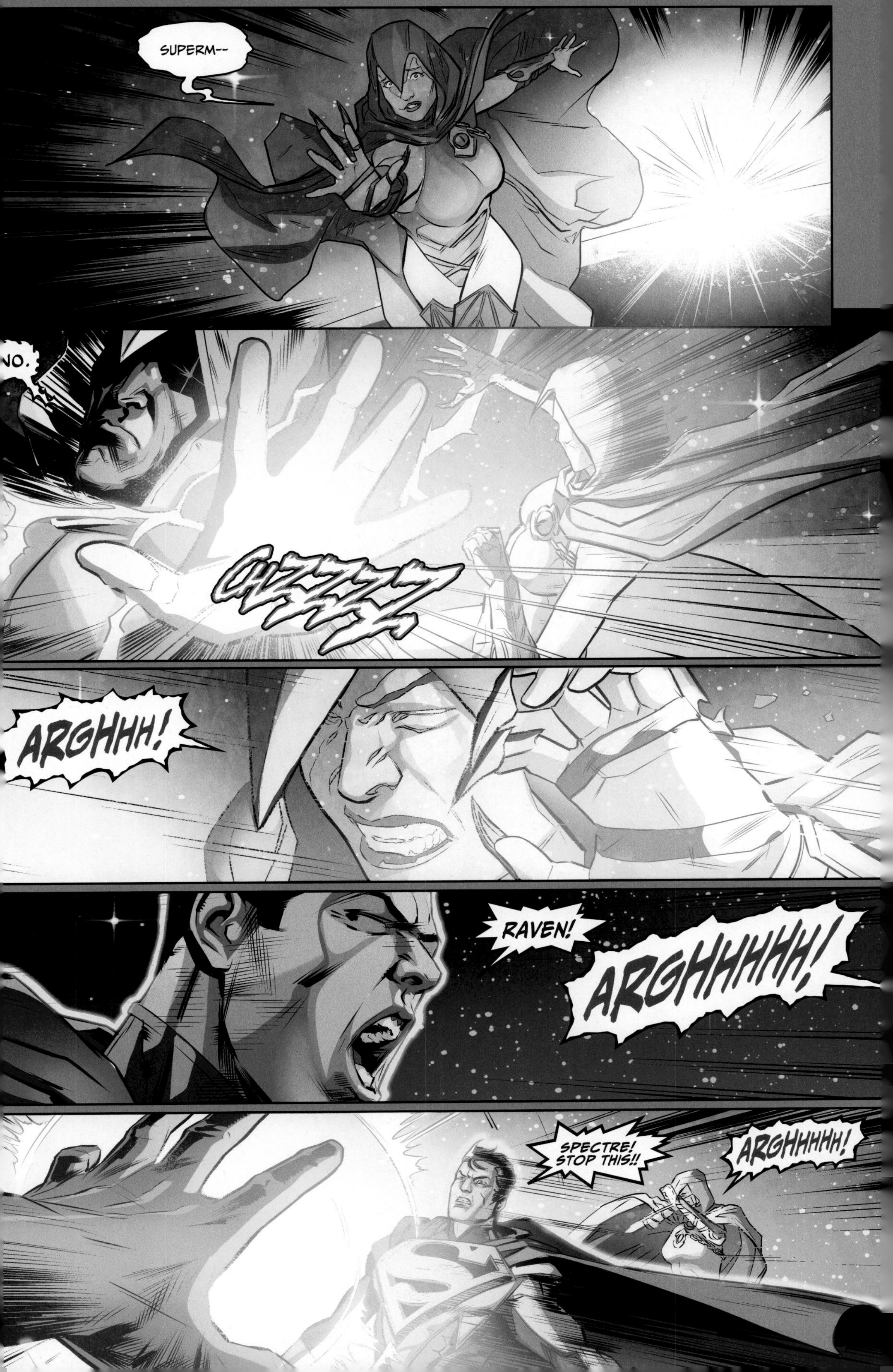
SUPERM--
NO.
CHZZZZ
ARGHHH!
RAVEN!
ARGHHHHH!
SPECTRE! STOP THIS!!
ARGHHHHH!

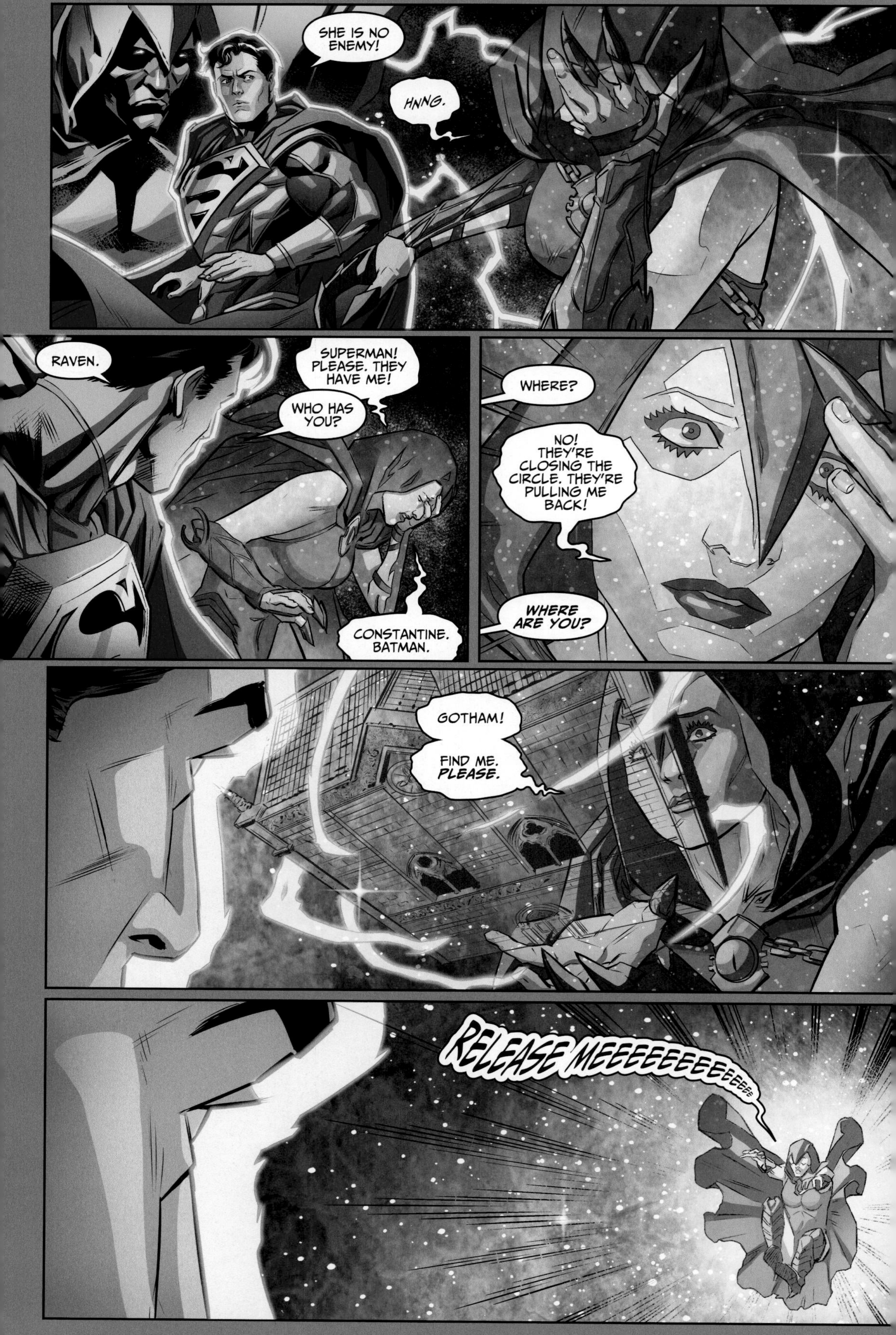
SHE IS NO ENEMY!
HNNG.
RAVEN.
SUPERMAN! PLEASE. THEY HAVE ME!
WHO HAS YOU?
CONSTANTINE. BATMAN.
WHERE?
NO! THEY'RE CLOSING THE CIRCLE. THEY'RE PULLING ME BACK!
WHERE ARE YOU?
GOTHAM!
FIND ME. PLEASE.
RELEASE MEEEEEEEEEEEEEE

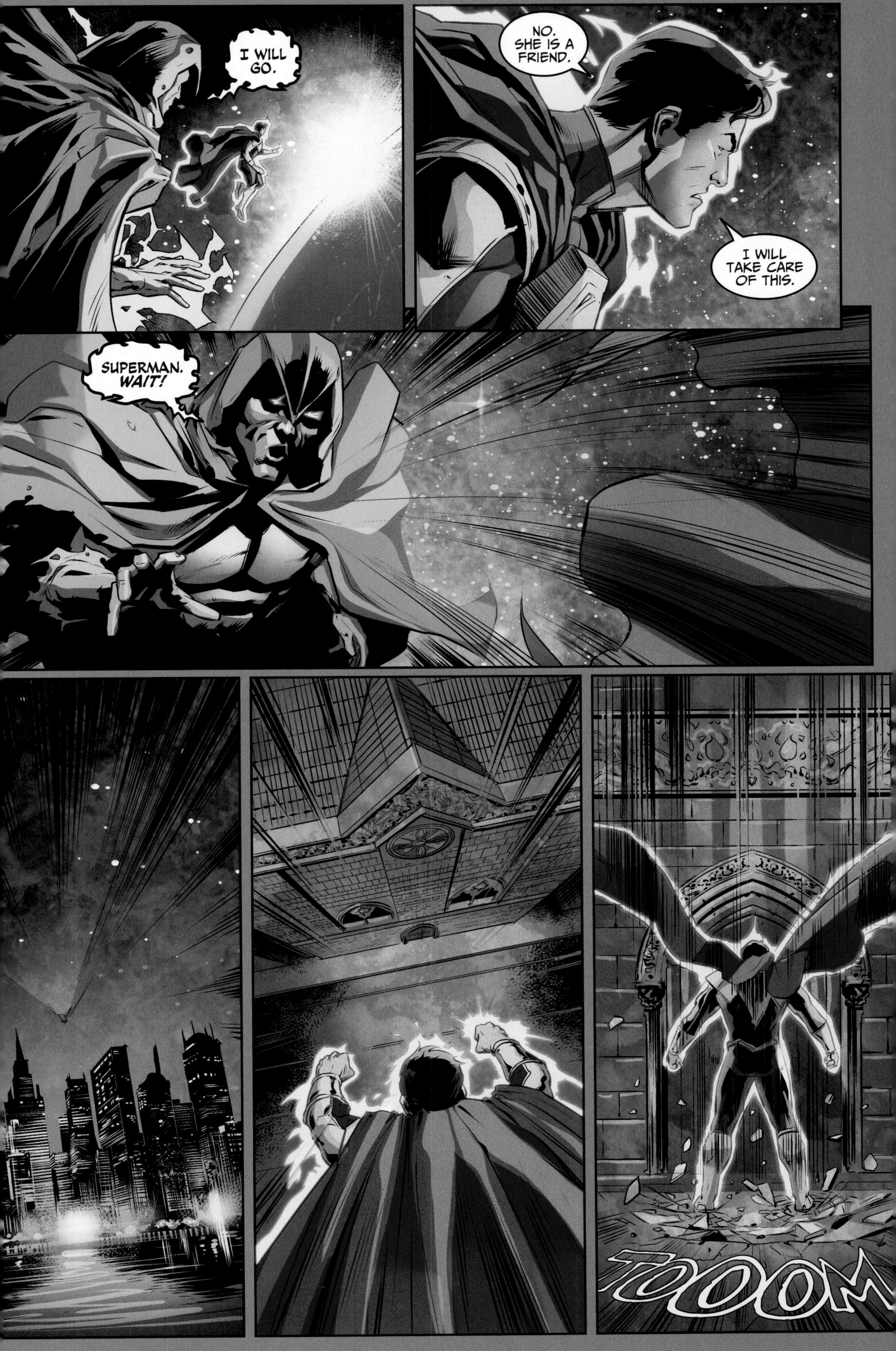
I WILL GO.
NO. SHE IS A FRIEND.
I WILL TAKE CARE OF THIS.
SUPERMAN. *WAIT!*
TOOOM

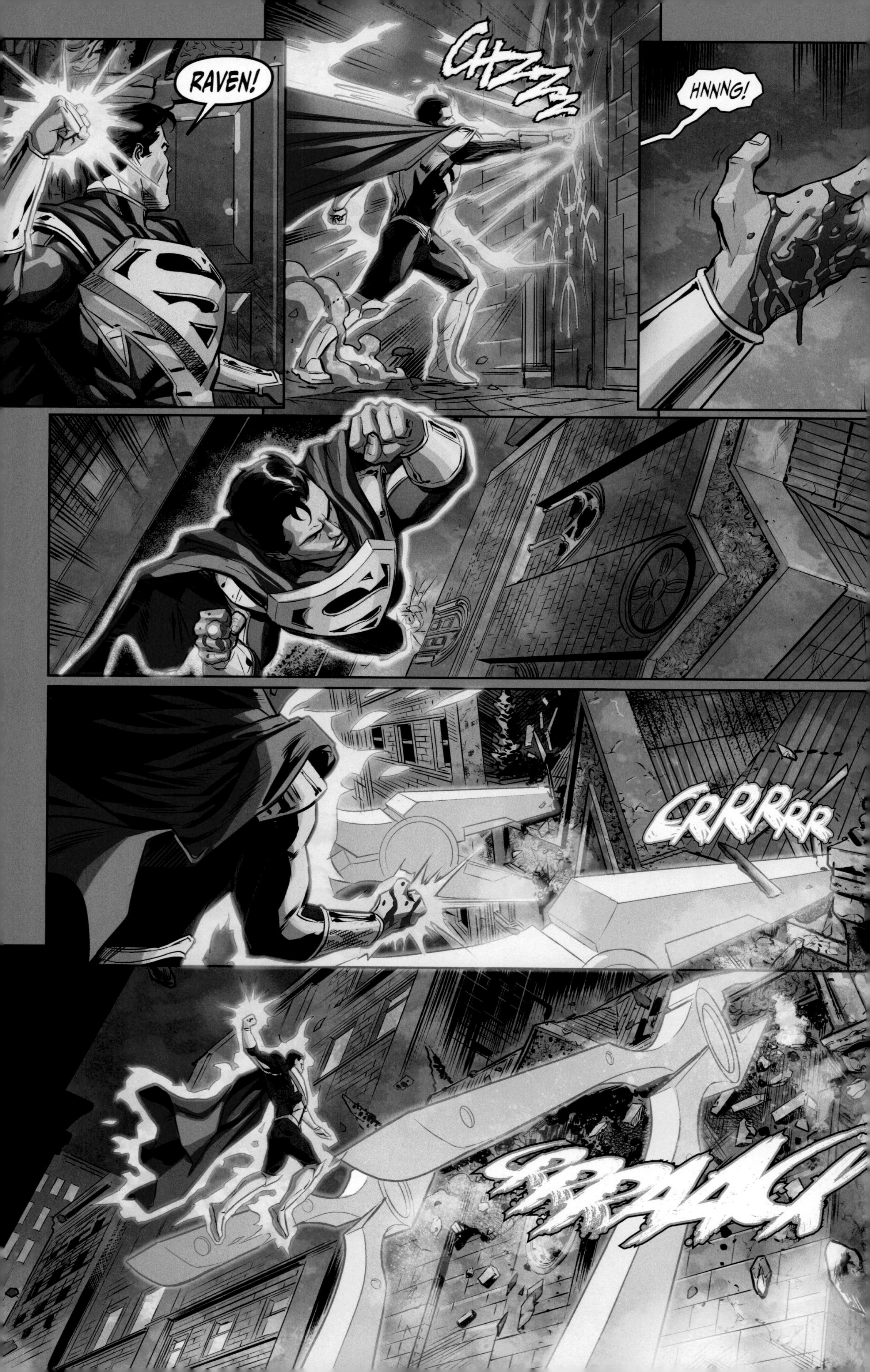
RAVEN!
CHZZZZ
HNNNG!
CRRRRR
SBRAAKA

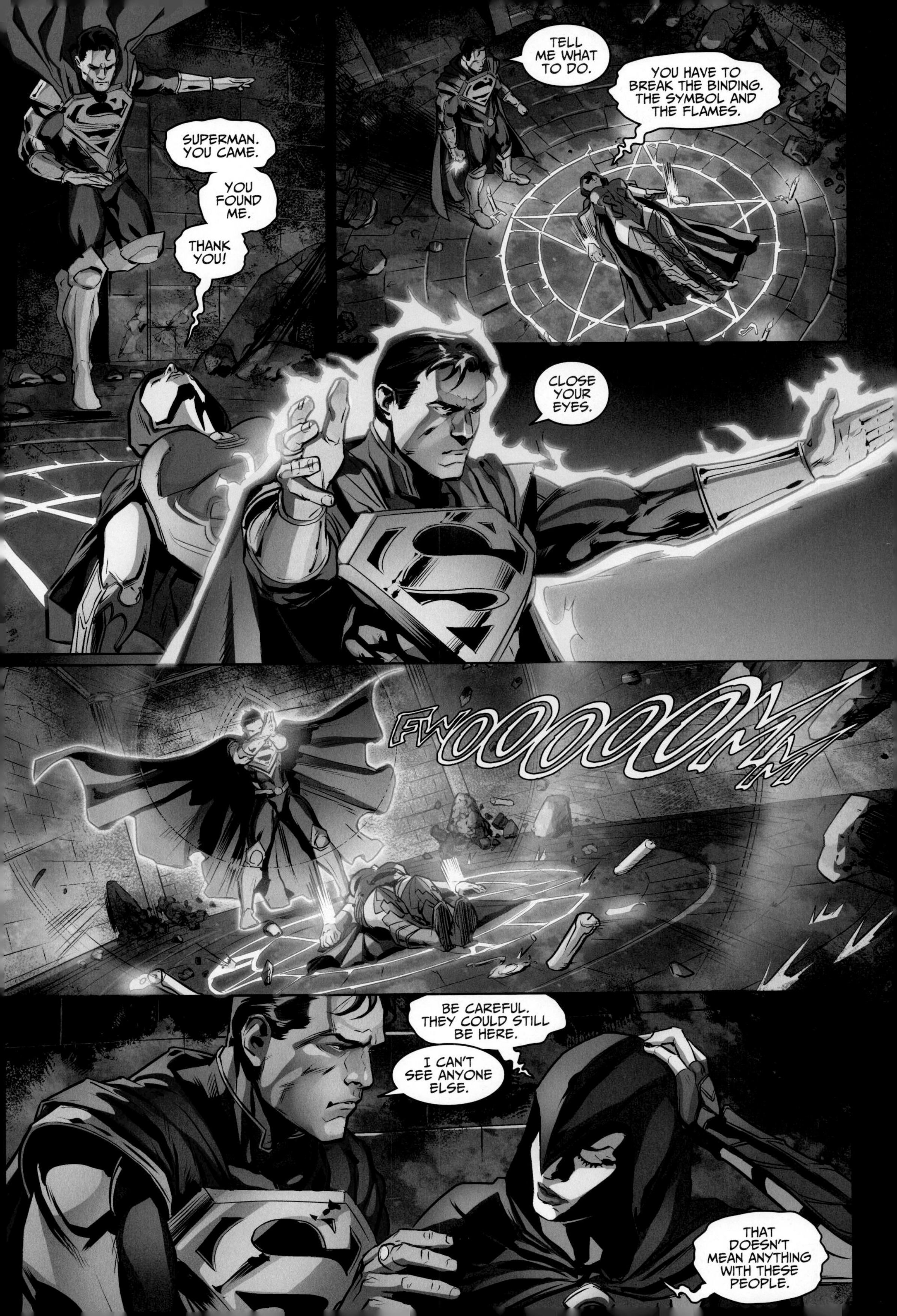
SUPERMAN. YOU CAME.
YOU FOUND ME.
THANK YOU!
TELL ME WHAT TO DO.
YOU HAVE TO BREAK THE BINDING. THE SYMBOL AND THE FLAMES.
CLOSE YOUR EYES.
FWOOOOOOM
BE CAREFUL. THEY COULD STILL BE HERE.
I CAN'T SEE ANYONE ELSE.
THAT DOESN'T MEAN ANYTHING WITH THESE PEOPLE.

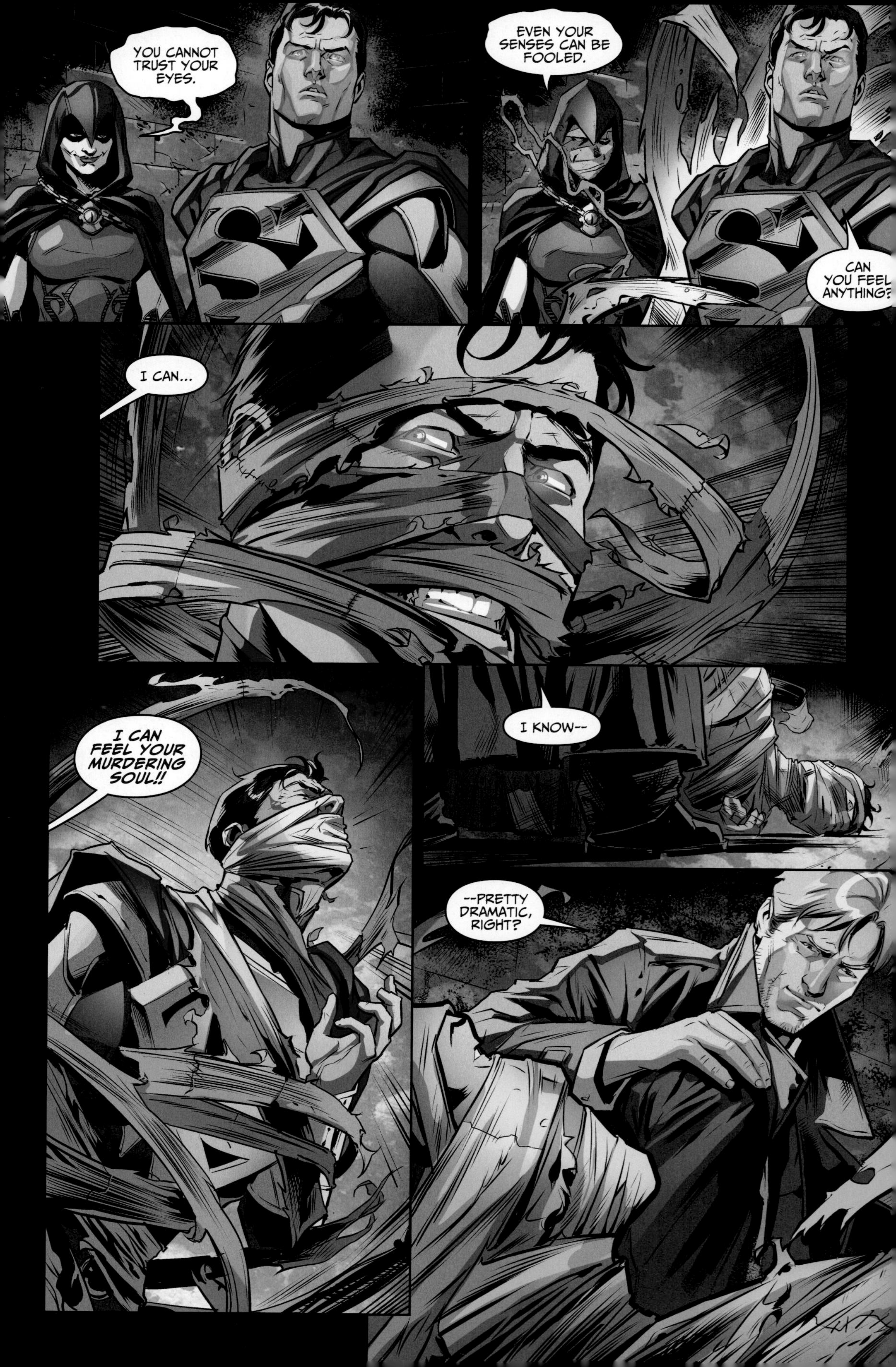
YOU CANNOT TRUST YOUR EYES.
EVEN YOUR SENSES CAN BE FOOLED.
CAN YOU FEEL ANYTHING?
I CAN...
I CAN FEEL YOUR MURDERING SOUL!!
I KNOW--
--PRETTY DRAMATIC, RIGHT?

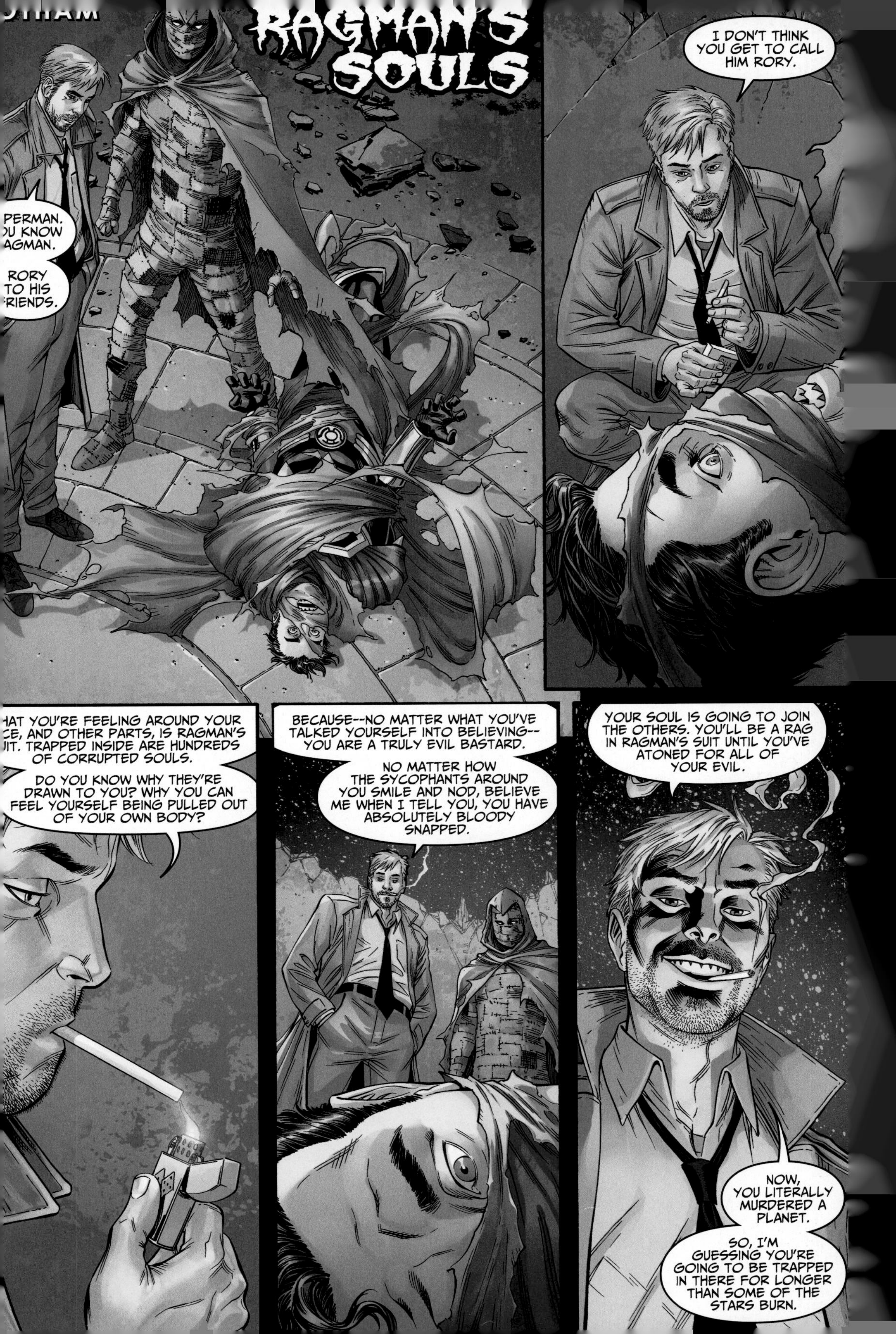
RAGMAN'S SOULS
PERMAN. OU KNOW AGMAN.
RORY TO HIS FRIENDS.
I DON'T THINK YOU GET TO CALL HIM RORY.
HAT YOU'RE FEELING AROUND YOUR CE, AND OTHER PARTS, IS RAGMAN'S UIT. TRAPPED INSIDE ARE HUNDREDS OF CORRUPTED SOULS.
DO YOU KNOW WHY THEY'RE DRAWN TO YOU? WHY YOU CAN FEEL YOURSELF BEING PULLED OUT OF YOUR OWN BODY?
BECAUSE--NO MATTER WHAT YOU'VE TALKED YOURSELF INTO BELIEVING--YOU ARE A TRULY EVIL BASTARD.
NO MATTER HOW THE SYCOPHANTS AROUND YOU SMILE AND NOD, BELIEVE ME WHEN I TELL YOU, YOU HAVE ABSOLUTELY BLOODY SNAPPED.
YOUR SOUL IS GOING TO JOIN THE OTHERS. YOU'LL BE A RAG IN RAGMAN'S SUIT UNTIL YOU'VE ATONED FOR ALL OF YOUR EVIL.
NOW, YOU LITERALLY MURDERED A PLANET.
SO, I'M GUESSING YOU'RE GOING TO BE TRAPPED IN THERE FOR LONGER THAN SOME OF THE STARS BURN.

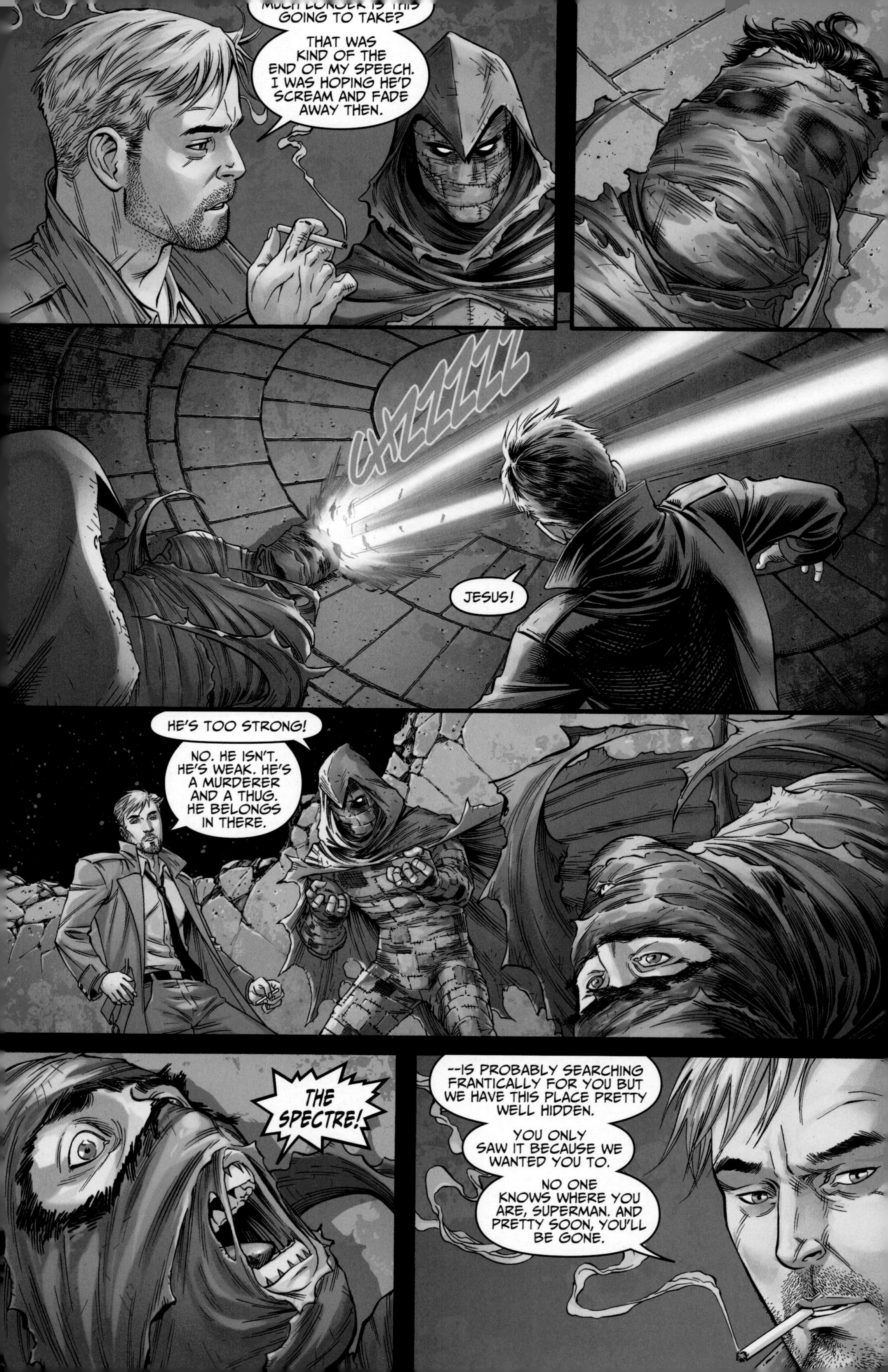
MUCH LONGER IS THIS GOING TO TAKE?
THAT WAS KIND OF THE END OF MY SPEECH. I WAS HOPING HE'D SCREAM AND FADE AWAY THEN.
CHZZZZZZ
JESUS!
HE'S TOO STRONG!
NO. HE ISN'T. HE'S WEAK. HE'S A MURDERER AND A THUG. HE BELONGS IN THERE.
THE SPECTRE!
--IS PROBABLY SEARCHING FRANTICALLY FOR YOU BUT WE HAVE THIS PLACE PRETTY WELL HIDDEN.
YOU ONLY SAW IT BECAUSE WE WANTED YOU TO.
NO ONE KNOWS WHERE YOU ARE, SUPERMAN. AND PRETTY SOON, YOU'LL BE GONE.

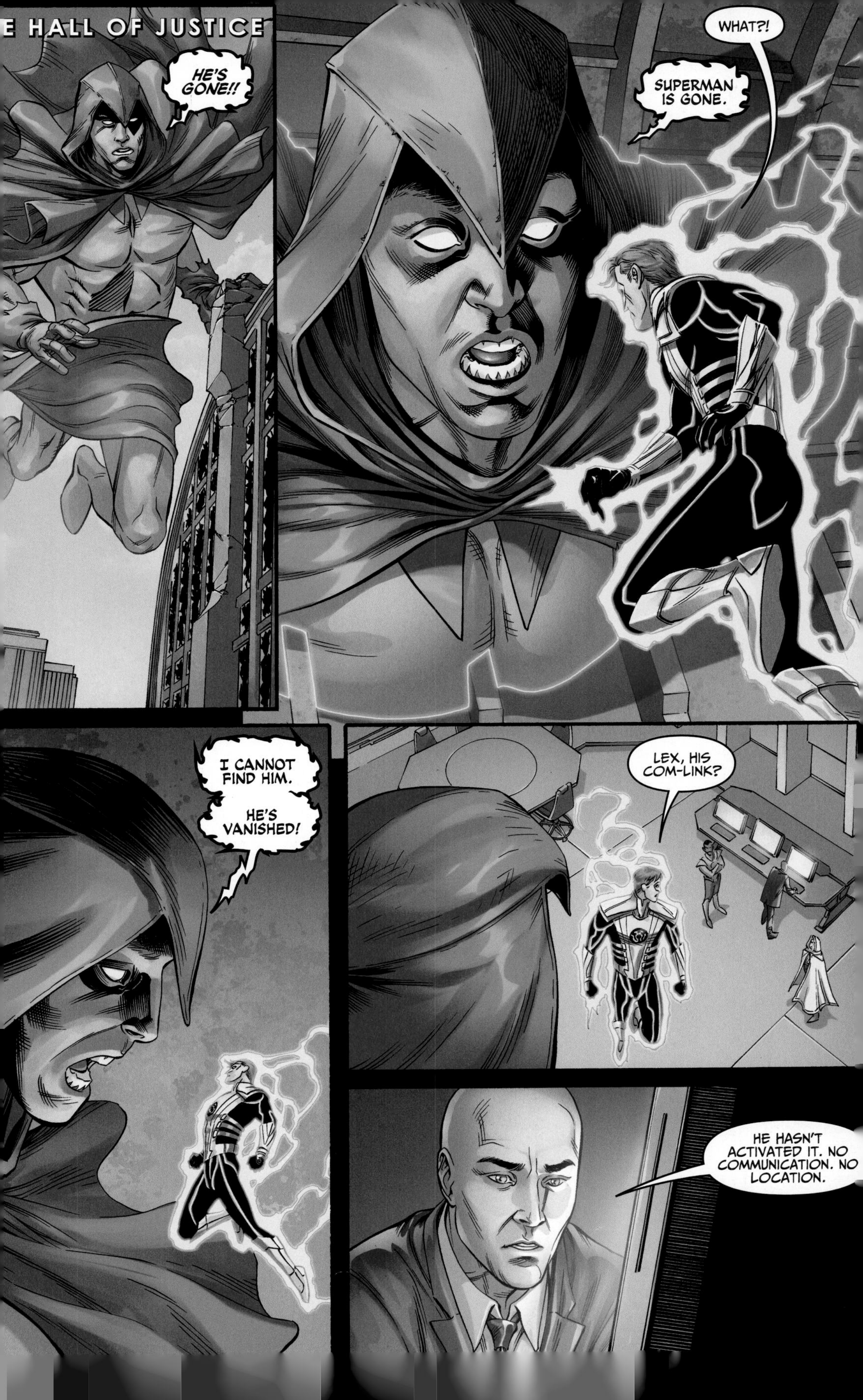
E HALL OF JUSTICE
HE'S GONE!!
SUPERMAN IS GONE.
WHAT?!
I CANNOT FIND HIM.
HE'S VANISHED!
LEX, HIS COM-LINK?
HE HASN'T ACTIVATED IT. NO COMMUNICATION. NO LOCATION.

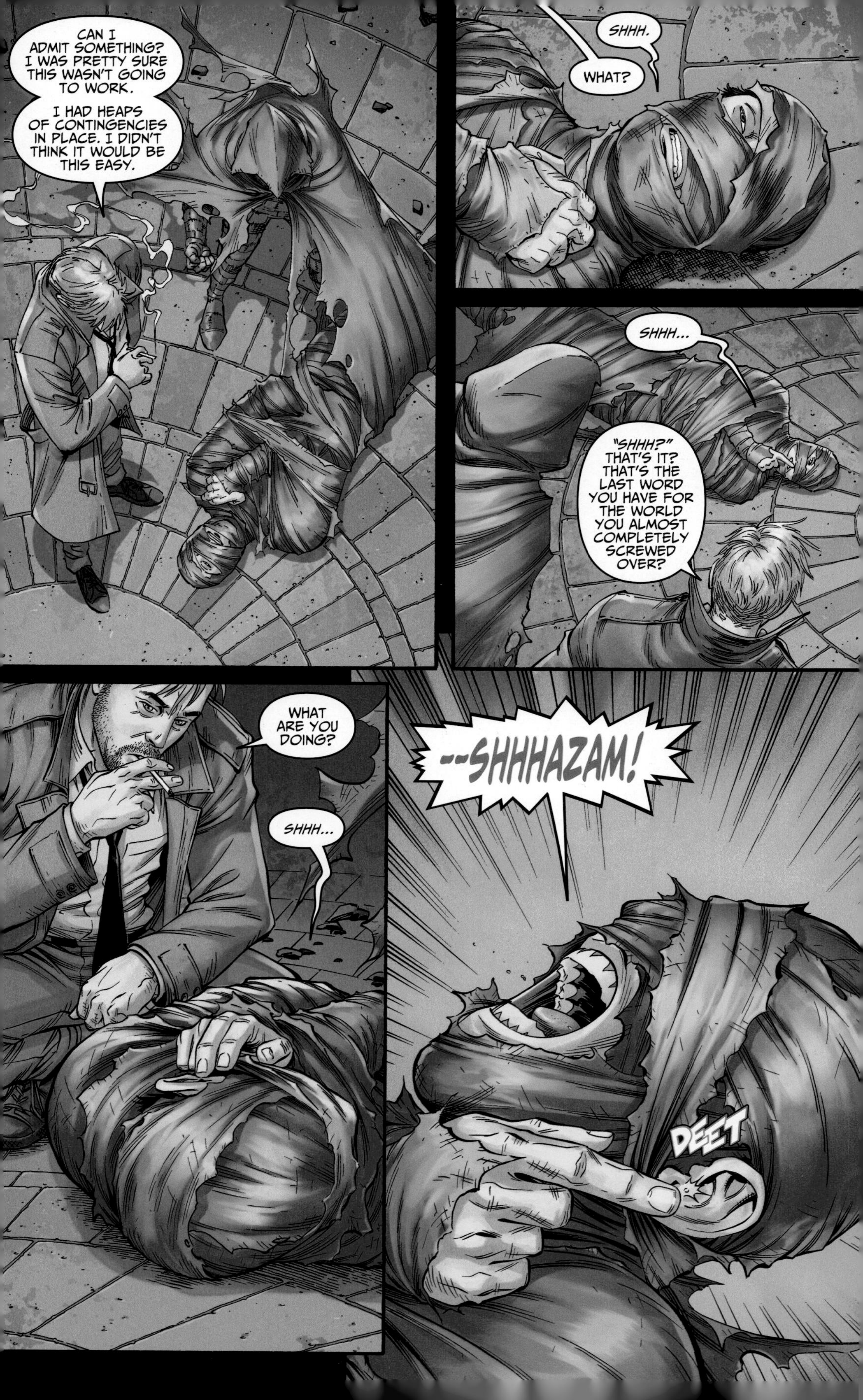
CAN I ADMIT SOMETHING? I WAS PRETTY SURE THIS WASN'T GOING TO WORK.
I HAD HEAPS OF CONTINGENCIES IN PLACE. I DIDN'T THINK IT WOULD BE THIS EASY.
SHHH.
WHAT?
SHHH...
"SHHH?" THAT'S IT? THAT'S THE LAST WORD YOU HAVE FOR THE WORLD YOU ALMOST COMPLETELY SCREWED OVER?
WHAT ARE YOU DOING?
SHHH...
--SHHHAZAM!
DEET

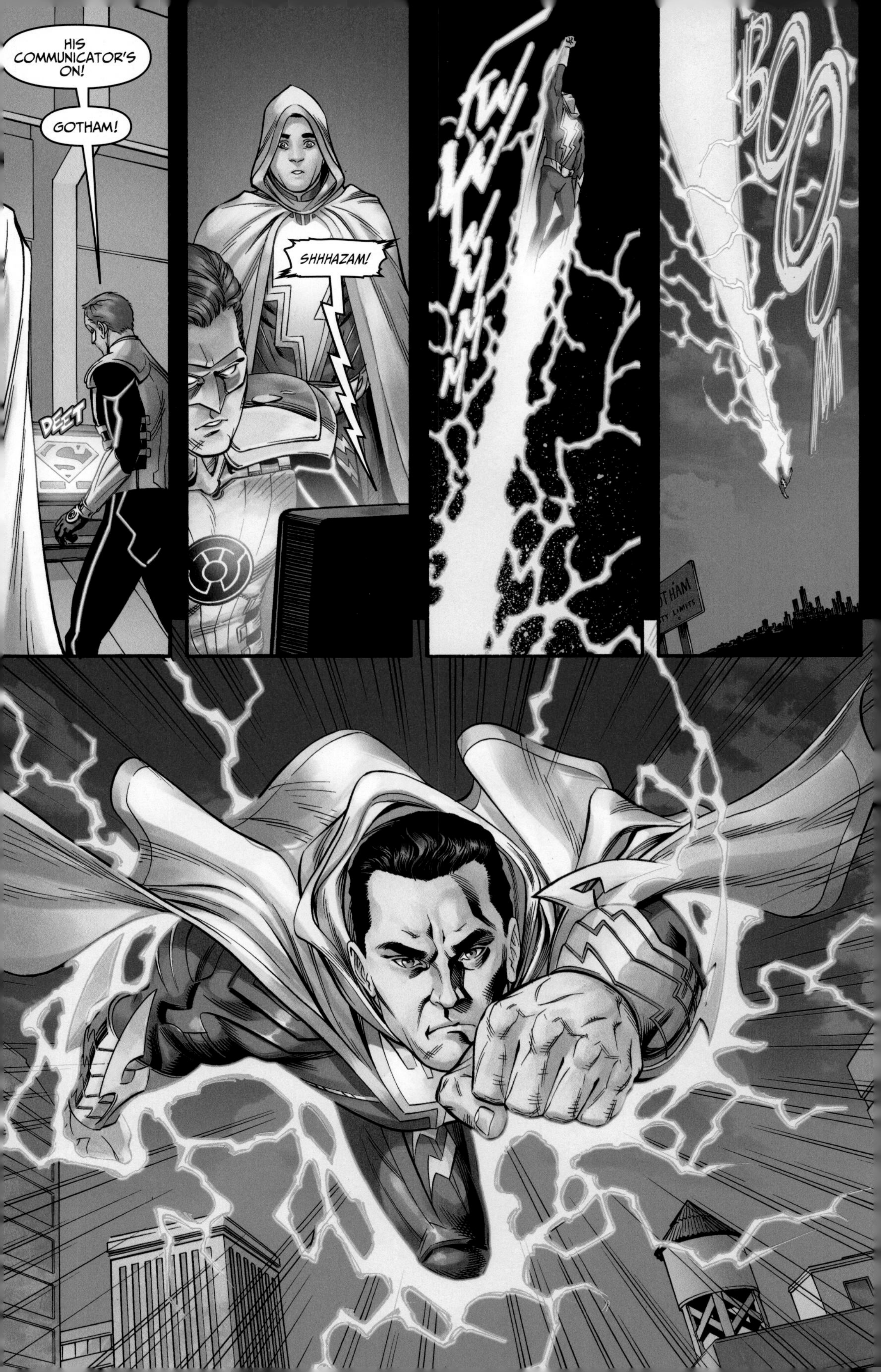
HIS COMMUNICATOR'S ON!
GOTHAM!
DEET
SHHHAZAM!

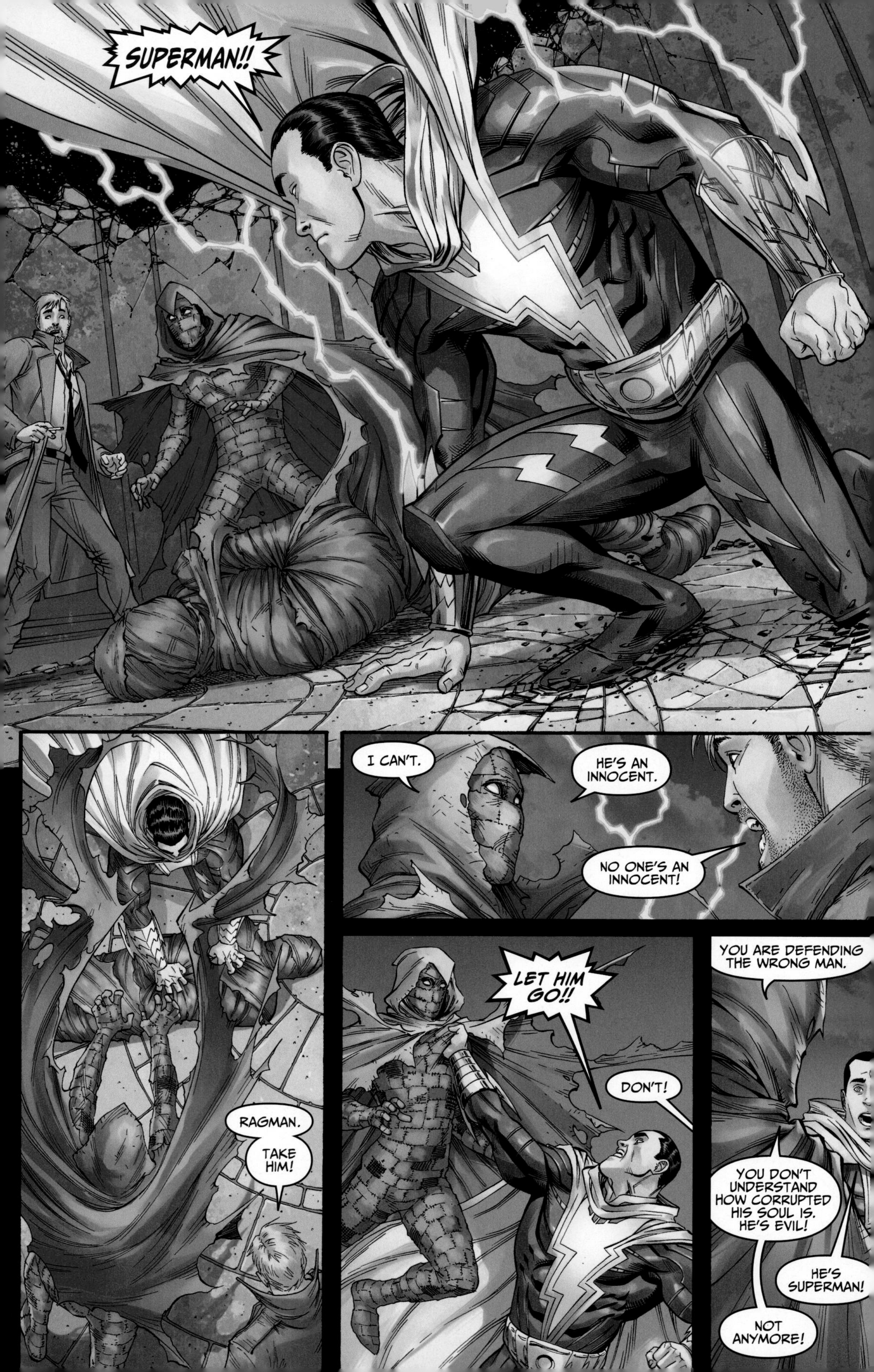
SUPERMAN!!
RAGMAN.
TAKE HIM!
I CAN'T.
HE'S AN INNOCENT.
NO ONE'S AN INNOCENT!
LET HIM GO!!
DON'T!
YOU ARE DEFENDING THE WRONG MAN.
YOU DON'T UNDERSTAND HOW CORRUPTED HIS SOUL IS. HE'S EVIL!
HE'S SUPERMAN!
NOT ANYMORE!

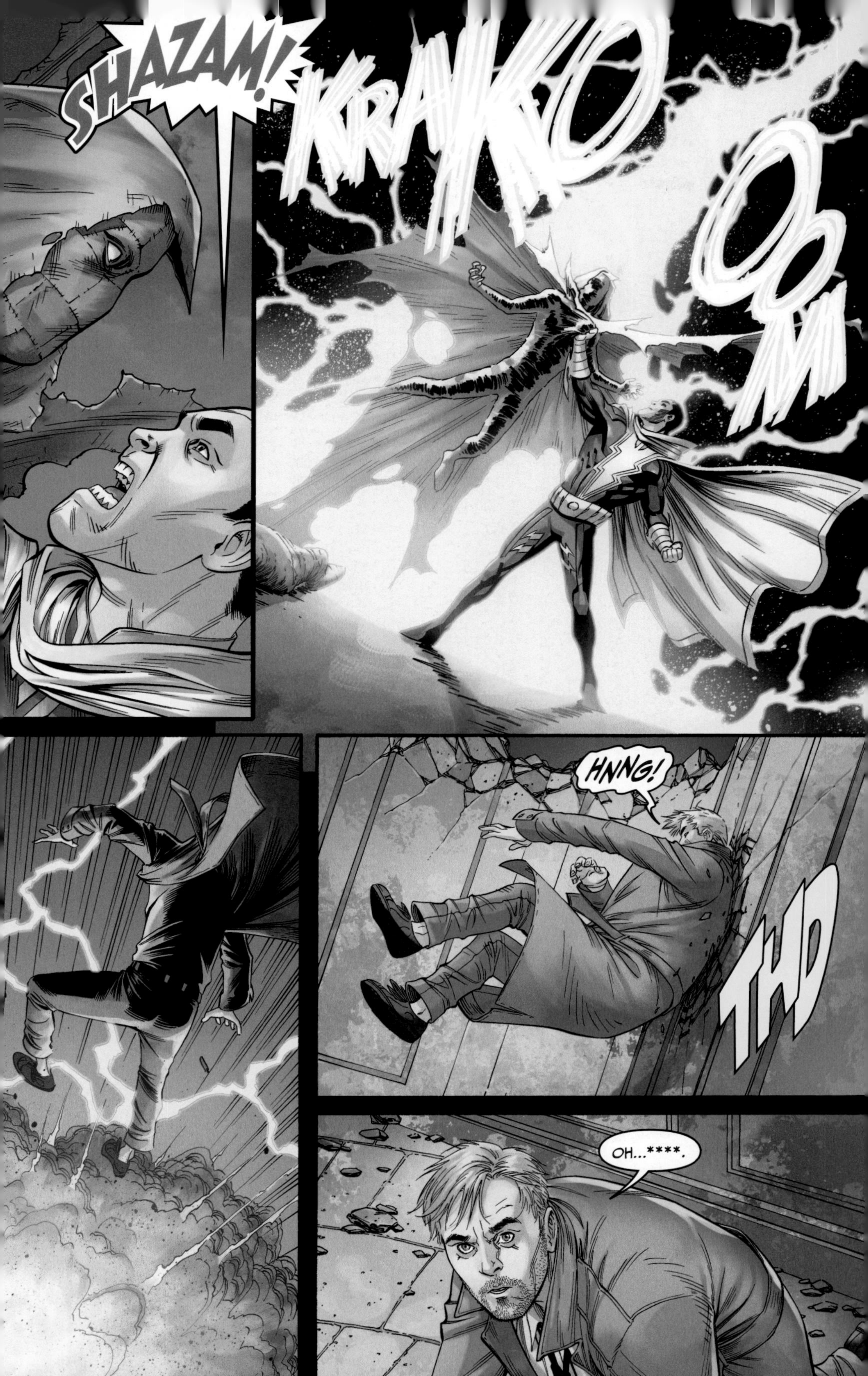
SHAZAM!
KRAKKOOOOM
HNNG!
THD
OH...****.

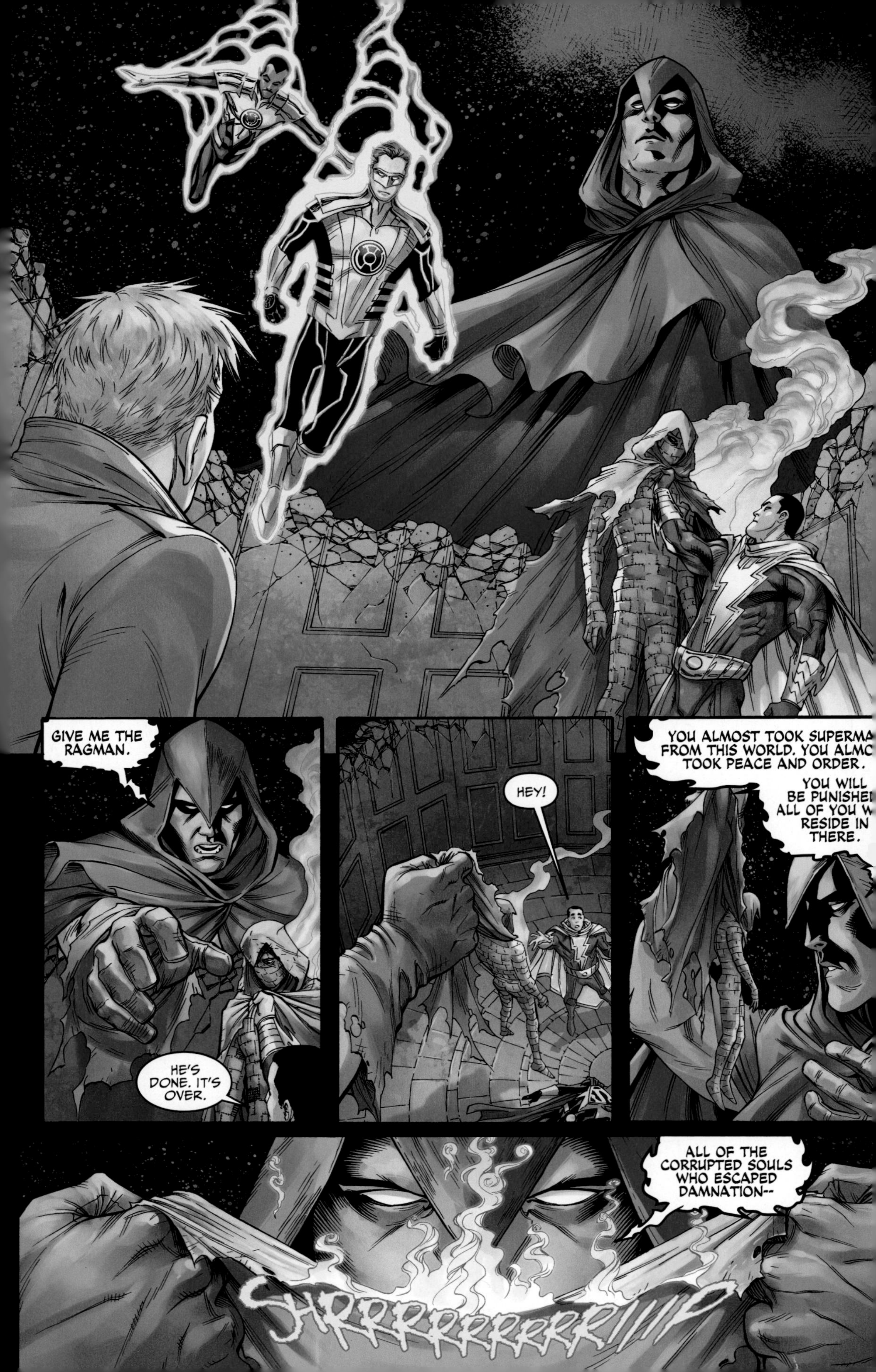
GIVE ME THE RAGMAN.
HE'S DONE. IT'S OVER.
HEY!
YOU ALMOST TOOK SUPERMA
FROM THIS WORLD. YOU ALMO
TOOK PEACE AND ORDER.
YOU WILL
BE PUNISHE
ALL OF YOU W
RESIDE IN
THERE.
ALL OF THE CORRUPTED SOULS WHO ESCAPED DAMNATION--
SHRRRRRRRRRRIIIP

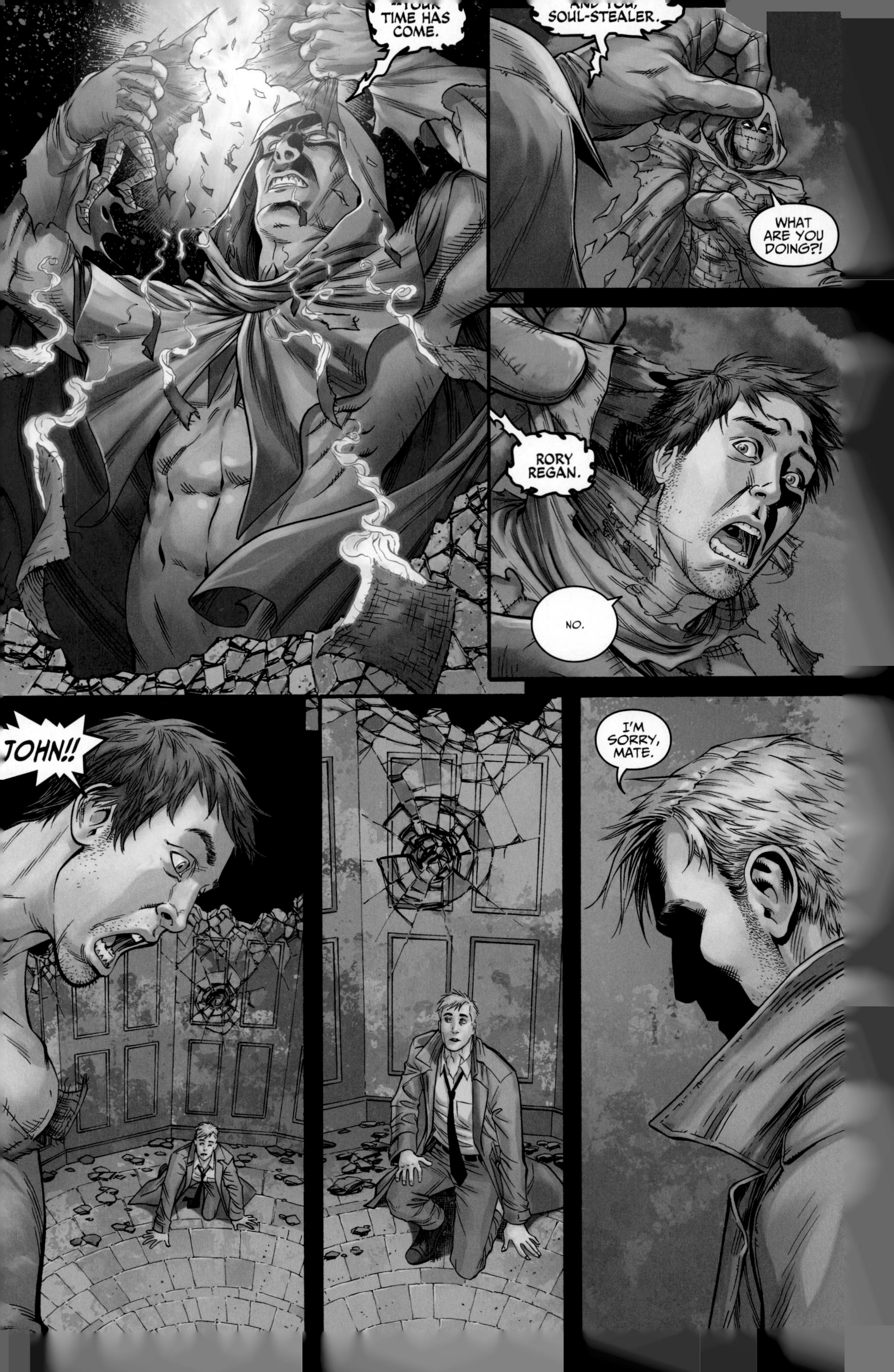
TIME HAS COME.
SOUL-STEALER.
WHAT ARE YOU DOING?!
RORY REGAN.
NO.
JOHN!!
I'M SORRY, MATE.

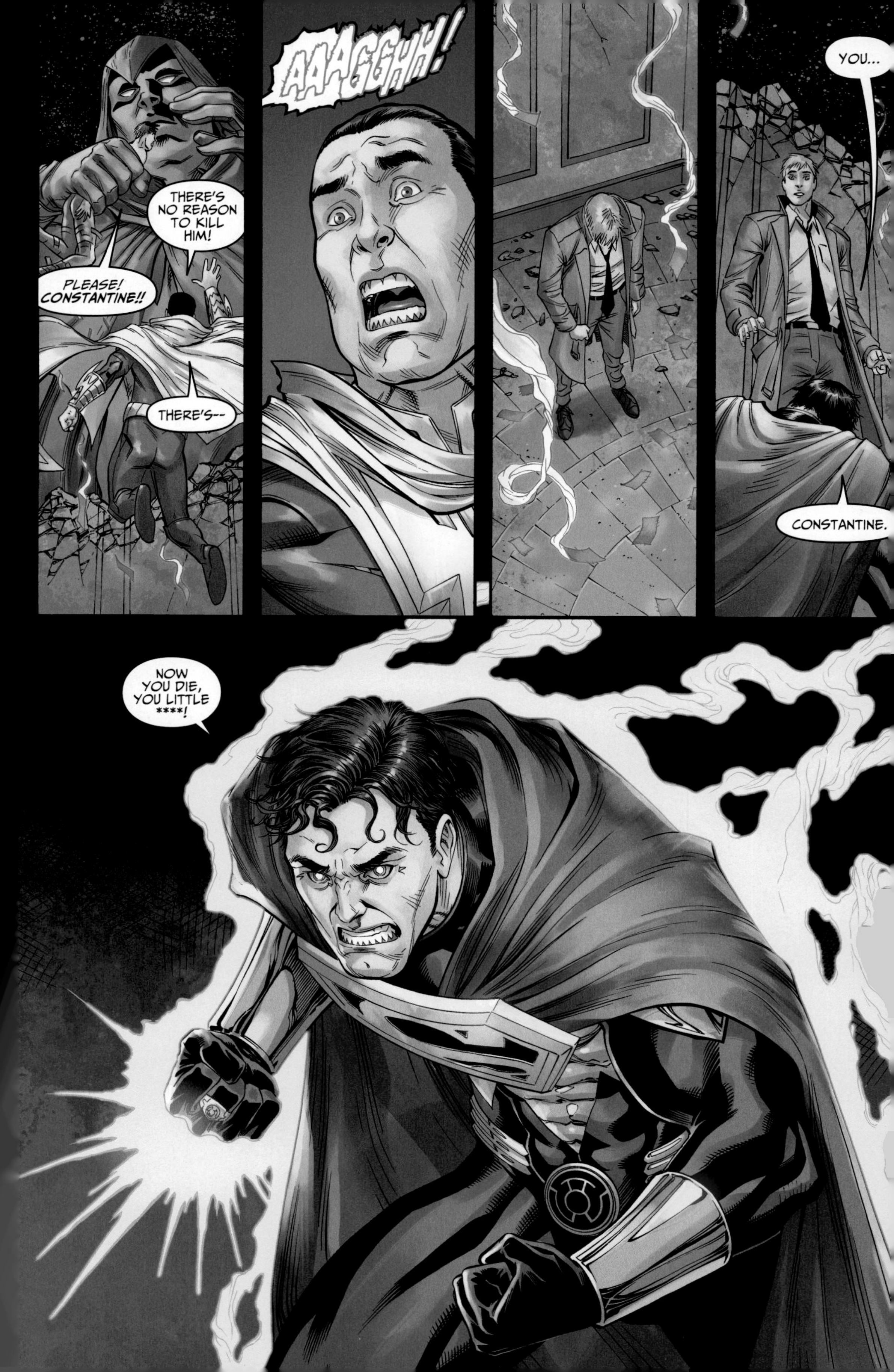
THERE'S NO REASON TO KILL HIM!
PLEASE! CONSTANTINE!!
THERE'S--
AAAGGHH!
YOU...
CONSTANTINE.
NOW YOU DIE, YOU LITTLE ****!

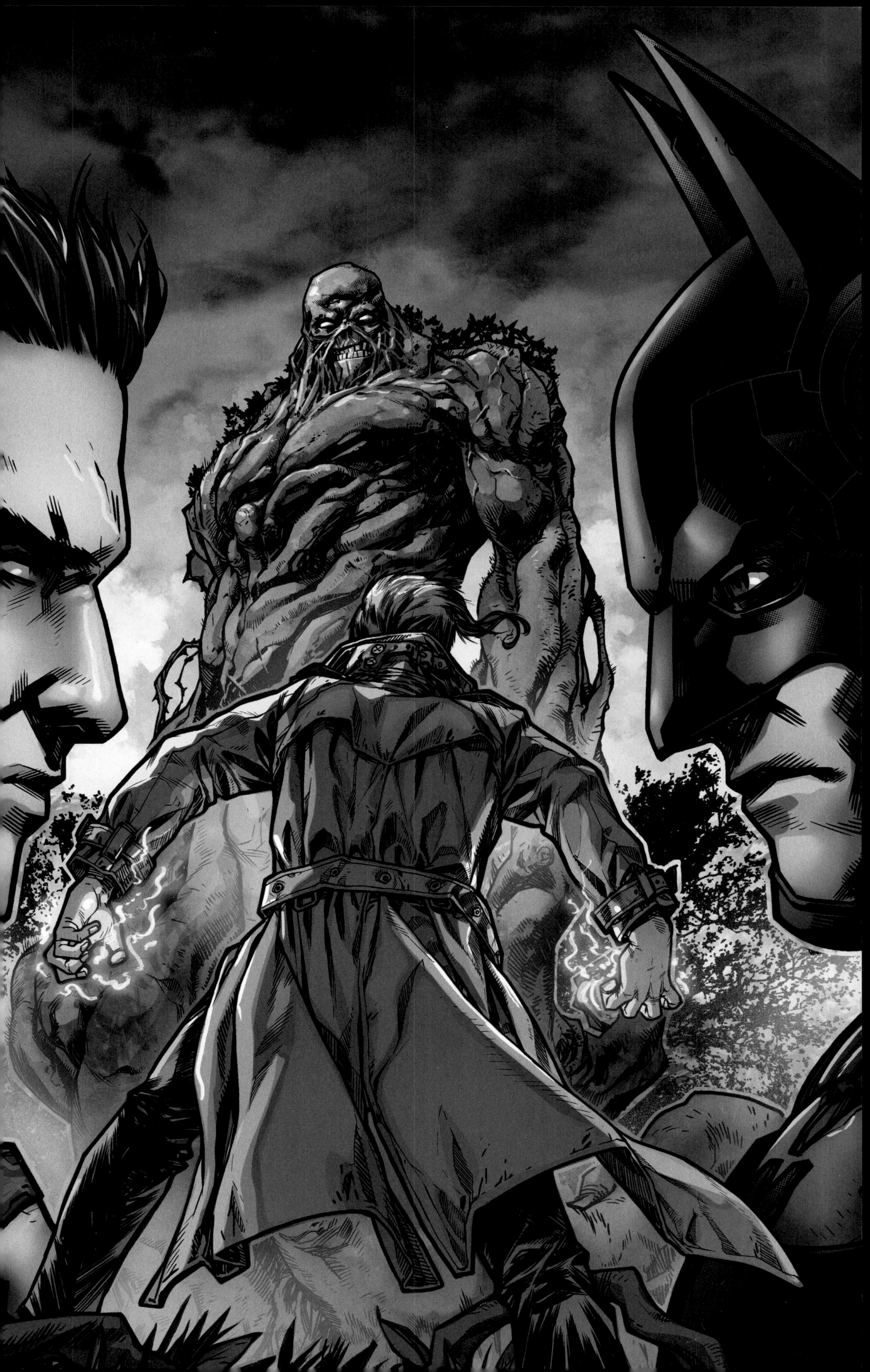

"Dead Man" **Bruno Redondo & Juan Albarran** Artists **Rex Lokus** Colorist
"Death of A Deadman" **Mike S. Miller** Artist **J. Nanjan** Colorist
Cover Art by **Neil Googe & Rex Lokus**

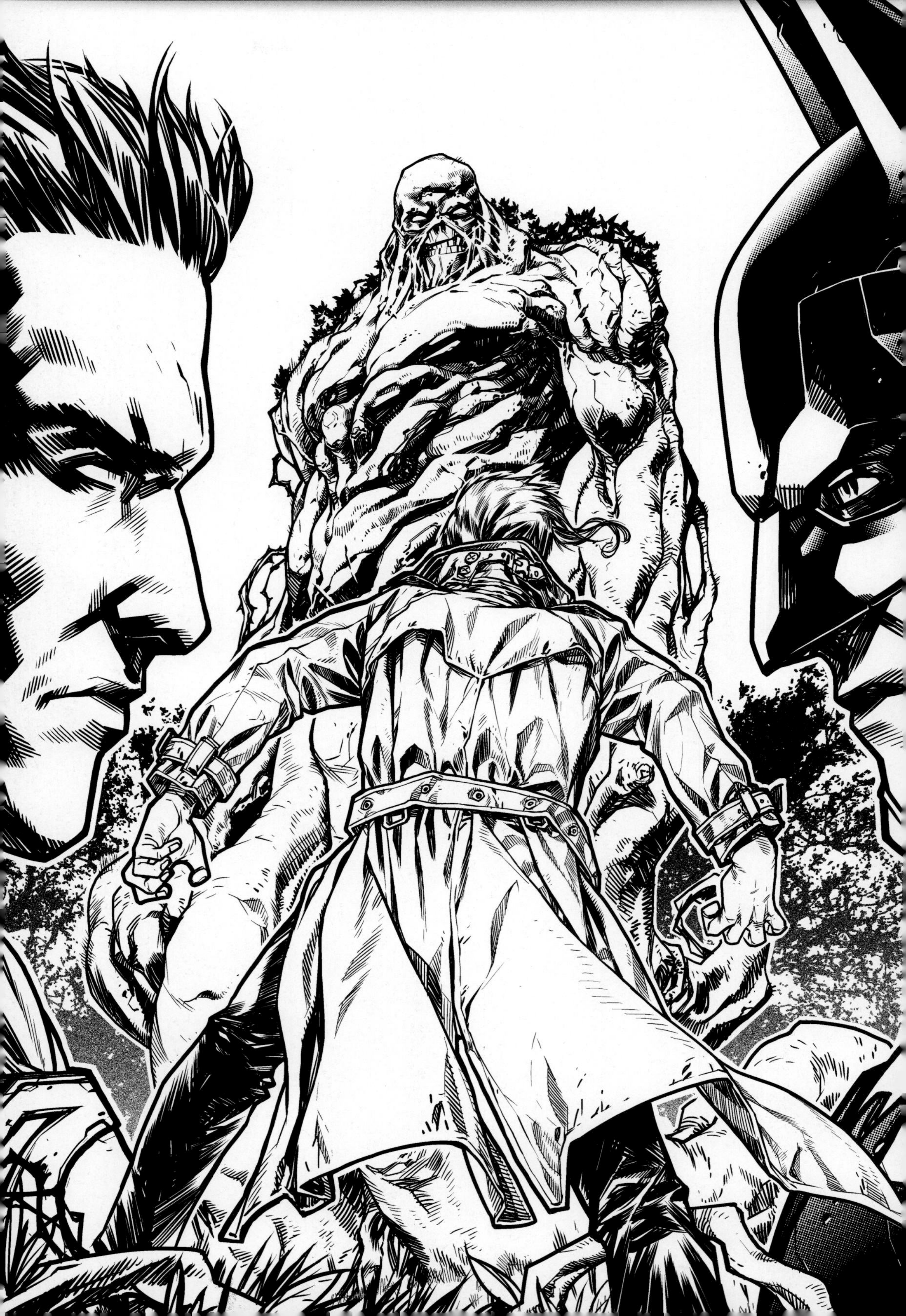

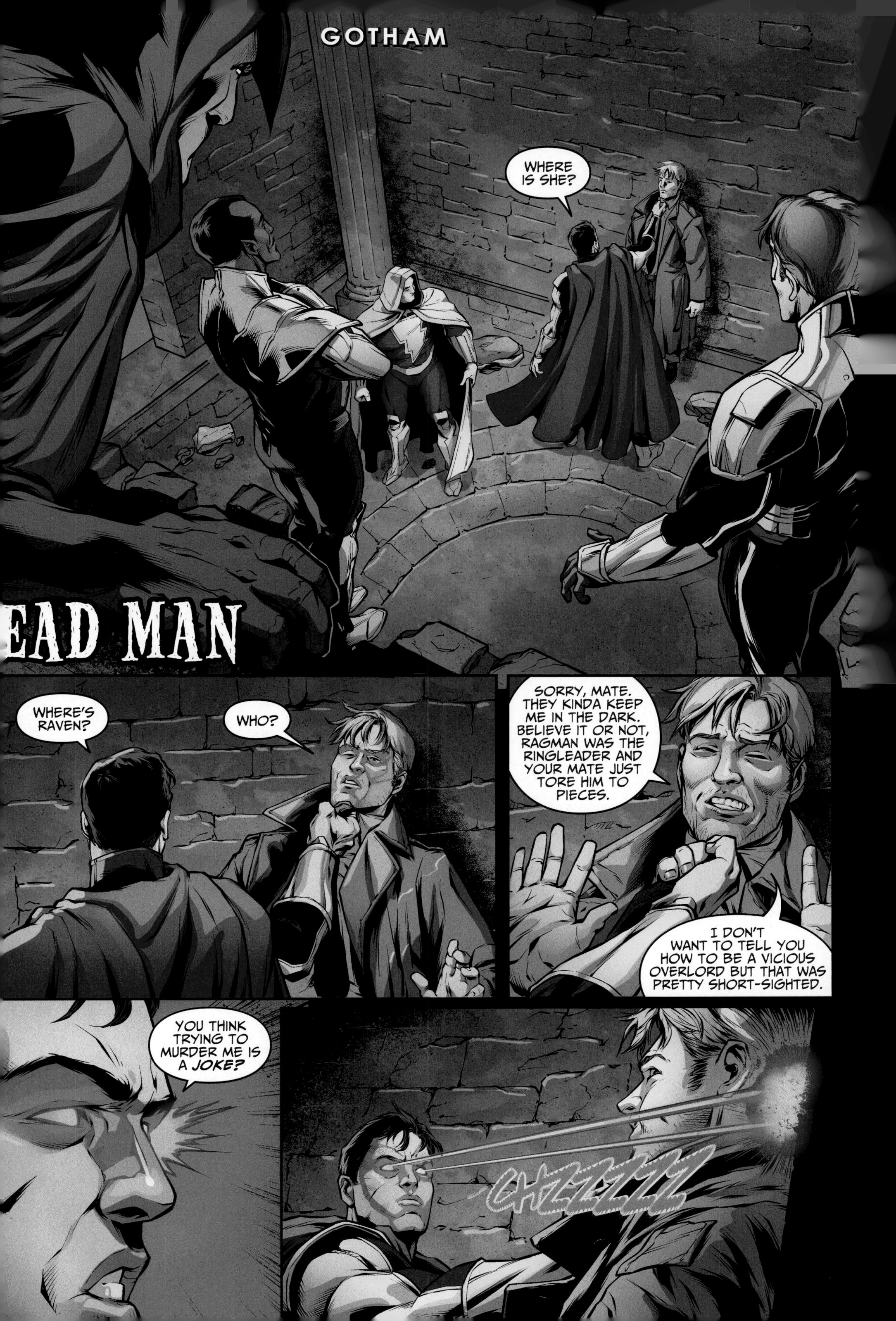

GOTHAM
WHERE IS SHE?
EAD MAN
WHERE'S RAVEN?
WHO?
SORRY, MATE. THEY KINDA KEEP ME IN THE DARK. BELIEVE IT OR NOT, RAGMAN WAS THE RINGLEADER AND YOUR MATE JUST TORE HIM TO PIECES.
I DON'T WANT TO TELL YOU HOW TO BE A VICIOUS OVERLORD BUT THAT WAS PRETTY SHORT-SIGHTED.
YOU THINK TRYING TO MURDER ME IS A JOKE?
CHZZZZ

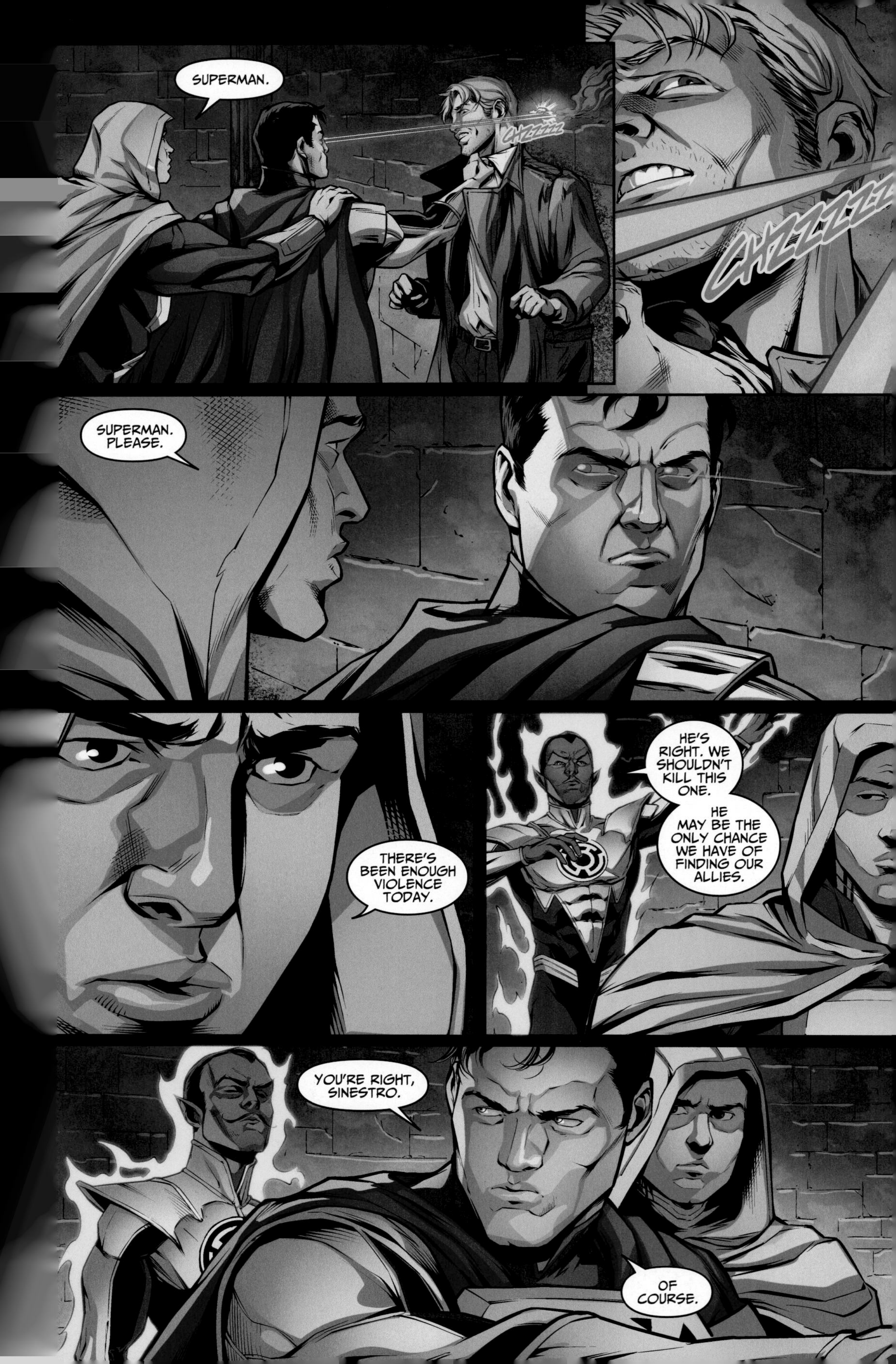
SUPERMAN.
CHZZZZ
CHZZZZZZ
SUPERMAN. PLEASE.
THERE'S BEEN ENOUGH VIOLENCE TODAY.
HE'S RIGHT. WE SHOULDN'T KILL THIS ONE.
HE MAY BE THE ONLY CHANCE WE HAVE OF FINDING OUR ALLIES.
YOU'RE RIGHT, SINESTRO.
OF COURSE.

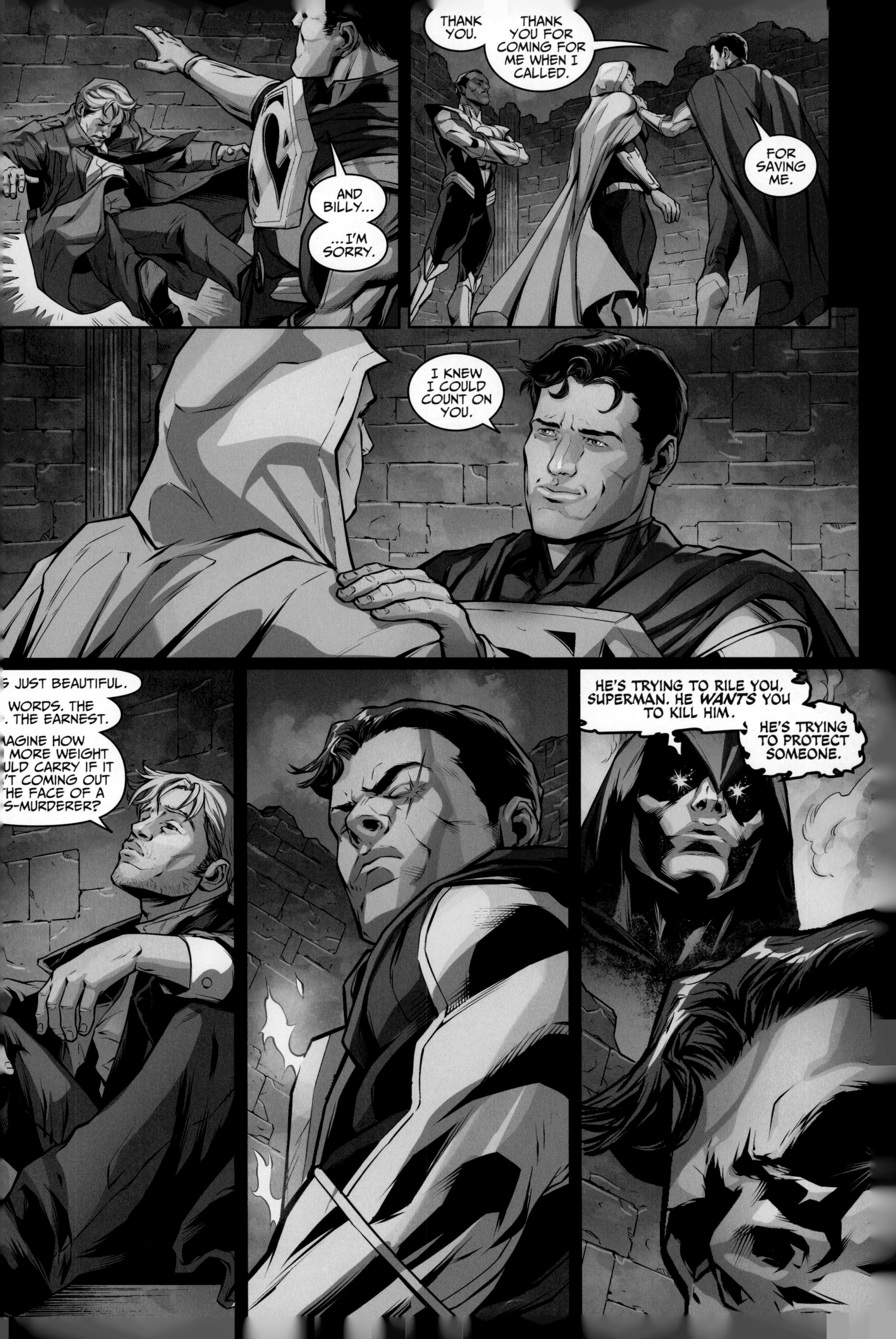
AND BILLY...
...I'M SORRY.
THANK YOU.
THANK YOU FOR COMING FOR ME WHEN I CALLED.
FOR SAVING ME.
I KNEW I COULD COUNT ON YOU.
S JUST BEAUTIFUL.
WORDS. THE . THE EARNEST.
AGINE HOW MORE WEIGHT ULD CARRY IF IT 'T COMING OUT THE FACE OF A S-MURDERER?
HE'S TRYING TO RILE YOU, SUPERMAN. HE *WANTS* YOU TO KILL HIM.
HE'S TRYING TO PROTECT SOMEONE.

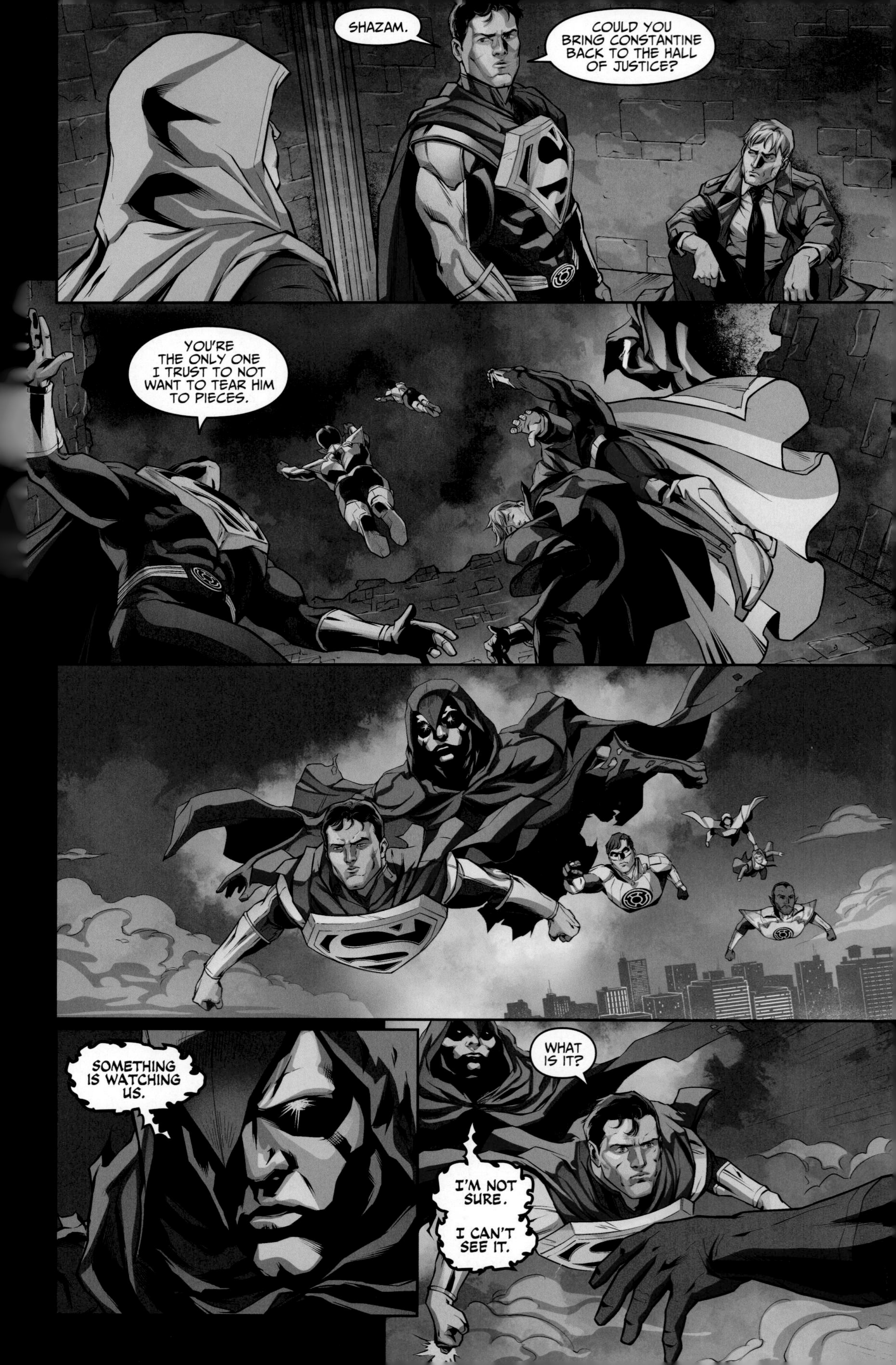
SHAZAM.
COULD YOU BRING CONSTANTINE BACK TO THE HALL OF JUSTICE?
YOU'RE THE ONLY ONE I TRUST TO NOT WANT TO TEAR HIM TO PIECES.
SOMETHING IS WATCHING US.
WHAT IS IT?
I'M NOT SURE.
I CAN'T SEE IT.

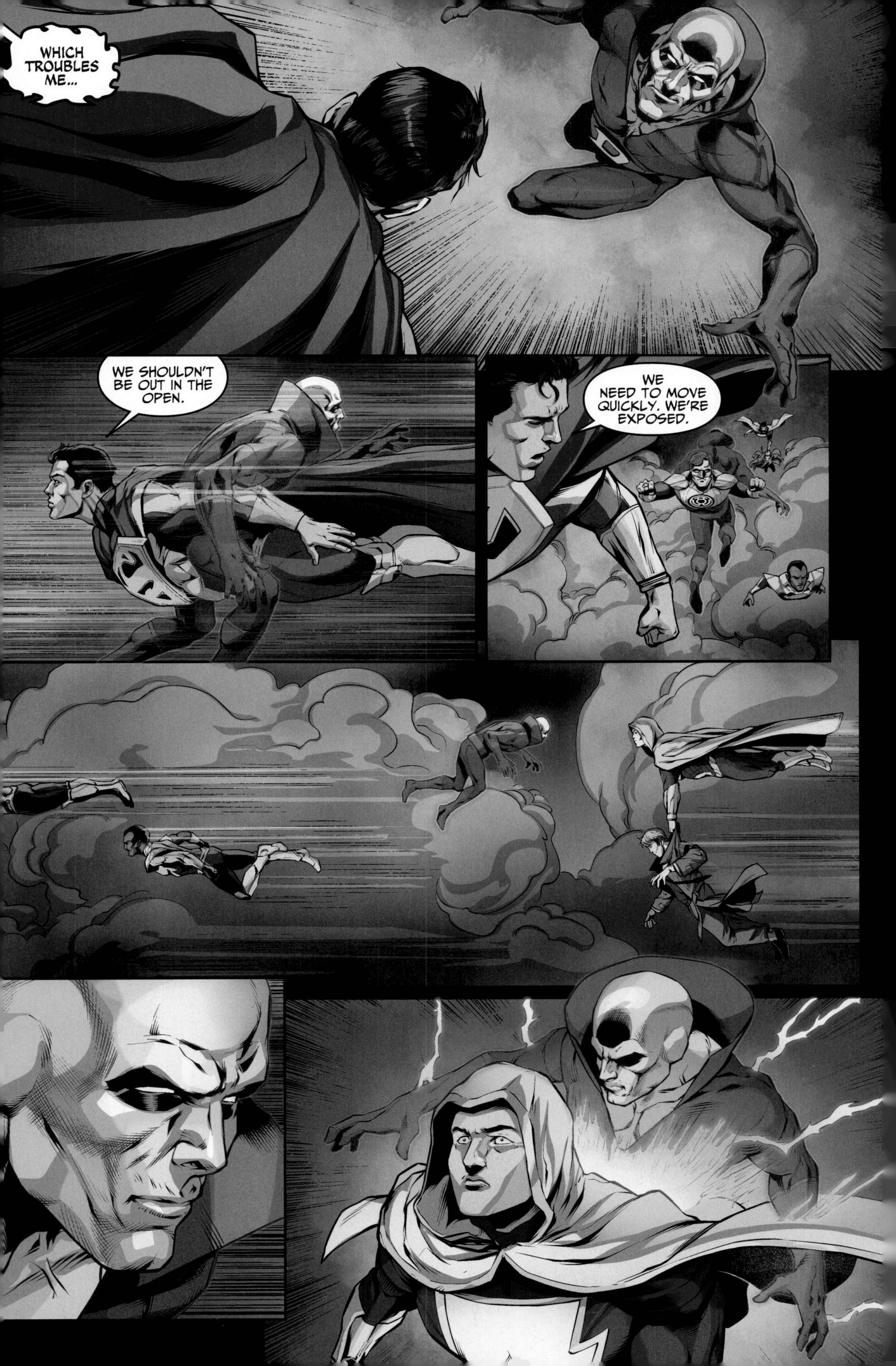
WHICH TROUBLES ME...
WE SHOULDN'T BE OUT IN THE OPEN.
WE NEED TO MOVE QUICKLY. WE'RE EXPOSED.

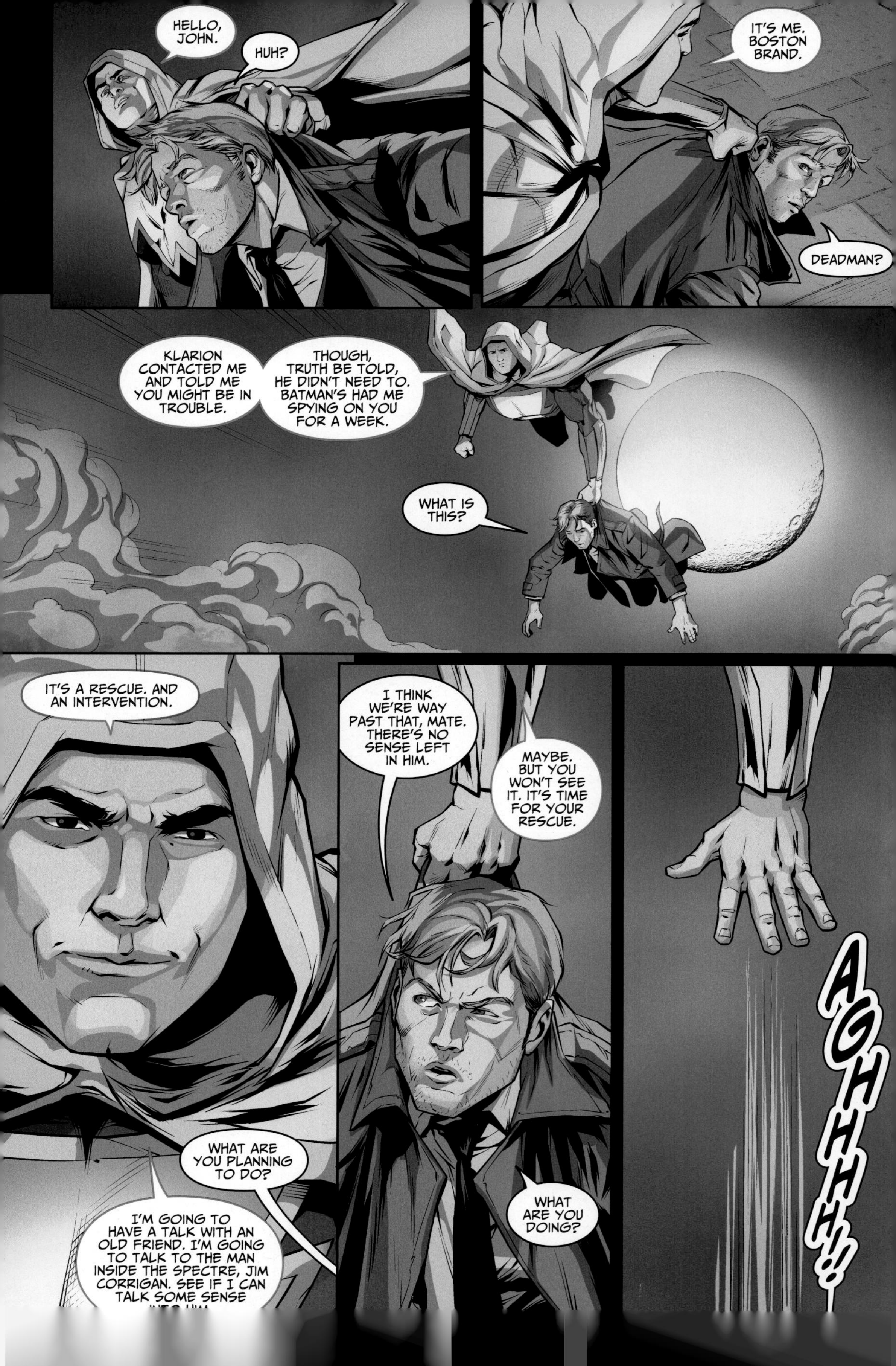
HELLO, JOHN.
HUH?
IT'S ME. BOSTON BRAND.
DEADMAN?
KLARION CONTACTED ME AND TOLD ME YOU MIGHT BE IN TROUBLE.
THOUGH, TRUTH BE TOLD, HE DIDN'T NEED TO. BATMAN'S HAD ME SPYING ON YOU FOR A WEEK.
WHAT IS THIS?
IT'S A RESCUE. AND AN INTERVENTION.
WHAT ARE YOU PLANNING TO DO?
I'M GOING TO HAVE A TALK WITH AN OLD FRIEND. I'M GOING TO TALK TO THE MAN INSIDE THE SPECTRE, JIM CORRIGAN. SEE IF I CAN TALK SOME SENSE
I THINK WE'RE WAY PAST THAT, MATE. THERE'S NO SENSE LEFT IN HIM.
MAYBE. BUT YOU WON'T SEE IT. IT'S TIME FOR YOUR RESCUE.
WHAT ARE YOU DOING?
AGHHHHH!

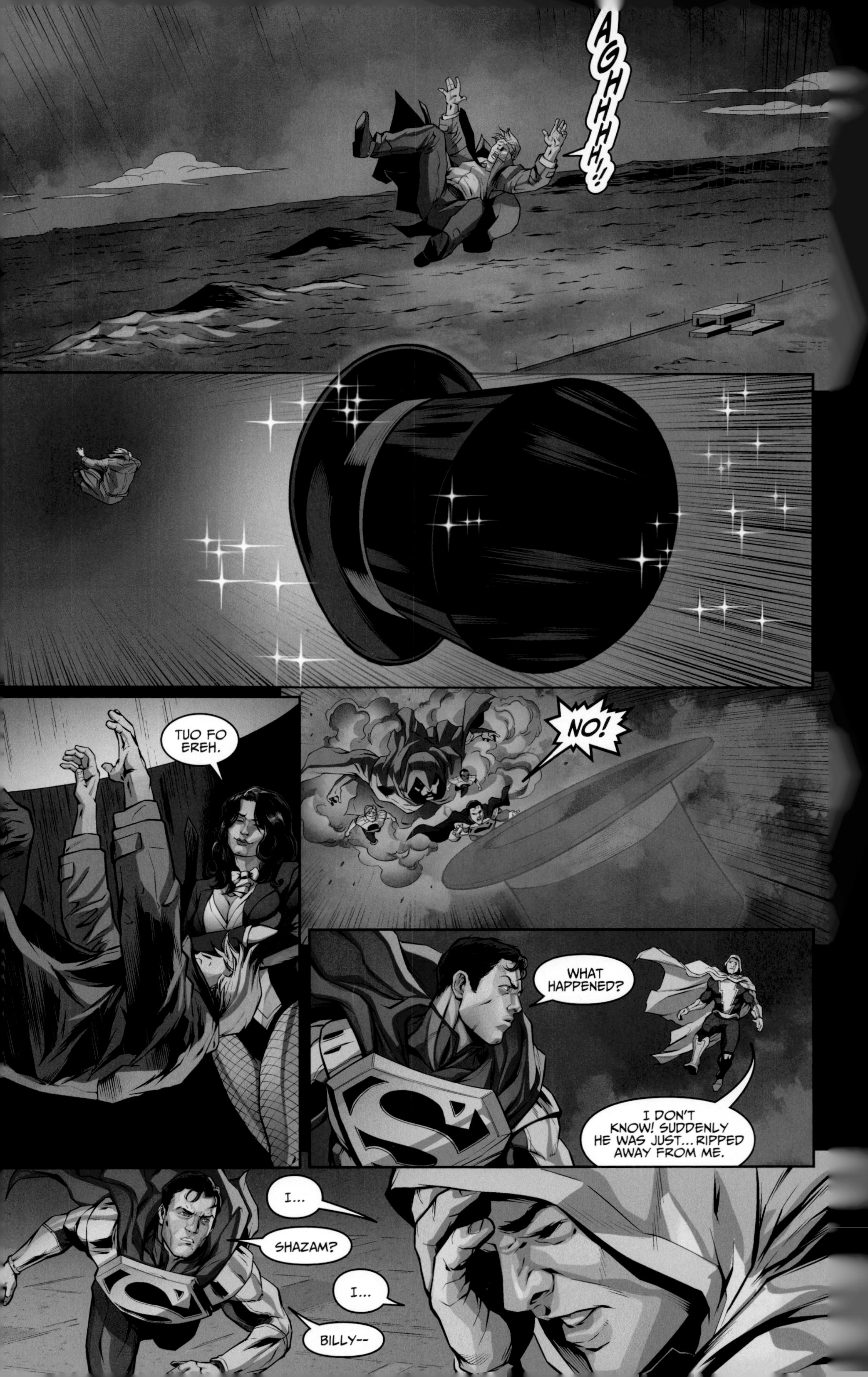
AGHHHH!!
TUO FO EREH.
NO!
WHAT HAPPENED?
I DON'T KNOW! SUDDENLY HE WAS JUST... RIPPED AWAY FROM ME.
I...
SHAZAM?
I...
BILLY--

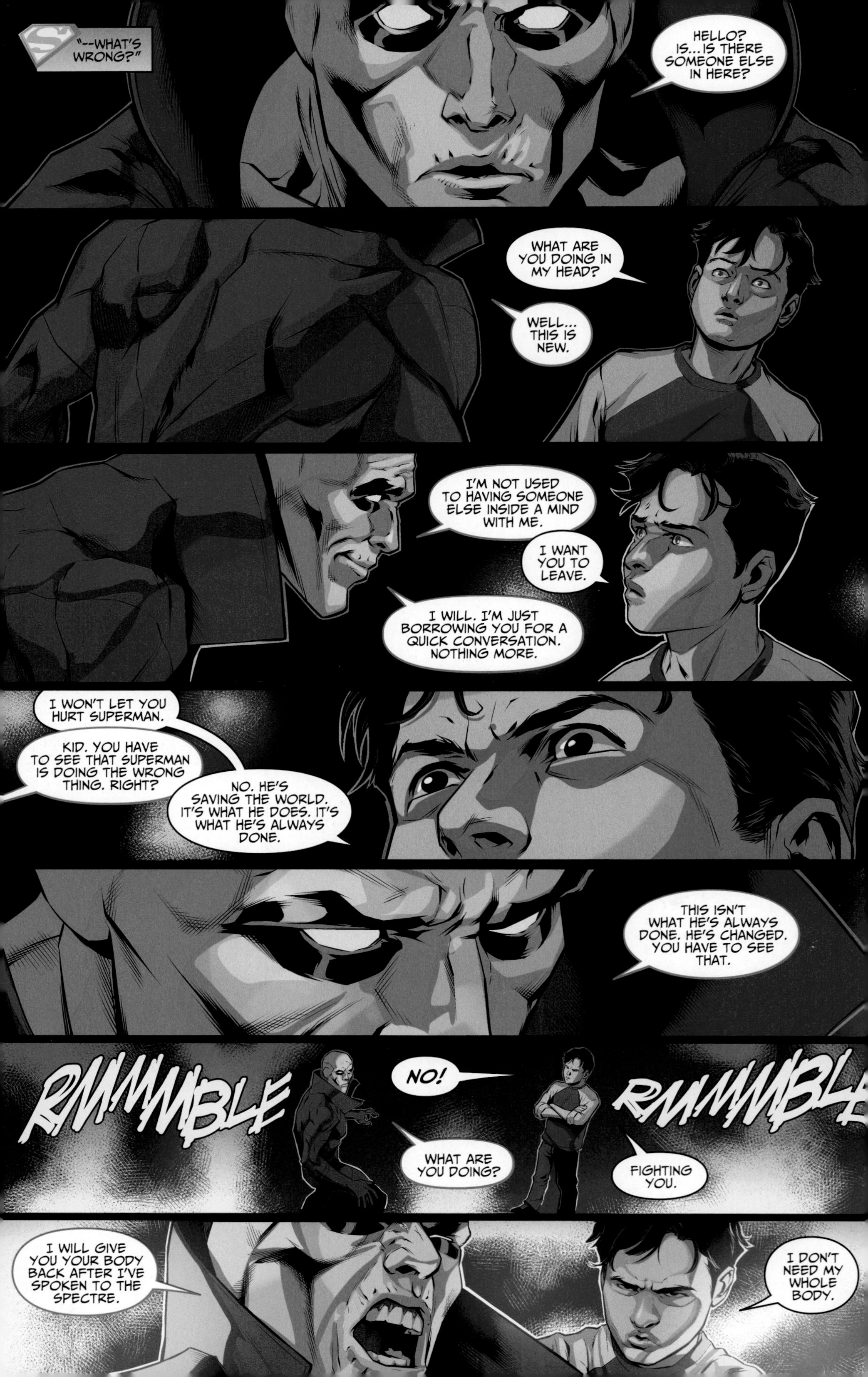
"--WHAT'S WRONG?"
HELLO? IS...IS THERE SOMEONE ELSE IN HERE?
WHAT ARE YOU DOING IN MY HEAD?
WELL... THIS IS NEW.
I'M NOT USED TO HAVING SOMEONE ELSE INSIDE A MIND WITH ME.
I WANT YOU TO LEAVE.
I WILL. I'M JUST BORROWING YOU FOR A QUICK CONVERSATION. NOTHING MORE.
I WON'T LET YOU HURT SUPERMAN.
KID. YOU HAVE TO SEE THAT SUPERMAN IS DOING THE WRONG THING. RIGHT?
NO. HE'S SAVING THE WORLD. IT'S WHAT HE DOES. IT'S WHAT HE'S ALWAYS DONE.
THIS ISN'T WHAT HE'S ALWAYS DONE. HE'S CHANGED. YOU HAVE TO SEE THAT.
RMMMBLE
NO!
RMMMBLE
WHAT ARE YOU DOING?
FIGHTING YOU.
I WILL GIVE YOU YOUR BODY BACK AFTER I'VE SPOKEN TO THE SPECTRE.
I DON'T NEED MY WHOLE BODY.

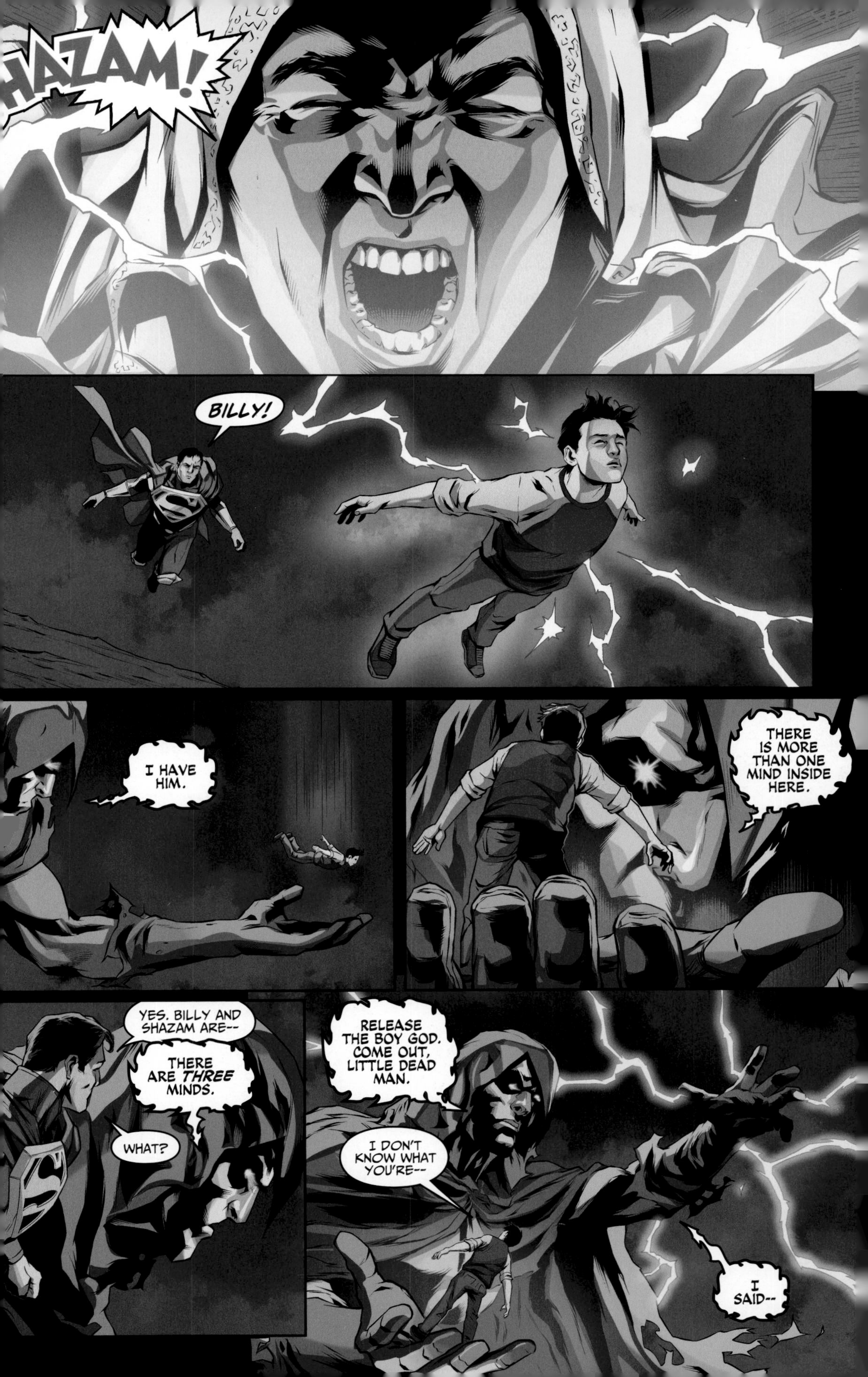
SHAZAM!
BILLY!
I HAVE HIM.
THERE IS MORE THAN ONE MIND INSIDE HERE.
YES. BILLY AND SHAZAM ARE--
THERE ARE *THREE* MINDS.
WHAT?
RELEASE THE BOY GOD. COME OUT, LITTLE DEAD MAN.
I DON'T KNOW WHAT YOU'RE--
I SAID--

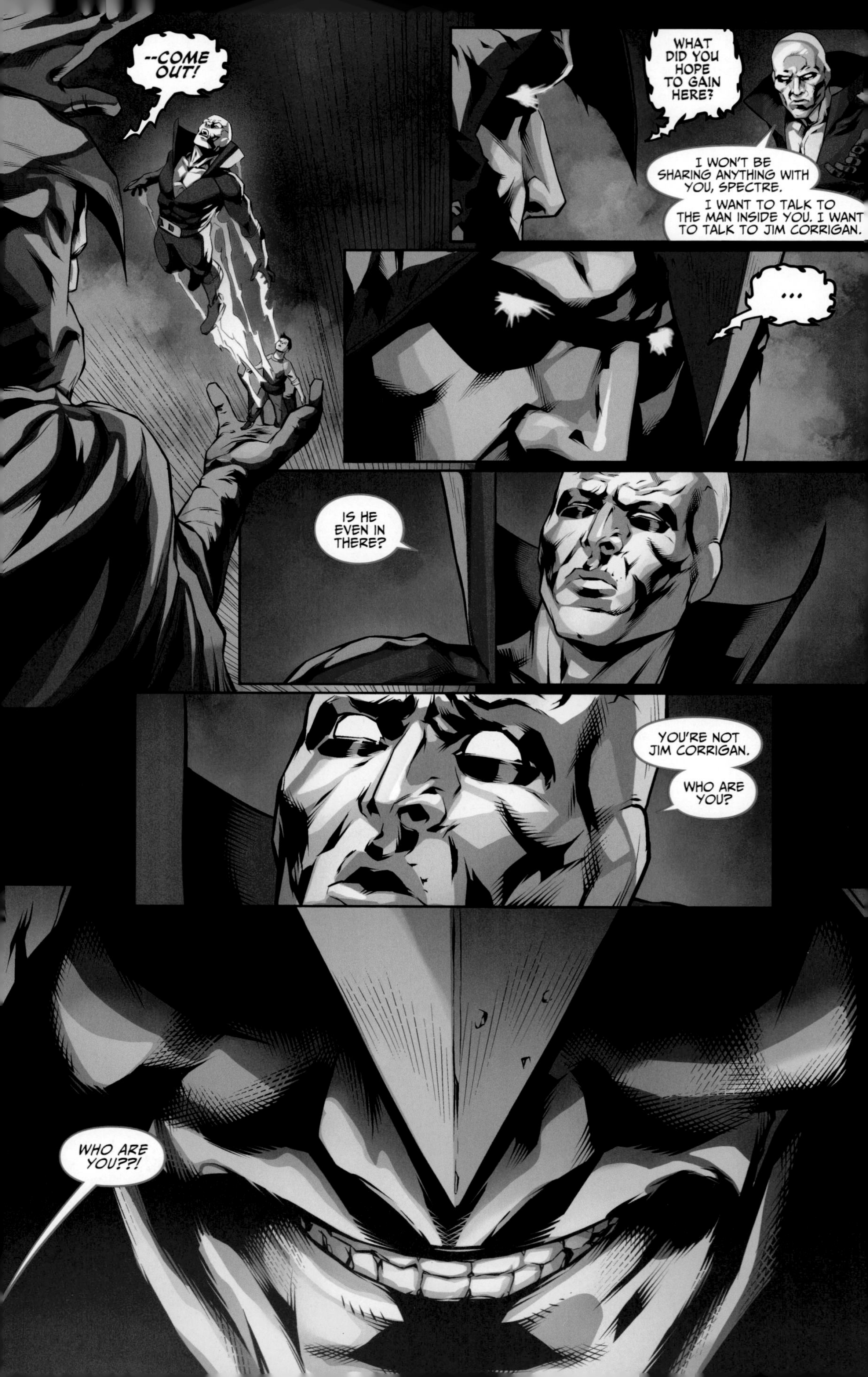
--COME OUT!
WHAT DID YOU HOPE TO GAIN HERE?
I WON'T BE SHARING ANYTHING WITH YOU, SPECTRE.
I WANT TO TALK TO THE MAN INSIDE YOU. I WANT TO TALK TO JIM CORRIGAN.
...
IS HE EVEN IN THERE?
YOU'RE NOT JIM CORRIGAN.
WHO ARE YOU?
WHO ARE YOU??!

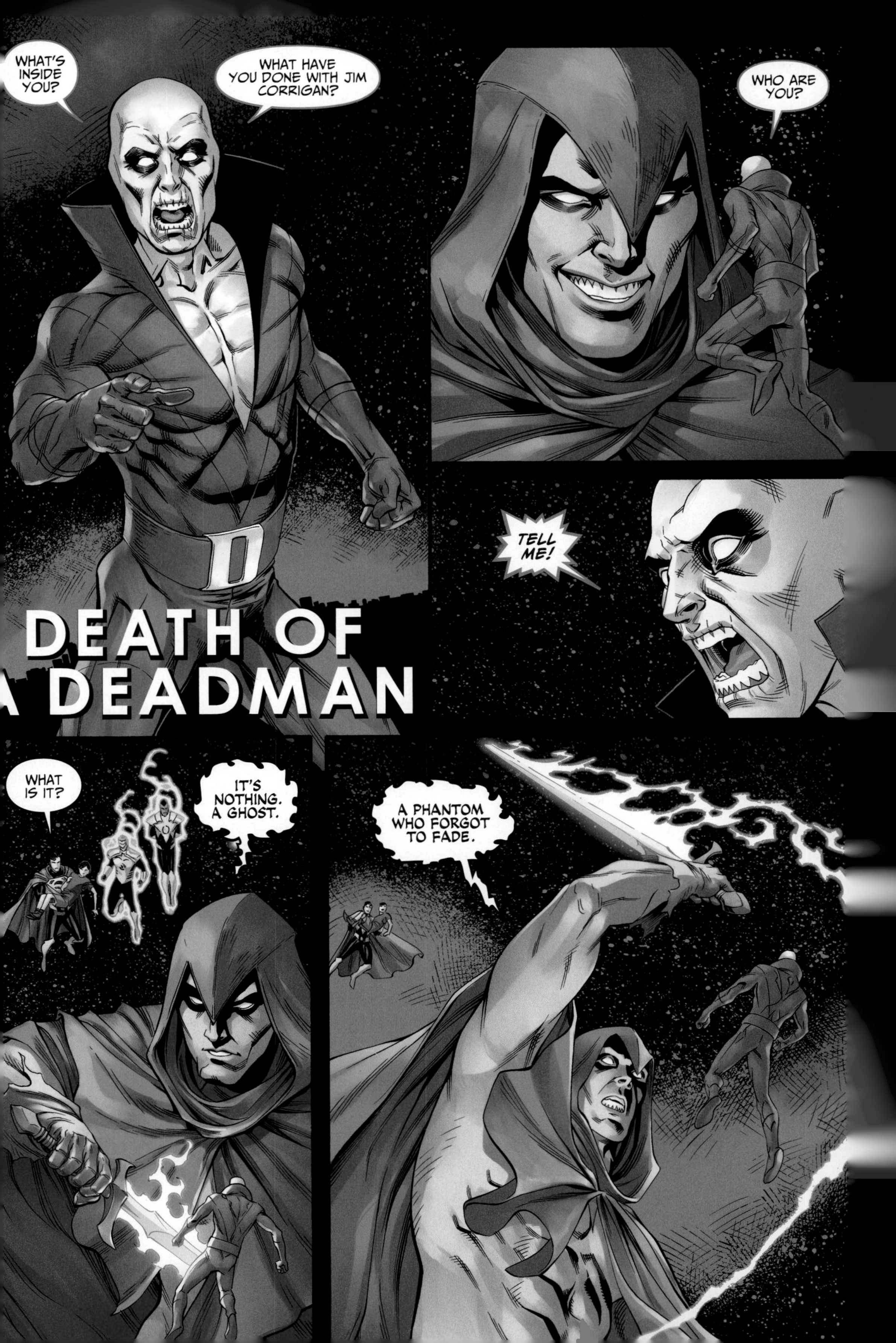
WHAT'S INSIDE YOU?
WHAT HAVE YOU DONE WITH JIM CORRIGAN?
WHO ARE YOU?
DEATH OF A DEADMAN
TELL ME!
WHAT IS IT?
IT'S NOTHING. A GHOST.
A PHANTOM WHO FORGOT TO FADE.

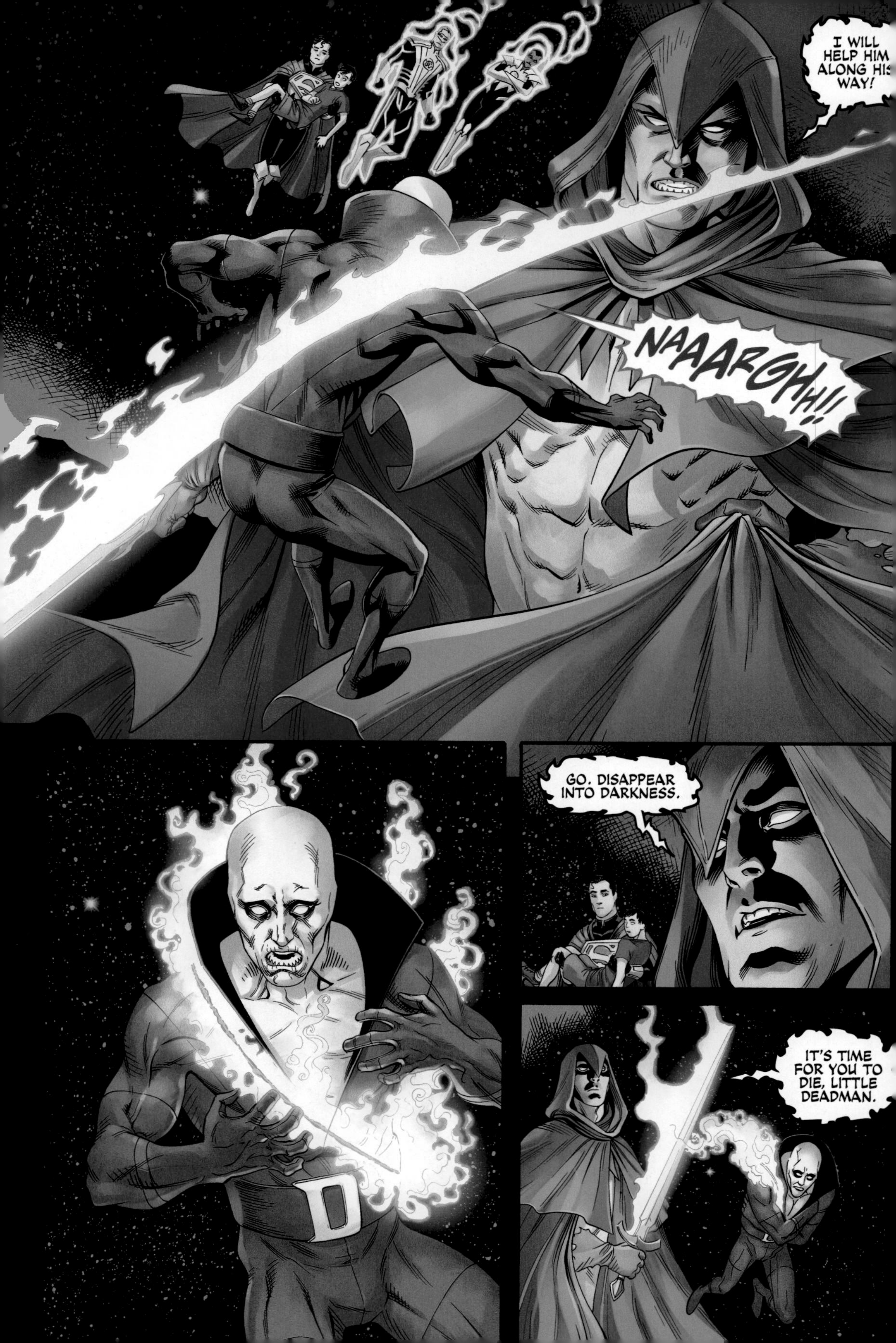
I WILL HELP HIM ALONG HIS WAY!
NAAARGHH!!
GO. DISAPPEAR INTO DARKNESS.
IT'S TIME FOR YOU TO DIE, LITTLE DEADMAN.

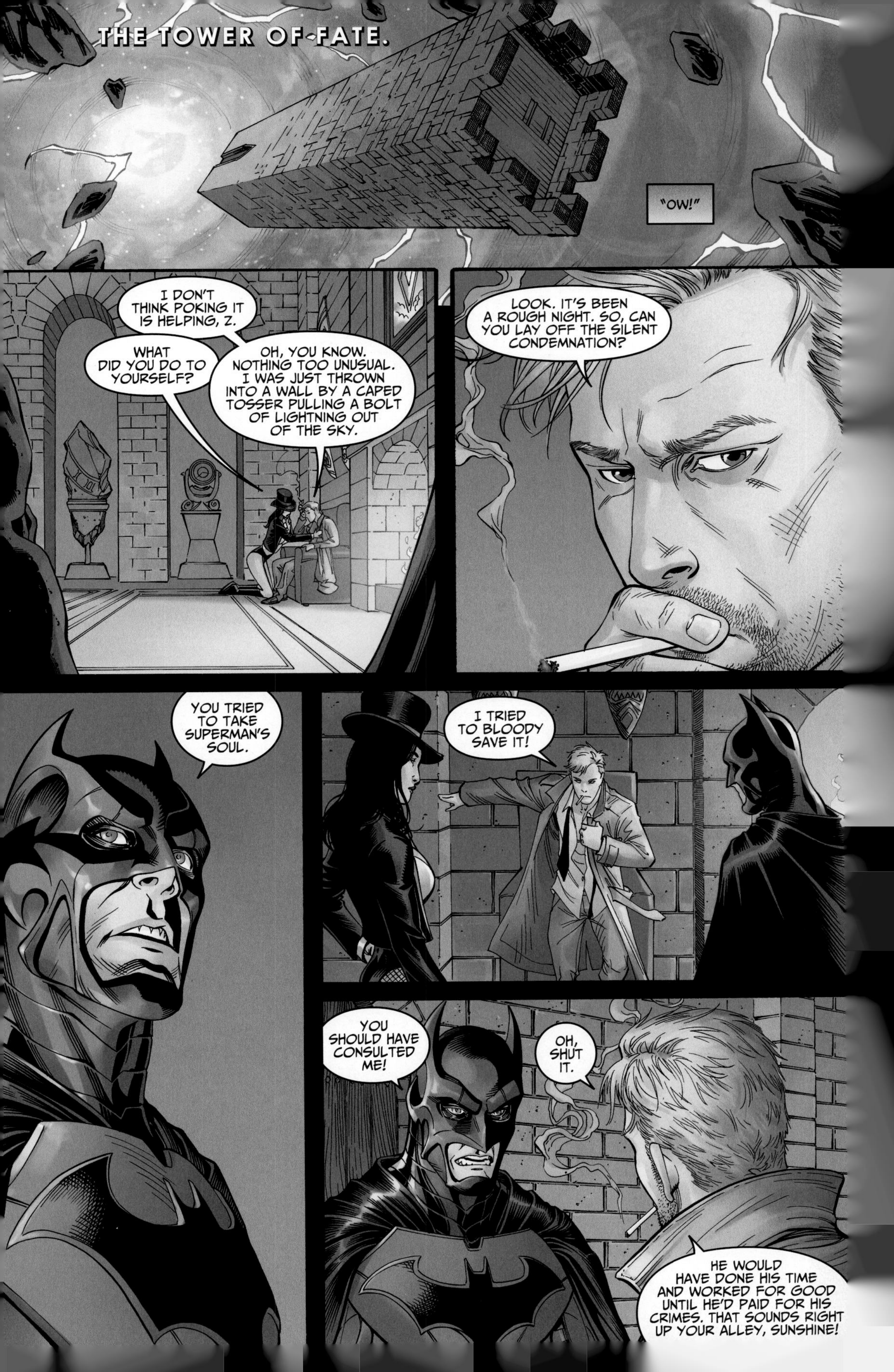
THE TOWER OF FATE.
"OW!"
I DON'T THINK POKING IT IS HELPING, Z.
WHAT DID YOU DO TO YOURSELF?
OH, YOU KNOW. NOTHING TOO UNUSUAL. I WAS JUST THROWN INTO A WALL BY A CAPED TOSSER PULLING A BOLT OF LIGHTNING OUT OF THE SKY.
LOOK. IT'S BEEN A ROUGH NIGHT. SO, CAN YOU LAY OFF THE SILENT CONDEMNATION?
YOU TRIED TO TAKE SUPERMAN'S SOUL.
I TRIED TO BLOODY SAVE IT!
YOU SHOULD HAVE CONSULTED ME!
OH, SHUT IT.
HE WOULD HAVE DONE HIS TIME AND WORKED FOR GOOD UNTIL HE'D PAID FOR HIS CRIMES. THAT SOUNDS RIGHT UP YOUR ALLEY, SUNSHINE!

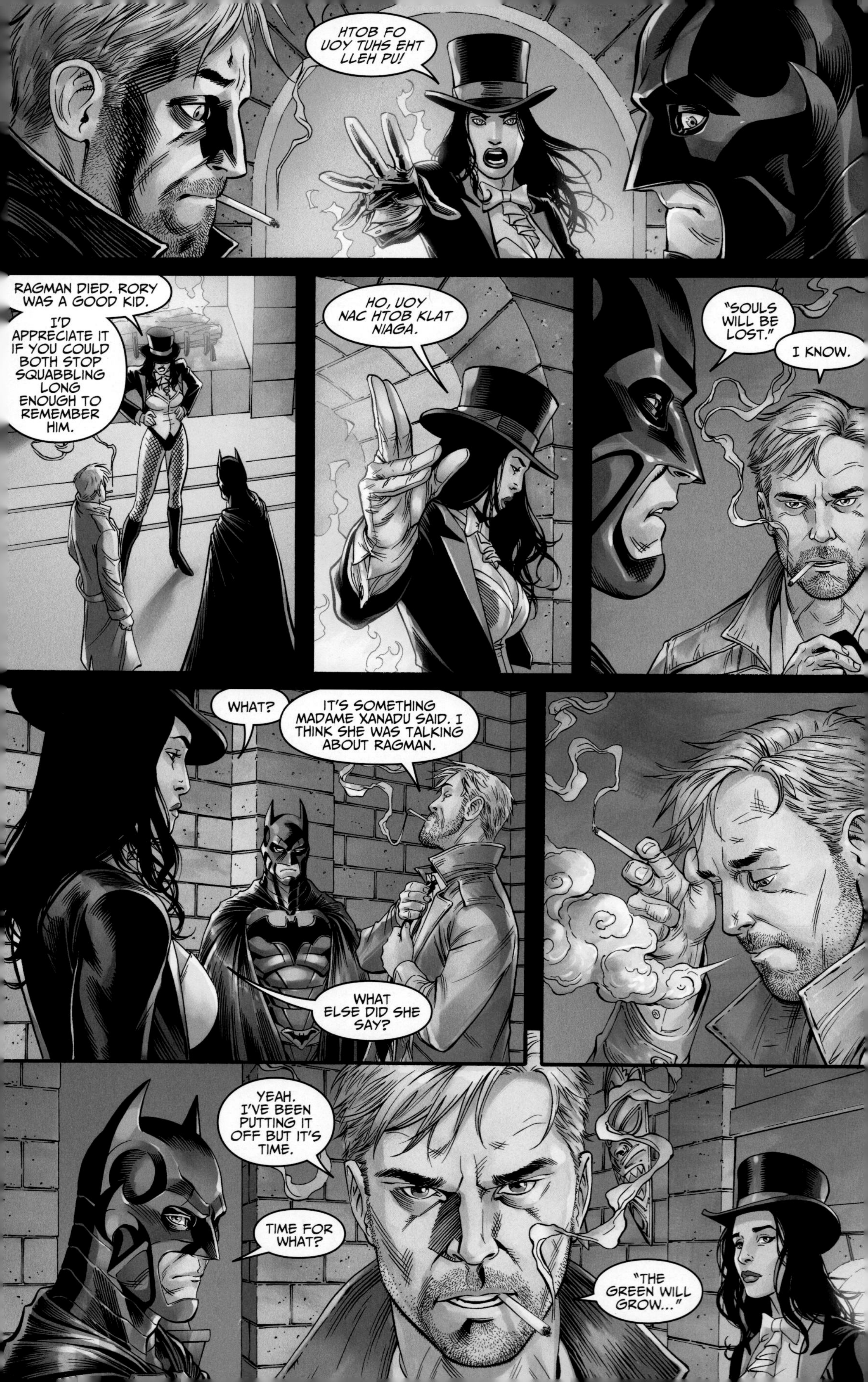
HTOB FO UOY TUHS EHT LLEH PU!
RAGMAN DIED. RORY WAS A GOOD KID.
I'D APPRECIATE IT IF YOU COULD BOTH STOP SQUABBLING LONG ENOUGH TO REMEMBER HIM.
HO, UOY NAC HTOB KLAT NIAGA.
"SOULS WILL BE LOST."
I KNOW.
WHAT?
IT'S SOMETHING MADAME XANADU SAID. I THINK SHE WAS TALKING ABOUT RAGMAN.
WHAT ELSE DID SHE SAY?
YEAH. I'VE BEEN PUTTING IT OFF BUT IT'S TIME.
TIME FOR WHAT?
"THE GREEN WILL GROW..."

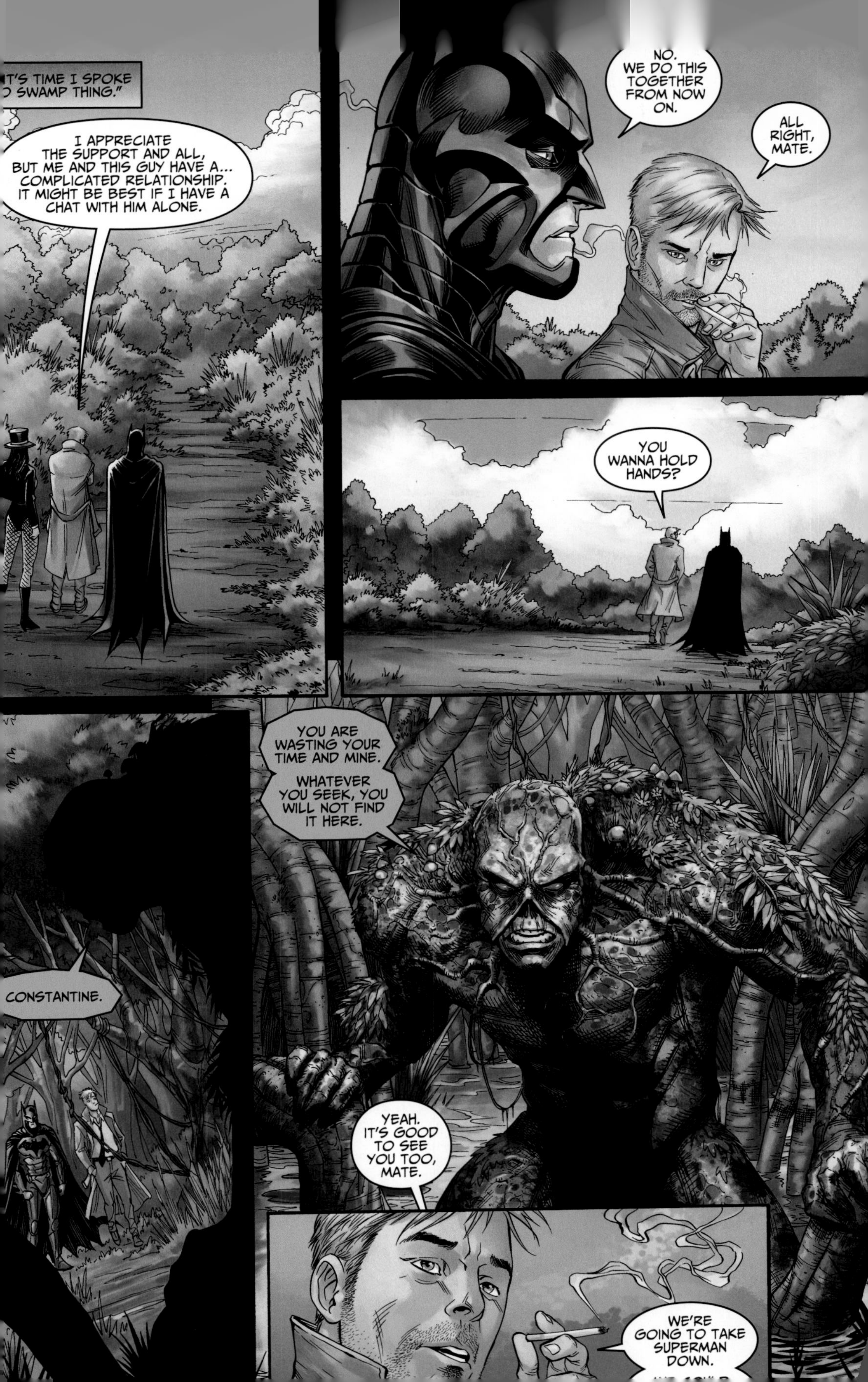

"T'S TIME I SPOKE
O SWAMP THING."
I APPRECIATE THE SUPPORT AND ALL, BUT ME AND THIS GUY HAVE A... COMPLICATED RELATIONSHIP. IT MIGHT BE BEST IF I HAVE A CHAT WITH HIM ALONE.
NO. WE DO THIS TOGETHER FROM NOW ON.
ALL RIGHT, MATE.
YOU WANNA HOLD HANDS?
CONSTANTINE.
YOU ARE WASTING YOUR TIME AND MINE.
WHATEVER YOU SEEK, YOU WILL NOT FIND IT HERE.
YEAH. IT'S GOOD TO SEE YOU TOO, MATE.
WE'RE GOING TO TAKE SUPERMAN DOWN.

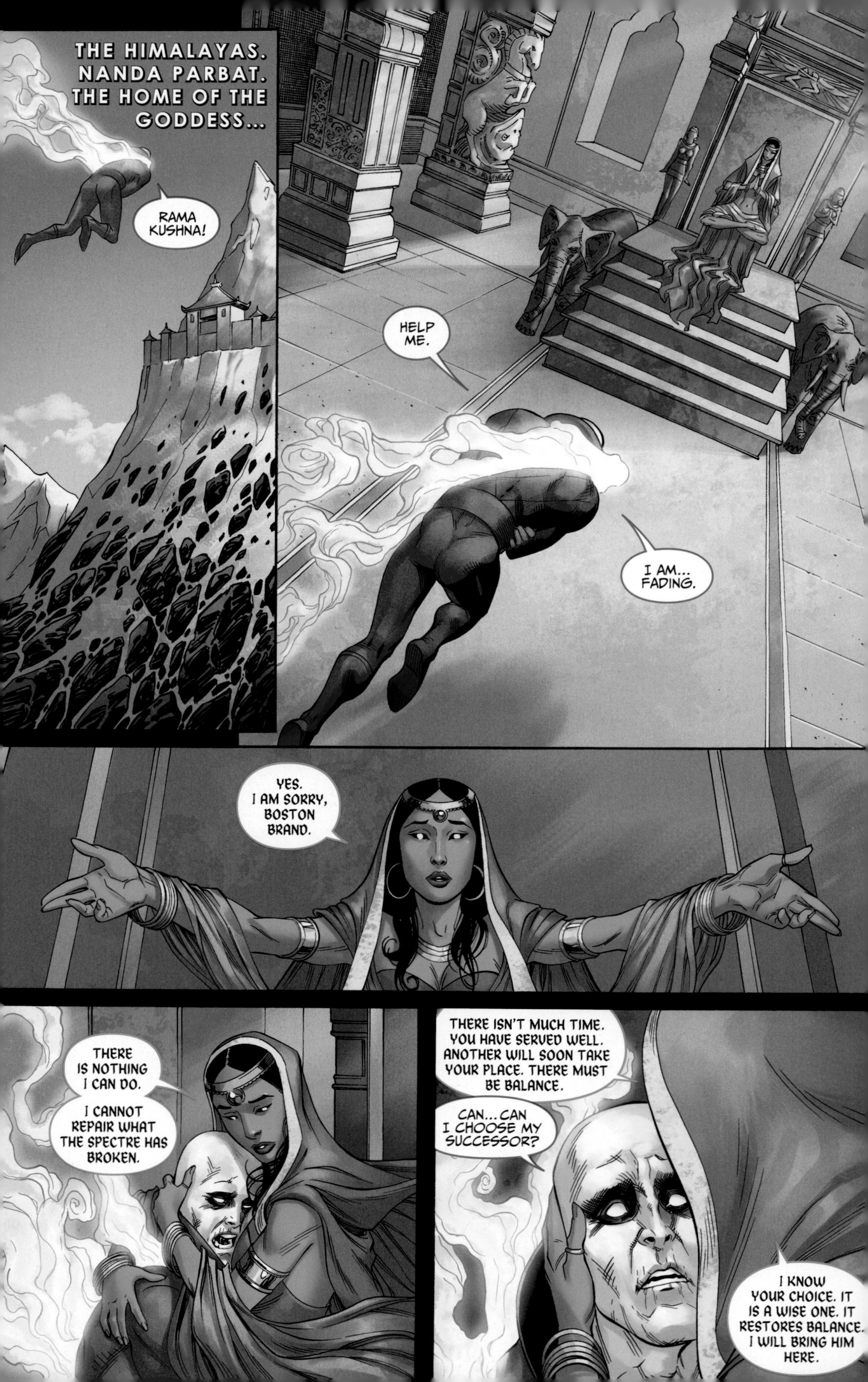

THE HIMALAYAS. NANDA PARBAT. THE HOME OF THE GODDESS...
RAMA KUSHNA!
HELP ME.
I AM... FADING.
YES. I AM SORRY, BOSTON BRAND.
THERE IS NOTHING I CAN DO.
I CANNOT REPAIR WHAT THE SPECTRE HAS BROKEN.
THERE ISN'T MUCH TIME. YOU HAVE SERVED WELL. ANOTHER WILL SOON TAKE YOUR PLACE. THERE MUST BE BALANCE.
CAN... CAN I CHOOSE MY SUCCESSOR?
I KNOW YOUR CHOICE. IT IS A WISE ONE. IT RESTORES BALANCE. I WILL BRING HIM HERE.

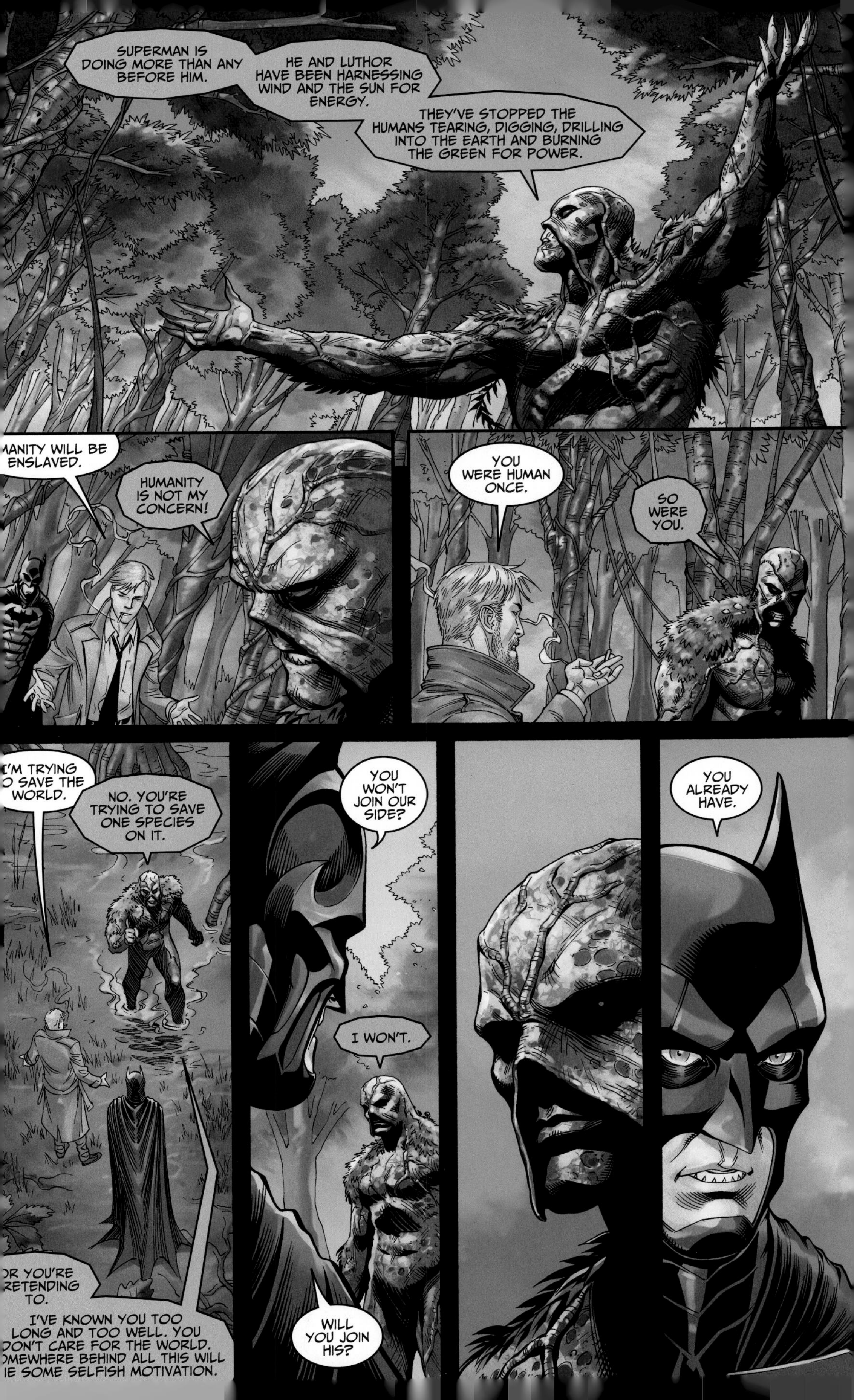
SUPERMAN IS DOING MORE THAN ANY BEFORE HIM.
HE AND LUTHOR HAVE BEEN HARNESSING WIND AND THE SUN FOR ENERGY.
THEY'VE STOPPED THE HUMANS TEARING, DIGGING, DRILLING INTO THE EARTH AND BURNING THE GREEN FOR POWER.
MANITY WILL BE ENSLAVED.
HUMANITY IS NOT MY CONCERN!
YOU WERE HUMAN ONCE.
SO WERE YOU.
I'M TRYING O SAVE THE WORLD.
NO. YOU'RE TRYING TO SAVE ONE SPECIES ON IT.
OR YOU'RE RETENDING TO.
I'VE KNOWN YOU TOO LONG AND TOO WELL. YOU DON'T CARE FOR THE WORLD. OMEWHERE BEHIND ALL THIS WILL IE SOME SELFISH MOTIVATION.
YOU WON'T JOIN OUR SIDE?
I WON'T.
WILL YOU JOIN HIS?
YOU ALREADY HAVE.

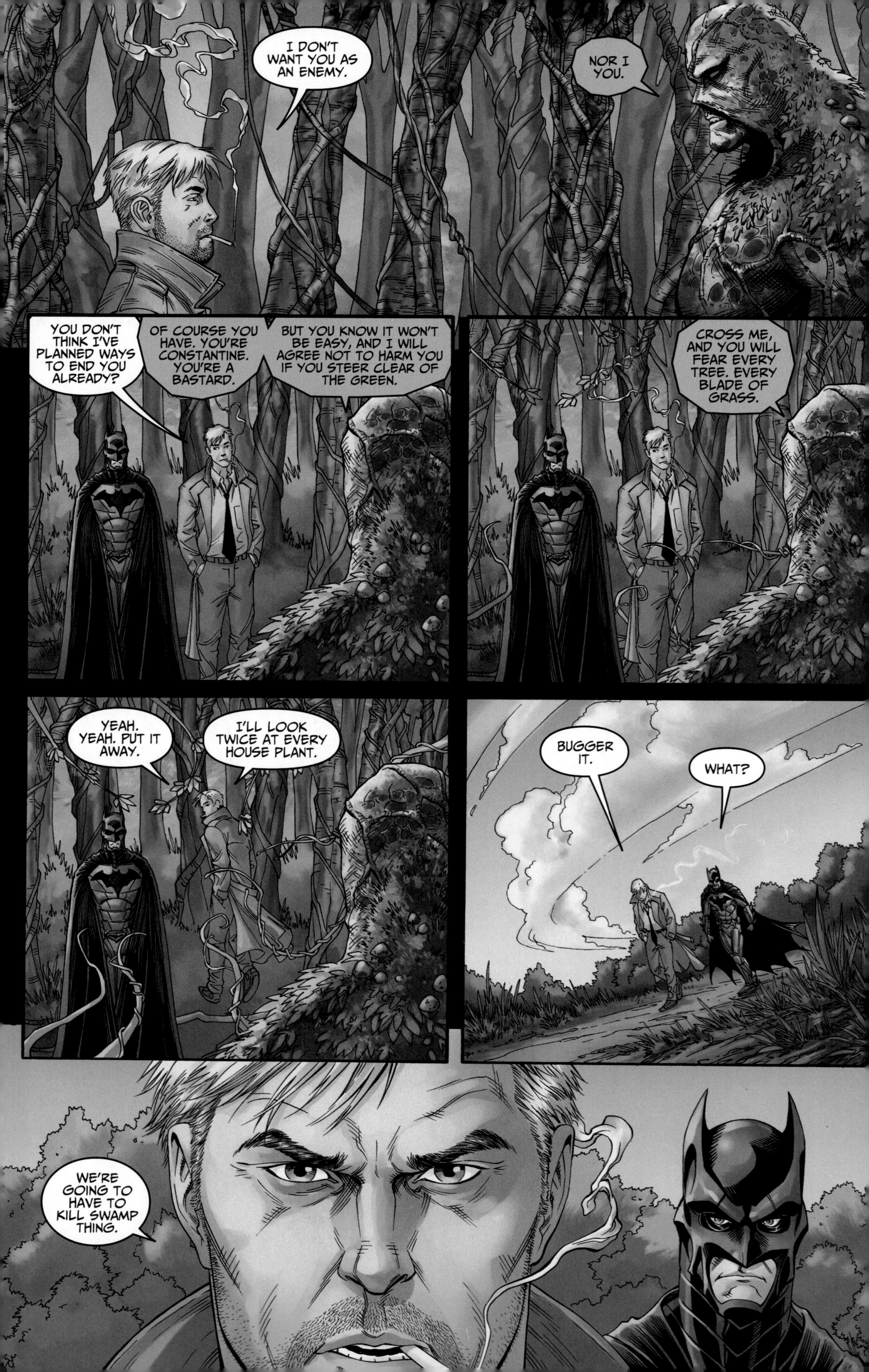
I DON'T WANT YOU AS AN ENEMY.
NOR I YOU.
YOU DON'T THINK I'VE PLANNED WAYS TO END YOU ALREADY?
OF COURSE YOU HAVE. YOU'RE CONSTANTINE. YOU'RE A BASTARD.
BUT YOU KNOW IT WON'T BE EASY, AND I WILL AGREE NOT TO HARM YOU IF YOU STEER CLEAR OF THE GREEN.
CROSS ME, AND YOU WILL FEAR EVERY TREE. EVERY BLADE OF GRASS.
YEAH. YEAH. PUT IT AWAY.
I'LL LOOK TWICE AT EVERY HOUSE PLANT.
BUGGER IT.
WHAT?
WE'RE GOING TO HAVE TO KILL SWAMP THING.

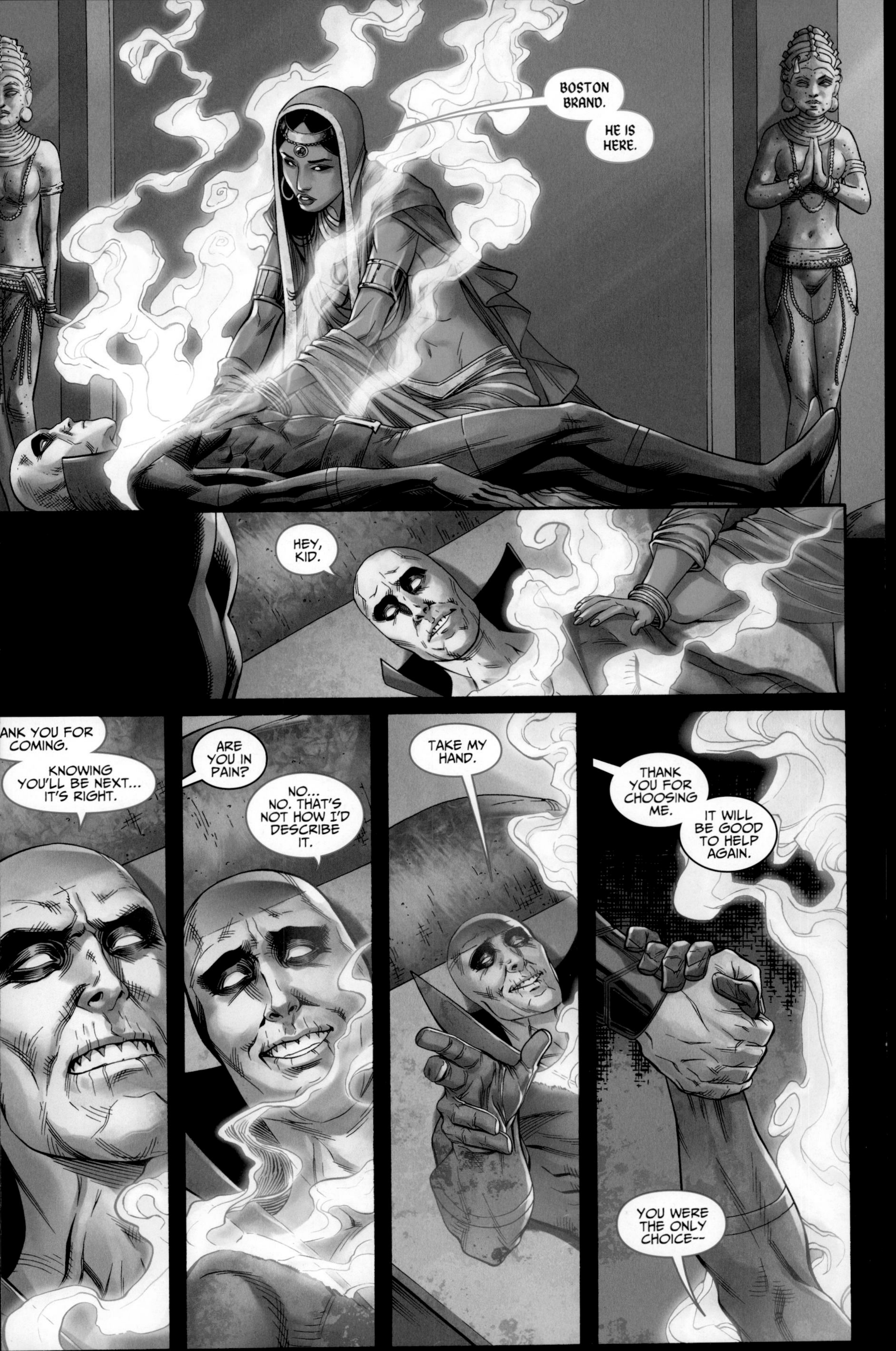
BOSTON BRAND.
HE IS HERE.
HEY, KID.
ANK YOU FOR COMING.
KNOWING YOU'LL BE NEXT... IT'S RIGHT.
ARE YOU IN PAIN?
NO... NO. THAT'S NOT HOW I'D DESCRIBE IT.
TAKE MY HAND.
THANK YOU FOR CHOOSING ME.
IT WILL BE GOOD TO HELP AGAIN.
YOU WERE THE ONLY CHOICE--

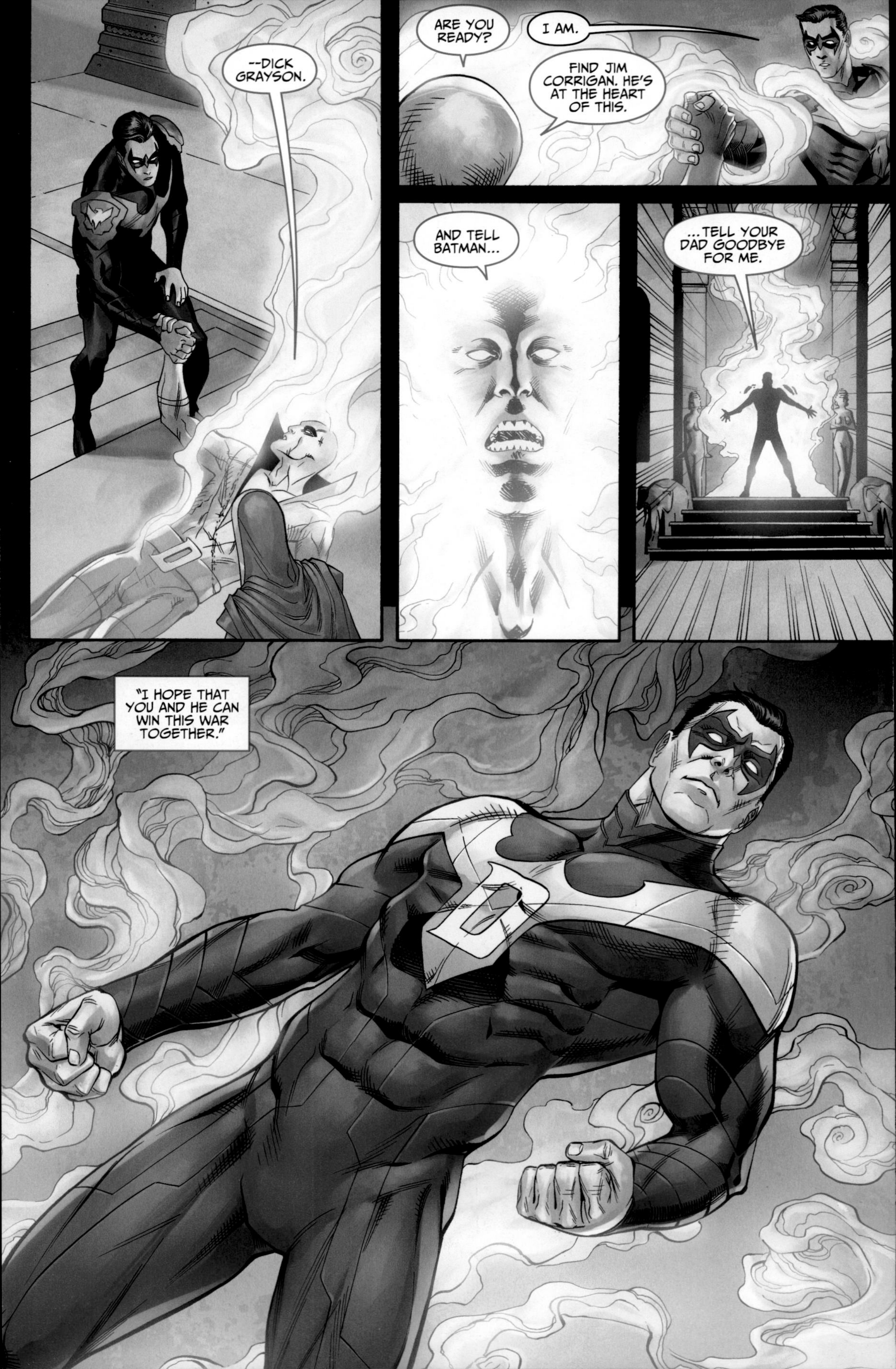
--DICK GRAYSON.
ARE YOU READY?
I AM.
FIND JIM CORRIGAN. HE'S AT THE HEART OF THIS.
AND TELL BATMAN...
...TELL YOUR DAD GOODBYE FOR ME.
"I HOPE THAT YOU AND HE CAN WIN THIS WAR TOGETHER."

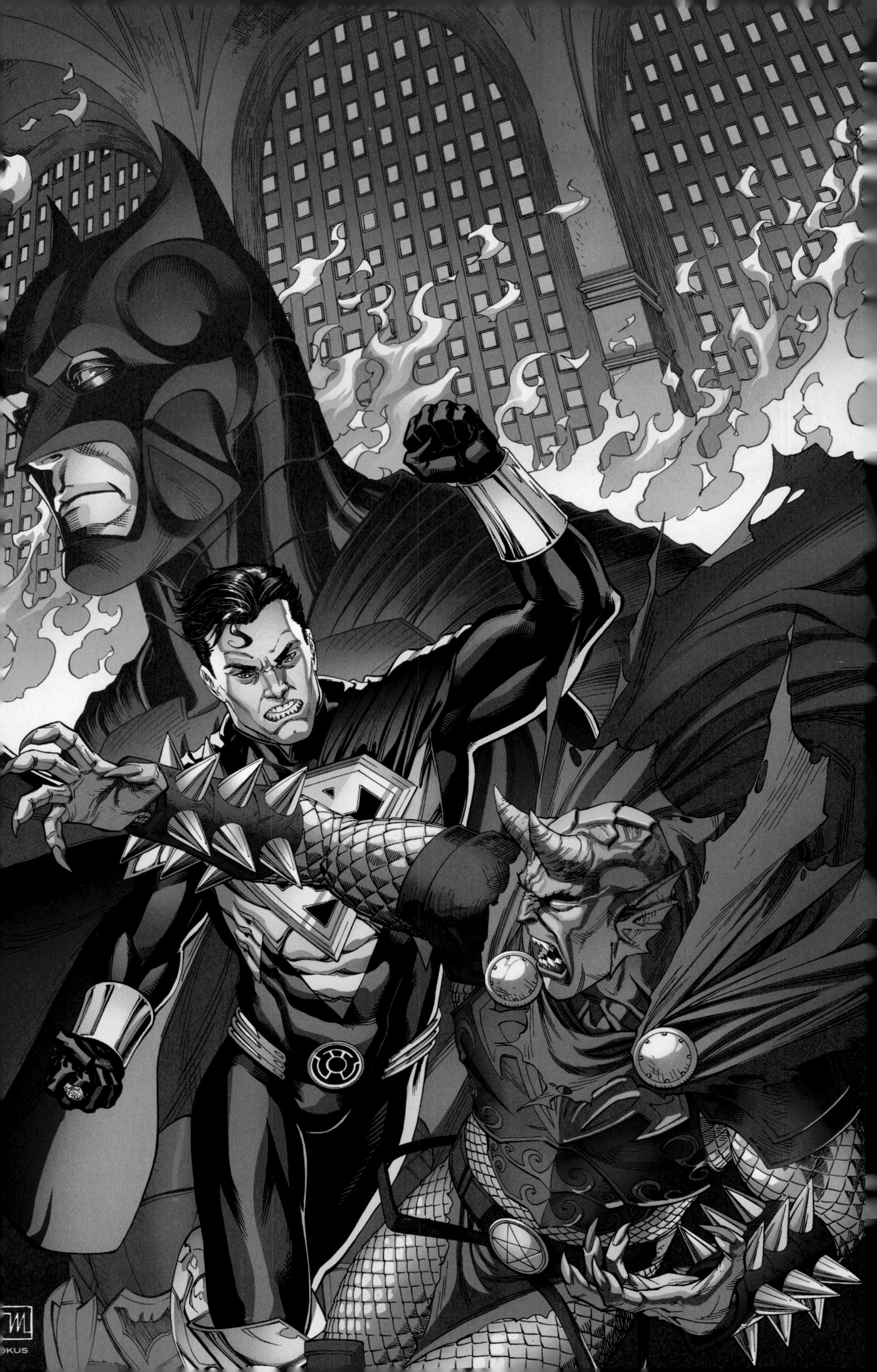

"Raise the Demon" **Bruno Redondo & Xermanico** Artists **Rex Lokus** Colorist
"Secret Weapon" **Mike S. Miller,Bruno Redondo & Juan Albarran** Artist **Rex Lokus** Colorist
Cover Art by **Mike S. Miller & Rex Lokus**

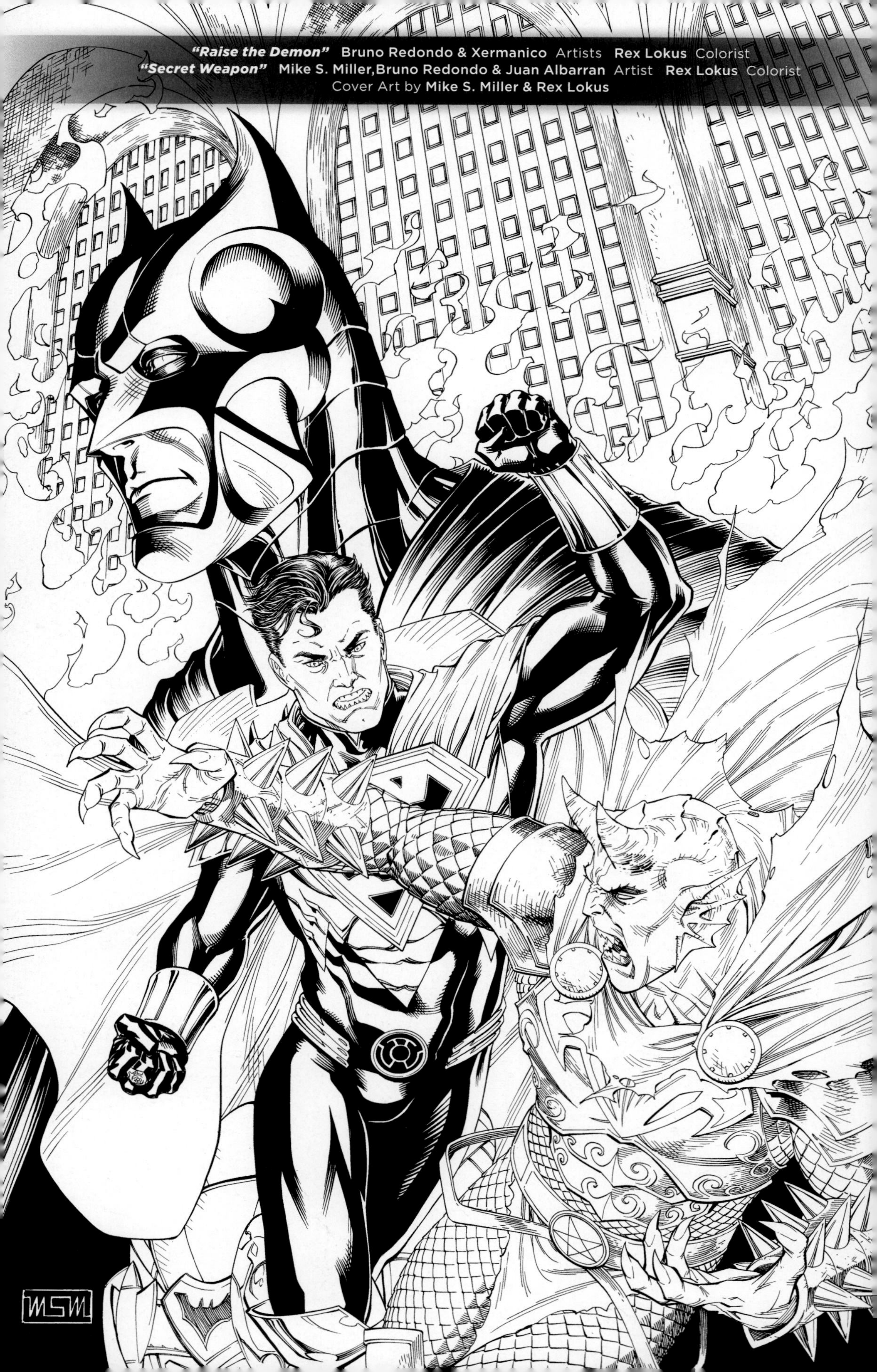

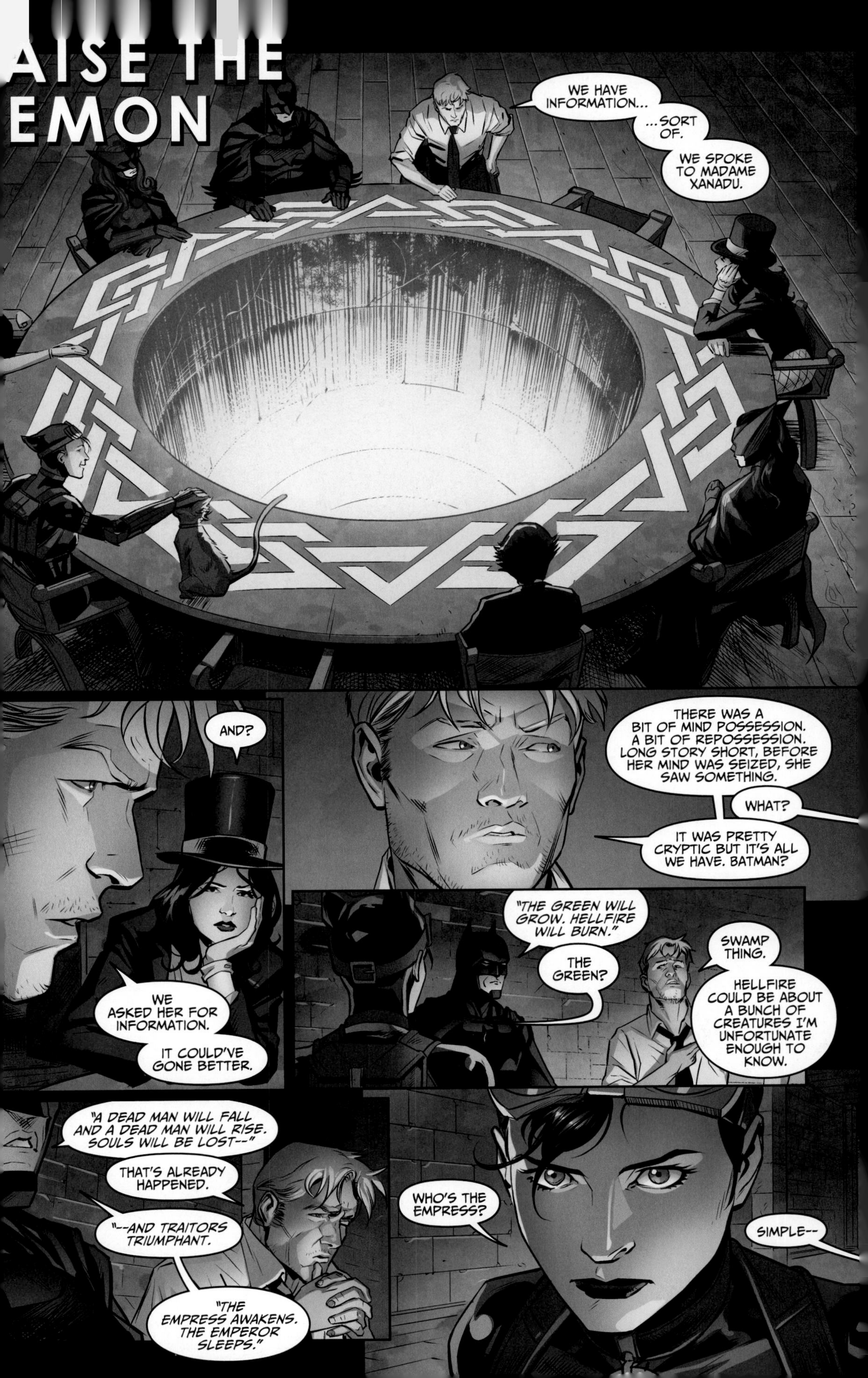
AISE THE
EMON
WE HAVE INFORMATION...
...SORT OF.
WE SPOKE TO MADAME XANADU.
AND?
WE ASKED HER FOR INFORMATION.
IT COULD'VE GONE BETTER.
THERE WAS A BIT OF MIND POSSESSION. A BIT OF REPOSSESSION. LONG STORY SHORT, BEFORE HER MIND WAS SEIZED, SHE SAW SOMETHING.
WHAT?
IT WAS PRETTY CRYPTIC BUT IT'S ALL WE HAVE. BATMAN?
"THE GREEN WILL GROW. HELLFIRE WILL BURN."
THE GREEN?
SWAMP THING.
HELLFIRE COULD BE ABOUT A BUNCH OF CREATURES I'M UNFORTUNATE ENOUGH TO KNOW.
"A DEAD MAN WILL FALL AND A DEAD MAN WILL RISE. SOULS WILL BE LOST--"
THAT'S ALREADY HAPPENED.
"--AND TRAITORS TRIUMPHANT.
"THE EMPRESS AWAKENS. THE EMPEROR SLEEPS."
WHO'S THE EMPRESS?
SIMPLE--

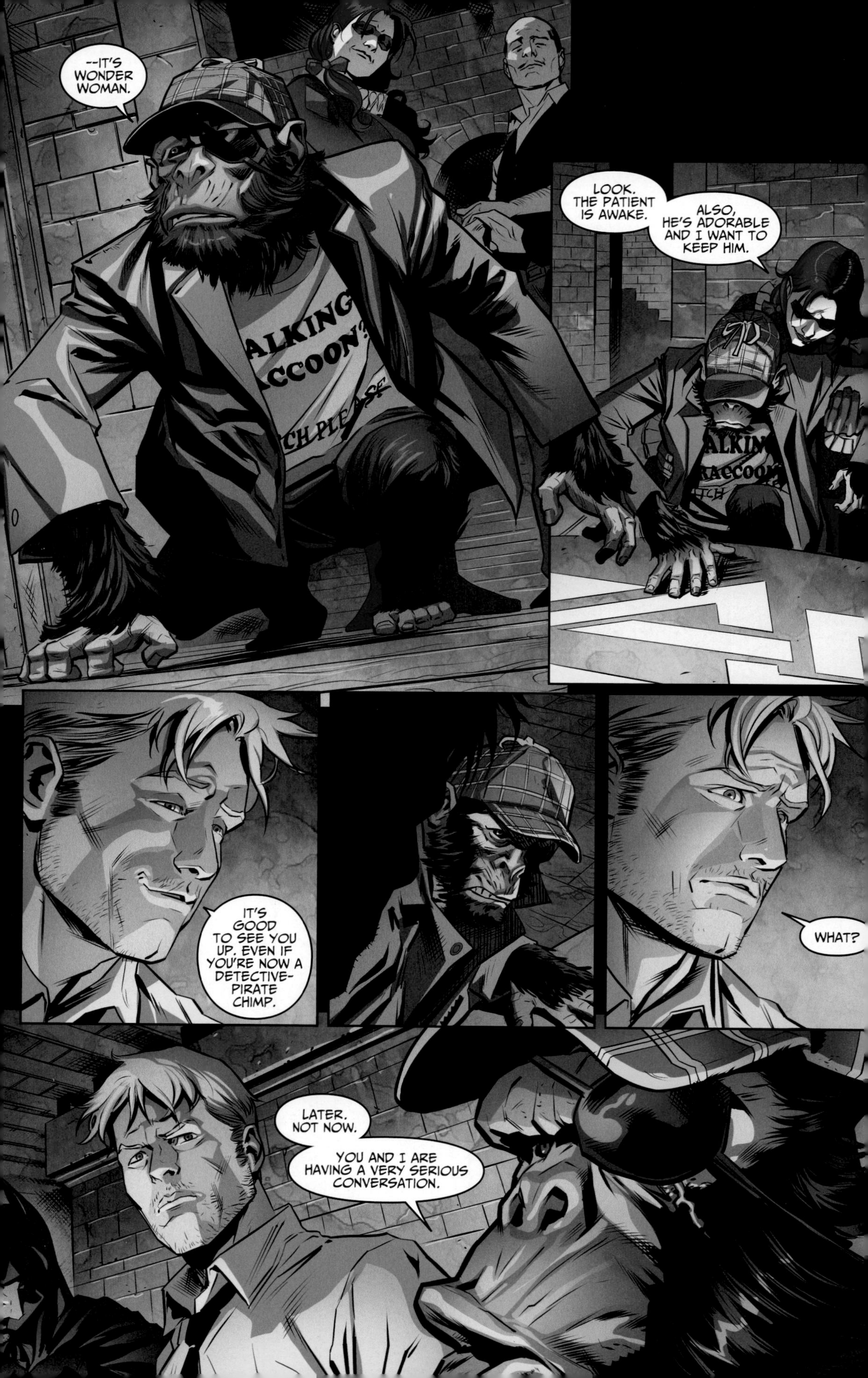
--IT'S WONDER WOMAN.
LOOK. THE PATIENT IS AWAKE.
ALSO, HE'S ADORABLE AND I WANT TO KEEP HIM.
IT'S GOOD TO SEE YOU UP. EVEN IF YOU'RE NOW A DETECTIVE-PIRATE CHIMP.
WHAT?
LATER. NOT NOW.
YOU AND I ARE HAVING A VERY SERIOUS CONVERSATION.

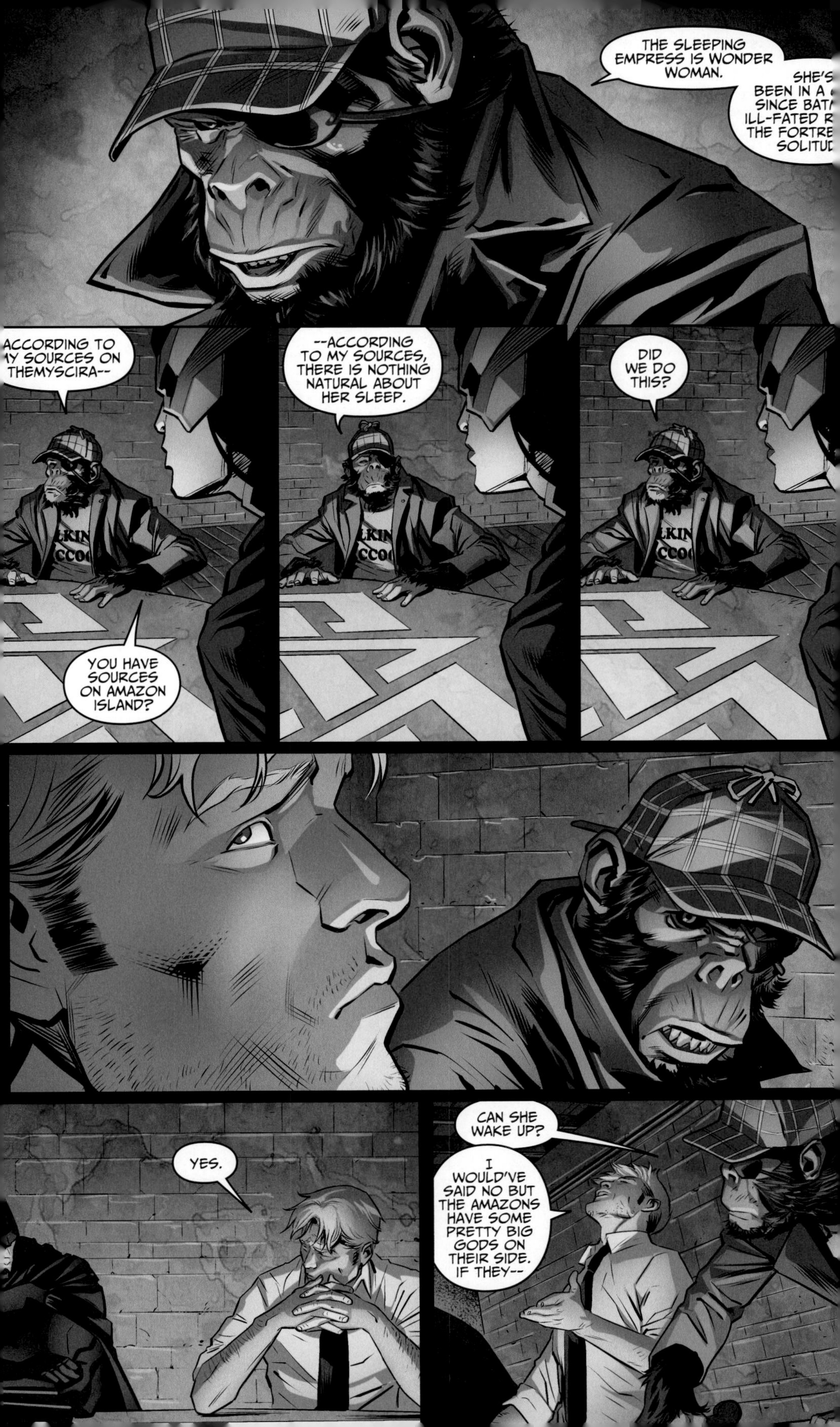
THE SLEEPING EMPRESS IS WONDER WOMAN.
SHE'S BEEN IN A SINCE BAT ILL-FATED R THE FORTRE SOLITUD
ACCORDING TO MY SOURCES ON THEMYSCIRA--
YOU HAVE SOURCES ON AMAZON ISLAND?
--ACCORDING TO MY SOURCES, THERE IS NOTHING NATURAL ABOUT HER SLEEP.
DID WE DO THIS?
YES.
CAN SHE WAKE UP?
I WOULD'VE SAID NO BUT THE AMAZONS HAVE SOME PRETTY BIG GODS ON THEIR SIDE. IF THEY--

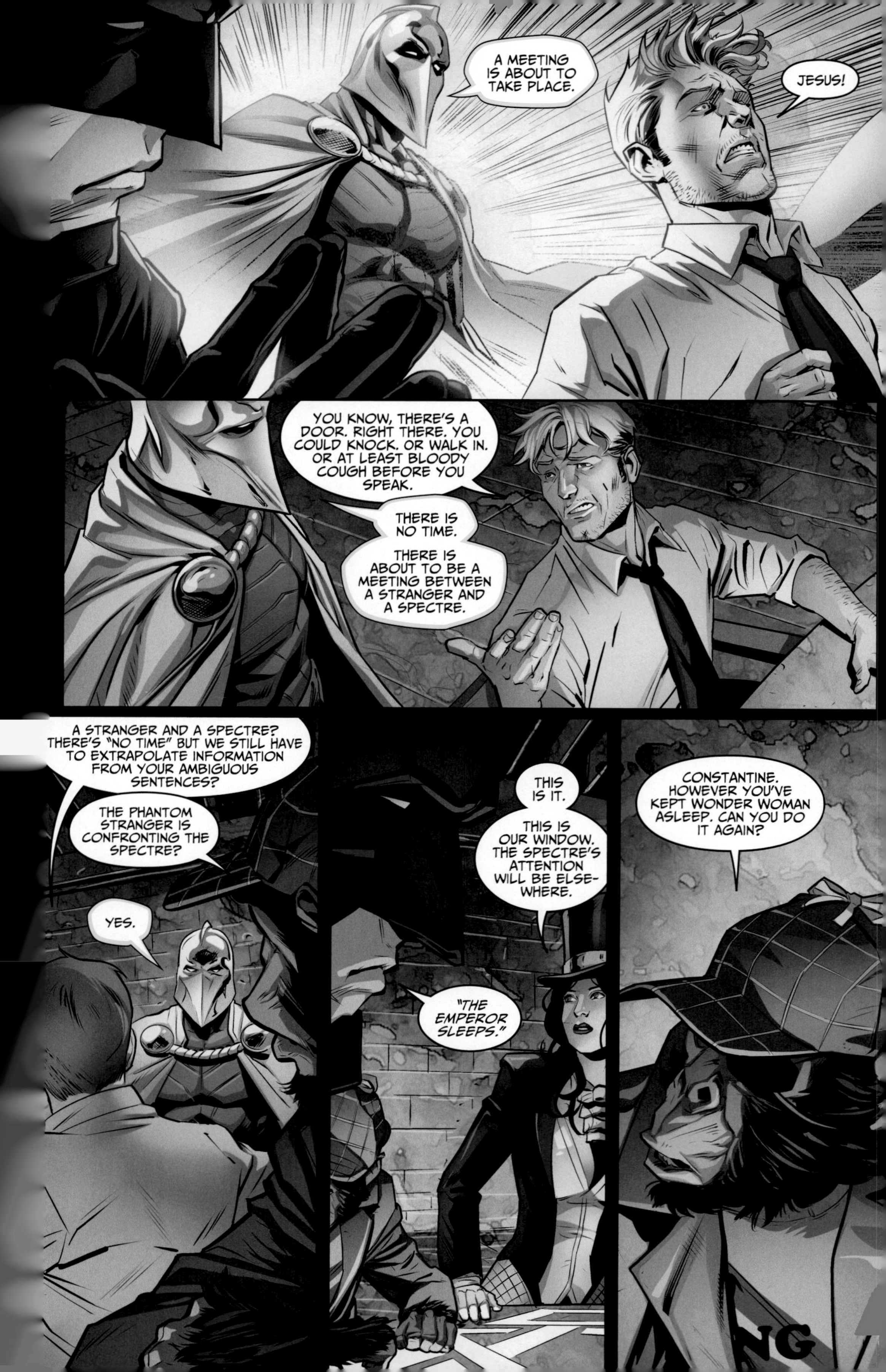
A MEETING IS ABOUT TO TAKE PLACE.
JESUS!
YOU KNOW, THERE'S A DOOR. RIGHT THERE. YOU COULD KNOCK. OR WALK IN. OR AT LEAST BLOODY COUGH BEFORE YOU SPEAK.
THERE IS NO TIME.
THERE IS ABOUT TO BE A MEETING BETWEEN A STRANGER AND A SPECTRE.
A STRANGER AND A SPECTRE? THERE'S "NO TIME" BUT WE STILL HAVE TO EXTRAPOLATE INFORMATION FROM YOUR AMBIGUOUS SENTENCES?
THE PHANTOM STRANGER IS CONFRONTING THE SPECTRE?
YES.
THIS IS IT.
THIS IS OUR WINDOW. THE SPECTRE'S ATTENTION WILL BE ELSE-WHERE.
"THE EMPEROR SLEEPS."
CONSTANTINE. HOWEVER YOU'VE KEPT WONDER WOMAN ASLEEP. CAN YOU DO IT AGAIN?

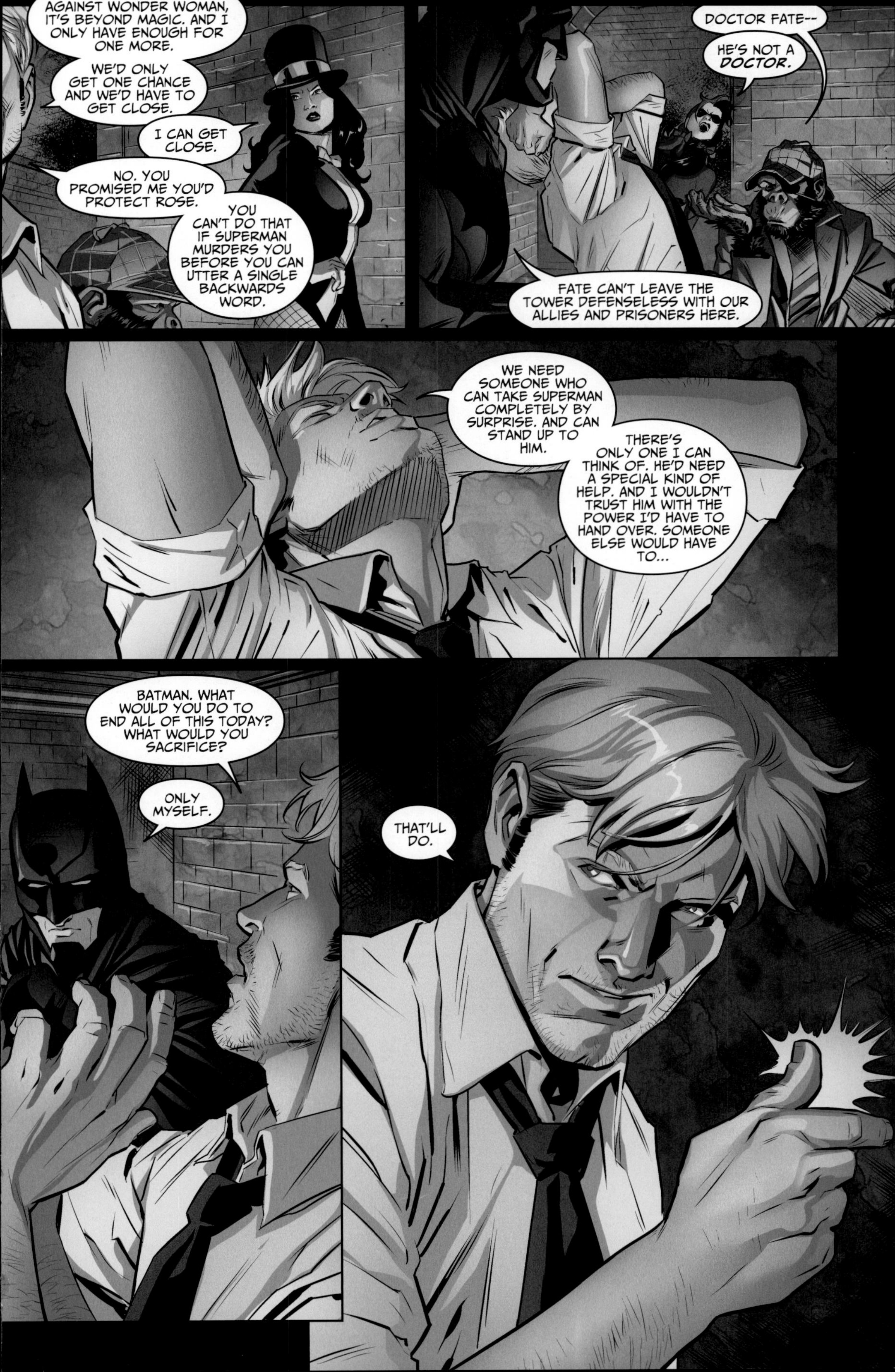
WHAT I USED AGAINST WONDER WOMAN, IT'S BEYOND MAGIC. AND I ONLY HAVE ENOUGH FOR ONE MORE.
WE'D ONLY GET ONE CHANCE AND WE'D HAVE TO GET CLOSE.
I CAN GET CLOSE.
NO. YOU PROMISED ME YOU'D PROTECT ROSE.
YOU CAN'T DO THAT IF SUPERMAN MURDERS YOU BEFORE YOU CAN UTTER A SINGLE BACKWARDS WORD.
DOCTOR FATE--
HE'S NOT A *DOCTOR.*
FATE CAN'T LEAVE THE TOWER DEFENSELESS WITH OUR ALLIES AND PRISONERS HERE.
WE NEED SOMEONE WHO CAN TAKE SUPERMAN COMPLETELY BY SURPRISE. AND CAN STAND UP TO HIM.
THERE'S ONLY ONE I CAN THINK OF. HE'D NEED A SPECIAL KIND OF HELP. AND I WOULDN'T TRUST HIM WITH THE POWER I'D HAVE TO HAND OVER. SOMEONE ELSE WOULD HAVE TO...
BATMAN. WHAT WOULD YOU DO TO END ALL OF THIS TODAY? WHAT WOULD YOU SACRIFICE?
ONLY MYSELF.
THAT'LL DO.

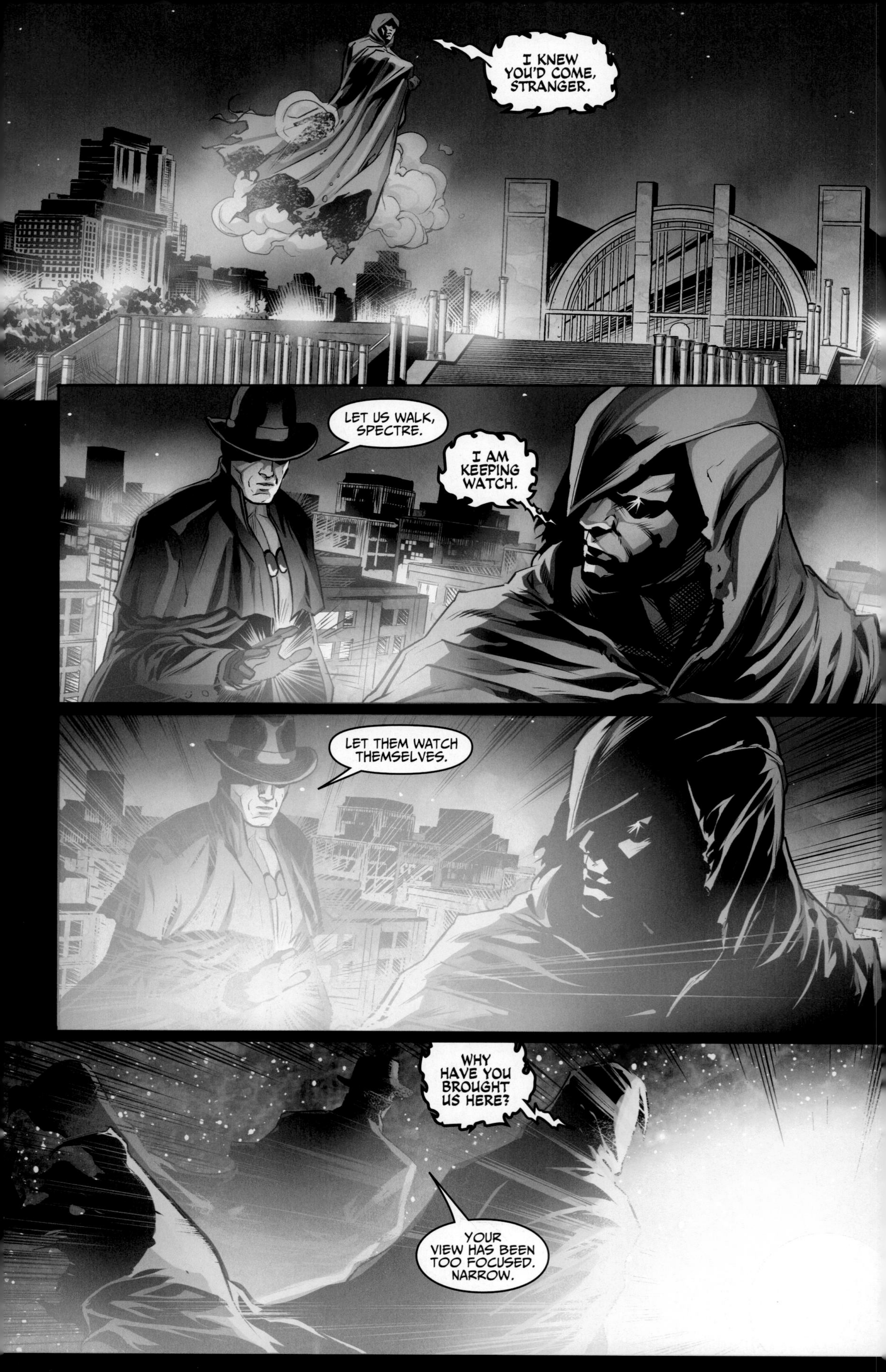
I KNEW YOU'D COME, STRANGER.
LET US WALK, SPECTRE.
I AM KEEPING WATCH.
LET THEM WATCH THEMSELVES.
WHY HAVE YOU BROUGHT US HERE?
YOUR VIEW HAS BEEN TOO FOCUSED. NARROW.

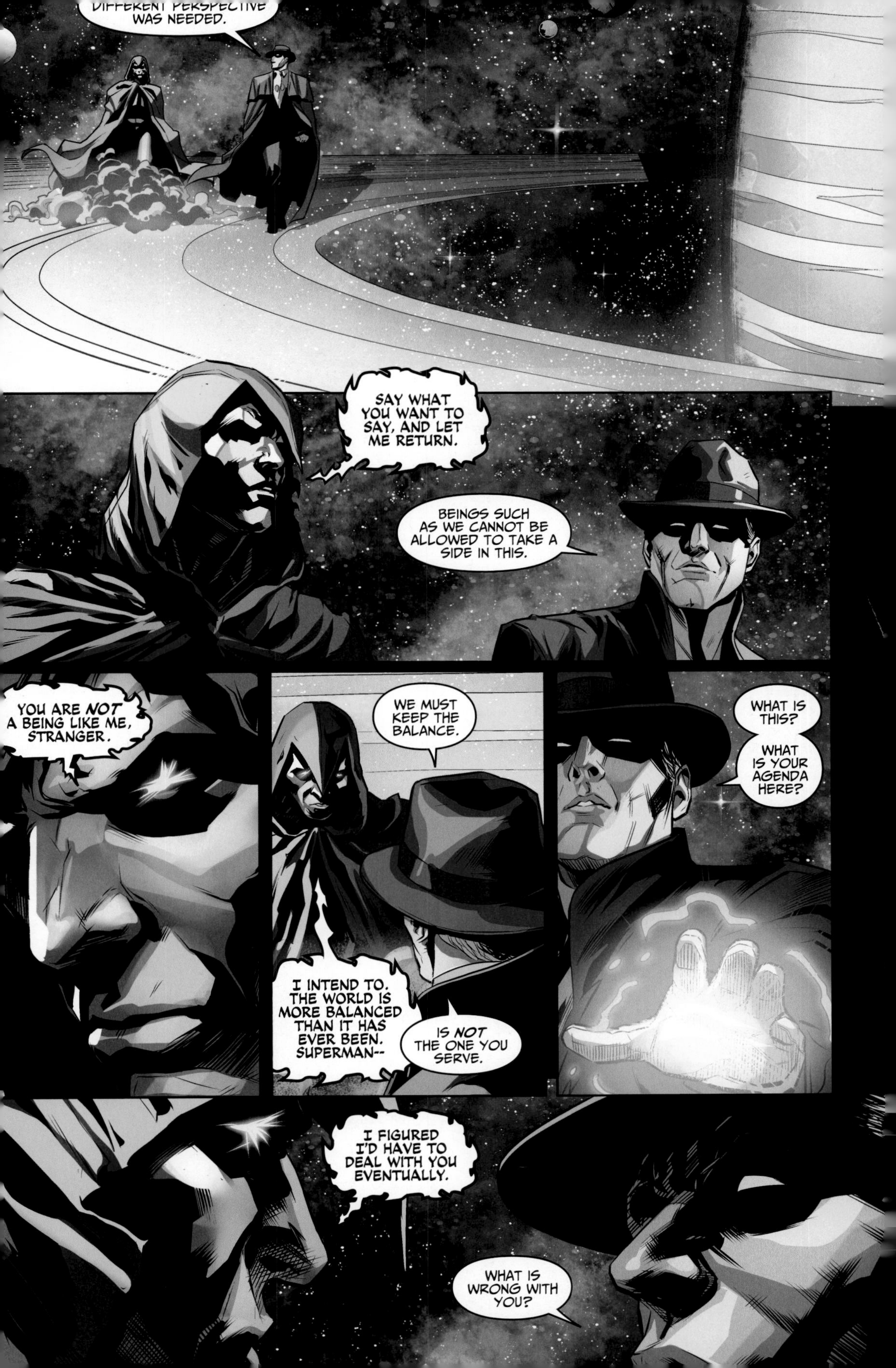
DIFFERENT PERSPECTIVE WAS NEEDED.
SAY WHAT YOU WANT TO SAY, AND LET ME RETURN.
BEINGS SUCH AS WE CANNOT BE ALLOWED TO TAKE A SIDE IN THIS.
YOU ARE *NOT* A BEING LIKE ME, STRANGER.
WE MUST KEEP THE BALANCE.
I INTEND TO. THE WORLD IS MORE BALANCED THAN IT HAS EVER BEEN. SUPERMAN--
IS *NOT* THE ONE YOU SERVE.
WHAT IS THIS?
WHAT IS YOUR AGENDA HERE?
I FIGURED I'D HAVE TO DEAL WITH YOU EVENTUALLY.
WHAT IS WRONG WITH YOU?

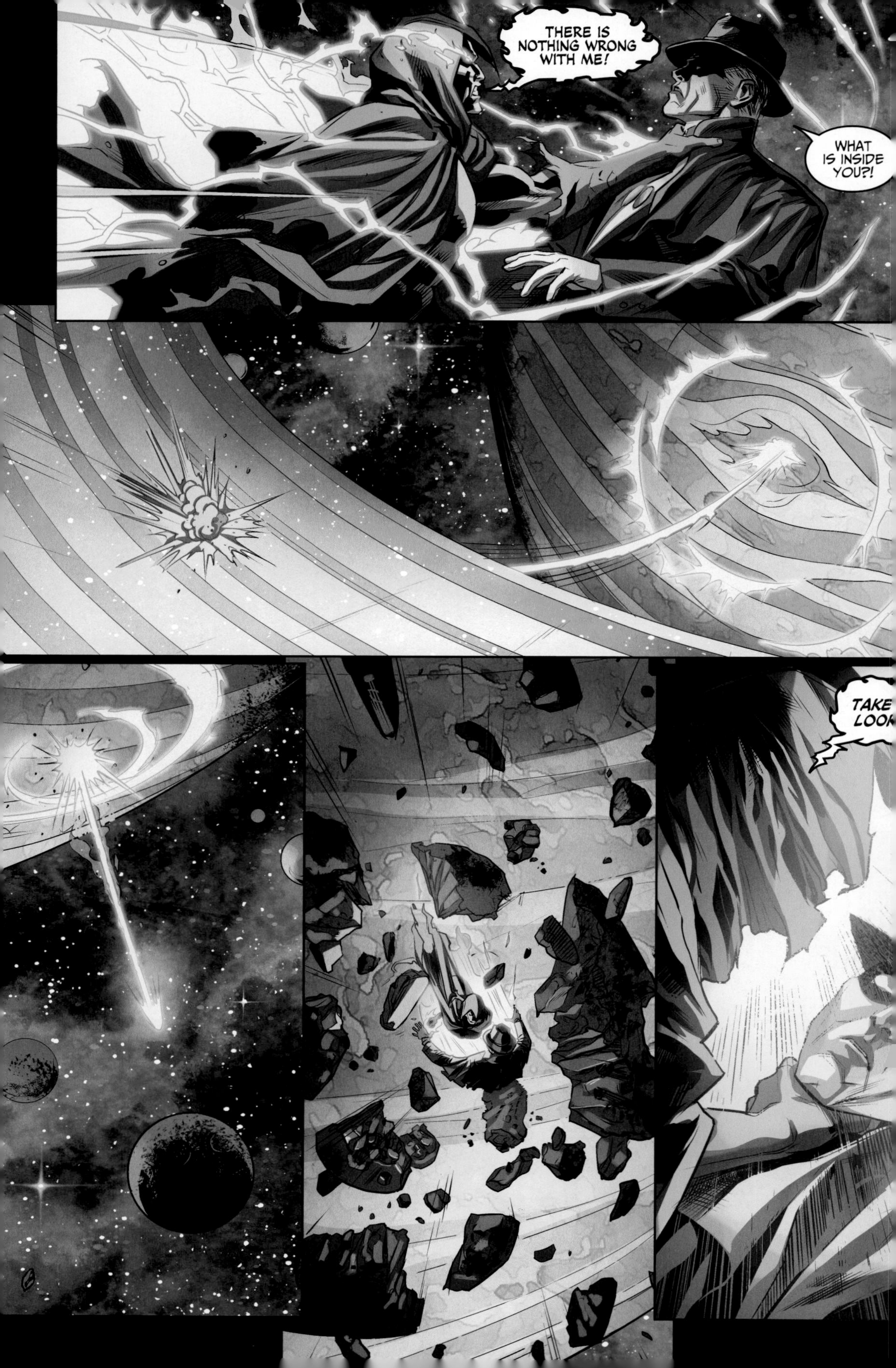
THERE IS NOTHING WRONG WITH ME!
WHAT IS INSIDE YOU?!
TAKE LOOK

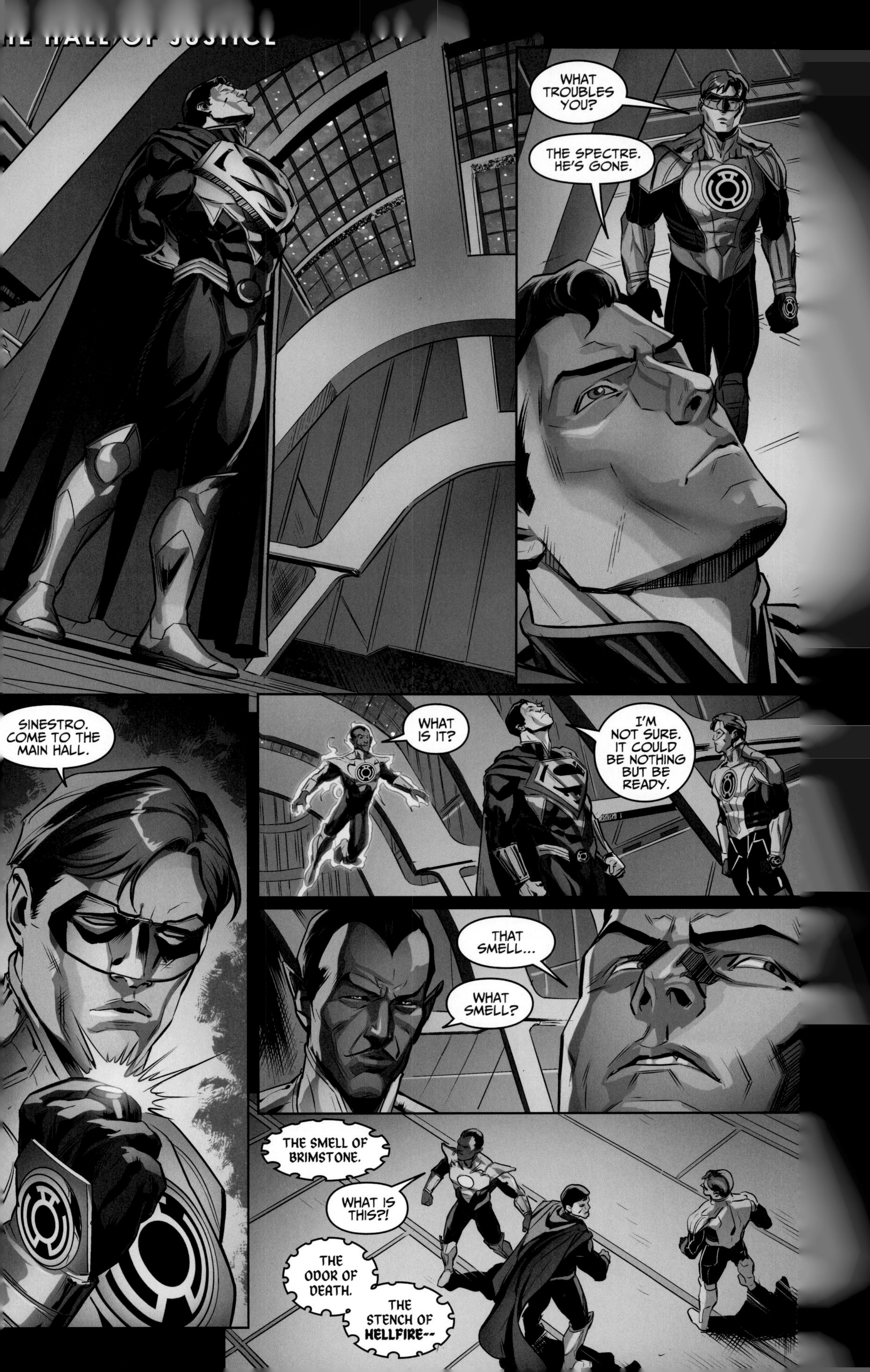
HE HALL OF JUSTICE
WHAT TROUBLES YOU?
THE SPECTRE. HE'S GONE.
SINESTRO. COME TO THE MAIN HALL.
WHAT IS IT?
I'M NOT SURE. IT COULD BE NOTHING BUT BE READY.
THAT SMELL...
WHAT SMELL?
THE SMELL OF BRIMSTONE.
WHAT IS THIS?!
THE ODOR OF DEATH.
THE STENCH OF **HELLFIRE**--

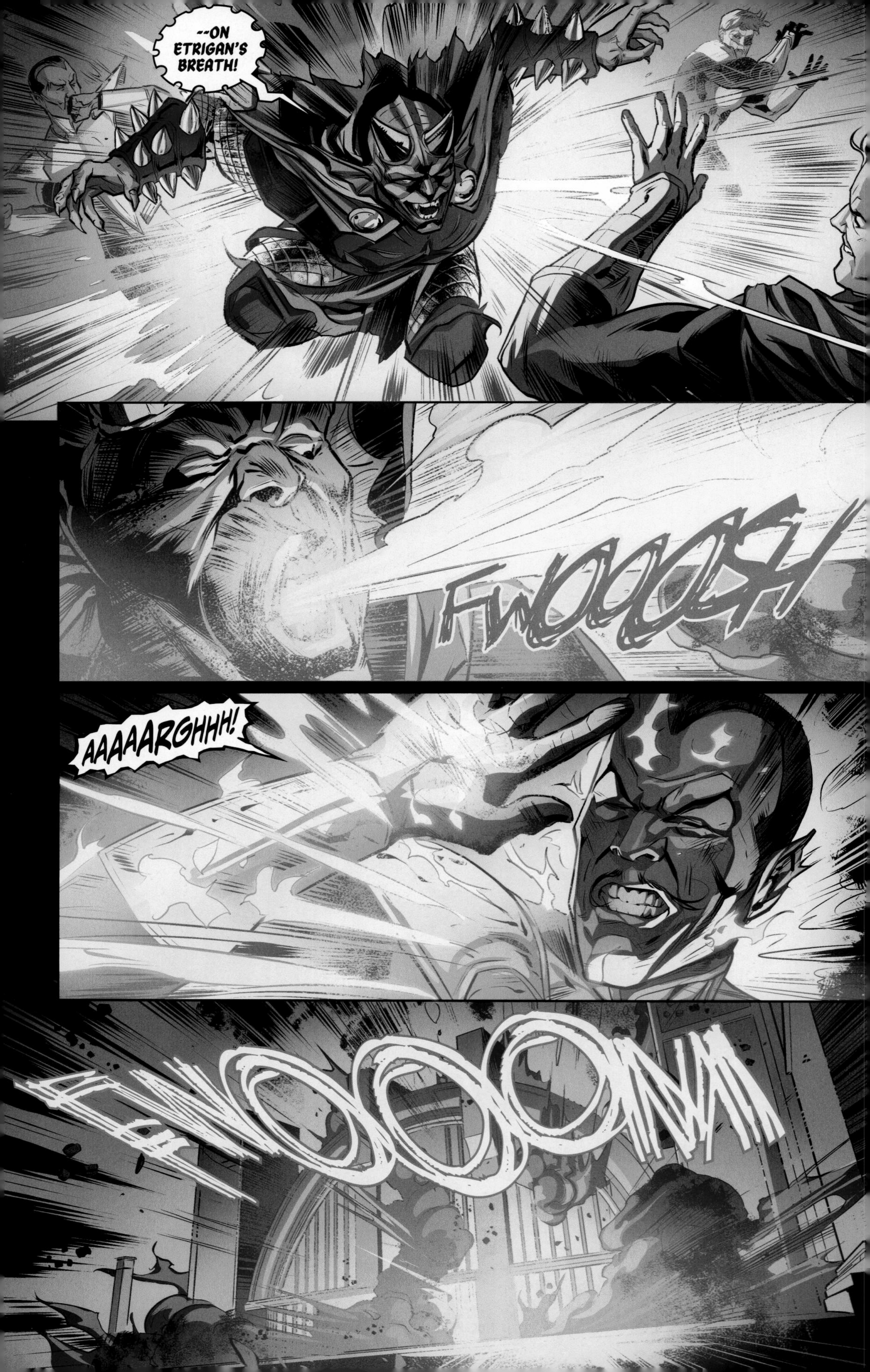
--ON ETRIGAN'S BREATH!
FWOOOSH
AAAAARGHHH!
FWOOOOM

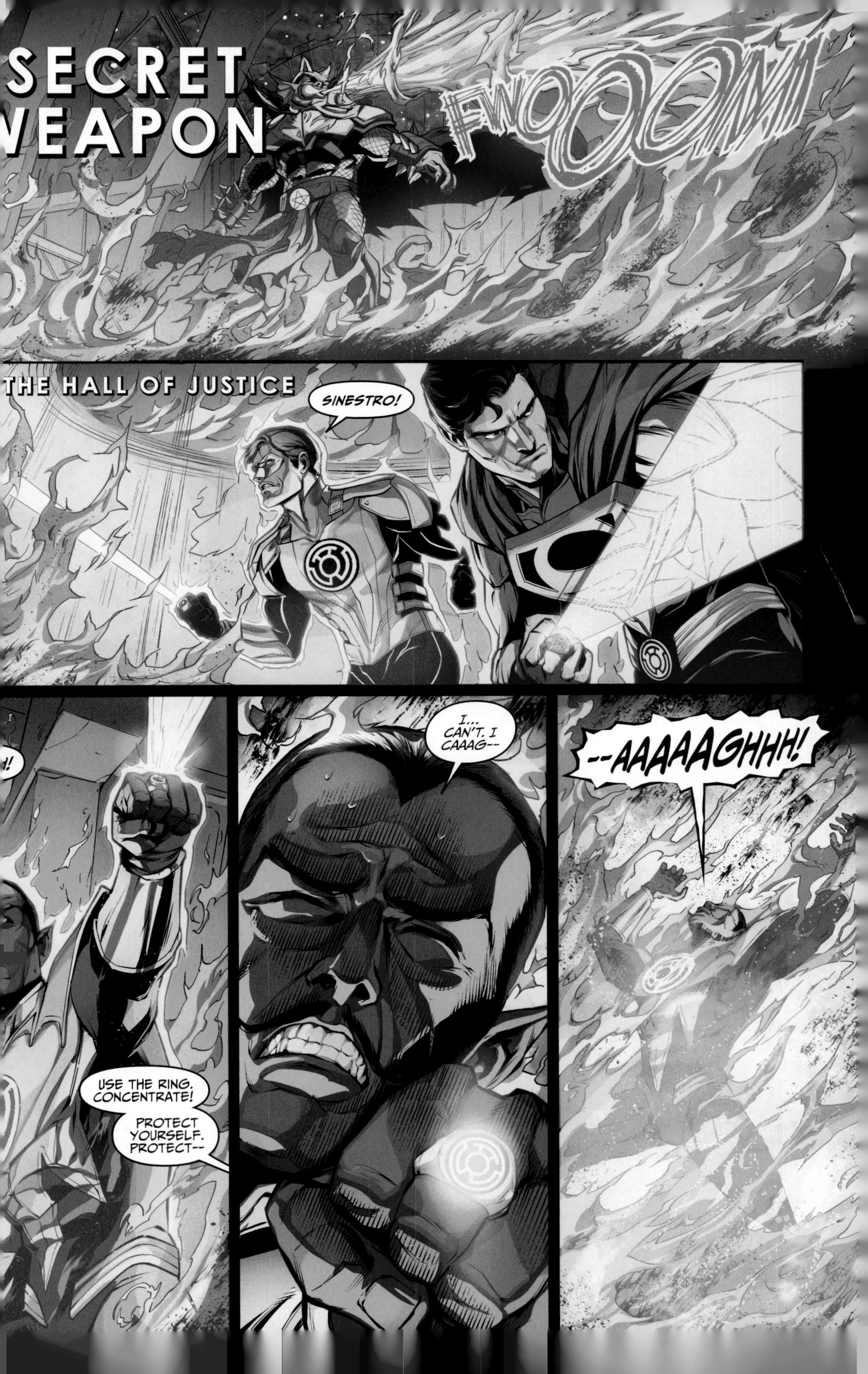
SECRET WEAPON
FWOOOOM!
THE HALL OF JUSTICE
SINESTRO!
USE THE RING. CONCENTRATE!
PROTECT YOURSELF. PROTECT--
I... CAN'T. I CAAAG--
--AAAAAGHHH!

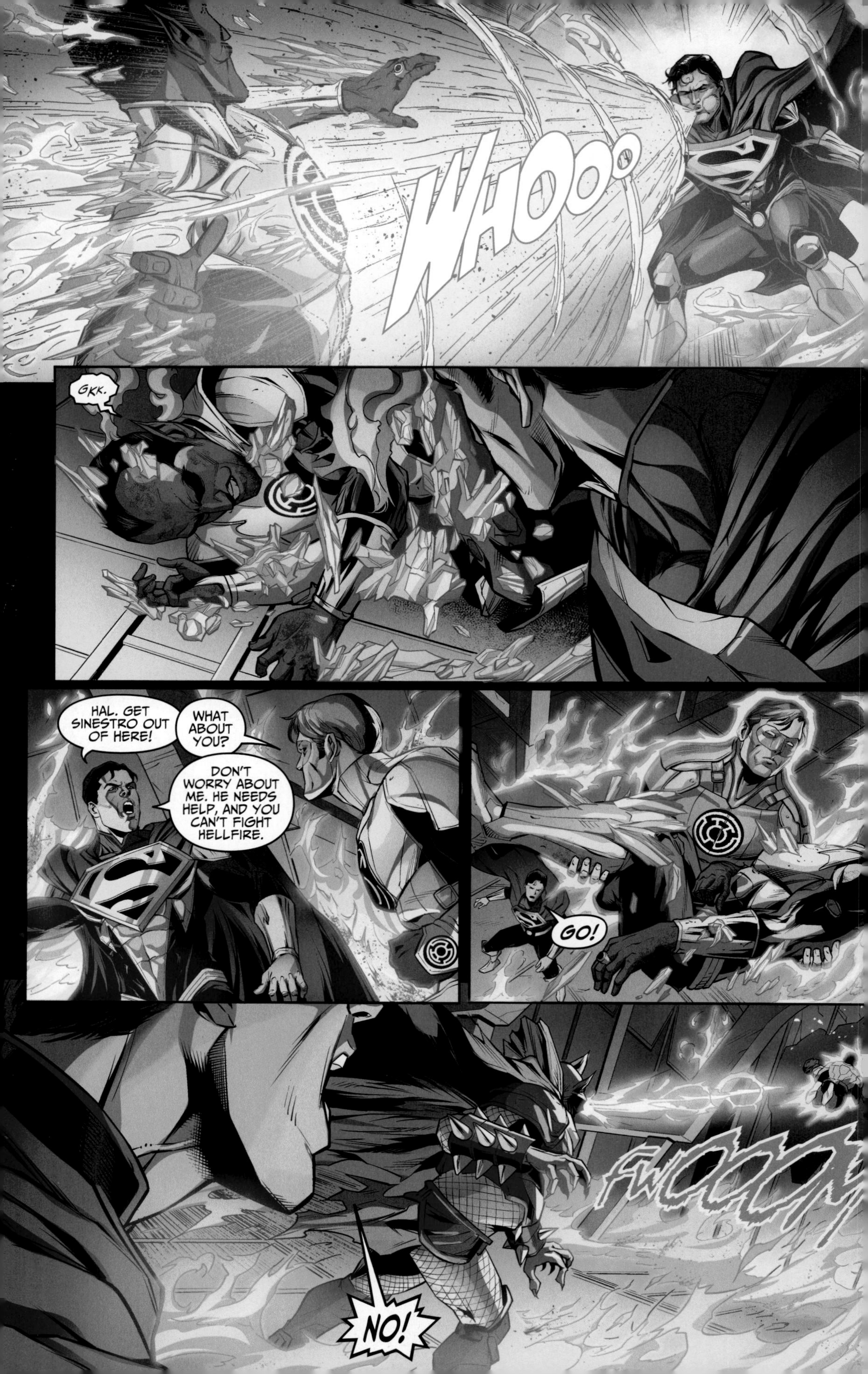
WHOOOO
GKK.
HAL. GET SINESTRO OUT OF HERE!
WHAT ABOUT YOU?
DON'T WORRY ABOUT ME. HE NEEDS HELP, AND YOU CAN'T FIGHT HELLFIRE.
GO!
FWOOOM
NO!

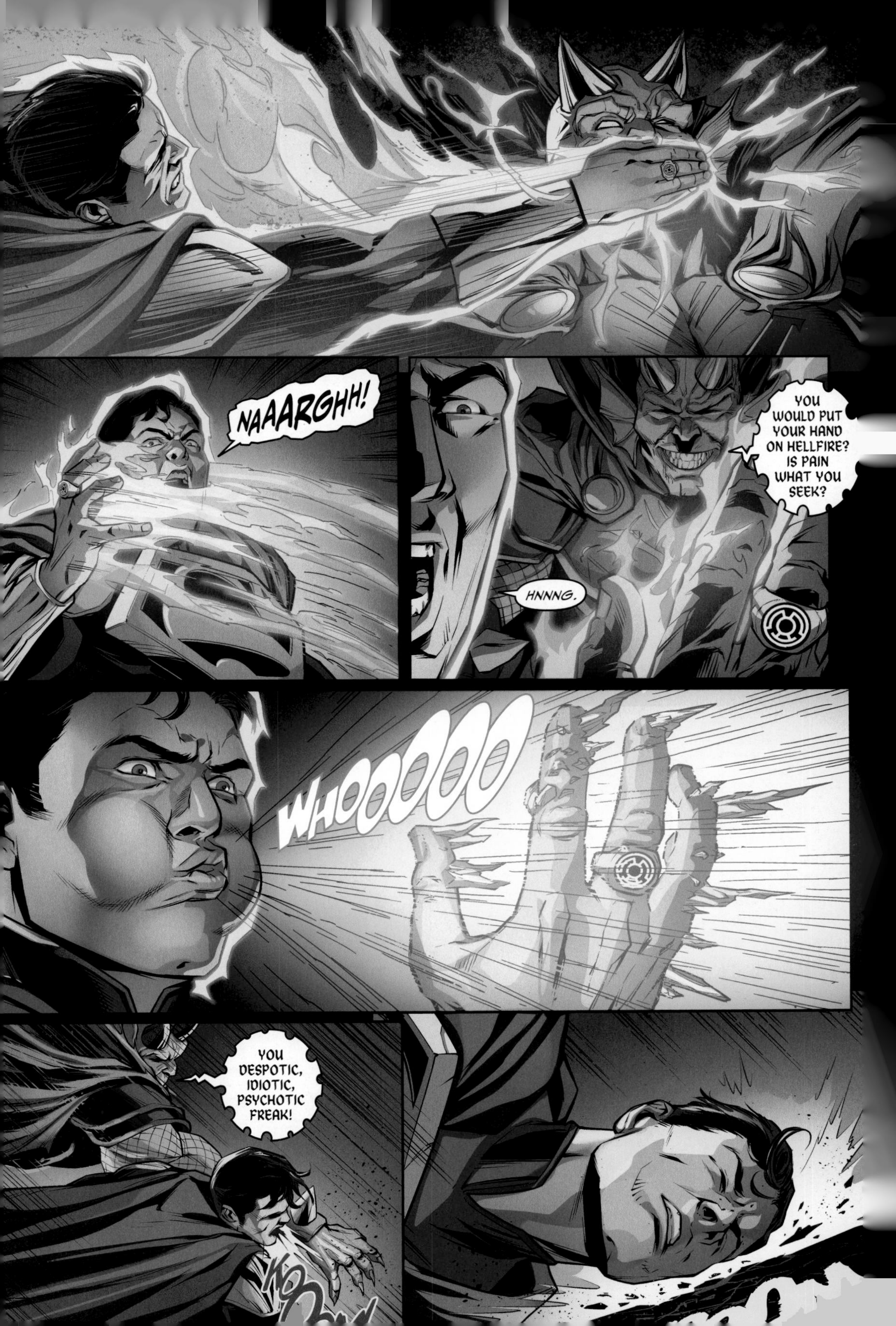

NAAARGHH!
YOU WOULD PUT YOUR HAND ON HELLFIRE? IS PAIN WHAT YOU SEEK?
HNNNG.
WHOOOOOO
YOU DESPOTIC, IDIOTIC, PSYCHOTIC FREAK!

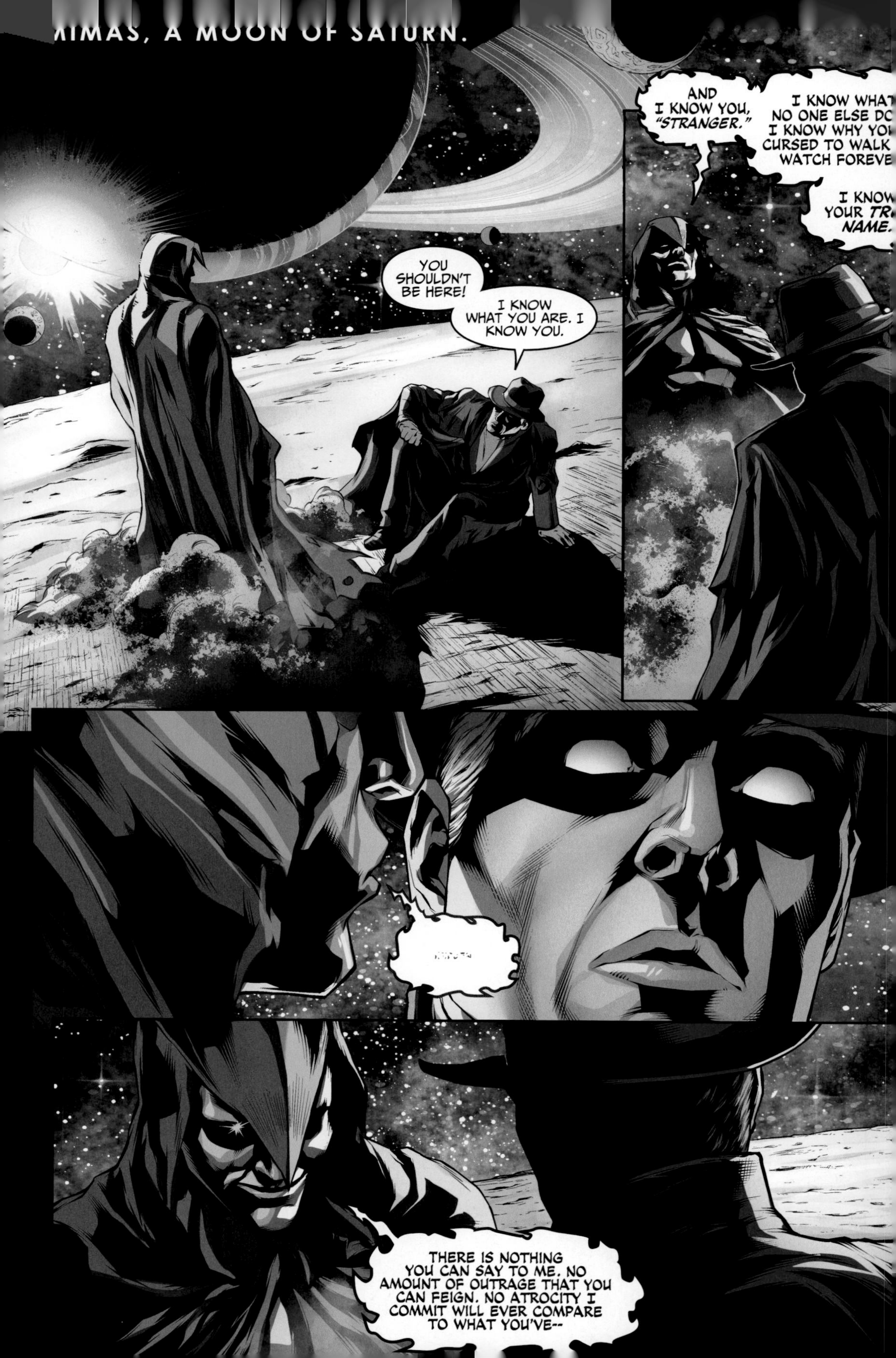
MIMAS, A MOON OF SATURN.
YOU SHOULDN'T BE HERE!
I KNOW WHAT YOU ARE. I KNOW YOU.
AND I KNOW YOU, "STRANGER."
I KNOW WHAT NO ONE ELSE DO I KNOW WHY YO CURSED TO WALK WATCH FOREVE
I KNOW YOUR TR NAME.
THERE IS NOTHING YOU CAN SAY TO ME. NO AMOUNT OF OUTRAGE THAT YOU CAN FEIGN. NO ATROCITY I COMMIT WILL EVER COMPARE TO WHAT YOU'VE--

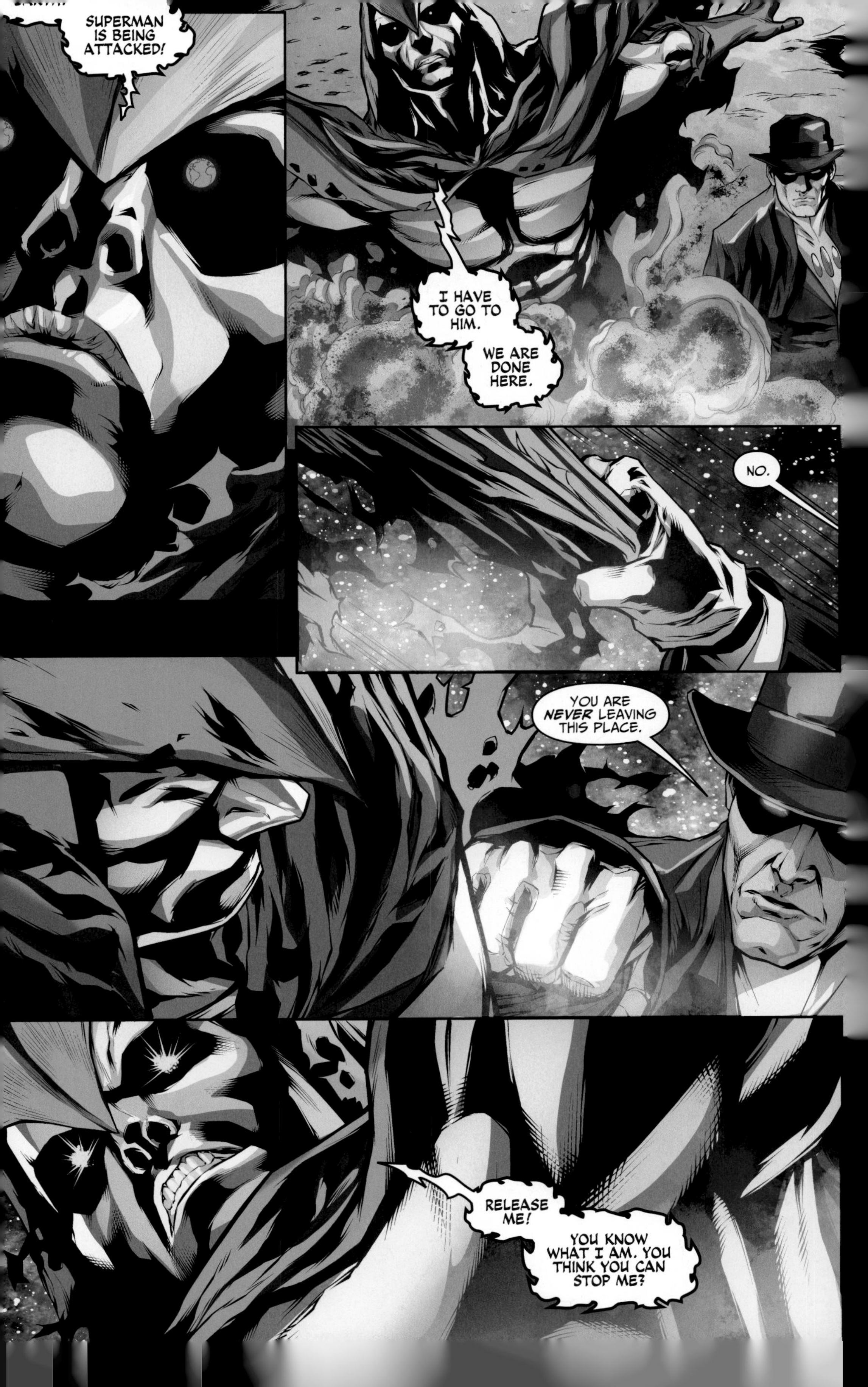
SUPERMAN IS BEING ATTACKED!
I HAVE TO GO TO HIM.
WE ARE DONE HERE.
NO.
YOU ARE *NEVER* LEAVING THIS PLACE.
RELEASE ME!
YOU KNOW WHAT I AM. YOU THINK YOU CAN STOP ME?

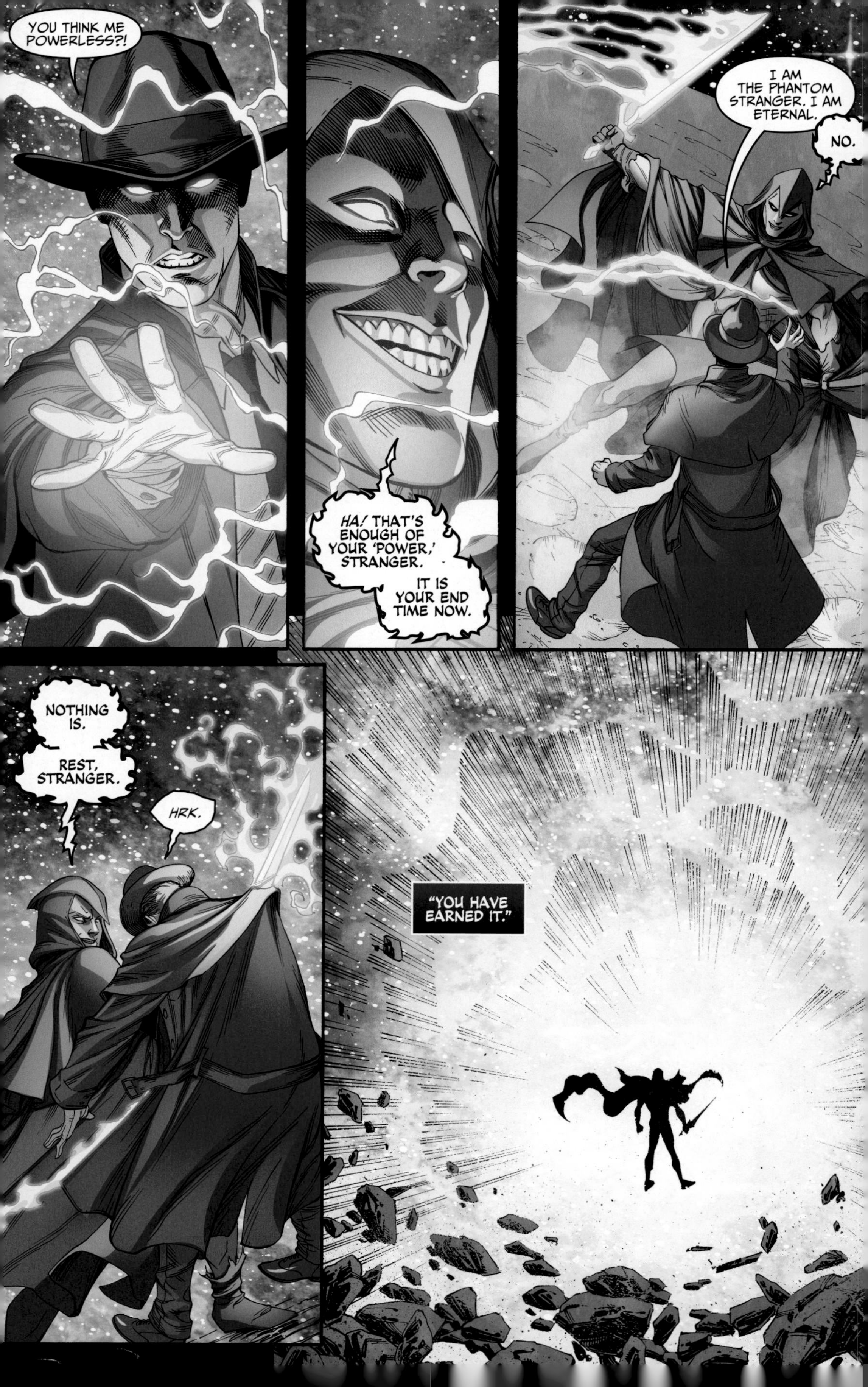
YOU THINK ME POWERLESS?!
HA! THAT'S ENOUGH OF YOUR 'POWER,' STRANGER.
IT IS YOUR END TIME NOW.
I AM THE PHANTOM STRANGER. I AM ETERNAL.
NO.
NOTHING IS.
REST, STRANGER.
HRK.
"YOU HAVE EARNED IT."

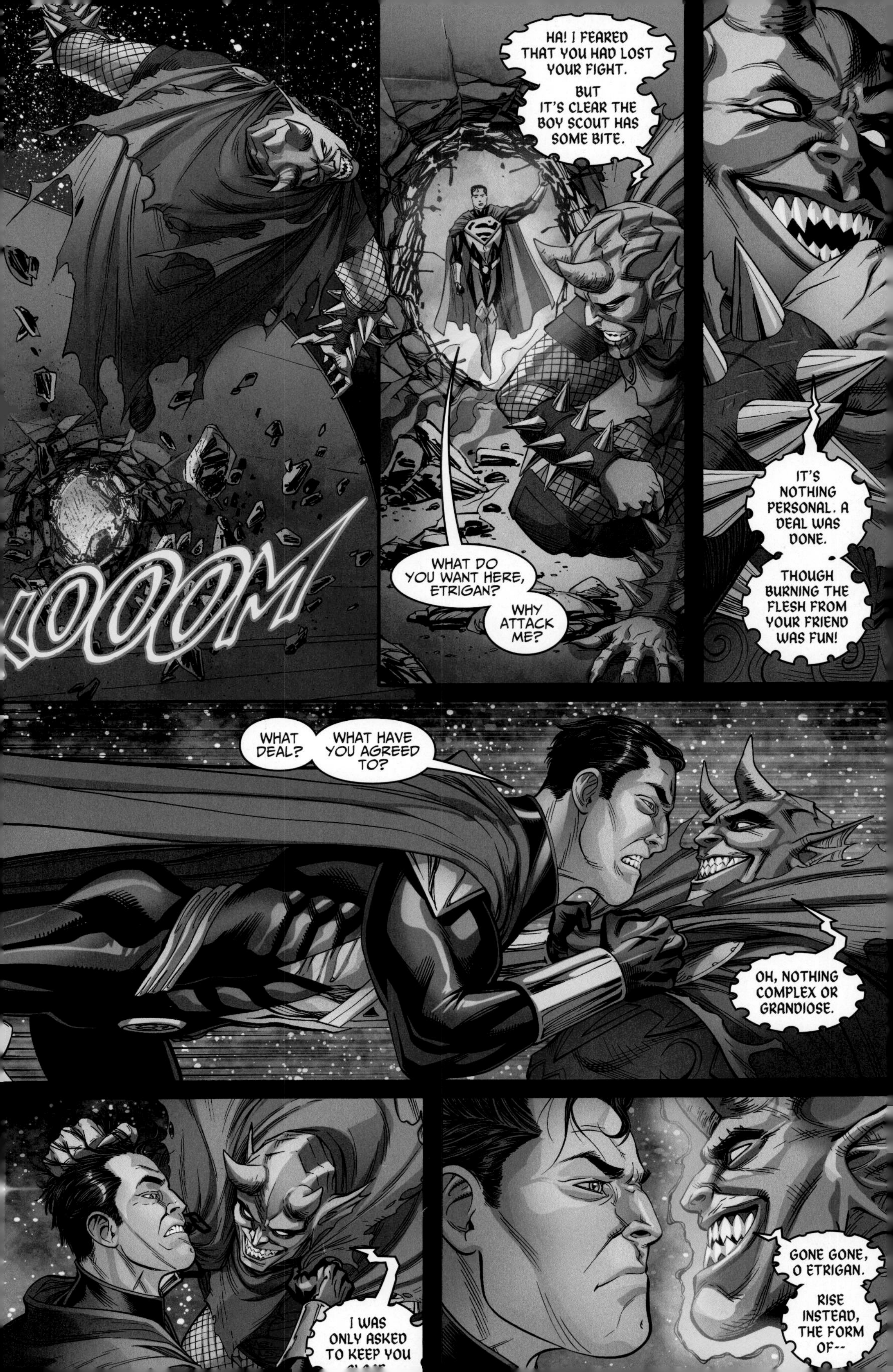
OOOM
HA! I FEARED THAT YOU HAD LOST YOUR FIGHT.
BUT IT'S CLEAR THE BOY SCOUT HAS SOME BITE.
WHAT DO YOU WANT HERE, ETRIGAN?
WHY ATTACK ME?
IT'S NOTHING PERSONAL. A DEAL WAS DONE.
THOUGH BURNING THE FLESH FROM YOUR FRIEND WAS FUN!
WHAT DEAL?
WHAT HAVE YOU AGREED TO?
OH, NOTHING COMPLEX OR GRANDIOSE.
I WAS ONLY ASKED TO KEEP YOU
GONE GONE, O ETRIGAN.
RISE INSTEAD, THE FORM OF--

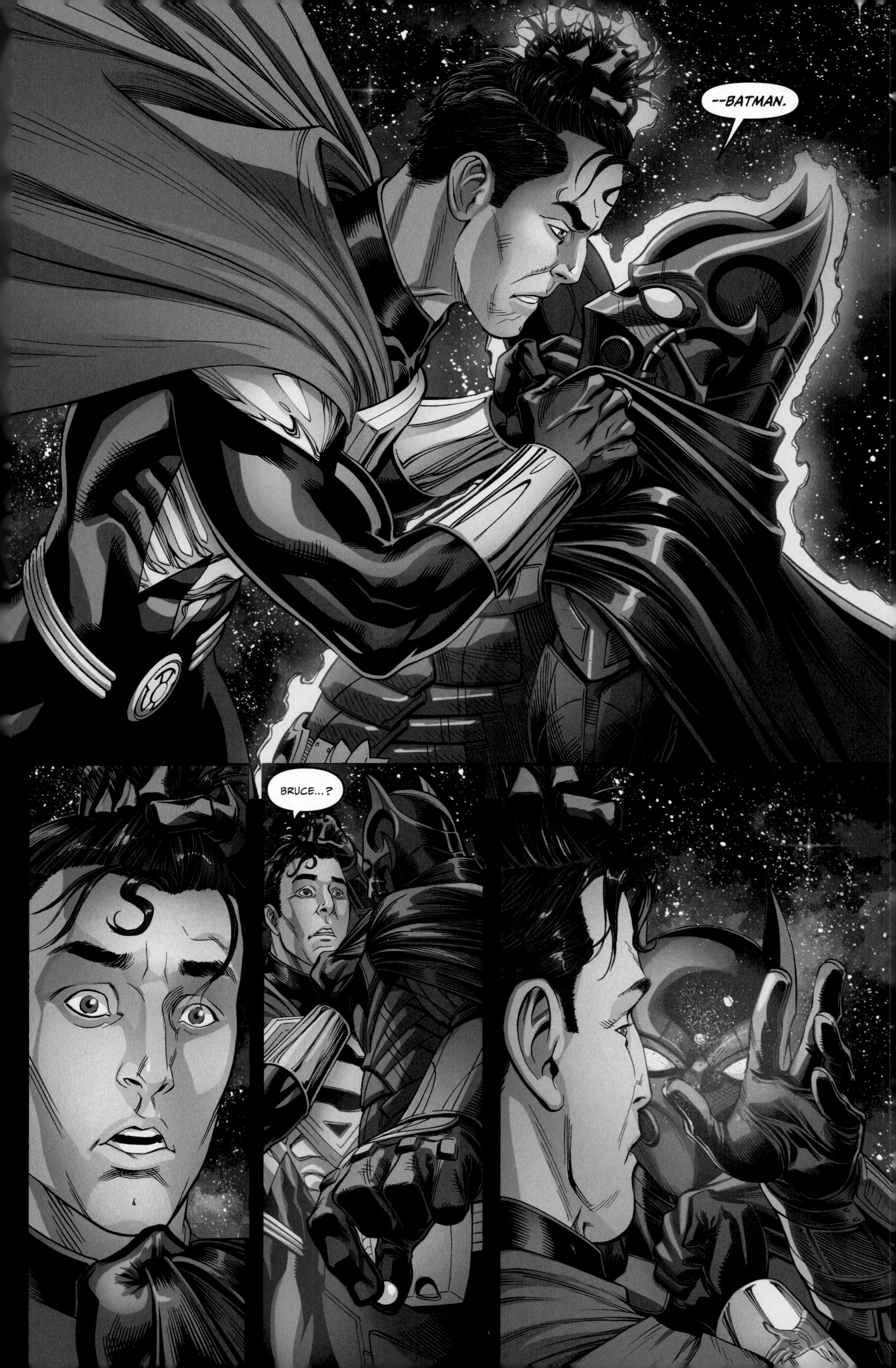
--BATMAN.
BRUCE...?

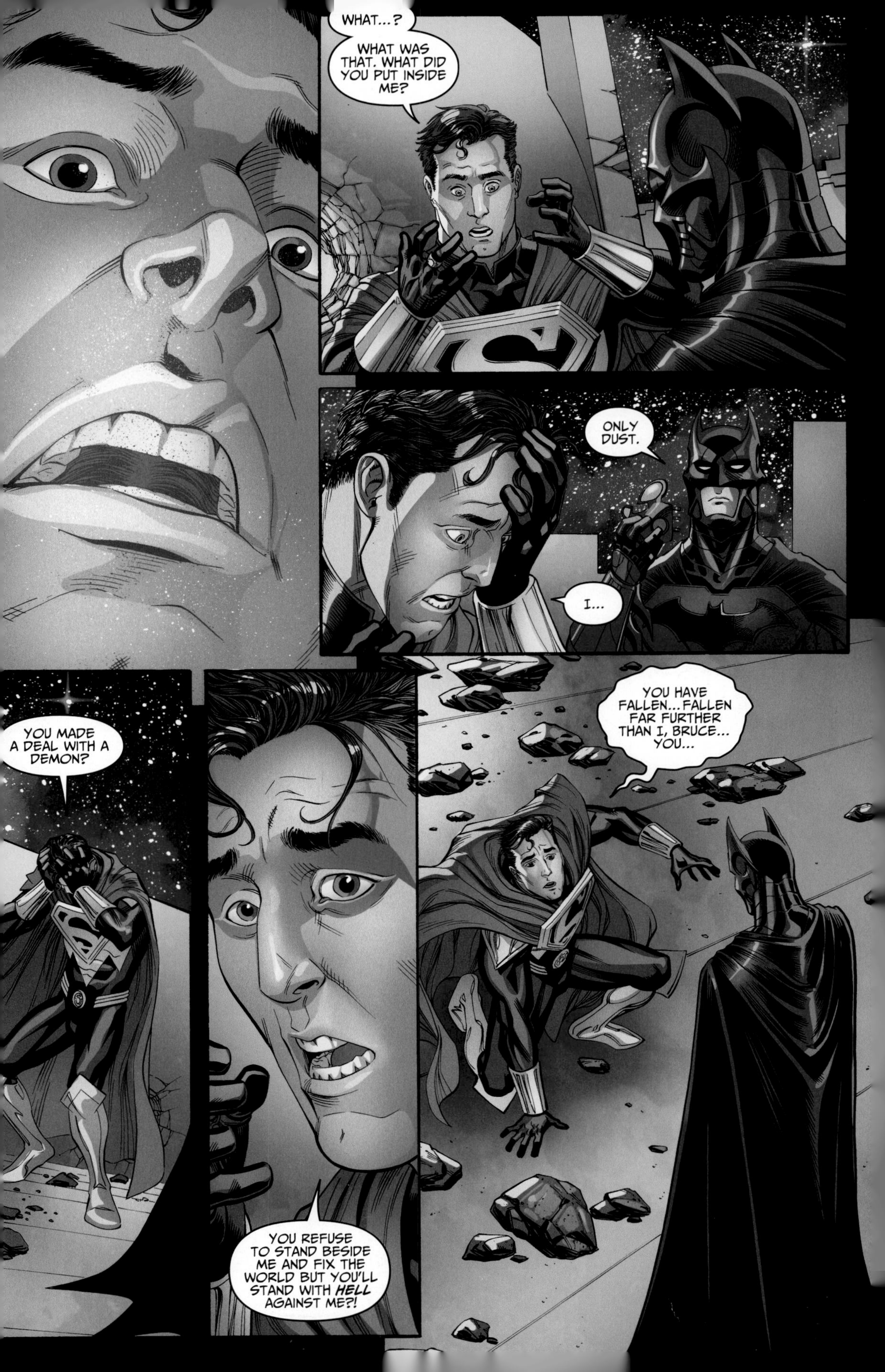
WHAT...?
WHAT WAS THAT. WHAT DID YOU PUT INSIDE ME?
ONLY DUST.
I...
YOU MADE A DEAL WITH A DEMON?
YOU REFUSE TO STAND BESIDE ME AND FIX THE WORLD BUT YOU'LL STAND WITH *HELL* AGAINST ME?!
YOU HAVE FALLEN...FALLEN FAR FURTHER THAN I, BRUCE... YOU...

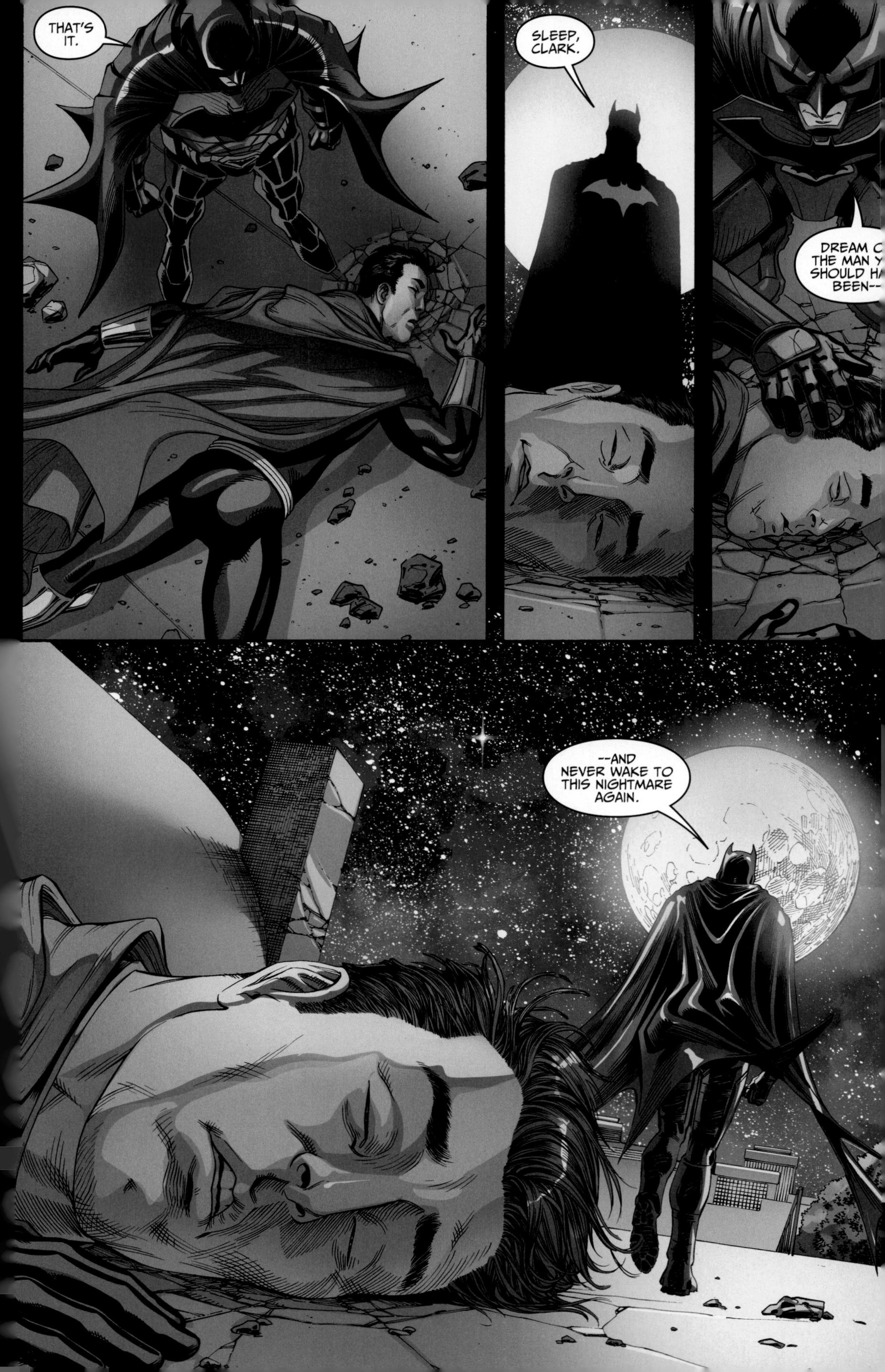
THAT'S IT.
SLEEP, CLARK.
DREAM THE MAN SHOULD BEEN--
--AND NEVER WAKE TO THIS NIGHTMARE AGAIN.

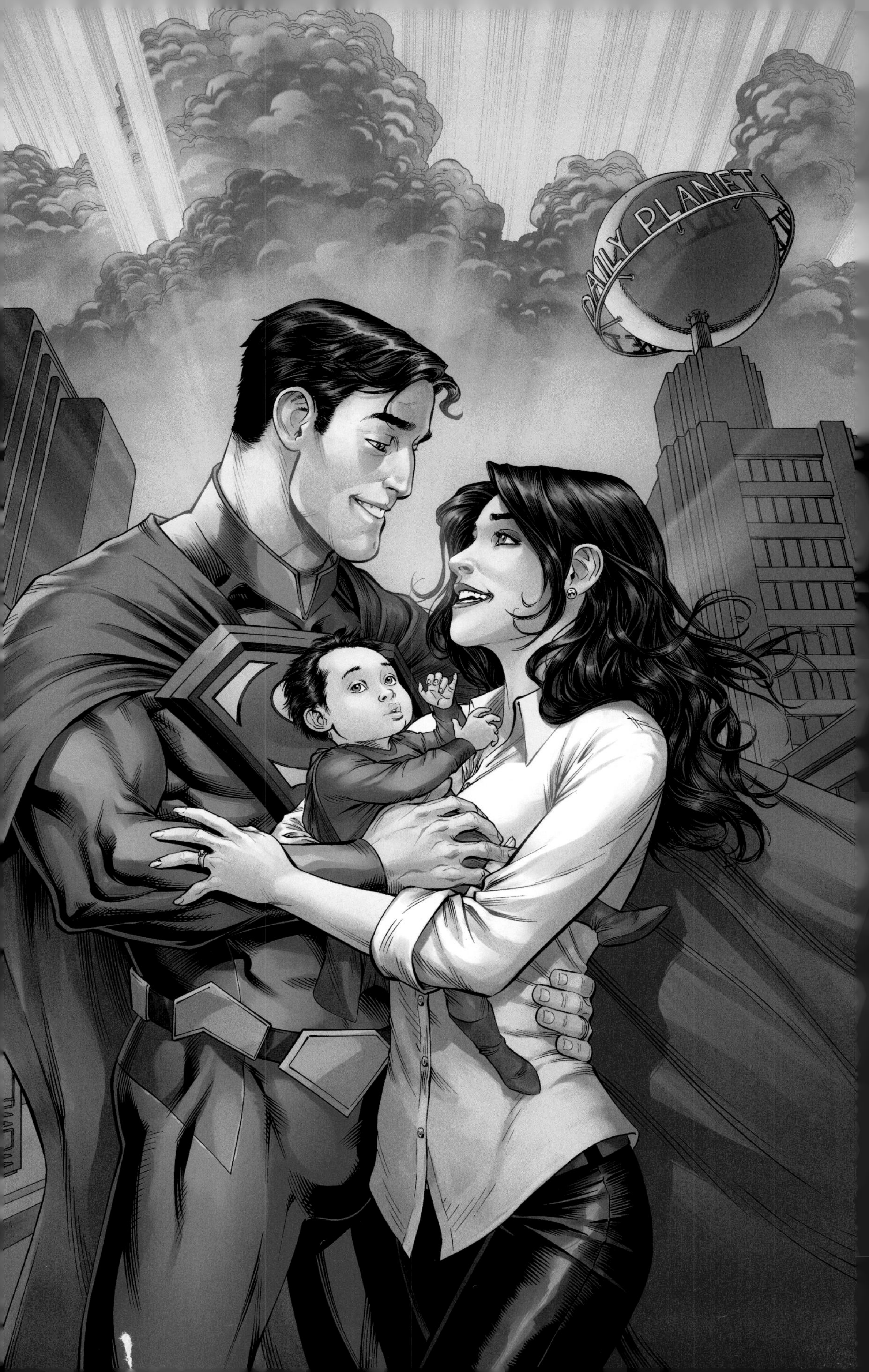
DAILY PLANET

"For the Man Who's Lost Everything" **Bruno Redondo, Xermanico, & Juan Albarran** Artists
Rex Lokus Colorist Cover Art by **Mike S. Miller & J. Nanjan**

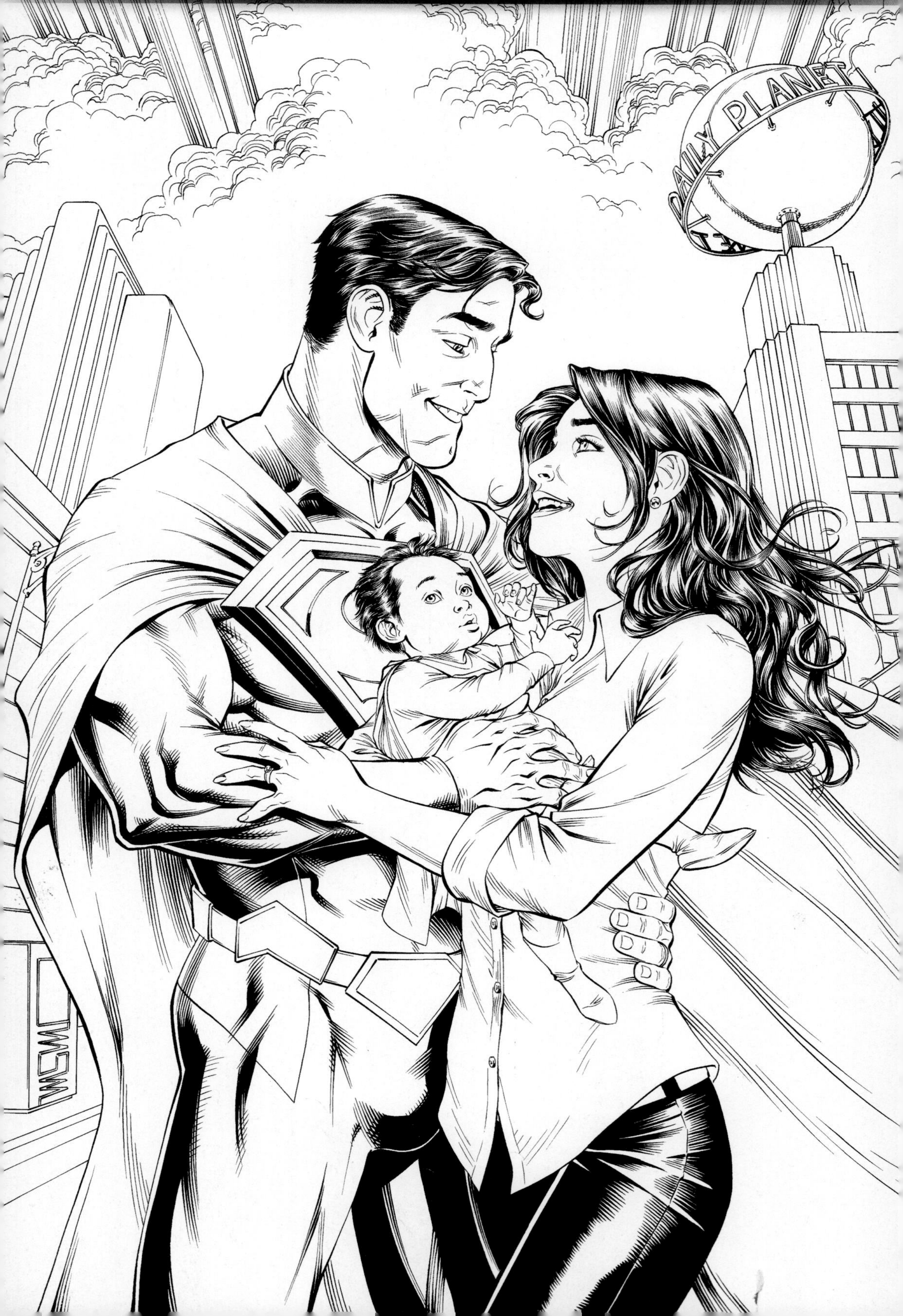
AILY PLANET

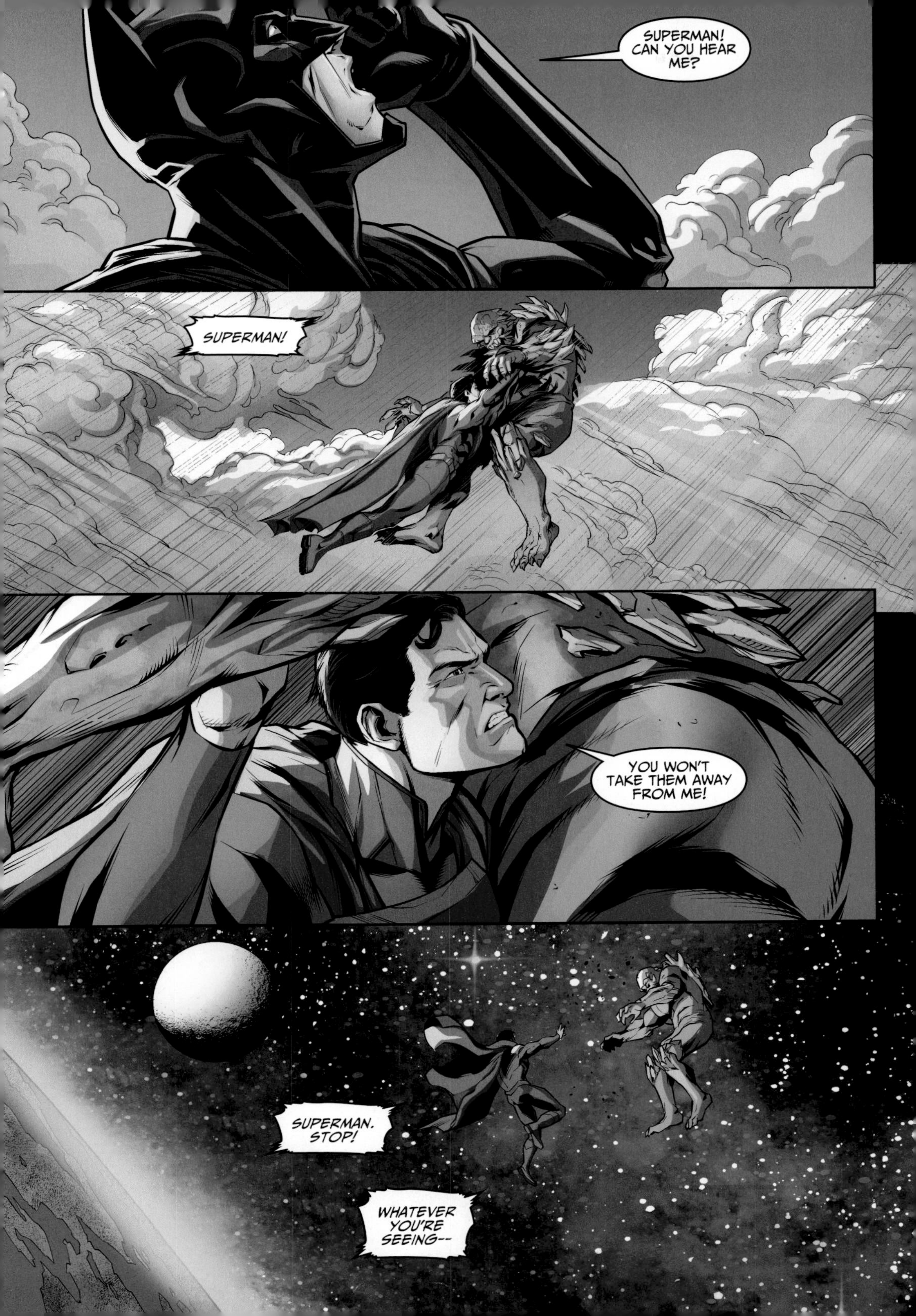
SUPERMAN! CAN YOU HEAR ME?
SUPERMAN!
YOU WON'T TAKE THEM AWAY FROM ME!
SUPERMAN. STOP!
WHATEVER YOU'RE SEEING--

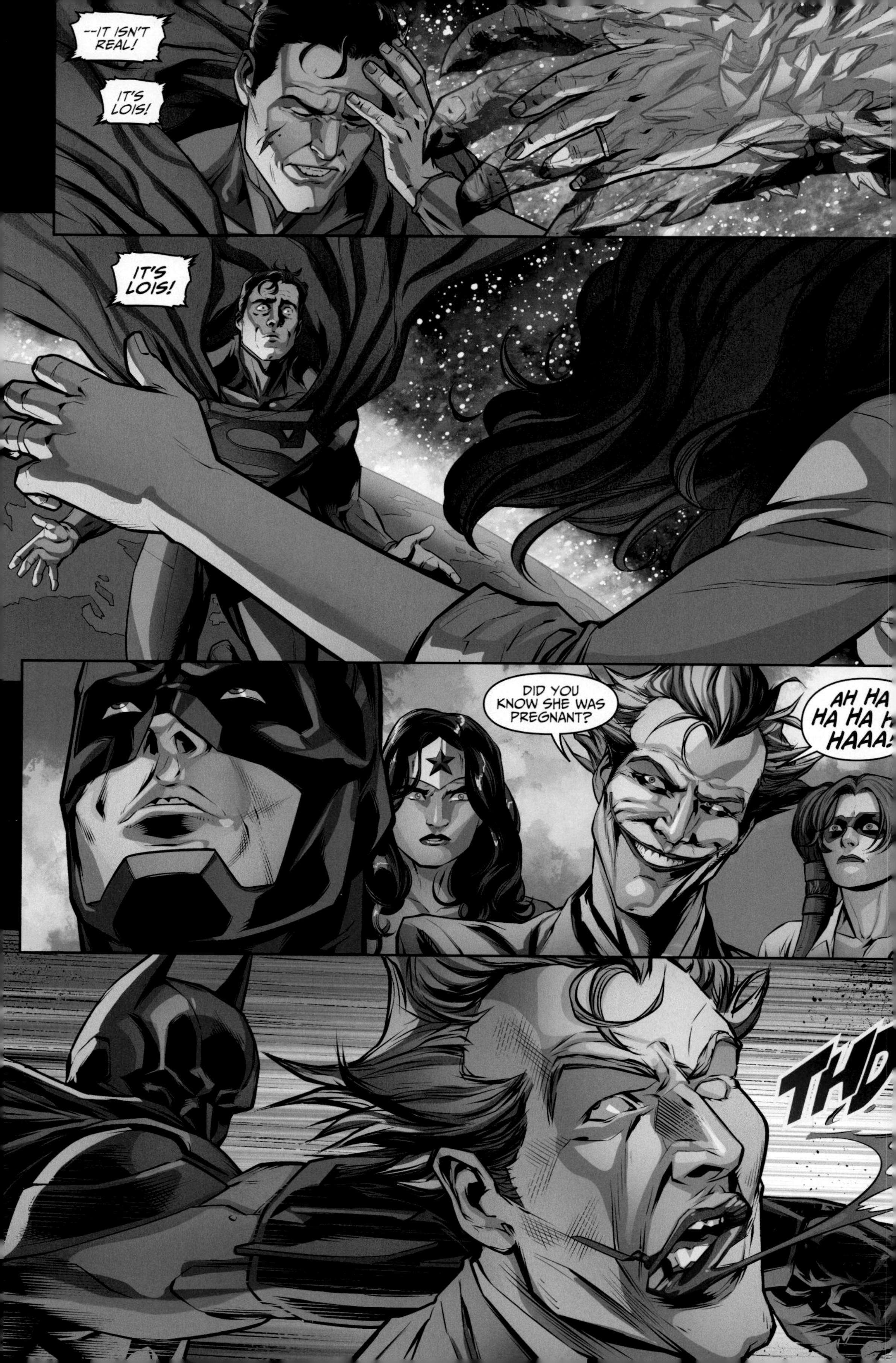
--IT ISN'T REAL!
IT'S LOIS!
IT'S LOIS!
DID YOU KNOW SHE WAS PREGNANT?
AH HA HA HA H HAAA!

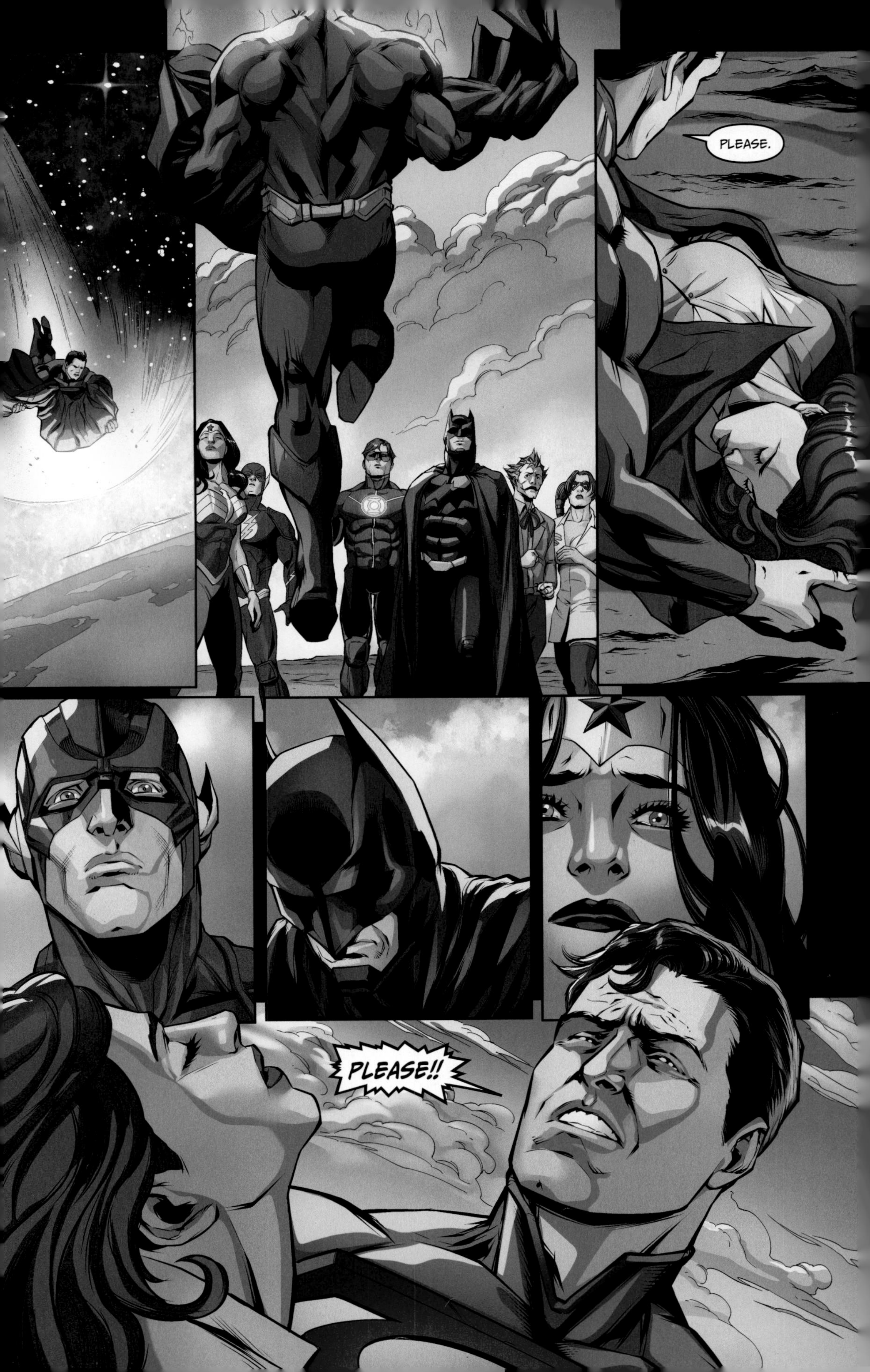
PLEASE.
PLEASE!!

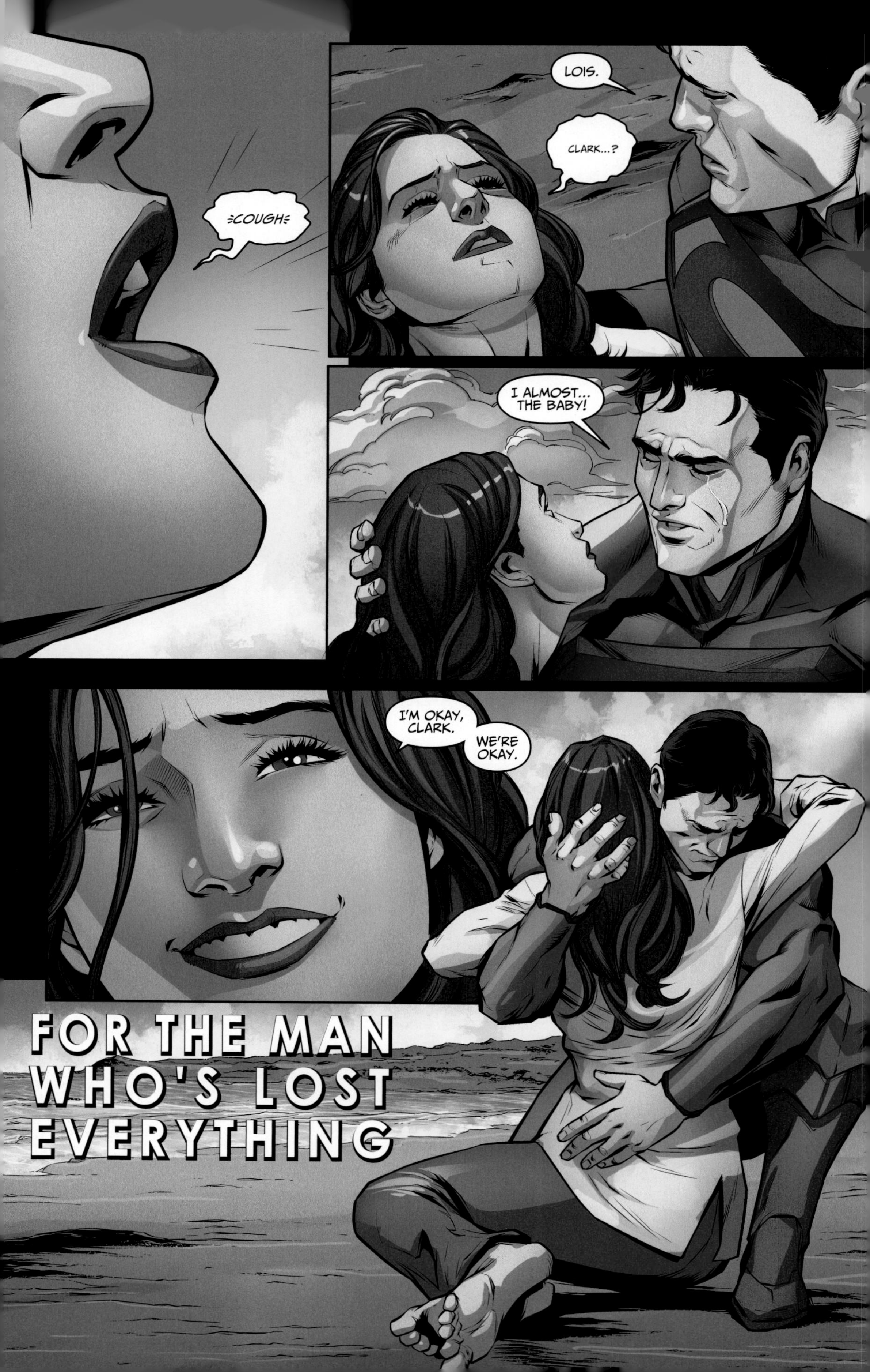

COUGH
LOIS.
CLARK...?
I ALMOST... THE BABY!
I'M OKAY, CLARK.
WE'RE OKAY.
FOR THE MAN WHO'S LOST EVERYTHING

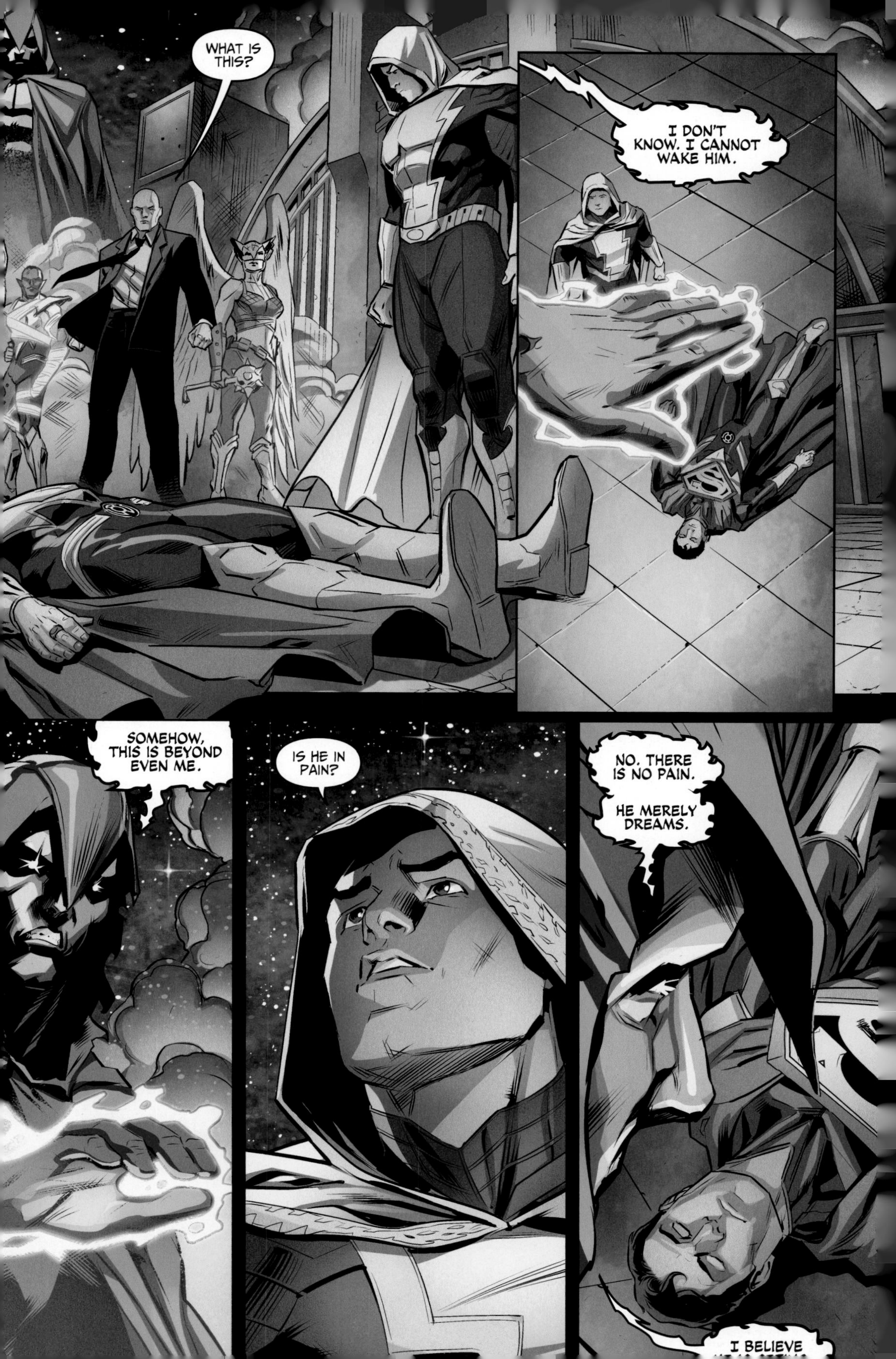
WHAT IS THIS?
I DON'T KNOW. I CANNOT WAKE HIM.
SOMEHOW, THIS IS BEYOND EVEN ME.
IS HE IN PAIN?
NO. THERE IS NO PAIN.
HE MERELY DREAMS.
I BELIEVE

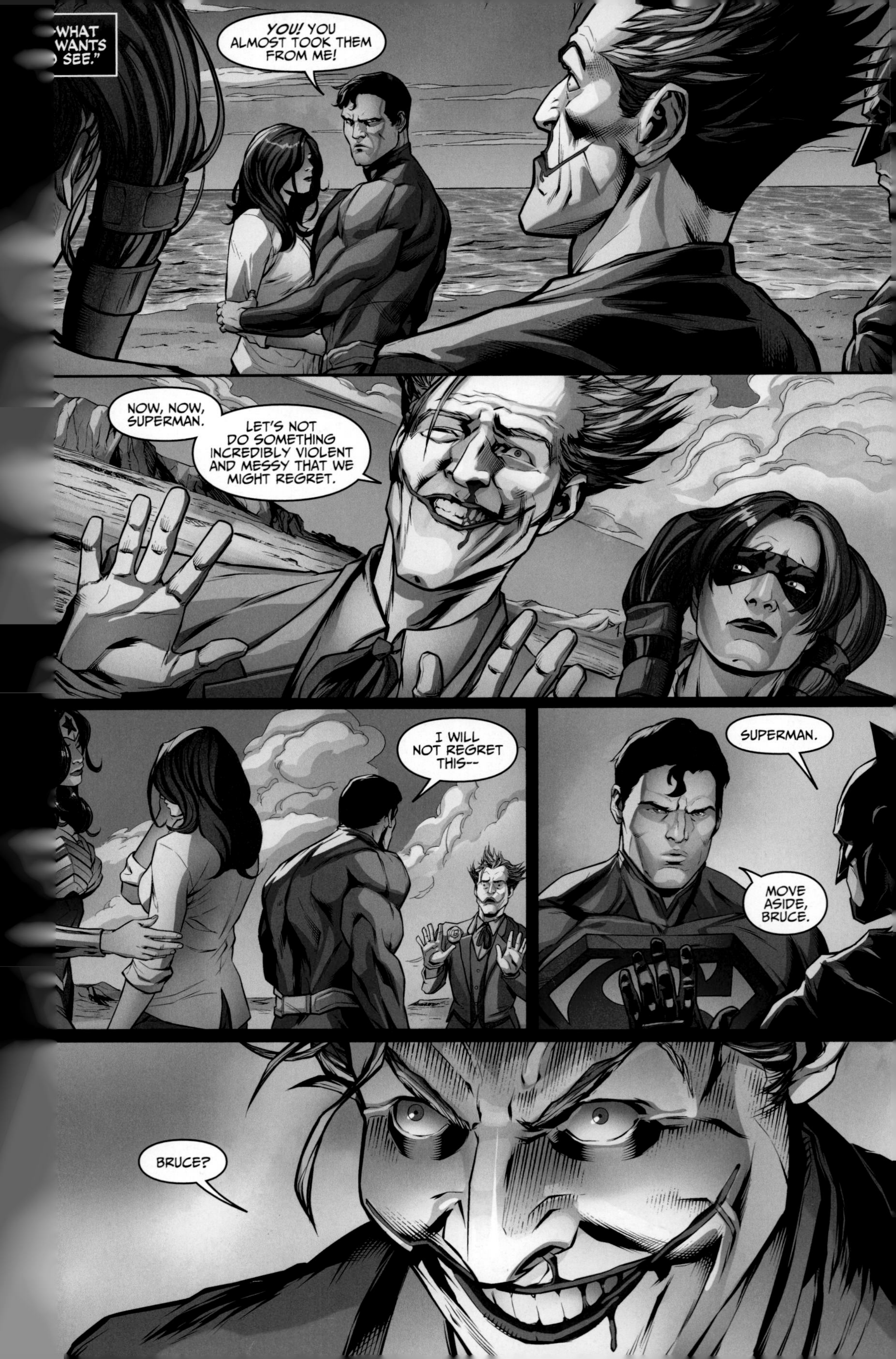

"WHAT WANTS SEE."
YOU! YOU ALMOST TOOK THEM FROM ME!
NOW, NOW, SUPERMAN.
LET'S NOT DO SOMETHING INCREDIBLY VIOLENT AND MESSY THAT WE MIGHT REGRET.
I WILL NOT REGRET THIS--
SUPERMAN.
MOVE ASIDE, BRUCE.
BRUCE?

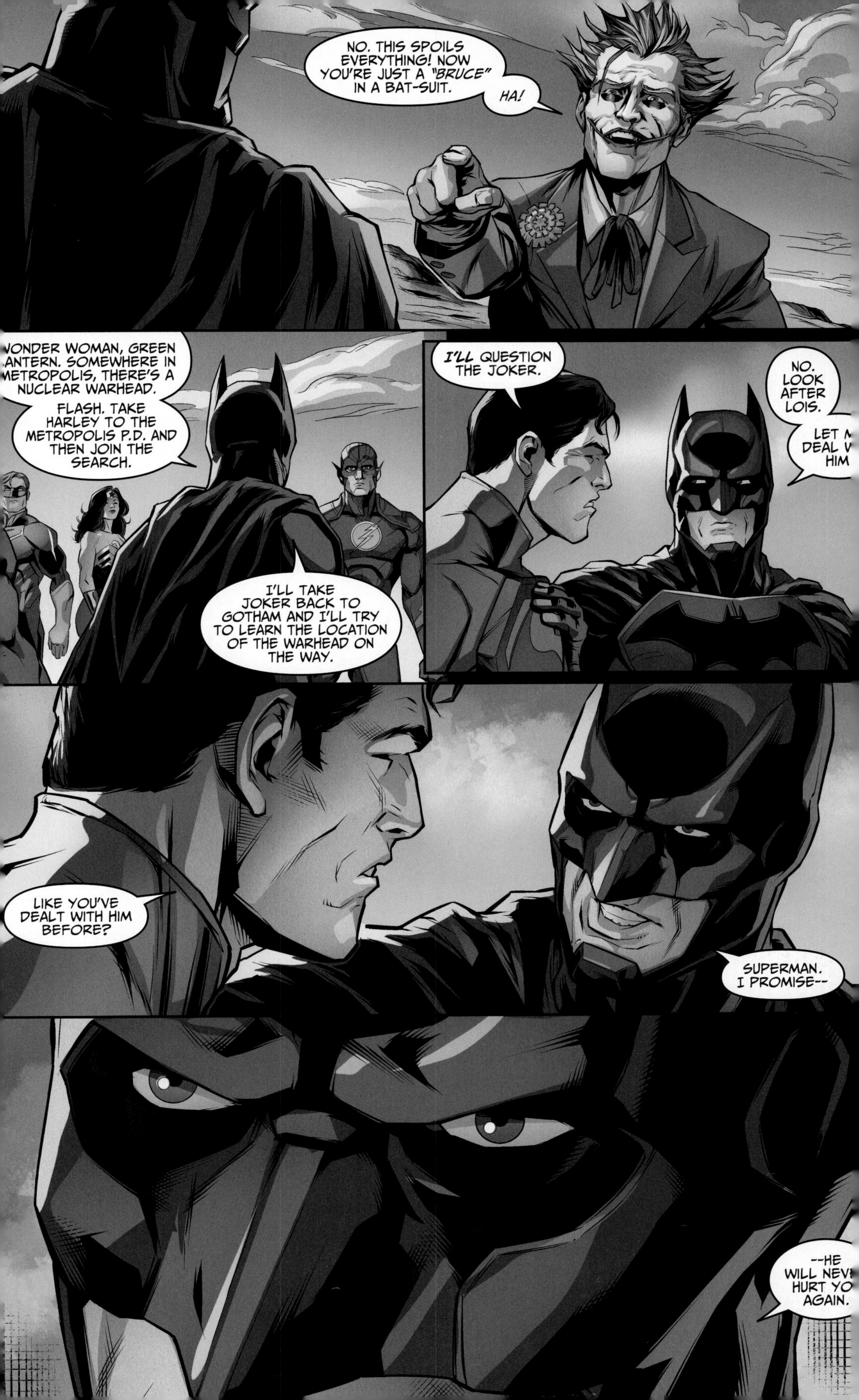
NO. THIS SPOILS EVERYTHING! NOW YOU'RE JUST A "BRUCE" IN A BAT-SUIT.
HA!
WONDER WOMAN, GREEN ANTERN. SOMEWHERE IN METROPOLIS, THERE'S A NUCLEAR WARHEAD.
FLASH. TAKE HARLEY TO THE METROPOLIS P.D. AND THEN JOIN THE SEARCH.
I'LL TAKE JOKER BACK TO GOTHAM AND I'LL TRY TO LEARN THE LOCATION OF THE WARHEAD ON THE WAY.
I'LL QUESTION THE JOKER.
NO. LOOK AFTER LOIS.
LET M DEAL W HIM
LIKE YOU'VE DEALT WITH HIM BEFORE?
SUPERMAN. I PROMISE--
--HE WILL NEVE HURT YO AGAIN.

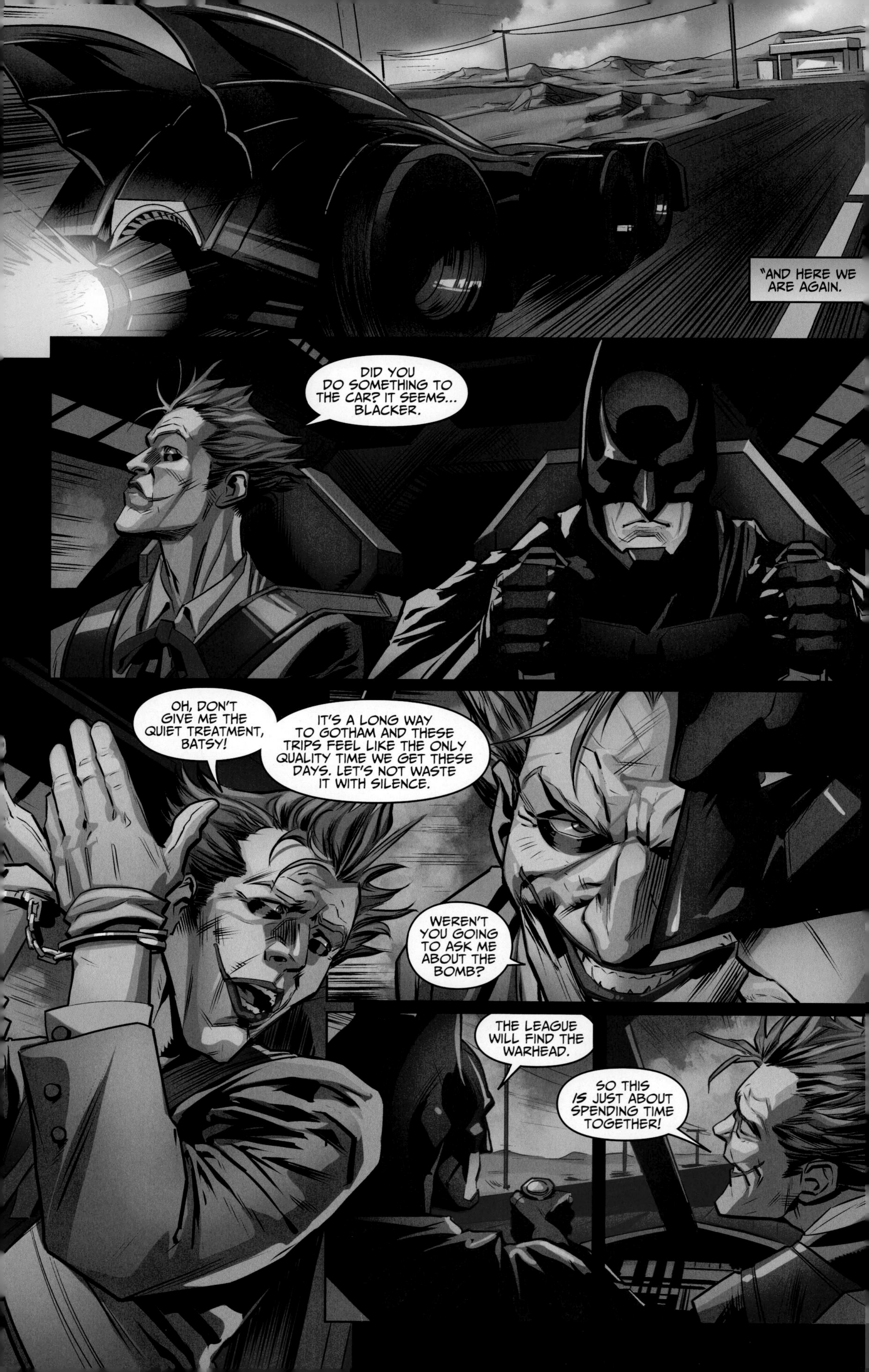
"AND HERE WE ARE AGAIN.
DID YOU DO SOMETHING TO THE CAR? IT SEEMS... BLACKER.
OH, DON'T GIVE ME THE QUIET TREATMENT, BATSY!
IT'S A LONG WAY TO GOTHAM AND THESE TRIPS FEEL LIKE THE ONLY QUALITY TIME WE GET THESE DAYS. LET'S NOT WASTE IT WITH SILENCE.
WEREN'T YOU GOING TO ASK ME ABOUT THE BOMB?
THE LEAGUE WILL FIND THE WARHEAD.
SO THIS *IS* JUST ABOUT SPENDING TIME TOGETHER!

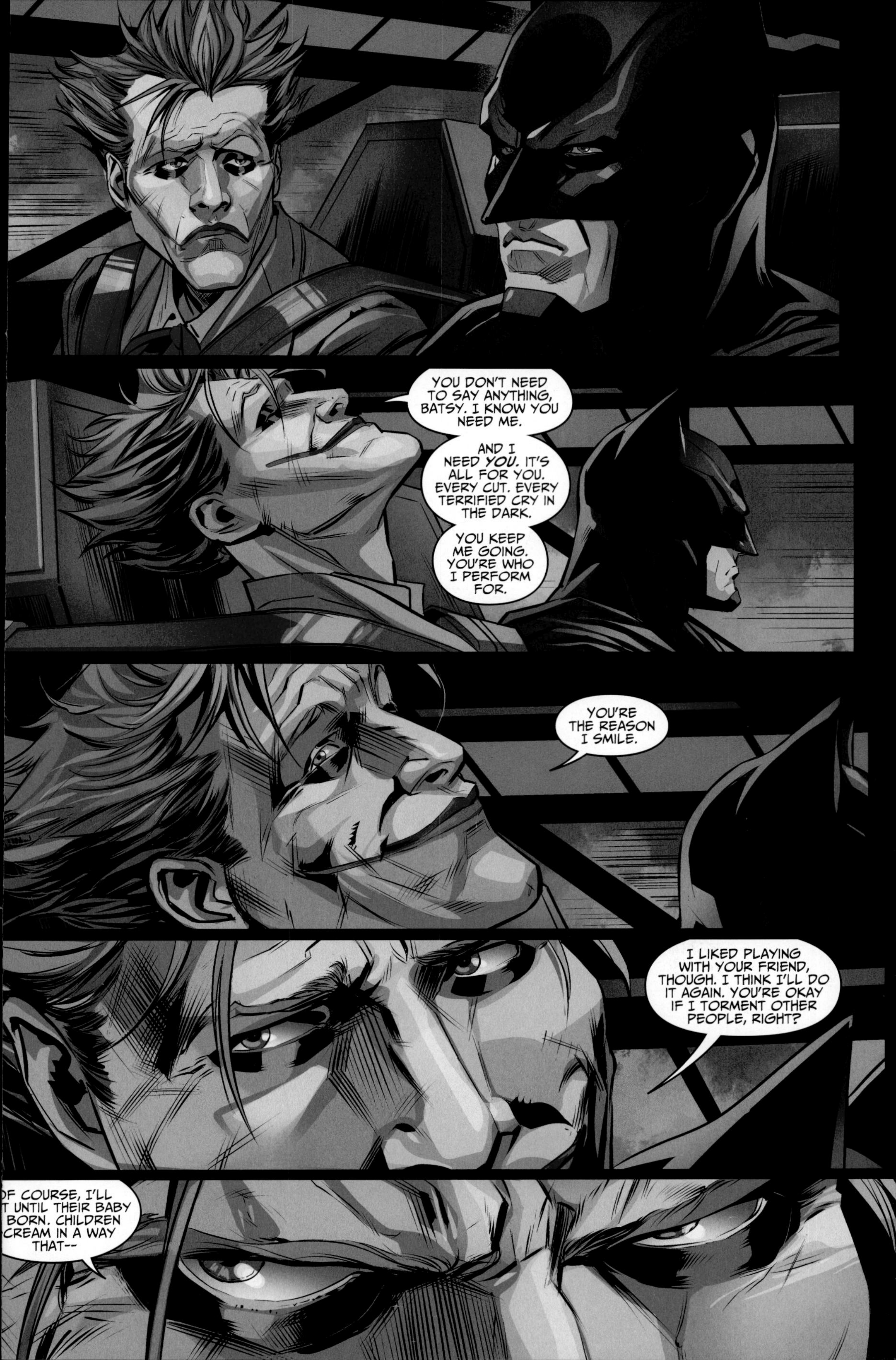

YOU DON'T NEED TO SAY ANYTHING, BATSY. I KNOW YOU NEED ME.
AND I NEED *YOU.* IT'S ALL FOR YOU. EVERY CUT. EVERY TERRIFIED CRY IN THE DARK.
YOU KEEP ME GOING. YOU'RE WHO I PERFORM FOR.
YOU'RE THE REASON I SMILE.
I LIKED PLAYING WITH YOUR FRIEND, THOUGH. I THINK I'LL DO IT AGAIN. YOU'RE OKAY IF I TORMENT OTHER PEOPLE, RIGHT?
OF COURSE, I'LL T UNTIL THEIR BABY BORN. CHILDREN CREAM IN A WAY THAT--

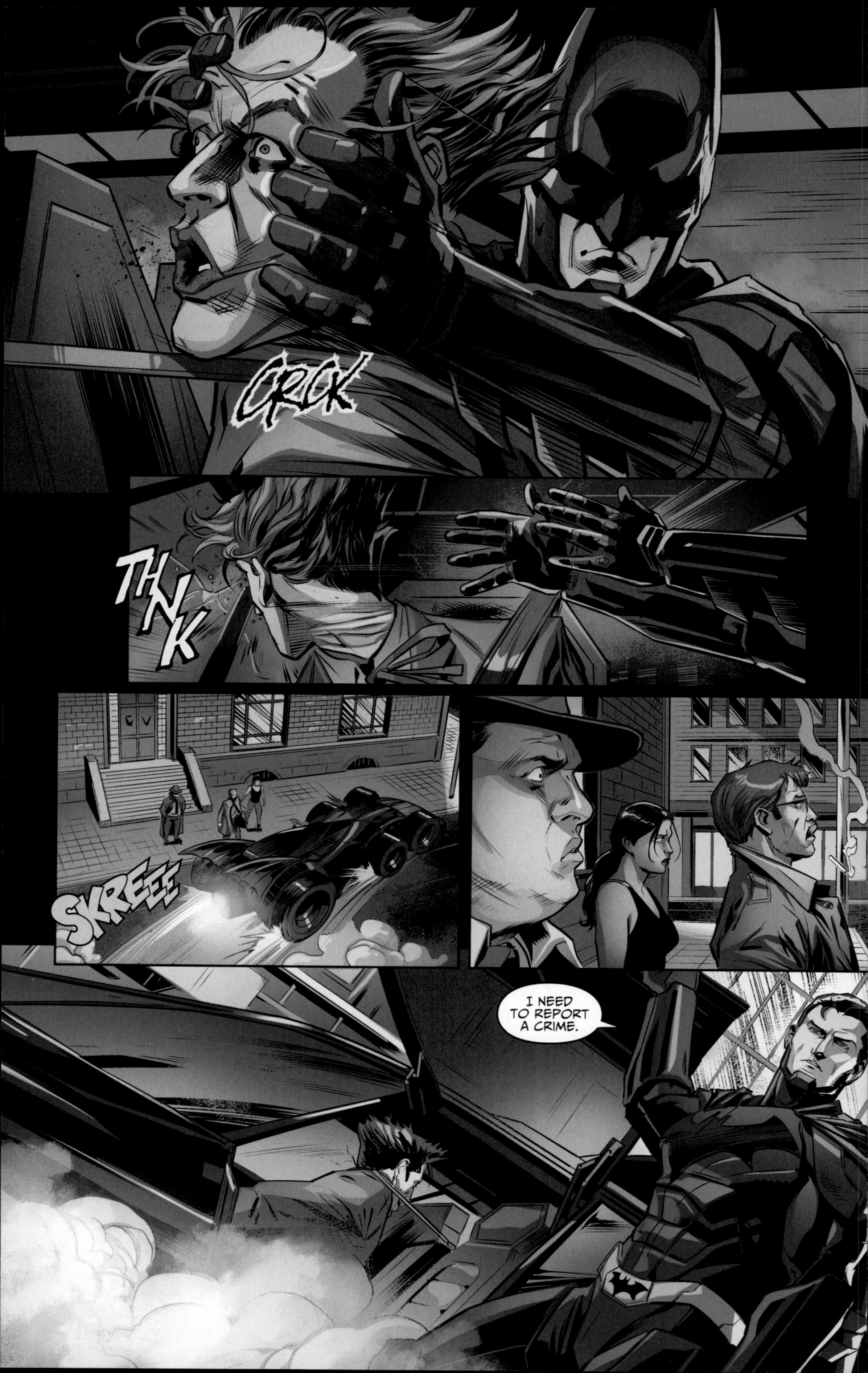
CRICK
THNK
SKREEE
I NEED TO REPORT A CRIME.

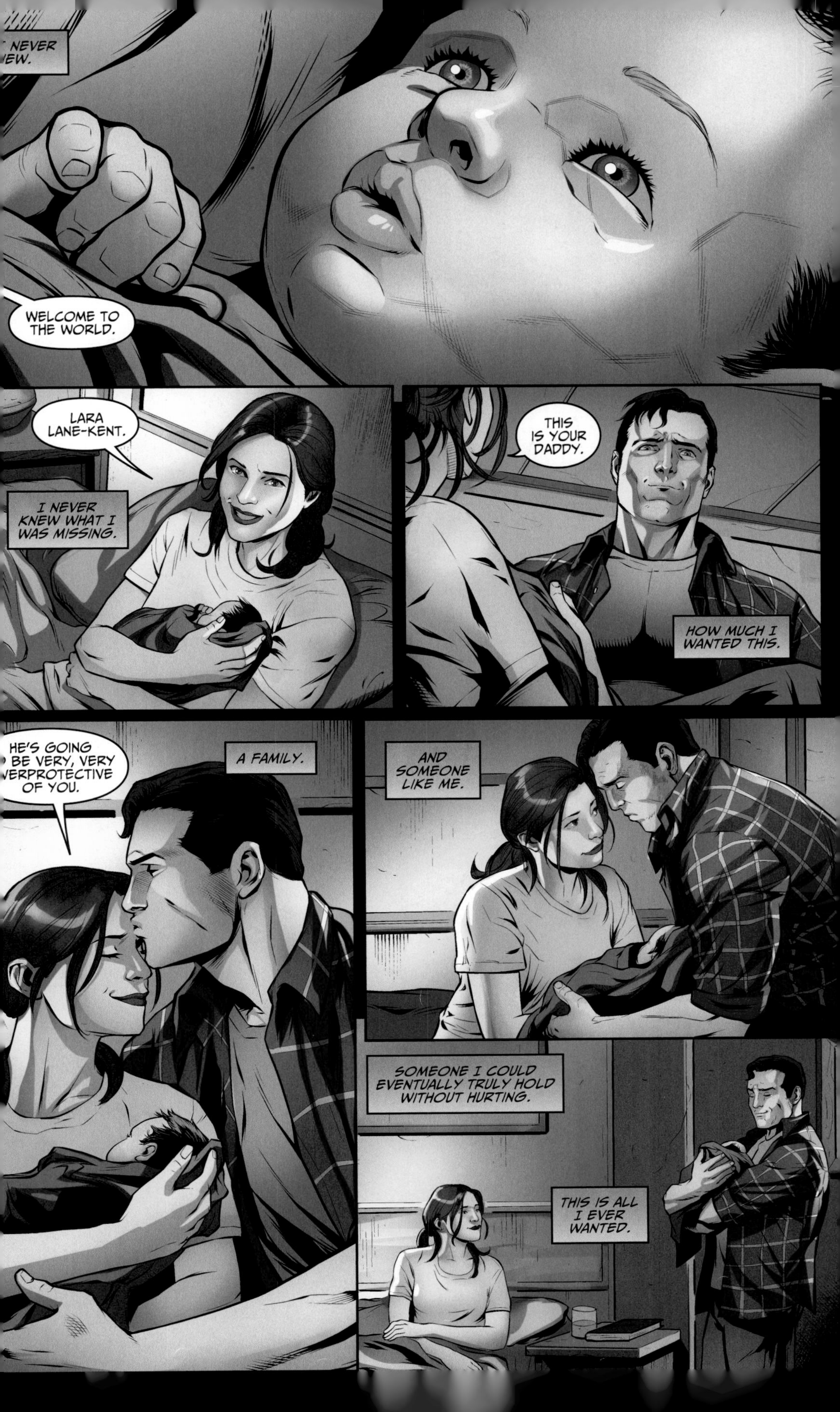

NEVER
EW.
WELCOME TO THE WORLD.
LARA LANE-KENT.
I NEVER KNEW WHAT I WAS MISSING.
THIS IS YOUR DADDY.
HOW MUCH I WANTED THIS.
HE'S GOING
BE VERY, VERY
VERPROTECTIVE OF YOU.
A FAMILY.
AND SOMEONE LIKE ME.
SOMEONE I COULD EVENTUALLY TRULY HOLD WITHOUT HURTING.
THIS IS ALL I EVER WANTED.

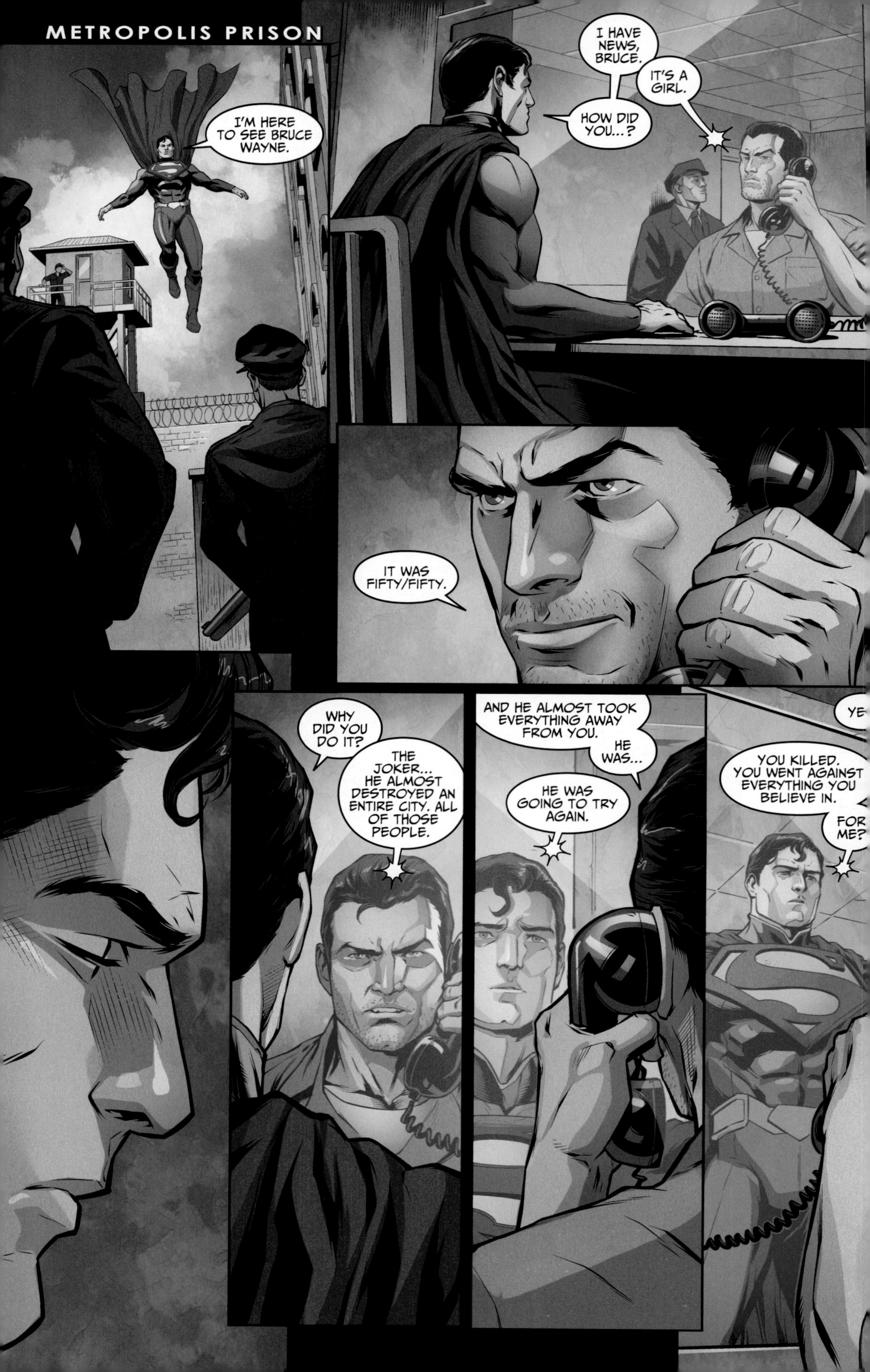
METROPOLIS PRISON
I'M HERE TO SEE BRUCE WAYNE.
I HAVE NEWS, BRUCE.
HOW DID YOU...?
IT'S A GIRL.
IT WAS FIFTY/FIFTY.
WHY DID YOU DO IT?
THE JOKER... HE ALMOST DESTROYED AN ENTIRE CITY. ALL OF THOSE PEOPLE.
AND HE ALMOST TOOK EVERYTHING AWAY FROM YOU.
HE WAS...
HE WAS GOING TO TRY AGAIN.
YOU KILLED. YOU WENT AGAINST EVERYTHING YOU BELIEVE IN.
FOR ME?

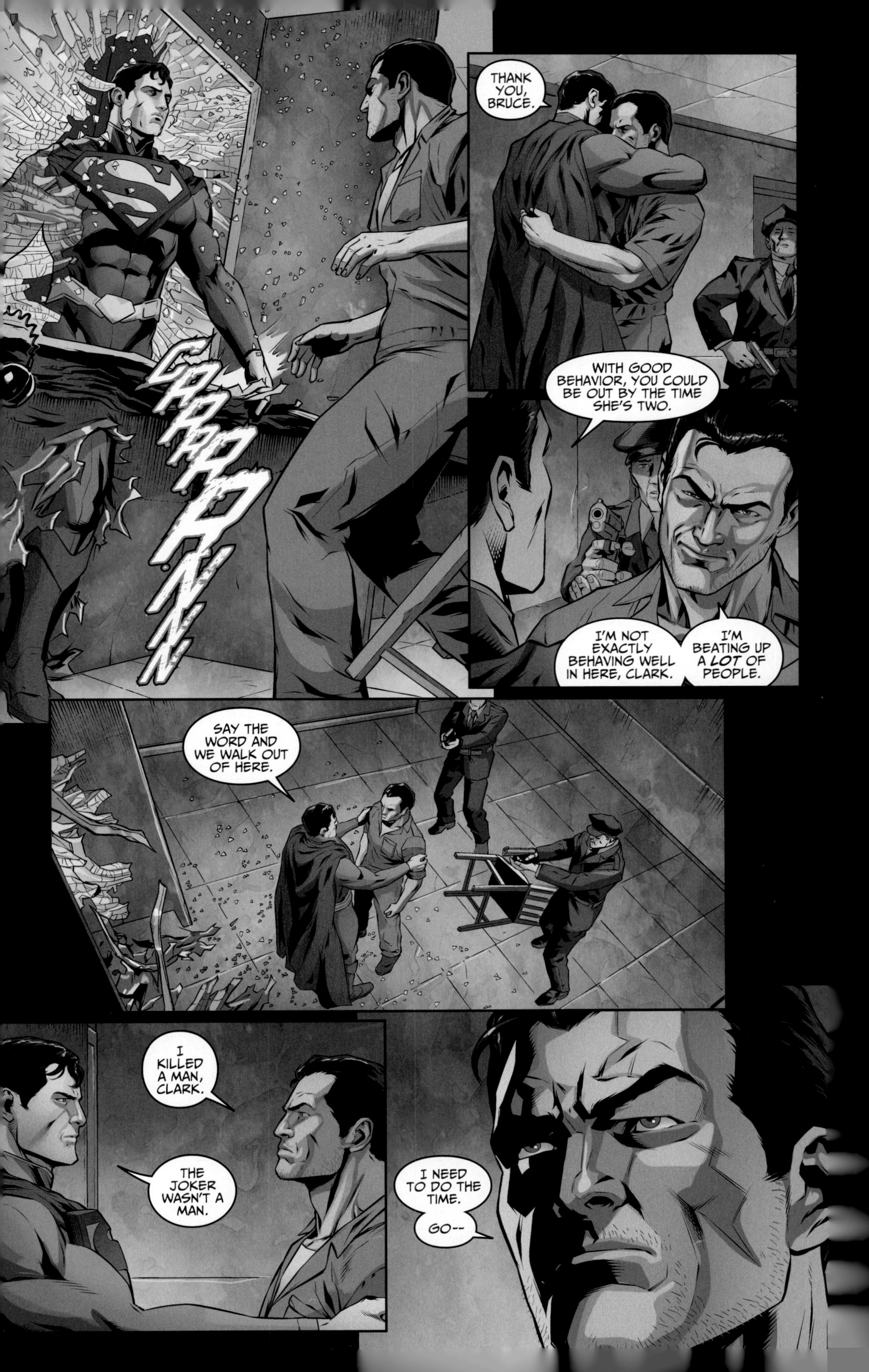
GRRRRNNN
THANK YOU, BRUCE.
WITH GOOD BEHAVIOR, YOU COULD BE OUT BY THE TIME SHE'S TWO.
I'M NOT EXACTLY BEHAVING WELL IN HERE, CLARK.
I'M BEATING UP A LOT OF PEOPLE.
SAY THE WORD AND WE WALK OUT OF HERE.
I KILLED A MAN, CLARK.
THE JOKER WASN'T A MAN.
I NEED TO DO THE TIME.
GO--

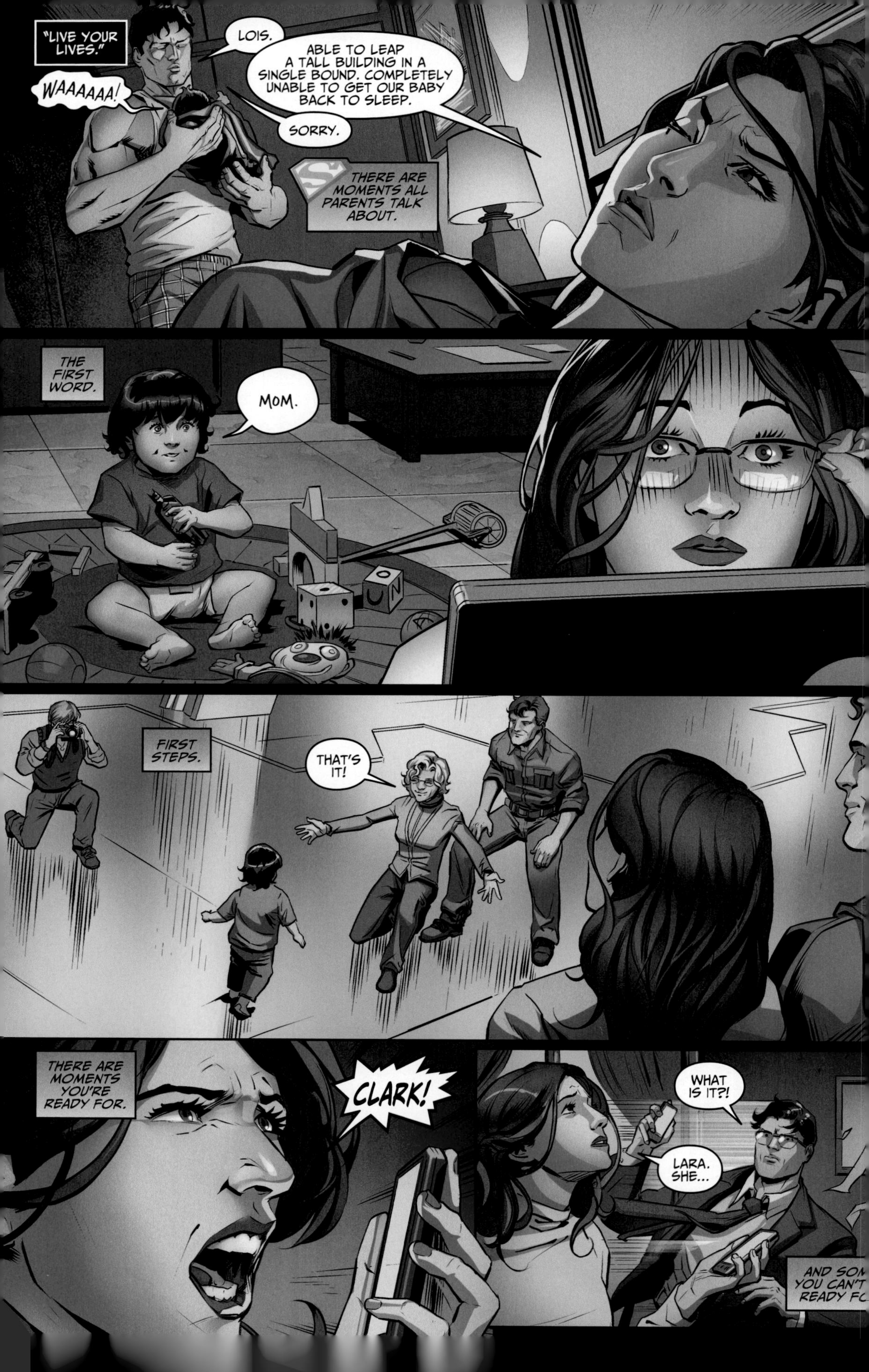
"LIVE YOUR LIVES."
WAAAAAA!
LOIS.
ABLE TO LEAP A TALL BUILDING IN A SINGLE BOUND. COMPLETELY UNABLE TO GET OUR BABY BACK TO SLEEP.
SORRY.
THERE ARE MOMENTS ALL PARENTS TALK ABOUT.
THE FIRST WORD.
MOM.
FIRST STEPS.
THAT'S IT!
THERE ARE MOMENTS YOU'RE READY FOR.
CLARK!
WHAT IS IT?!
LARA. SHE...

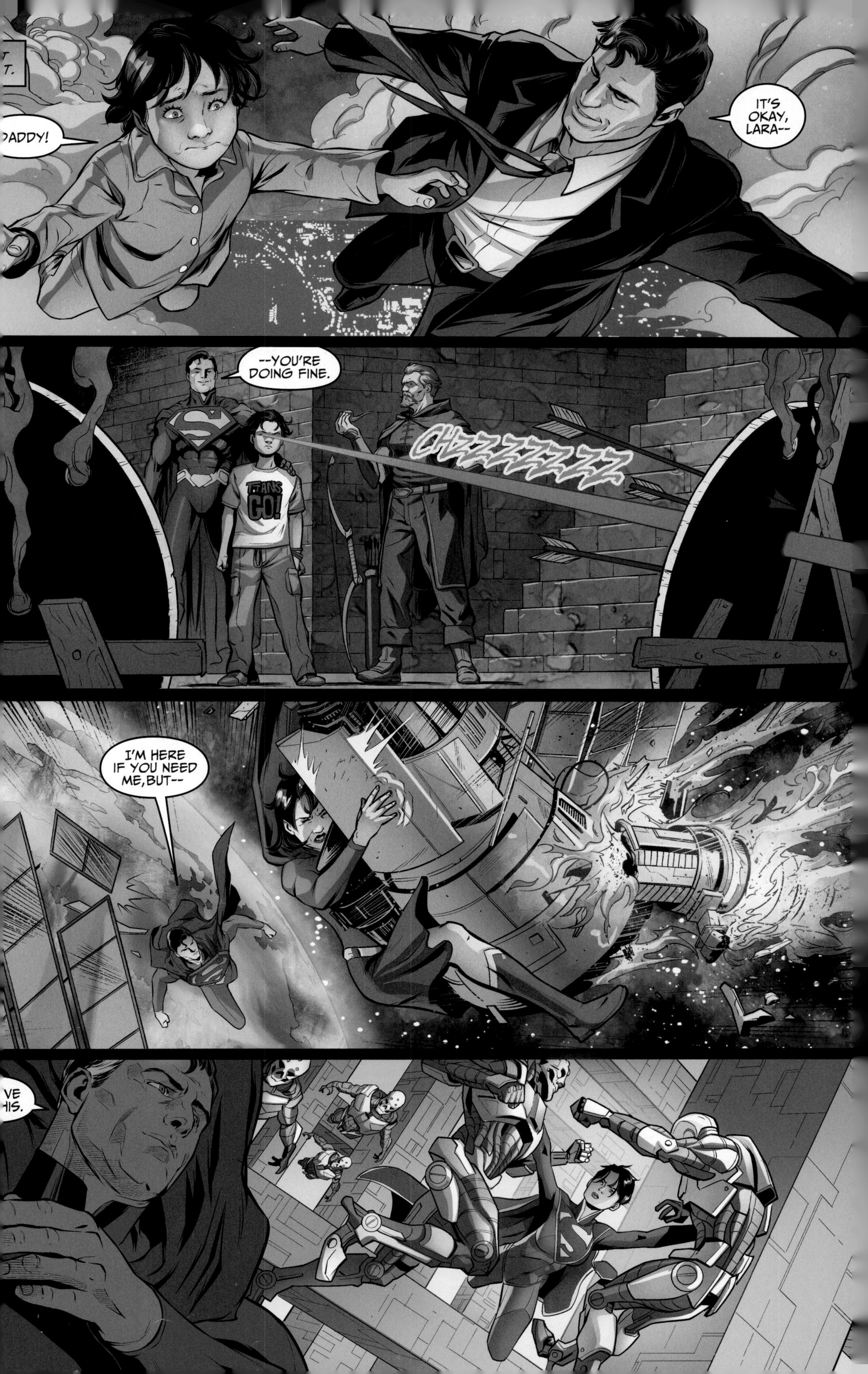
DADDY!
IT'S OKAY, LARA--
--YOU'RE DOING FINE.
CHZZZZZZZ
I'M HERE IF YOU NEED ME, BUT--

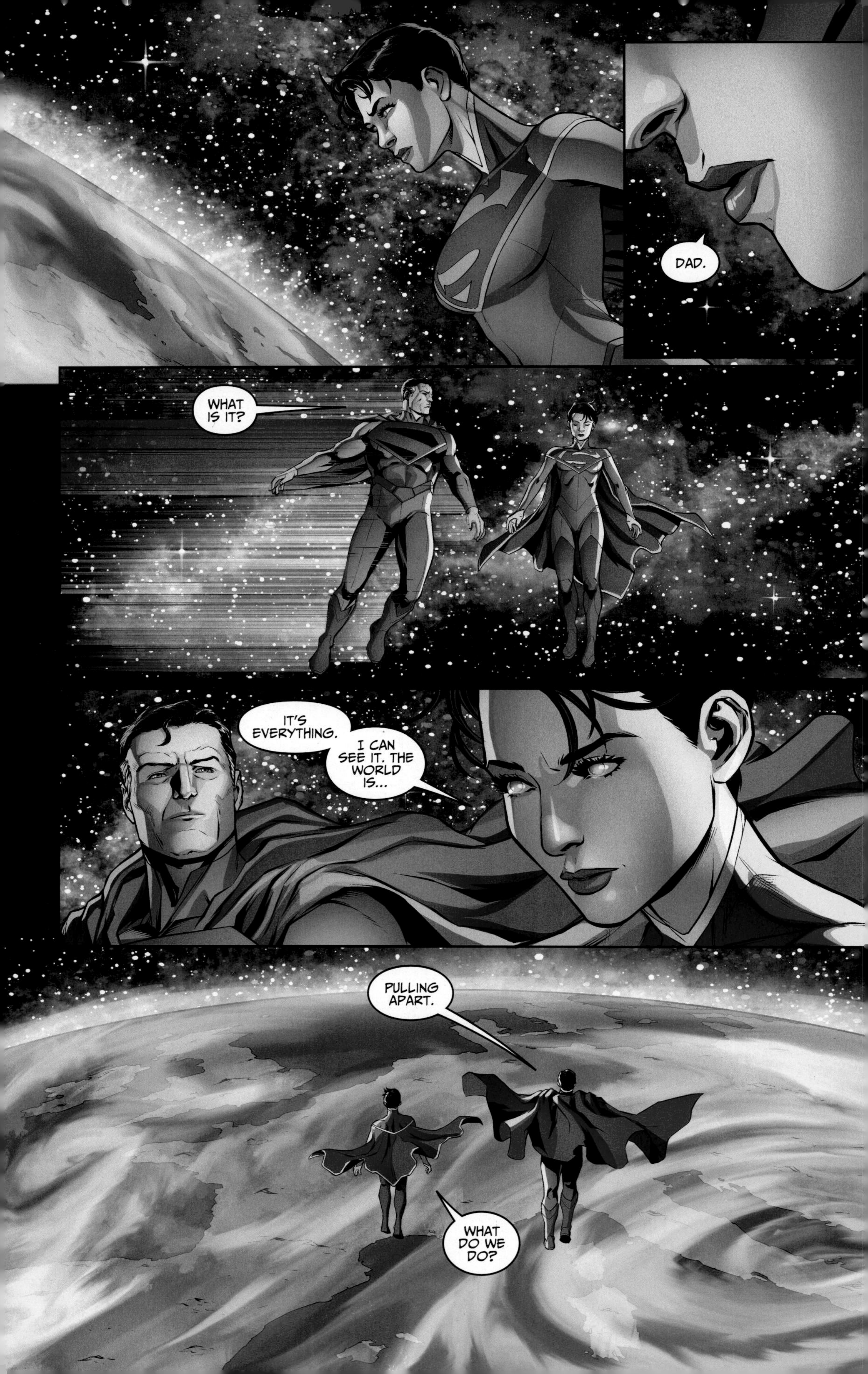
DAD.
WHAT IS IT?
IT'S EVERYTHING.
I CAN SEE IT. THE WORLD IS...
PULLING APART.
WHAT DO WE DO?

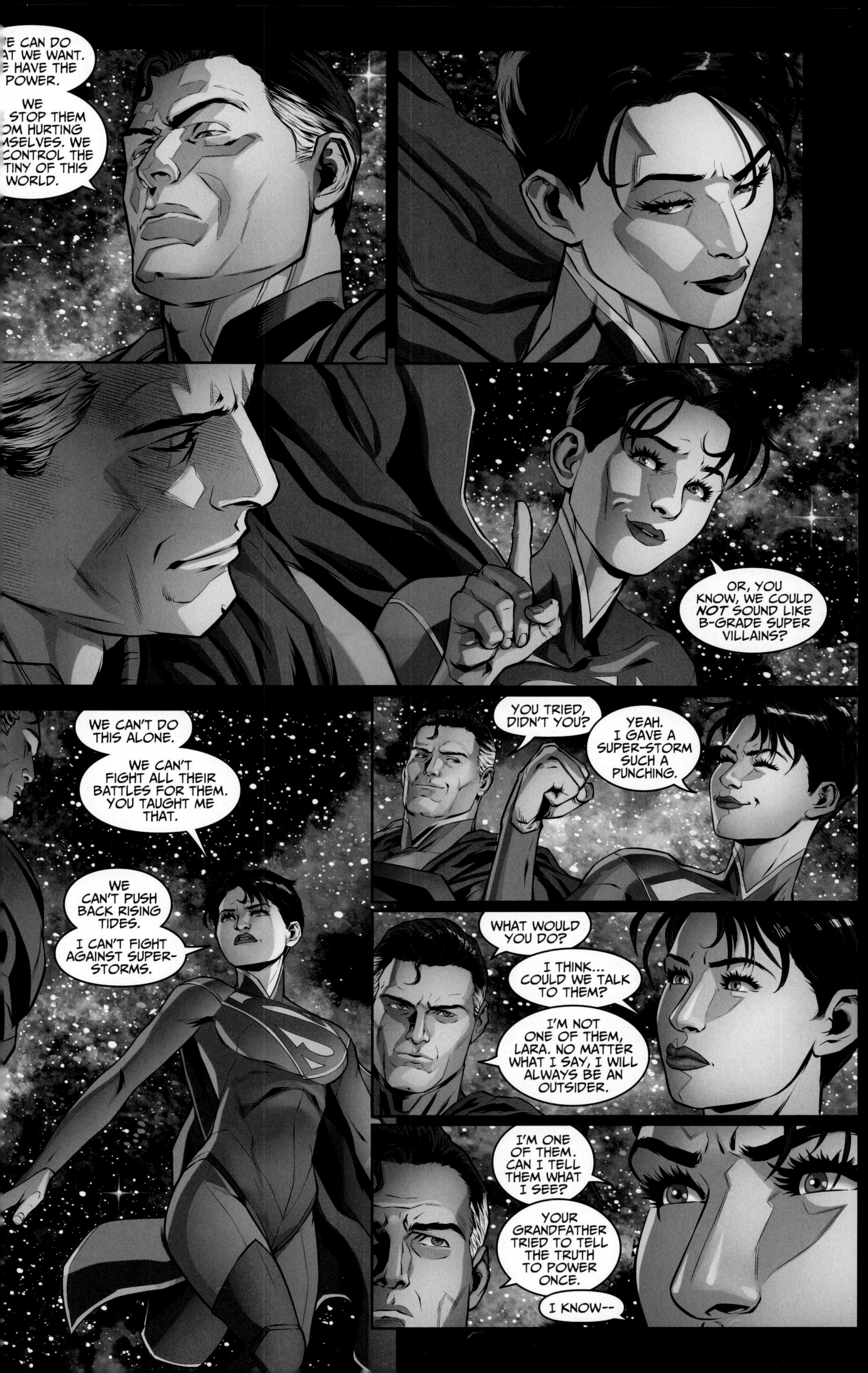
E CAN DO AT WE WANT. E HAVE THE POWER.
WE STOP THEM OM HURTING MSELVES. WE CONTROL THE TINY OF THIS WORLD.
OR, YOU KNOW, WE COULD NOT SOUND LIKE B-GRADE SUPER VILLAINS?
WE CAN'T DO THIS ALONE.
WE CAN'T FIGHT ALL THEIR BATTLES FOR THEM. YOU TAUGHT ME THAT.
WE CAN'T PUSH BACK RISING TIDES.
I CAN'T FIGHT AGAINST SUPER-STORMS.
YOU TRIED, DIDN'T YOU?
YEAH. I GAVE A SUPER-STORM SUCH A PUNCHING.
WHAT WOULD YOU DO?
I THINK... COULD WE TALK TO THEM?
I'M NOT ONE OF THEM, LARA. NO MATTER WHAT I SAY, I WILL ALWAYS BE AN OUTSIDER.
I'M ONE OF THEM. CAN I TELL THEM WHAT I SEE?
YOUR GRANDFATHER TRIED TO TELL THE TRUTH TO POWER ONCE.
I KNOW--

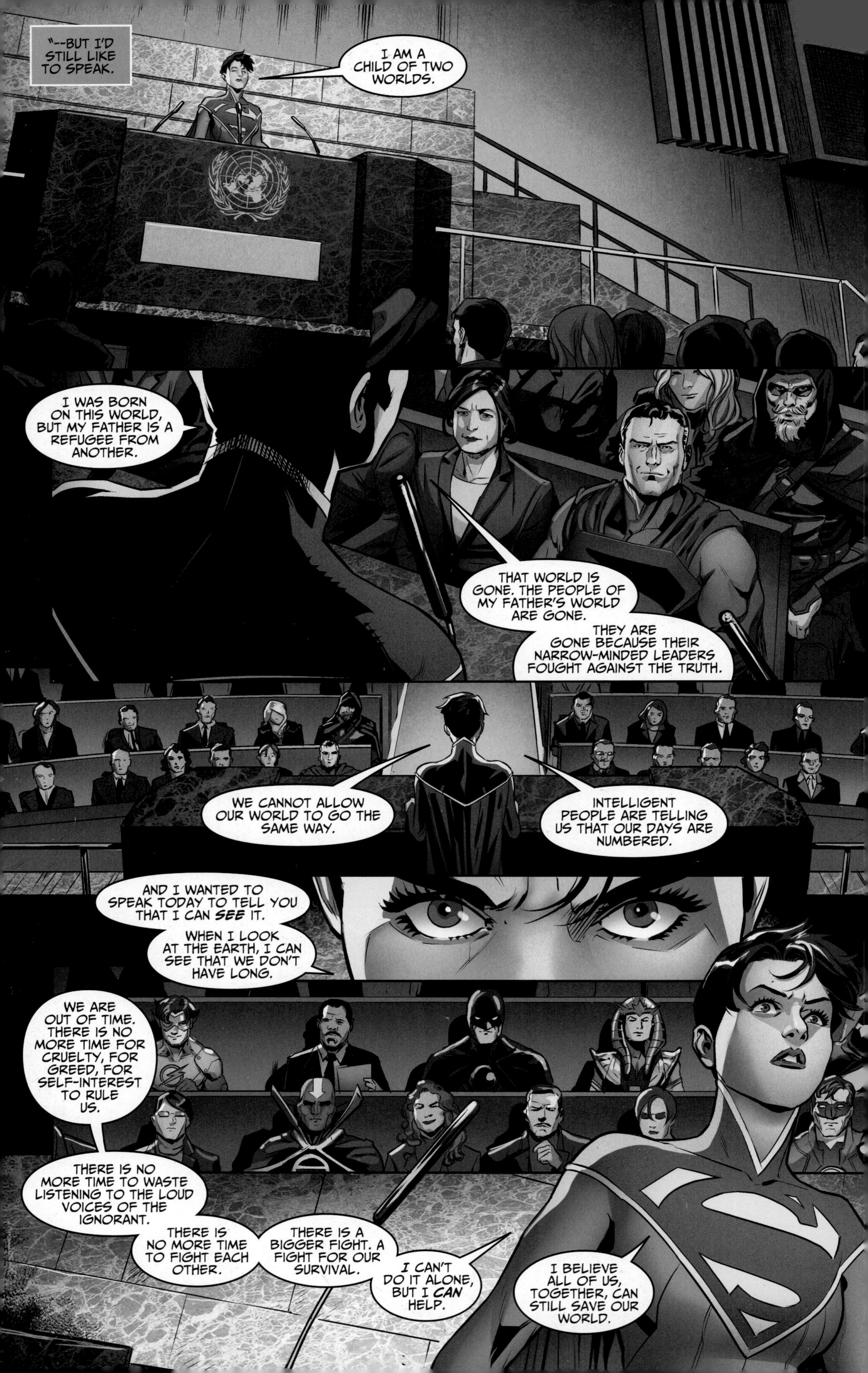
"--BUT I'D STILL LIKE TO SPEAK.
I AM A CHILD OF TWO WORLDS.
I WAS BORN ON THIS WORLD, BUT MY FATHER IS A REFUGEE FROM ANOTHER.
THAT WORLD IS GONE. THE PEOPLE OF MY FATHER'S WORLD ARE GONE.
THEY ARE GONE BECAUSE THEIR NARROW-MINDED LEADERS FOUGHT AGAINST THE TRUTH.
WE CANNOT ALLOW OUR WORLD TO GO THE SAME WAY.
INTELLIGENT PEOPLE ARE TELLING US THAT OUR DAYS ARE NUMBERED.
AND I WANTED TO SPEAK TODAY TO TELL YOU THAT I CAN ***SEE*** IT.
WHEN I LOOK AT THE EARTH, I CAN SEE THAT WE DON'T HAVE LONG.
WE ARE OUT OF TIME. THERE IS NO MORE TIME FOR CRUELTY, FOR GREED, FOR SELF-INTEREST TO RULE US.
THERE IS NO MORE TIME TO WASTE LISTENING TO THE LOUD VOICES OF THE IGNORANT.
THERE IS NO MORE TIME TO FIGHT EACH OTHER.
THERE IS A BIGGER FIGHT. A FIGHT FOR OUR SURVIVAL.
I CAN'T DO IT ALONE, BUT I ***CAN*** HELP.
I BELIEVE ALL OF US, TOGETHER, CAN STILL SAVE OUR WORLD.

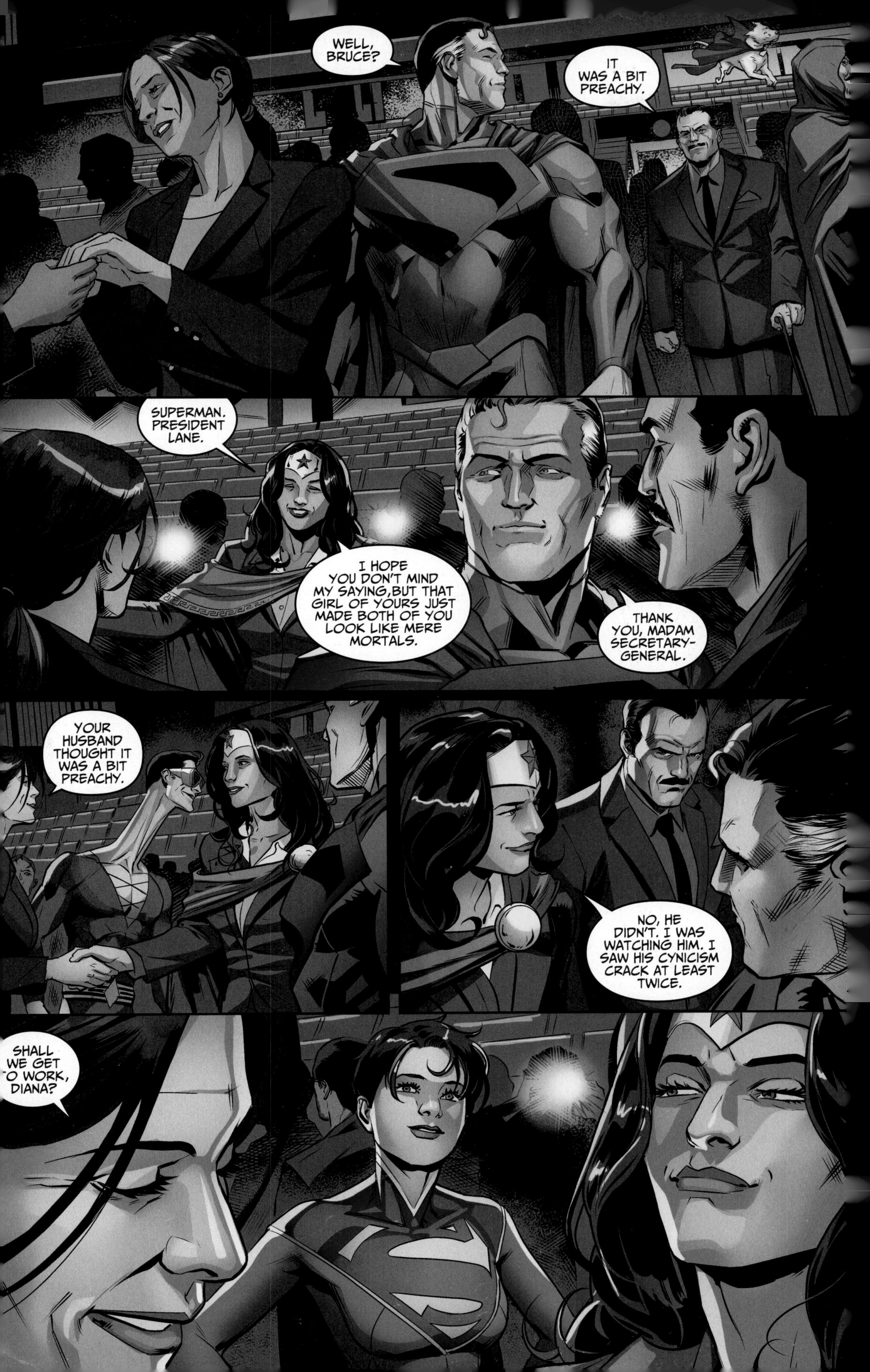
WELL, BRUCE?
IT WAS A BIT PREACHY.
SUPERMAN. PRESIDENT LANE.
I HOPE YOU DON'T MIND MY SAYING, BUT THAT GIRL OF YOURS JUST MADE BOTH OF YOU LOOK LIKE MERE MORTALS.
THANK YOU, MADAM SECRETARY-GENERAL.
YOUR HUSBAND THOUGHT IT WAS A BIT PREACHY.
NO, HE DIDN'T. I WAS WATCHING HIM. I SAW HIS CYNICISM CRACK AT LEAST TWICE.
SHALL WE GET TO WORK, DIANA?

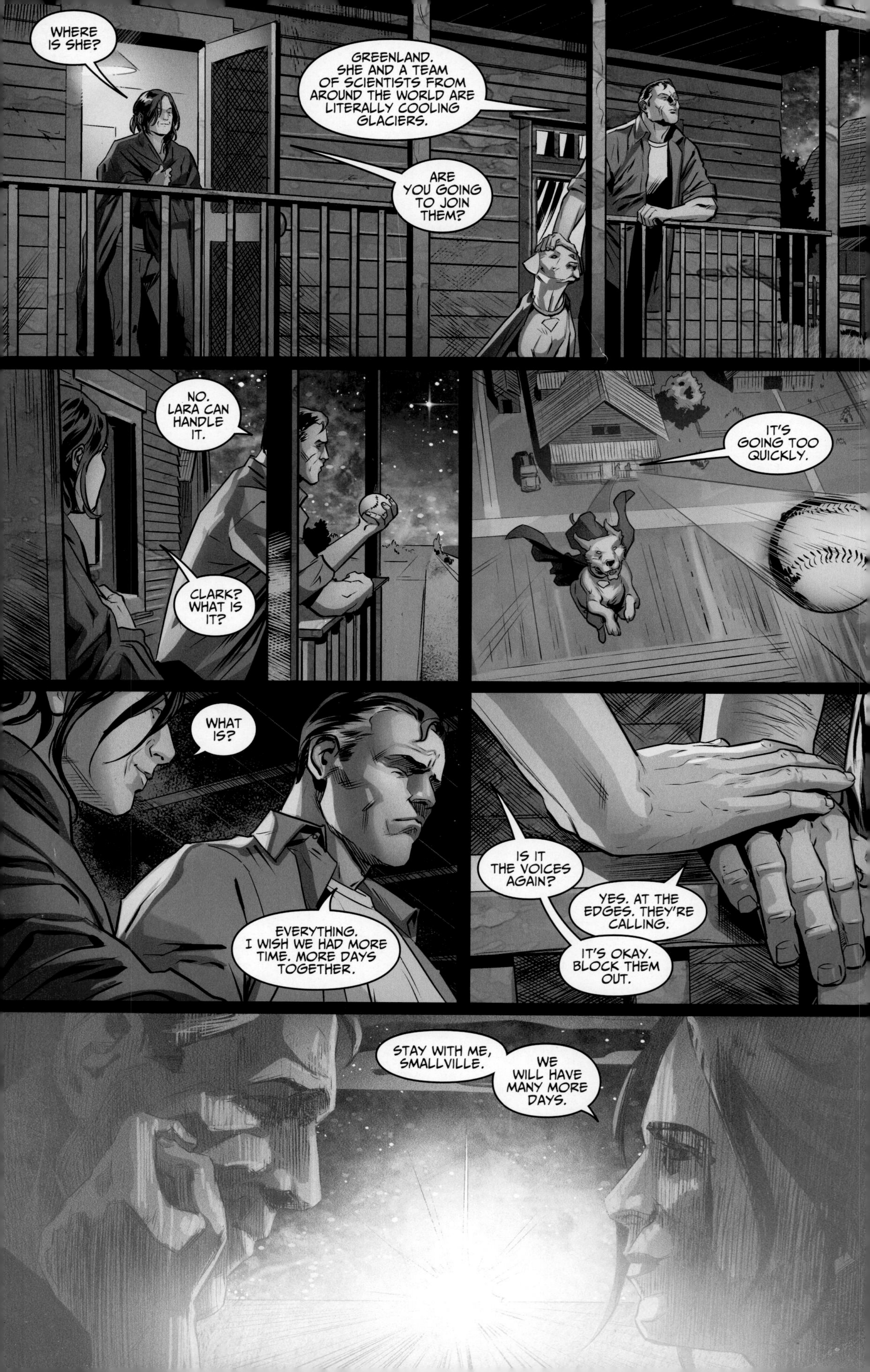
WHERE IS SHE?
GREENLAND. SHE AND A TEAM OF SCIENTISTS FROM AROUND THE WORLD ARE LITERALLY COOLING GLACIERS.
ARE YOU GOING TO JOIN THEM?
NO. LARA CAN HANDLE IT.
CLARK? WHAT IS IT?
IT'S GOING TOO QUICKLY.
WHAT IS?
EVERYTHING. I WISH WE HAD MORE TIME. MORE DAYS TOGETHER.
IS IT THE VOICES AGAIN?
YES. AT THE EDGES. THEY'RE CALLING.
IT'S OKAY. BLOCK THEM OUT.
STAY WITH ME, SMALLVILLE.
WE WILL HAVE MANY MORE DAYS.